Muslim Communities Reemerge

Central Asia Book Series

Muslim Communities Reemerge

Historical Perspectives on Nationality, Politics, and Opposition in the Former Soviet Union and Yugoslavia

Andreas Kappeler, Gerhard Simon, Georg Brunner,

Editors of the German edition

Edward Allworth, *Editor of the English edition*

Translations from the German & French by Caroline Sawyer

DUKE UNIVERSITY PRESS *Durham and London 1994*

*Die Muslime in der Sowjetunion und in Jugoslawien,
Identität-Politik-Widerstand*
English supplemented and translated edition,
Central Asia Book Series, 1994,
Duke University Press, Durham, North Carolina
Typeset in Trump Medieval by Tseng Information Systems
Library of Congress Cataloging-in-Publication Data appear
on the last printed page of this book.
The editors wish to thank the Volkswagen Foundation for
its financial support in organizing the conference. They also
thank the Bundesinstitut für ostwissenschaftliche und
internationale Studien for its financial assistance for the
printing of the German edition and for the translation of the
German and French-language chapters into English.

Contents

Excellent !!

Central Asia Book Series

Political analysts often referred, during 1991–92, to what they called the disintegration of the Soviet Union and of Yugoslavia. Perhaps the term *integration* aptly applied to political structure and system, but that application of the verb *integrate* suggests more than the situation warrants about a deeper sharing of ideas and values. Integration usually conveys nuances of unity, solidarity, willing cooperation, and harmony among human groups—religious, ethnic, racial, or regional. To what degree might the term *integration* accurately characterize the condition or aspiration of most nationalities held under the control of Russia or Serbia up to the start of the breakup?

The Russian and Serbian style of integration usually implied negative, rather than affirmative, equality. To some extent, that occurred because the leadership of the dominant groups insisted upon discriminating between nationalities in ways that frequently inflicted disabilities upon some or all of them. And, among most highly placed leaders, such integration lacked the underlying idealism that elsewhere motivated efforts to end racial segregation and apartheid.

Ideological leaders also publicly announced policies guaranteeing freedom of religion and its separation from schools and state. Nonetheless, the Soviet government and ruling Communist Party closely supervised any licensed religious establishment. Simultaneously, they acted vigorously to propagate atheism and to destroy the capacity of any religion to support or integrate its community of believers. And, in the Soviet case, religion received no official recognition in the definition of nationality. In Yugoslavia, despite Marxist scruples, religion complicated the concept of nationality greatly.

Recent actions taken by the former constituent republics in the religious and political fields of both shattered states of Southern Europe and Eurasia confirm the failure of the Marxist regimes to achieve real unity among their subject nationalities. Despite the leaders' manipulation of words and symbols, the style of integration instituted by them failed to win the minds and loyalties of most people. Consequently, an inquiry that offers enlightenment and overcomes skepticism regarding the situation that prevailed in lands controlled by Russia and Serbia in the decades leading up to the 1990s requires clear insight and an approach aided by more specific, accurate terminology than the Soviet or Yugoslav political idiom cared to provide.

Muslim Communities Reemerge concentrates upon two states which, early in their existence, had designated themselves "federated" in the special Marxist vocabulary. A political glossary published in Central Asia while public Islam remained strong there ignored V. I. Lenin's earlier doubts regarding the suitability of federation for a Marxist state. According to this source, the word *federation* meant "a union, a unity of several governments which conduct their own internal affairs independently." Though independence, like other key concepts in Marxist political thought, bore a special nuance in a class society, the sense of this entry seems simple and clear. But that application disappeared before long.

Some six decades later, the political lexicon issued in Central Asia in Uzbek, but now entirely prepared in Russia, defined what it called the new type of federation effective both within the region and Union-wide. The definition makes no mention of independence but strongly implies integration according to Marxist-Leninist ideological precepts: "A socialist federation is a form of state fraternally built on the basis of the cooperation and of the mutual assistance of laboring people, [and] built on the basis of those socialist nations' and tribes' joining together, [and] of their republics' fully equal legality, liberty, and on the basis of their joining together voluntarily in a single socialist state" (M. Häsän, *Ozbekchä siyasi-ijtima'i lughät*, Tashkent: Ozbekistan Däolät Näshriyati, 1926, p. 47; L. A. Onikov and N. V. Shishlin, comps., *Qisqacha siyasiy lughat*, translated from the Russian edition of 1980, Tashkent: "Ozbekistan," 1983, pp. 360–61).

In the standard Soviet usage, federation expressed a deep irony when it described a polity consisting of united states that preserve their independence within known boundaries. That conflict between reality and fiction caused officials to reiterate at every opportunity that the principal republics under the Soviet and Yugoslav governments remained free and sovereign. The given definition also virtually required spokesmen and spokeswomen to maintain the pretense that the eponymous nation-alities whose names labeled many of those constituent republics in the two states shared in the freedom advertised by ideologists. The nation-alities as well as their religious communities usually found themselves participating, however unwillingly, in the charade that in the aggregate people possessed the right to choose their type of government and their expressions of faith.

"Disassembly" rather than "disintegration" better describes the pro-cess that so rapidly progressed throughout the regions recently still called the Union of Soviet Socialist Republics and the Federal Republic of Yugoslavia. Current evidence of this disassociation could hardly exert a more persuasive impact than the present group of studies does upon the thinking of scholars and students of religious and ethnic affairs. The present volume challenges the version of integration and federation long propagated by the governments of the Soviet and Yugoslavian states. Thus, this book also offers essential preparation in political theory for anyone following the events unfolding since 1990 in the former Soviet Union and Yugoslavian Republic.

The Central Asia Book Series intends to continue issuing serious studies using indigenous Central Asian languages, as in this volume, and to emphasize the publishing of books by individual authors. It also provides readers with relevant collections of documents, eye-witness ac-counts, and reference materials that can make lasting contributions to knowledge about the region. The area's cultural, economic, and political terrain stretches broadly eastward from the Caspian Sea at least as far as Dunhuang and Komul (Hami) in Eastern Turkistan (Xinjiang).

Edward Allworth, General Editor of the Series,
Columbia University
Andras J. E. Bodrogligeti, Advisory Editor,
University of California, Los Angeles
Richard N. Frye, Advisory Editor, Harvard University

Preface to the English-Language Edition

The terrible events afflicting the Muslims in Bosnia-Herzegovina and other parts of the former Federal Republic of Yugoslavia (FRY) as well as those in the Tajikistan Republic (TR) during the first years of the 1990s started to occur shortly after the publication of the German edition of this book. The editors have revised only the prefatory and introductory material; the chapters themselves remain virtually the same. The special importance of this work as a substantial scholarly guide to understanding the meaning of the trauma that has overtaken the Muslims in the former FRY and TR has convinced the editors and Duke University Press that the German version should remain intact and that an English edition should appear at this time. Readers will recognize the fact, therefore, that the authors wrote their chapters not long before the ethnic cleansing began in the FRY and the killing erupted in Tajikistan's protracted civil war.

Besides displaying directly in English the scholarship of a number of prominent European authors whose work deserves greater dissemination than it receives in North America and other English-speaking areas, this translated edition of *Die Muslime in der Sowjetunion und in Jugoslawien, Identität–Politik–Widerstand* (1989), offers other significant rewards to the North American reader. It puts information about numerous recent publications before the student and scholar. These publications appear in the reference-note system at the end of each chapter and in the biographies of the contributors. Readers will find works by a variety of authors from the two, now fragmented, countries. These pages also list many writings by the authors and editors of this edition, now entitled *Muslim Communities Reemerge: Historical Perspectives on Nationality, Politics, and Opposition in the Former Soviet Union and Yugoslavia.* In this way, the book substantially adds to the recent bibliography from leading scholars concerning the subject of Islam in the two former states. To enrich that list of titles, the authors brought their brief biographical sketches up to date in May 1992.

In addition to publishing the six manuscripts as they were originally written in English, this edition offers a translation of the eight chapters first composed in German or French, here well rendered into English by Ms. Caroline Sawyer, a Ph.D. candidate in Middle Eastern, especially Turkic, studies at Columbia University. With two exceptions, the original chapters remain without much alteration. Professors Edward J. Lazzerini and Sabrina Petra Ramet, with the agreement of the editors and for certain technical reasons, have substituted somewhat different, but very appropriate, chapters for this version of the joint study.

Transliterations from Russian follow the system in *Nationalities of the Soviet East: Publications and Writing Systems* (1971) by Edward Allworth. Renditions from Iranian and Turkic languages correspond generally, though not exactly, to the tables shown in that same volume. Some chapters show Slavic versions of a few Arabic terms as well as the standard transliterated forms, without macrons. Serbian titles, names, and words remain as presented in the German edition of this volume, with suitable diacritical marks. Croatian-language titles appear in their original Roman alphabet. References to Western European-language material published in the Roman alphabet also remain untransliterated.

Muslim Communities Reemerge

Introduction

Gerhard Simon

During recent years, Islam's increasingly important role in international affairs has captured considerable attention among a broad audience. Because Islam has proved to be an unexpectedly strong political and spiritual force in many areas of the world, it has presented a challenge to the concepts of progress and modernity as defined by the West. The political, social, and spiritual manifestations of Islam are often at odds with Western legal and social structures, and with the value systems underlying them.

Nevertheless, despite the attention that has been focused on Islam in the Arab world and in Asia, Islam's millions of adherents in the former Soviet Union and other communist states have largely remained "forgotten Muslims," an apt expression from the title of a book by Alexandre Bennigsen and Chantal Lemercier-Quelquejay: *Les musulmanes oubliés. L'Islam en URSS aujourd'hui* (Paris 1981). In recent years, however, the Afghanistan War and conflicts between nationalities such as the war between Armenians and Azerbaijanians, civil war in Tajikistan, and the Crimean Tatar movement have started to direct public interest more strongly toward the Muslims of the former Soviet Union.

This volume was originally produced as one of the few publications in German to treat the historical and contemporary situation of Islam in communist countries. It is the result of a conference that took place in Schlangenbad in May 1987. It was organized by the Committee for Nationality and Regional Problems in the Soviet Union, East-Central, and South Eastern Europe, in conjunction with the German Society for Eastern European Studies. Here, for the first time in the German-speaking world, historians of Eastern Europe and political scientists and scholars focusing upon Western Asia came together from Western

Europe and North America in an interdisciplinary academic conference to discuss the problems of Islam in communist countries. The presentations from that conference were revised and brought up to date for the German edition.

Among the communist states, the former Soviet Union and ex-Yugoslavia were those with the greatest percentage of Muslims. The USSR, furthermore, included more than 50 million traditionally Islamic people. It was one of the world's largest Muslim states. This book marks an initial attempt to compare the past and very recent situations of the Muslim population of the former Soviet Union with those of their coreligionists in ex-Yugoslavia. In both of those countries, a communist party (CP) claimed the right to consign nations and religions to the dustbin of history. Moreover, prior to 1948, the Yugoslav CP was not only heavily dependent on the CPSU, Titoist Yugoslavia also saw itself as an exemplary Stalinist state. The essays in this volume suggest that the position of Islam in the society and politics of both countries was characterized by a set of common features.

The articles by Hans Bräker and Alexandre Popović treat in passing the fact that the Soviet Union and Yugoslavia have had similar reasons for taking Islam into account in the realm of foreign policy. Yugoslavia was one of the leading powers in the movement of nonaligned states which included a substantial number of Muslim states; the USSR was the neighbor of numerous Muslim states in Asia. International relations, however, do not provide the main focus of this volume.

One of the most significant similarities discussed is the increasing strength of ethnic and religious identification of the Muslims in Yugoslavia and the USSR, with their distinctive histories and cultures, over the course of the past three decades. The growing significance of Islam as a religious, ethnic, and cultural factor in people's consciousness, policies, and political actions bears witness, on the one hand, to the power of Islam that is also evident in many countries outside the sphere of communist influence. On the other hand, this trend also points to the weakness and diminishing effectiveness of the socialist political system. The eventual demise of religion within the socialist system and the obsolescence of nations as political factors were not the only ideological expectations of socialism that have remained unfulfilled. Decreasing effectiveness in socialist economies has gone hand in hand with a crisis of legitimacy of the one-party dictatorship, so that communist parties were no longer in a position to wield power against nations and religious communities. On the contrary, they sought among these groups—selectively, of course—support and aid toward the consolidation of their rule.

In the case of Yugoslavia, liberalization of policy toward religions, in addition to increasing federalization of the political system, resulted in the increasing influence of nations and religions following the 1960s. The Soviet Union hesitated to take similar steps. From the beginning of the 1980s, in fact, the anti-Islamic campaign had been stepped up, and was a concomitant rapprochement with the Russian Orthodox Church. The emergence of *perestroika* (rebuilding), however, and the defeat of Soviet forces in Afghanistan, led to increased pressure from below toward concessions to nations and religious communities.

One fundamental theme of this book is the encounter between the European world—especially in the Russian and Soviet states—with the world of Islam, and the multidimensional conflicts resulting from that encounter. One feature of these tensions involves the opposition between European conceptualization and Islamic reality. The concepts of *nation* and *religion* have been formulated on the basis of European experience, and their application to Islamic societies can only be ambiguous and imprecise. In Islam, the religious community is also a political body and vice versa. Religious and legal-political norms are inseparable; a Protestant sort of separation between church and state is unthinkable in Islamic culture.

This volume is divided into three sections, according to theme. The first treats the problem of ethnic-religious identity and nation-building. Here, the Muslims of the Soviet Union and Yugoslavia are not presented—as is often the case in scholarship and journalism—merely as groups that are dependent on and manipulated by political centers. Rather, this section attempts to understand the history and culture of these peoples in their own right. In this undertaking, it becomes clear that the current problems cannot be understood without reaching back into history—not merely into that of the twentieth century, but into the entire tradition of these communities. This volume, consequently, provides broad scope for historical discussion.

Nation-building, in the European sense, was never completed among the Muslim population of the Soviet Union or Yugoslavia. National affiliation was always superseded, and thus limited, by the ʿumma, the community of all Muslim believers. Among people with traditional tribal divisions, particularly among the Turkic people who remained nomadic well into the twentieth century, loyalty to the clan also entered into the picture. In that case, national consciousness was further restricted. It is an apparent paradox that such national development as has occurred among the Muslims there has been the unexpected and, for the political authorities, undesired result of the nationality policies of communist parties.

In his discussion of national development among the Uzbeks and

Tajiks, Bert G. Fragner demonstrates that, until the twentieth century, the concepts of *Tajik, Sart,* and *Uzbek* primarily designated social and, to some extent, linguistic affiliation, rather than nationality. Remnants of centuries-old Persian-Turkic bilingualism still exist among the agricultural and urban population of Transoxiana. The creation of Uzbekistan by the Soviet regime in 1924 was a masterpiece of *Realpolitik,* by means of which several ends were attained. On the one hand, Pan-Turkic movements, of which the central authorities did not approve, were hobbled, but a small compensation was also offered to the Turkistanists. Amidst the withdrawal of Pan-Turkist claims and hopes, the rise of Tajik national sentiment, systematically promoted, was a natural ally, so to speak, for the Soviet regime.

According to the central thesis of Edward J. Lazzerini, the Islamic revival movement (*Jadidism*) in the Russian Empire was brought into being by the decline of the Islamic world that began in the eighteenth century. Worldwide Islam demonstrated its inability to cope with the political, economic, and cultural challenges posed by the Western world. In contrast to the classical Islamic revival movements of earlier centuries, the Jadids felt cut off from access to a lost Golden Age of Islam. To a large extent, they sought to escape the crisis through cultural synthesis with the Russian Empire. Borrowing from European progress, it was thought, would restore Islam to its status as a competitive force. From that time onward, the ideas of Jadidism in Russia reappeared in cultural variations throughout the Islamic world.

Among other features of his discussion of the national development of the Azerbaijanis, Tadeusz Swietochowski examines the background of the Azerbaijani-Armenian conflict since the "Tatar-Armenian War" of 1905 and the clashes involving Nagorno-Karabagh during and after the Revolution of 1917. In Azerbaijan, the Bolsheviks also became co-founders of the nation, by granting legitimacy to the national concerns of a small sector of Western-influenced intellectuals with secular education, supporting them against society at large, which was imbued with Pan-Turkism and Pan-Islamism. Between 1941 and 1945, the Soviet regime promoted Azerbaijanian irredentism in Iran. After the beginning of the 1980s and the deterioration of relations with Ayatollah Khomeini's dictatorship, the Soviets permitted Azerbaijani intellectuals apparently unlimited freedom to propagandize in favor of "One Azerbaijan" made up of the parts divided by the Araxes River into Azerbaijan proper and Iranian Azerbaijan.

The chapter by Azade-Ayşe Rorlich comes to the conclusion that two Tatar nations exist: the Volga Tatars and the Crimean Tatars. Since the 1950s, the Crimean Tatar people, small in number, has been binding its community together as a nation in a campaign of a scope unprecedented in Soviet history. A few media devoted to Crimean Tatar issues and renewed possibilities for instruction in the Crimean Tatar mother tongue also have contributed to the growing cultural and historical awareness among them. Leading Jadids have emerged from among the Volga Tatars as well as from Crimean Tatars. After the Revolution of 1917, national communism, aspiring to unite social revolution with national liberation, had a distinct following among both nationalities. To a considerable extent, the national consciousness of the Volga Tatars is defined by the claim that they are descendants of the Khanate of Kazan, whose territory reached far into the modern-day Tatar Autonomous Republic.

Edward Allworth investigates the problem of the ethnic and religious elements in contemporary Uzbek drama. The publication of the German edition of this volume represented the first time this subject had been discussed in the German language. Modern Central Asian plays are, above all, the means of transmission of traditional moral values concerning the family, justice, generosity, responsibility, and forgiveness. Other strong values include the unity of justice and leadership, as well as the fact that political and social leaders should come from the same ethnic and regional provenance as the ruled. In the course of the purges that swept through Central Asia starting in 1983, some of these values were denounced as nepotism and clannishness, which gave further fuel to arguments favoring the obliteration of local ruling elites. Dr. Allworth also stresses the fact that an abundance of expressly ethnic signals in this dramatic tradition does not necessarily supply evidence for a strongly defined national consciousness; it may simply be the mark of a bad dramatist. Concealed and subtle ethnic signals may communicate to the audience much more effectively.

The most unusual case of nation-forming, from both the European and the communist perspectives, is that treated by Sabrina P. Ramet in her discussion of the nation of the Muslims of Serbian and Croatian ethnic background in Bosnia. From the 1960s, the CP of Yugoslavia officially recognized the Muslims of Bosnia as a nation. Rather than being intended as a concession to the Islamic faith, this acknowledgement was supposed to give Muslims a quasi-secular identity. In fact, Muslim nationalism intensified significantly beginning in the late 1960s. A strict division between profane and sacred Islam was impossible. After the breakup of Yugoslavia and the war among Serbs, Croats, and Muslims over Bosnia-Herzegovina, it may turn out that the Muslim nation of Bosnia cannot survive as a unit and will be divided between the "big brothers."

The second section of this volume generally investigates the perspective from the top, treating governments' views of Muslims. The third section offers a view from below, with the theme of resistance movements of the Muslims in opposition to colonialism and assimilation.

Andreas Kappeler offers an essay about the policy of the Russian government toward Muslims from the sixteenth century until the end of Czarist times. He advances the thesis that pragmatic flexibility characterized this policy. The Czarist government did pursue objectives of subjugation and control by means of force and repression, yet, as a rule, it was not interested in swift assimilation of non-Russians. To a great extent, furthermore, the Russian regime did not intervene in socio-cultural matters. Consequently, up to the eighteenth century, part of the local elites were co-opted into the Russian ruling classes. Russian rule over Muslim subjects was thus largely indirect. It must be conceded that there were, however, isolated periods of intolerance, forced religious conversion, and intrusion into traditional social order.

The Soviet administration's policy stands out in sharp contrast to those of its predecessors. The regime brutally endeavored to destroy social structures and religious and cultural values that had existed for centuries. The government did this through forced collectivization of agriculture and compulsory settlement of nomads. In his chapter, Hans Bräker demonstrates that, despite these destructive policies, Islam survived as a cultural force and a religious-spiritual orientation. In fact, during the past two decades, Islam has been on the upswing as a way of life, a cultural identity, and a religion within the territory of the former Soviet Union.

One reason for this trend can be seen in the fact that the anti-Islamic policy of Soviet authorities failed to take Islam's particular nature into account. Following the lines of policy deployed against the Russian Orthodox Church, the political leaders destroyed Islamic religious institutions and dispersed the clergy. They failed to recognize that Islam is much less dependent on hierarchy and ecclesiastical structures than are the major Christian denominations. Islam in the Soviet Union, as in Yugoslavia, was able to coexist with socialism by attributing the principles of socialism to the Prophet. Socialism had set out to destroy Islam, but it happened that Islam contributed essentially to destroying socialism.

Georg Brunner elaborates the sharp differences between the apparent federalism in the Soviet Union and the progressive appropriations of federal authority by the republics and provinces in Yugoslavia. Although Marshal Tito initially hailed the Soviet model, decentralization of state and party went into effect in 1948, transforming Yugoslavia into a de facto confederation. After 1988, the demand for decentralization was also voiced in the Soviet Union, although the traditionally Islamic Soviet republics were not in the forefront of this movement. Dr. Brunner's investigation of the jurisdictional status of the Muslims in both of these federative systems shows regional Muslim peculiarities—in so far as they exist—generally were directed against Islamic principles, in contrast to defined Islamic legal practices. No stable coalescence of interests has taken place among the regional entities of Bosnia and Kosovo, which may have to do with the fact that, on the Albanian side of the Kosovo conflict, Islamic interests are subordinated to those of nationality.

Wolfgang Höpken traces the evolution of the CP of Yugoslavia from the rigid dogma of an ethnically unified Yugoslav nation to recognition of the Bosnian Muslims as a nation. The Bosnians are distinguished not only by the fact that they speak two different languages, Serbian or Croatian, but that their number includes the Macedonian Muslims from outside Bosnia's boundaries, though not the Muslim Albanians and Turks of Yugoslavia. The Bosnian "nation," an example of the persistence of religious faith within a communist state, issues from a late stage of nation-building. Whether this peculiar religion-based nation will survive after the war in Bosnia-Herzegovina and the redrawing of political boundaries remains to be seen.

The four essays in the third section of the book consider various aspects of Islamic self-assertion and resistance. Ewe Halbach points out that *jihad* involves more than "holy war." In the nineteenth and twentieth centuries, jihad against the European powers had been mainly defensive and had involved both ethnic self-assertion as well as "holy war." As a most pertinent example, the chapter considers the resistance of the North Caucasus tribes against the Russian Empire in the mid-nineteenth century. This jihad—like other similar defensive struggles both within and outside of the Russian Empire—drew its strength from organized Sufism. The theocratic state of Imam Shamil set the Shari'a against traditional tribal law. The theocratic state had an integrative effect that served to break down the social organization of the tribes.

Richard Lorenz's chapter about the anti-Soviet Basmachi movement in Central Asia, and particularly in Ferghana, has as its primary focus the economic, social, and political bases of the Basmachi movement. By 1917, cotton farmers in these areas had already begun to sink into poverty, and their conditions grew even worse after the events of October 1917, with the new leaders' confiscation of the entire cotton harvest. During the years of War Communism, 1918 to 1921, the harshly anti-Islamic policies of the Russian Bolshevik Soviets in Central Asia drove the Muslims to the Basmachis. Their struggle was brought down not only because of the superior military forces of the Red Army, but also because of the lack of military and political unity among the insurgents.

Marie Broxup's essay treats the trends toward politicization of Islam in the former Soviet Union. One of the roots of Islamic revival is *mirasism*, the rediscovery of the national legacy of past eras, when Central Asia was the center of the Islamic world. From this perspective, the cultural and political legacy is inseparable from that of religion. As a consequence, nonbelievers often practice religious rituals, thus making clear their non-European and non-Russian national and cultural affiliations. Sufi Islam (*muridism*) in the North Caucasus, following in the tradition of the anti-Russian struggles of the nineteenth century, was regarded by Soviet authorities as a potential force for political opposition. The Afghanistan War led to a series of local jihad actions in southern Tajikistan. The need to restrain the advance of militant Islam, which seemed uncontrollable, was yet another reason for the Soviet Union's pressing interest in bringing the War in Afghanistan to an end. After the breakup of the USSR, civil war split Tajikistan into several regions, each dominated by the local elite. Certain regions and their political leaders strove for a public order established on basic Islamic principles. This is, in one respect, proof of the strength of Islam in Tajikistan and, at the same time, of the weakness of national cohesion there.

Alexandre Popović considers the problems of Islam's politicization in the former Yugoslavia. Since the 1970s, evidence has emerged of the radicalization of Muslim nationalism in Bosnia. Its proponents included, first, the intellectuals of Bosnia-Herzegovina, who enjoyed the protection of local party leaders and who tended toward glorification and mystification of a distinct culture and local history. The second group held to a form of Islamic religious radicalism and was accused by its opponents of seeking the overthrow of the contemporary social order and the institution of an Islamic republic.

The editors have not been able to try to bring consistency into the authors' detailed assessments and interpretations. Alongside the numerous points of agreement, the reader will discover points of controversy regarding important questions. For example, the policies of the Czarist government are judged quite differently by Dr. Rorlich and Dr. Kappeler. The drawing-up of national boundaries in Central Asia in 1924, leading to the creation of separate republics, receives differing assessments from Drs. Fragner and Brunner. Dr. Höpken and Dr. Popović categorize the recognition of the Bosnian Muslims as a nation in different ways and accord it differing values.

These diverse interpretations reflect contemporary controversies in research, where the three essential elements of Muslim national development and identity are loyalty to religion in the framework of the ʿumma, to language and nation in the framework of the republics, and to tribe. Each carries different weight. Discussion of these issues is active indeed and is affected by current dramatic events in the political arena. The authors and editors of this volume seek to contribute to this discussion and to encourage further attention to these complex problems—issues that continually grow in significance.

Some overlap of content is inevitable. The reader will find information about the national development of the Bosnian Muslims, for instance, in Dr. Ramet's contribution as well as in Dr. Höpken's. These disadvantages of overlap have been judged of little weight when compared to the advantages of having each essay retain its internal coherence.

Part I *Nation Building*

1. The Nationalization of the Uzbeks and Tajiks

Bert G. Fragner

I

According to a report in *Der Spiegel*, May 11, 1987, the Tehran periodical of the "Party of the Islamic Republic" (the leading party at that time, now dissolved) had made a statement some time earlier to the effect that, from the Iranian point of view, the Soviet Socialist Republics of Uzbekistan, Tajikistan, Turkmenistan, and parts of Georgia were regarded as areas to be liberated. The statement claimed that those territories had been seized illegitimately from the Iranian state of that time by czarist Russia in the nineteenth century. Had this information been correct, the new rulers of Iran would have been articulating in semi-official form a claim that had already been part of the repertoire of the radical, nationalistic ideology of so-called Pan-Iranism for centuries.

The political and historical substance of this claim is false, for the most part. From the sixteenth to the nineteenth centuries, the sovereigns of the Iranian highlands did in fact reclaim Georgia, Armenia, and northern Azerbaijan, as well as the southern regions of Daghistan and Turkmenistan, and ruled them for some time. During the past three thousand years, Uzbekistan and Tajikistan, that is, the classical cultural domain of Transoxiana, between the Oxus/Amu Darya and the Jaxartes/Sir-Darya, along with the Pamir mountains and their headland, were incorporated only rarely and for relatively brief periods by any state with its center in the Iranian highlands.[1]

From a cultural perspective, Transoxiana has assuredly been, since antiquity, one of the cradles of Iranian civilization, both in its socio-cultural and, for a considerable period, its linguistic aspects. It was in Transoxiana that the political structures of Khwarazm and Sogdia developed:

these cultural areas had been in existence since ancient times and were by far the best-known domains of Iranian culture of Central Asian antiquity and of the early Middle Ages. From Transoxiana, too, came important impulses for the creation of the classical New Persian literary language during the ninth and tenth centuries A.D.[2] Those with a legitimate share in this common inheritance include all the speakers of the modern variants of New Persian: Farsi (hitherto referred to as "Persian") in Iran, Dari in Afghanistan, and Tajik in the Soviet Union. In contrast, however, no common "political inheritance" can be construed, despite the best efforts to do so.

Since the high Middle Ages, Transoxiana, the Mawaraunnahr of the Arabic-Islamic geographers, was a site of migration and settlement for Turkic ethnic and racial groups from Inner Asia. As a result of the gradual process of migration, between the fifteenth and early twentieth centuries there was a complex, contradictory, and dynamic condition of symbiosis among a great number of ethnic groups. During the reign of Timur and his successors, who made Transoxiana their political center during the late fourteenth and fifteenth centuries, this socio-historical symbiosis took on the features that remain characteristic of the region even today.

Eastern Turkic speakers constituted the military basis of the Timurid regime, which explains their political dominance. There is no doubt that they represented the main beneficiaries of the Timurid state's policies of raiding and taxation. Their military and tribal leaders, the so-called amirs, formed a type of aristocratic class in Transoxiana. The settled urban populace, however, was still influenced by Iranian socio-cultural forms from a linguistic point of view, through Persian, and in general this was also the case for the farmers living on the plains. The remote and mountainous terrain of the Pamirs, then as now, was to some extent a refuge for very diverse Iranian peoples.

The particular structure of Central Asian nomadism among both riders and herders, into which the present study cannot venture, in the long term caused the continuing settlement of Turkic individuals and small groups, who were in most cases detached from their tribal bonds. With the adoption of the ways of life of traditional settled peoples, they to a large extent also took on the cultural systems of the same: patterns of settlement, agricultural and economic traditions, typical Iranian urbanism, and, not least, intellectual culture.

Public administration, including finance, was completely derived from the traditions of the Irano-Islamic Middle Ages. Persian prevailed as the court and administrative language and also furnished the elite court and high culture with a linguistic medium of communication that held great prestige. As in its other regions of diffusion, from Anatolia to India, however, Persian was in no way the universal mother tongue, but for a long time it functioned as a language of communication among different regions and groups—a lingua franca.

The organization of the Timurid state took into account this basic socio-ethnic condition. It recognized two deliberative governing bodies of the sovereign: a so-called "Persian Divan": the assembly of bureaucrats and financial specialists, and the "Divan of the Amirs," in which military and political problems were debated. The language of transaction of the former was Persian, of the latter, Turkic. The Persian Divan fixed its signature with the designation *Divan-e Tajikan* (in Persian) and *Sart Divani* or *Tajik Divani* (in Turkic).[3]

In the Turkic usage of Transoxiana in the late Middle Ages, the terms *Sart* and *Tajik* designated, above all, a socio-cultural group. The term *Tajik* was also used in this sense throughout the area where Persian was used, which is partially the case even today. It was therefore in no way a distinctly ethnic appellation. To a much greater extent, it denoted nontribal agricultural and urban social groups with an Iranian cultural background who had been settled for centuries, in order to distinguish them from nomadic or transhumant groups that were organized by clans. In the highlands of Iran and Central Asia from the late Middle Ages onward, the clans were most often—although by no means always—ethnic Turkic people. This is the distinction referred to by the common and polarizing phrase in traditional Persian historiography *"Tork o Tajik,"* distinguishing the Turkic clans, politically and militarily dominant for centuries, from the settled social groups acculturated to New Persian. The populations who spoke Persian but who were tribally organized (for example, the Bakhtiyaris of Central Iran or the Hazaras of the Afghan mountains) were never included in the concept of *Tajik*. The term was often used pejoratively by the militant Turkic clan aristocracy. In Afghanistan, *Tajik* now functions as an ethnic designation for Persian speakers there: especially on the part of the tribally organized Pashtu, it is in fact a signification of the otherness of nontribal settled peoples; in no way does it extend to all the Persian speakers of the country. The ethno-linguistic self-designation of the Afghan Persian speakers, moreover, is not *Tajik*, but is commonly *Farsivan* (roughly, "Persian-like").

In Central Asia, too, the term *Tajik*, like its synonym *Sart*, was for centuries not primarily an ethnic designation but a socio-cultural category. The nominal precursors of the modern Tajiks belonged to the settled, nontribal or detribalized groups of the population that were influenced by Iranian culture. The use of the Persian language was not the dominant criterion for the definition of either *Sart* or *Tajik*. Even in the twentieth century the inhabitants of the Pamirs who were influenced exclusively by Iranian rather than Turkic preferred for themselves the ethno-linguistic designation *Farsigu* over *Tajik*, which they regarded as perjorative, to the extent that they used Persian and not one of the Iranian languages known as "Pamir languages." Consequently, the notions *Tajik* and *Sart* arose in situations where the populations so termed came into contact with militant, tribally organized ethnics, mainly of Turkic descent, and had to coexist with them.[4]

These interethnic relationships in Transoxiana, already evident in the fifteenth century, were characteristic of the region up to the beginning of the twentieth century—over the span of half a millenium. There are two fundamental observations to be made in this regard:

1. Concerning the linguistic situation: In the course of the cultural Iranization of the agrarian, urban, and court strata, another Eastern Turkic language, Chaghatay, developed and spread. From the fifteenth century onward it held high prestige alongside Persian. Like Ottoman, this Turkic court language was replete with lexical and even syntactical elements from Persian literary language. Through borrowings from classical Persian literary traditions, a rich Chaghatay artistic literature came into existence in Transoxiana, making its way thence into other Turkic-speaking regions as far away as Kazan on the Volga, the Crimea, and even the Ottoman Empire. Persian, with similar breadth of distribution, made linguistic contact with Afghanistan and, above all, with Islamic India possible for the people of Transoxiana. For political reasons there was less contact with Iran, which had become increasingly isolated from neighboring Sunni regions after having adopted Twelver Shiism in the sixteenth century. In Transoxiana an unusual condition of bilingualism arose, in which the knowledge of both Turkic and Persian became characteristic of its settled population.[5]

2. The military and political sovereignty of Transoxiana passed from the hands of the Timurids to another power: the leaders of the Turkic clan federation of the Uzbeks, who replaced Timurid rule. From a linguistic point of view they were not Eastern Turks, but rather so-called Northern Turks, and were thus related to the Kazakhs, Bashkirs, and Tatars. Nonetheless, they adapted themselves to the socio-cultural and linguistic realities of Transoxiana. Subsequently, two states that were ruled by elites of the Uzbek clans came into existence: Bukhara and, on the territory of ancient Khwarazm, Khiva. In the eighteenth century a third was added: the khanate of Khokand in Farghana and in the northern river-oases of the Sir Darya (Jaxartes).

Although in Khiva the significance of the Persian language declined, following a long preference for Chaghatay, in both of the other states, especially Bukhara, Persian retained its status as the official language of the court and administration. It was only after the Russian conquest in the nineteenth century, in consequence of which the people of Transoxiana came into closer contact with other Turkic-speaking peoples of Russia, that the linguistic balance of Persian and Chaghatay began to shift gradually toward Turkic.

Toward the end of the nineteenth century the situation was as follows: the Northern Turkic clans of the Uzbeks and their elites represented an honored quasi-nobility that had increasingly lost power owing to Russian colonialism. The agrarian and urban Sarts were held in low esteem by the Uzbeks: European observers around the turn of the twentieth century report cultural Iranization among the Sarts, but at the same time they point to a trend toward increased use of Eastern Turkic dialects related to Chaghatay. Exceptions to this rule, however, were Samarkand, a Russian city since 1867, and the Amirate of Bukhara, which was able to maintain its inner autonomy under an Uzbek dynasty until 1920—and relatively so as a Soviet People's Republic until 1924. The eastern part of this amirate (the range of the Pamir Mountains with its foothills) remained essentially Iranian. The majority of the Sarts of Farghana were similarly bilingual, although to a certain degree Persian was more prevalent.

Among Russian political observers, as well as among Russian orientalists (Nikolai Ostroumov), the word *Sart*, hitherto a traditional synonym for *Tajik*, became an ethnic designation for the settled populations who now increasingly spoke Turkic but were even more predominantly bilingual, being misconstrued in opposition to the Uzbek clans. In addition, reports from around 1900, particularly Russian ones, tended to use the word *Tajik* for native people presumed to be primarily Persian-speaking. Nikolai Ostroumov, mentioned above, concluded that the Eastern Turkic colloquial language of Transoxiana—the direct predecessor of modern-day Uzbek—was "Sart." The native people had never used that term for it, however. In effect, therefore, Ostroumov created a fictive "Sart" Turkic, which even found a place as a category in the Russian census.[6]

II

Toward the end of the nineteenth century, the ideas of the Muslim Turkic nationalists, under the broad heading of Jadidism, and especially Turkism and Pan-Turkism, swept into the colonial administrative region of Russian Turkistan and, following some delay, overtook both the protectorate states of Bukhara and Khiva. In this context, the existing multicultural situation of Central Asia did not furnish favorable conditions for the propagation of nationalist ideas, nor even Pan-Turkic ones. To a significant degree, settled society in Transoxiana was socially and culturally distinct from the almost exclusively tribal nomadic society of the Northern Turkic (Kipchak) Kazakhs and the Southern Turkic (Oghuz) Turkmens. Within Transoxiana the clan aristocracy of the Uzbeks—nontranshumant but linguistically Northern Turkic like the Kazakhs—distinguished themselves from the socio-culturally separate group of bilingual Sarts (Tajiks), who were influenced by Eastern Turkic dialects, Chaghatay literature, and Persian.

The perjorative meaning which the Uzbeks had long given the words *Sart* and *Tajik* was taken into colonial Russian usage. Before the 1917 Revolution, the word *Sart* acquired the unfavorable meaning of "Turkistani natives," collectively, just as the Russians in Azerbaijan at that time employed the disparaging epithet *Tatar* for the Turkic-speaking Muslims living there.

While some intellectuals of Central Asia accepted the reformist ideas of Jadidism, which had been brought by the Tatars of the Volga and the Crimea, as well as having come from Ottoman Turkey, its nationalist and Turkicist variant could only be partially implemented, by what might be called "Turkistanists," who dreamt of the consolidation of the ethnic mosaic of Central Asia into a homogeneous "Nation of Turkistan." This nation was to be dominated linguistically by Eastern Turkic, construed as a modern pendant on the necklace of now-archaic Chaghatay. Furthermore, the acceptance of the designation "Turkistan" for the whole of Central Asia was nothing other than the adoption of a concept molded by the Russian colonial administration. The word *Turkistan* traditionally had referred only to the oasis lands bordering the northern bank of the Sir Darya. The Russian administration was the first to extend the word's denotation to the region of the Governor-generalship of Turkistan.

The regionalist-nationalist activists of the Northern Turkic Kazakhs and the Southern Turkic Turkmens did not feel that they were identified in such a "Greater Turkistan" concept, nor did the Sarts (or rather Tajiks) inside Transoxiana, who did not want to renounce their Persian cultural background. The Turkmens had had their own tradition of script and literature since the eighteenth century, and the Kazakh written language had come into existence earlier in the nineteenth century. In contrast to the Turkic of Transoxiana, neither had derived from Eastern Turkic.[7]

For this reason a second type of Jadidism came into play in Central

Asia: rather than pursuing nationalistic goals of reform, this form of Jadidism sought modernization and cultural revolution, and it proposed the preservation of ethnic pluralism. It took a critical stance toward the Turkic inclinations of many Jadidists. The champions of Turkicism demanded the abandonment of Persian and its dialects—reviled as "backward" and "reactionary"—in favor of the creation of a Turkic tongue, derived from Eastern Turkic, as the standard educated language of the whole society. Their opponents, however, insisted on the retention of Persian as the authentic cultural language of Transoxiana and the Pamirs, at least as the region's second language.

Apart from these differences, the common orientation of all of these reformist intellectuals was opposition to the yoke of Russian colonialism, as well as to the local regimes in both protectorates of Bukhara and Khiva, which were seen as archaic and reactionary. The gradual increase in the popularity of the reformist movements among the local populace led to more and more radical engagement against czarist foreign domination.[8]

Under the influence of the Young Turk Revolution in the Ottoman Empire, the nationalist-Turkist orientation of the enlightened intellectuals of Central Asia gained increasing ascendancy over other groups. Their ideological goals were unambiguously formulated and were put forward as the sole path to better mobilization of their adherents, since they drew on ideological and political experience and discourse that extended from the Tatar reform movements on the Volga and in the Crimea to the Ottoman Young Turks.

III

The declared intention of the new Soviet powers to solve the "National Question" finally, definitively—without running counter to the Soviet interest in perpetuating their own power—led to the polarization of the nationalist discussion among Transoxianan intellectuals. This situation must be seen in the context of the Soviet system's abandonment by large sectors of the population in the early nineteen twenties, which trend was expressed by the manifold movements of so-called Basmachiism.[9] During the first years after the 1917 Revolution, Soviet authority was felt by many local peoples to be a new variety of foreign domination, but one that went so far as to declare a programmatic objective of interference with and alteration of the traditional social structure of Transoxiana.

After the mastery of the military problems with which the Soviet regime found itself confronted during the Civil War in Turkistan in the early twenties, the new rulers consolidated control, effecting the "national partition" of Central Asia. From 1922 to 1923, at the latest, nearly all adherents of Turkist ideals were express opponents of the Soviet regime, whether between the Volga and the Urals or in Central Asia. Consequently, the Soviet leadership had to combat the program and the political effectiveness of the "Turkistanists," along with any proposed goals of the unification of Turkistan as a territory and a state and the homogenization of a "single nation of Turkistan" (including not only Transoxiana, but also the Kazakhs, Kirghiz, and Turkmens), as well as the goal of unifying such a proposed nation as a Turkic-speaking one.

Here it must be emphasized that the concrete socio-historical circumstances of the segmented, multiethnic and multicultural society of Central Asia and of its heartland, Transoxiana, having evolved over the course of five hundred years, were not in harmony with the Pan-Turkist and nationalist conception of a nation of Turkistan that was to be unified territorially, socially, and linguistically. It is therefore understandable that within Transoxiana, as among many Kazakhs and Turkmens, there should be as much skepticism toward such a concept as there was support of the Turkistanists in their role as the vanguard of the anti-Soviet movements in the early twenties.

The matter was further complicated by the fact that large sectors of the local populace rejected the nationalists' modernist concepts, clashing as they did with the people's identification as members of the ʿUmma— the community of Muslims. Many rejected any modernist ideology as contrary to Islam, disregarding the fact that all these groups shared a thoroughgoing rejection of the new Soviet system. This local resistance to the modernist Turkistan nationalists was conditioned by internal facts of historical development and initially had nothing to do with a conscious accommodation to the objectives of Soviet policies of nationalization.

IV

In retrospect, the foundation of the Soviet Socialist Republic of Uzbekistan and the proclamation of an Uzbek nation by the Soviet regime appears to be a masterpiece of *Realpolitik*. Viewed from without, these measures stand in stark contrast to the goals of the Turkistanists. In actuality, however, following the defeat of the Basmachi movement in the mid-twenties, they offered many of the partisans opportunities for indigenous group identification. The opposition between Uzbek and Sart was set aside; the demeaning word *Sart* was forbidden; all were able to use the proud designation of *Uzbek*, whose etymology was popularly construed to be "one who is his own master." Chaghatay was declared to be a "nonlanguage," rather than a "nonperson." The newly created Uzbek language was initially based on the Uzbek clans' Northern Turkic dialects, similar to those of the Kazakhs; these were the dialects of the "genuine" Uzbeks. Beginning in the nineteen thirties, however, Uzbek shifted to an Eastern Turkic basis. Present-day standard Uzbek could be termed either *New Chaghatay* or, even better, *Post-Chaghatay*. For ideological reasons, however, in the Soviet view such a designation was impossible. Rather, the term *Old Uzbek* was decreed for Chaghatay, Transoxiana's literary language of five hundred years.

This was a highly questionable measure, since the Northern Turkic dialects thus became known as "Old Uzbek," even though they had existed for hundreds of years at considerable remove from Chaghatay and its dialects. In any case, the creation of the Uzbek territory/nation was diametrically opposed to the political objectives of the Turkistanists but, on the other hand, in its structure and methodology it was completely in keeping with the Turkistanists' arguments. The old state structures of Bukhara and Khiva (Khwarazm), with their regional and multiethnic definitions, were abolished once and for all, which had in fact been one of the demands of the Turkistanists.

The traditions of Transoxianan cultural life supplied substantial pre-requisites for the historical self-concept the Soviet regime sought for the newly created "Uzbek nation." As a fairly homogeneous legacy of late medieval Transoxiana, the Soviet Socialist Republic of Uzbekistan has thus far been able to present itself as a socio-historical continuation of Transoxianan culture, with greater historical justification than would have been the case with a state entity of "Greater Turkistan" (which, largely due to external factors, namely, Soviet power politics, was never created). In summary, the rejection of ethnic and social pluralism in favor of a unified, Turkic-speaking nation—indeed, a nation of "Uzbeks"— was a measure that was wholly consistent with the structures, if not the political objectives as well, of Turkist thought.

The opinion has been put forth that the Soviet leadership founded the Uzbekistan SSR as a compromise bid, so to speak: as a "Lesser Turkistan" restricted to the Transoxianan heartland. Whatever, today's Uzbekistan has undoubtedly become the locus of national identification and patriotic feeling for more than sixteen million people in Transoxiana.[10]

V

What happened to the Transoxianan intellectuals who could not identify with the Turkistanist ideas of national and linguistic unification during the early twenties—who, after that time, as before, regarded the Iranian elements of the legacy of their land as an essential part of their culture?

In face of the pointed opposition between Soviet authorities and Turkistanist nationalists, in the early years of the Central Asian Civil War there was a noticeable convergence of interests, albeit a limited one, between the proponents of the Soviet policy of nationalities and the supporters of regional inclinations among the Muslim modernists in Central Asia. Such regional nationalists had gained a foothold in (Turkic-speaking) Azerbaijan in 1920 and had repudiated the defenders of a trans-regional imbedding of their land in a political Turkdom, as Tadeusz Swietochowski has recently shown.[11]

In Transoxiana it was above all the proponents of "Tajikdom," aligning themselves against Turkist objectives, who, favoring a convergence of interests, presented themselves to the Soviet regime as provisional partners. They were concerned to preserve the particular cultural dimensions of Transoxiana that derived from Persian, as against the Turkistanists' objectives of imposing political, linguistic, and cultural unity on the whole region. With regard to the designation of *Tajik* for the social group that was always the bearer of their cultural forms (including the Persian language), the cultural interests of a "Tajik people" were increasingly articulated.

One of the forerunners of this movement was Sadriddin Ayniy, an author, poet, and cultural politician who was originally a Jadidist. His writings indicate that the exclusive insistence on the Persian language was at first not the primary goal of this group. From around 1923 onward, however, the linguistic and political pressure of the Turkistan nationalists had the effect of making the defense of Persian more and more a central aspect of the program Ayniy and those of like mind had in view. Ayniy himself nevertheless was composing literary works in Uzbek even decades later. In view of the immediate circumstances of the foundation of Uzbekistan, described above, and because Soviet politicians persisted in the creation of single nations with linguistic and territorial unity (in accordance with Stalin's definition of the concept of *nation*), in the end the Tajik regionalists could do nothing but promulgate the Persian language as a "national language" in a very limited territory, which was realized in the founding of Tajikistan, first as an autonomous republic within Uzbekistan (October 14, 1924), and then some years later in the rank of a Union republic (October 5, 1929). The proclamation of Tajikistan took place, furthermore, against the resistance not only of the declared Turkistanists, but also on the part of some "New Uzbek" patriots.[12]

At first this development proceeded entirely within the notions of the makers of Soviet nationality policy. Away from Soviet eyes, however, it concealed for some time another inherent danger: the spread of "Pan-Iranism" among Tajik intellectuals, that is, the consciousness of deep commonality of the cultural and linguistic heritage of the Central Asian Persian-speakers with the people of Iran and Afghanistan. The political potential inherent in such an ideology, destabilizing for the Soviet regime, was well known by the Moscow authorities. From 1925, at the latest, with the Uzbeks meanwhile constituted as a nation with their own Turkic national language, the intellectuals who propounded a distancing of the Tajiks from the Uzbeks, were themselves to be distinguished culturally from the Iranians and Afghans as a special Central Asian/Iranian element. The concept of *Tajikistan* was now finally transformed into a national designation.

A normative Tajik language was subsequently established, distinct from classical Persian and with substantial consideration of the phonetic, lexical, morphological, and syntactic peculiarities of Central Asian speakers of Persian. From 1927 to 1940, the alphabet of this distinctive form of New Persian was a phonetic one based on the Roman alphabet; this was replaced by a Cyrillic alphabet in 1940, which is the one in use today. In contrast to traditional literary Persian, which continued to prevail in Iran and Afghanistan, language reform in the forms of standard Tajik has hitherto been obstructed by an abundance of Russianisms, neologisms based on calques from Russian and some new coinings, which have prevented reform along lines parallel to the language reform of Persian in Iran. Nevertheless, there remains a general orientation toward the language of classical Persian literature. Certain theoreticians and writers have reacted by looking back to various dialects as the basis of the new Tajik language—a matter of authentic "proletarian" linguistic elements. They have pushed toward tendencies such as that of the "Prolet Cult" but their efforts have been largely rejected.[13]

True to general nationalistic models, which throughout the world have always been historically derived, a specific Tajik national history had to be created for the securing of Tajik national consciousness within the Soviet framework. The objectives of such an effort were many. One was the task of tracing consistently the roots of the Tajik people at least back to late antiquity. In the Soviet outlook, the Tajiks are described as direct descendants of the pre-Islamic Central Asian Iranian Sogdians, and the blossoming of the literary language of New Persian in Eastern Iran and Transoxiana is presented as the Tajiks' primary historical accomplishment.

Such a view of history fulfills several different objectives: first, the Tajiks are presented as the oldest Transoxianan race, having wielded cultural influence on the region between the Oxus and the Jaxartes long before the Turks, who began to press forcefully into the region only in the tenth century. Secondly, with the argument of the Sogdian origin of the Tajiks, the Persians of the Iranian highlands are represented as being of a genuinely different race, being referred back to the "state people" of the pre-Islamic Sasanian Empire, which is consonant with modern Iranian nationalism.

In accordance with the Soviet-Tajik view of history, furthermore, the classical New Persian language appears as a literary language developed mainly by the Tajiks of Transoxiana and Khorasan and only later propagated by the actual "Persians." This teaching made it possible to declare all of classical Persian literature to be the cultural heritage of the Tajik people, regardless of the background of any particular poet.

A further effect of these historical principles arose from the fact that they were best adapted to securing for the Tajiks—only declared to be a nation twenty years earlier—the consciousness of a cultural group that had existed since time immemorial. Consequently, the collective designation *Tajik*, which had been a disparaging one until the time of the 1917 Revolution, was elevated to the status of a proud, lofty appellation for this nation in a Central Asian and Islamic cultural context.

As for the specifically Tajik, internal aspects of this image of national history: in the general Soviet outlook the writing of the history of the Tajik republic had to fulfill further criteria. From the twenties onward, the category of the "two streams" (dva potoka) was obligatory in Soviet cultural and historical research, as well as in the popularization of its results. The national historical and cultural legacy was not to be elaborated as a unified category, but rather in terms of the confrontation of ruling-class reactionary traditions with the nature of the "proletariat" or, where appropriate, "pre-proletariat."

The writing of national history was thus a basis for the establishment of the historical development of class struggle. Historical phenomena were always to be attributed to one of the two "streams" and judged as "progressive" or "reactionary." The discussion of these categories was from the beginning constrained by the ideological programs of the leadership of the CPSU. According to this outlook, in part even today, there is a general principle in effect in Soviet-Tajik history: the religion of Islam and its socio-cultural manifestations among the Tajiks should be stigmatized as fundamentally "reactionary."

From the nineteen thirties onward, class analysis of premodern societies had to fit the prescribed category of "feudalism." All developments that supplied the requisite conditions for the consolidation of Soviet power in Central Asia were to be judged as "progressive." With the propagation of "Soviet patriotism" in the forties and fifties this principle was further applied to political unification with Russia; that is, to czarist colonization of Central Asia. Contemporary regionalism and nationalism was to be quickly condemned as anti-Russian, hence "reactionary"; conversely, affirmations of "friendship" with the peoples of the USSR, and above all with the "Great Russian Brotherhood," were obligatory.

All of this serves to emphasize the fact that the Soviet-Tajik image of the national history that has emerged so far, and has been widely accepted and internalized in the region, was developed along a chain of constant contradictions. The separation from Turkic concepts, and from those based on an encompassing nation of "Turkistan" demanded the glorification of the Tajik-Iranian past in Central Asia. It is said that Joseph V. Stalin himself demonstrated that "the Tajik people has an ancient, distinct culture."[14] The period of Samanid rule in the tenth century, the time of first blossoming of the Persian-Tajik literary language, though "feudal" according to the generally prescribed guidelines, is esteemed to be a high point in the cultural formation of Tajikistan.

The labeling of the Islamization of the Tajiks as "a step backward in history" has produced suspicious analogies to modern Iranian national historicism, which is viewed with hostility. Pro-emancipation Jadid intellectuals of the prerevolutionary period (Ahmad Danish and his circle) were to some extent revered as enlightened forerunners of the revolution, and thus as Tajik national heroes. Until the present time, historians of Tajik culture have been faced with difficulties in that, while they extol Bukhara and Samarkand as centuries-old Tajik cultural centers, these cities belong to the neighboring Soviet Socialist Republic of Uzbekistan. To question the boundaries of the republics, however, was considered "bourgeois" nationalism, and hence anti-Soviet, with a single exception of Farghana's city of Khojand (Leninabad). Khojand's incorporation into the Tajik SSR, though it initially caused violent local disagreement, was later triumphantly cited as evidence for what were termed the flexible and democratic policies of Stalin's times. The requisite cultural and historical division of Tajik history from that of other Iranian peoples contrasts starkly with the concomitant melding of all classical Persian literature into "the cultural heritage" of the Tajik nation. The vanquishing of the multiethnic character of premodern Transoxiana through the creation of national Soviet states is revered as an important station along the path of progress. At the same time, however, former ethnic relationships serve as evidence for the "friendship" between the nation of the Tajiks—naturally much older—and that of the Uzbeks. The enumeration of other contradictions could fill several pages, and all go back to the historically based convergence of interests between the former defenders of Tajik national thought—against "Turkistanism"— with Soviet national policy.

All of this derives from two facts:

1. The self-identification of the Tajiks as a nation in the nineteen twenties bore from the very beginning significant historical features: sociocultural interpretations of the history of Central Asia as the constituent elements of Tajik national thought.

2. The development of Tajik national consciousness in the early twenties was accepted as fundamentally positive under Soviet nationality policy from the beginning.

To a large extent, then, historical discussion has dominated the national cultural existence of the Tajiks. The Soviet authorities have thus far continued to legitimize freedom of content for this discussion. It has been, and is still, carried on with strong public resonance on the part of journalists and writers, as well as specialists in history. It functions as an important matter of politics in the public life of the Tajikistan Soviet Socialist Republic and includes all aspects of its social and cultural history. In the larger Soviet context, it is not only Tajiks who participate in the discussion, but also other historians, orientalists, literary critics, archaeologists, and the like.[15]

The development of Tajik national consciousness under the conditions set by the Soviet regime has thus far found remarkably little expression in Western research. There are only a few monographs from the Soviet point of view explicitly concerned with Tajikistan.[16] In European study as well, Tajik nationalism is only treated in linear opposition to Soviet nationality policy. The affinities encountered from the beginning between the former defenders of "Tajikism" and the Soviet regime, and the resulting dialectical dynamic, are simply ignored. This is true to an even greater extent for investigations that deal with the nationalistic struggles of Soviet Turkic peoples—or, as they have often been called recently, "Soviet Muslims"—collectively. More or less explicitly transregional Pan-Turkist, Turkistanist, relatively "Muslim/nationalist communist" conceptions are put forth, in almost Manichaean fashion, as historically justified, autochthonous models of feasible national development in opposition to measures of the makers of Soviet nationality policy, which are judged to be artificial and arbitrary. This essay has attempted to illustrate that such arguments will not do justice to the complex historical context. The Soviet Socialist Republics of both Uzbekistan and Tajikistan exist in essentially plausible continuity with respect to the premodern cultural landscape of Transoxiana, as would have been the case as well with a nation of "Greater Turkistan" that included Kazakhs and Turkmens. Because of the enduring Turko-Iranian bilingualism and the many linguistic affinities between the two genetically distinct languages, communication between the two Soviet Socialist republics can be mutually intelligible, now as before.

Many Western authors have subsumed the Tajiks—even expressly—in the Turkic people; in doing so they have followed unconsciously and uncritically the premises of earlier Turkist nationalists who would see Central Asia's Persian speakers as merely linguistically alienated Turks. In this respect they are like the theoreticians of modern Turkey who declare that the Kurds are officially "Mountain Turks," having been alienated from their original and true language—Turkish—for a brief period of their history. The bizarre logic, along similar lines, of the present Bulgarian authorities for the systematic de-Turkicization of Bulgarian Muslims, also makes clear on what a low level the theoretical discussion of some Turkist nationalists took place during the early decades of this century.[17] This would also become clear, however, if investigators of the history of ideas and ideology of Russian and Soviet Muslims were to keep more in mind the non-Russian and non-Soviet components of their study. Among other Western Asian ideologies, scholars might consider the ideas—of great historical impact yet extraordinarily abstruse effect—of the Ottoman Pan-Turkist, Tekinalp, who at the turn of the century dreamed of a Turkic world empire that included Finland and Hungary in the west and Korea and Japan in the east and thus turned the heads of many young people of his time.

It is now time to become aware of the recent history and culture of Central Asian people as an object of study in its own right, rather than proceeding exclusively or predominantly from an outside perspective. The latter will be the case as long as analysts continue to regard the so-called Soviet Muslims only from the perspective of their anti-Soviet resistance and the ways in which they depend on the "Moscow Central," thus disregarding the fact that regions like Central Asia and the Caucasus have also experienced multifaceted inner development under Soviet auspices and that to a great extent this inner development is what determines the reality of life for the people who live there. Hegemonic dependency now dominates the greater portion of the human population; even the nations of Central Europe until recently were no exception. Historians would be ill-advised, however, to regard their history and culture from this angle alone and blind themselves to the richness of other aspects of human existence. A trend in this direction has become quite evident in Central Asian studies in the West for the past ten to twenty years. It should receive increasing support from all sides.[18]

Notes

1. Sogdia and Khwarazm were integral parts of the Iranian Achaemenid empire (559–330 B.C.); Sogdia constituted the sixteenth satrapy of this empire and also belonged to the Seleucid empire for a short period. This dual sovereignty did not extend north of the Amu Darya. The power of the Sasanians (226–651 A.D.) who had settled in the Iranian highlands encompassed Transoxiana only occasionally and temporarily. As a result of the Arabo-Muslim conquest (seventh century A.D.), both the Iranian highlands and Transoxiana were brought into the framework of the eastern domain of the Caliphate. The political power, however, was centered in Syria and, later, in Mesopotamia. The empire of the Islamic Iranian Samanids (ninth–tenth century A.D.) had its center in Transoxiana (with its capital at Bukhara), from whence its influence radiated over Eastern Iran. Thus, in terms of territory, the Samanids can be regarded as a genuinely Transoxianan political force.

For a short time in the eleventh century A.D. the Turkic Great Seljuks exercised sovereignty in Transoxiana. In the twelfth century they were displaced by the Transoxianan (even by name) Khwarazmshahs, also of Turkic origin. Under the Chinggisid Mongols (thirteenth and fourteenth centuries) the political separation of Iran from Transoxiana became complete: the Mongol Il-Khanids reigned in the Iranian highlands; Khwarazm belonged to the Golden Horde (its center on the lower Volga). The rest of Transoxiana, together with what is now known as Xinjiang, constituted the "Ulus Chaghatay," also Mongol. The three Mongol realms were in a state of permanent feud with one another. Timur and his successors (fourteenth and fifteenth centuries) regarded Transoxiana as their place of origin and treated Iranian regions as conquered territory. From the beginning of the sixteenth century onward, Iran and Transoxiana shared no common political objectives. The propagation of Twelver-Shiism by the Safavids (after 1500) created yet another divisive factor between Iran and Transoxiana, which remained Sunni. This schism has effect even to this day.

2. Gilbert Lazard, "The Rise of the New Persian Language," in *The Cambridge History of Iran*, vol. 4: *The Period from the Arab Invasions to the Saljugs*, ed. R. N. Frye (Cambridge, 1975), pp. 595–632. New Persian quickly established itself as the preeminent transregional language of communication in the "eastern" Islamic world, and thus in the Iranian highlands and in Transoxiana, but also among the Muslims of the Caucasus and in India and even, for some time, in Anatolia (at the time of the Seljuks of Rum and under the early Ottomans). For the Turkic people of Central Asia, as for

the Indian Muslims later, Persian was long the language of Islamic high culture. To a large extent it was the displacement of Arabic by Persian that had made possible this preference for Persian during the Middle Ages: not only as the medium of everyday speech and of courtly literature but, ultimately, also as the language of administration (Wilhelm Barthold, *Zwölf Vorlesungen über die Geschichte Mittelasiens* [Berlin, 1935], pp. 221, 225, and passim).

3. Hans Robert Roemer, *Staatsschreiben der Timuridenzeit. Das Šaraf-namä des Abdallah Marwarid in kritischer Auswertung. Persischer Text in Facsimile*, Veröffentlichung der Orientalischen Kommission, no. 3 (Wiesbaden, 1952), pp. 169ff.

4. Hans Heinrich Schaeder, "Türkische Namen der Iranier," in *Die Welt des Islams, Festschrift Friedrich Giese* (Leipzig, 1941), pp. 1–34; Vasili V. Bartol'd (Barthold), "Tadzhiki—istoricheskii ocherk," in *Akademik V. V. Bartol'd Sochinenie* 2/1 (Moscow, 1963), pp. 452–468; see also W. Barthold, "Tadjik," in *Enzyklopaedie des Islam* 4 (Leiden-Leipzig, 1908, 1913–1936), p. 648. For the term *Sart* and its centuries-long conflation with *Tajik*, cf. Schaeder, *infra*, and Barthold, *Zwölf Vorlesungen*, pp. 239, 243.

5. A. K. Borovkov, "Tadzhiksko-uzbekskoe dvukhiazýchie i vopros o vzaimovliianii tadzhikskogo i uzbekskogo iazýkov," in *Uchenýe zapiski instituta Vostokovedeniia* 4 (1952), pp. 165–200; Gerhard Doerfer, "Türkische Lehnwörter im Tadschikischen, *Abhandlungen für die Kunde des Morgenlandes* 37/3 (Wiesbaden, 1967); Jiri Bečka, "Tajik Literature from the 16th Century to the Present," in *History of Iranian Literature*, ed. Jan Rýpka (Dordrecht, 1968), pp. 483–605, particularly p. 488; V. Barthold, *Zwölf Vorlesungen*, p. 242 and passim. During the first half of this century, Panturkist and "Turkistani" nationalists propagated the idea that Persian had spread in Transoxiana only as an elite language of the educated. This argument, however, had no basis and was plainly an inadmissible transposition of linguistic relations in the Ottoman empire onto Central Asia, as ideological "wishful thinking" on the part of Turkist nationalists. Recent Soviet statistics provide no data for Persian-Turki (hence, Tajik-Uzbek) bilingualism. They only register the statements of those surveyed with regard to their mother tongue and the group to which they assign themselves, so that the percentage of the Tajik minority appears to be significantly below that of the population that is actually still bilingual, as the example of Samarkand reveals. Here the percentage of bilingual individuals (Uzbek-Tajik) may in fact reach nearly 70 percent, whereas the segment of those declaring themselves to be Tajik on the basis of mother tongue only comprised some 25 percent (Alexandre Bennigsen and S. Enders Wimbush, *Muslims of the Soviet Empire: A Guide* [London, 1985], pp. 86, 92f.). Soviet sociological research on bilingualism concentrates heavily in the area of Russian as a national language. With regard to the multilingualism of many regions where non-Russian languages prevailed, such as Transcaucasia, the Caucasus and parts of Siberia, they often neglect the widespread phenomenon of bilingualism, harking back as it often does to premodern relationships (*Present-Day Ethnic Processes in the USSR* [Moscow, 1977/1982], pp. 135–58).

6. On the political, religious and cultural conformation of the earliest Uzbek dynasty, that of the Shaybanids, see Ulrich Haarmann, "Staat und Religion in Transoxiana im fruhen 16. Jahrhundert," *Zeitschrift der Deutschen Morgenländischen Gesellschaft* 124 (1974): 332–369. The traditional priority of Turkic in Khwarazm (later the Khanate of Khiva) derives from the fact that, in contrast to the rest of Transoxiana

in the Mongol period, Khwarazm did not belong to the "Ulus Chaghatay" but to that domain's enemy, "Ulus Juchi"—the so-called Golden Horde. In consequence, for a long time Khwarazm oriented itself toward the lower Volga and was cut off from contact with the Persian-speaking regions of Transoxiana (Bukhara, Samarkand, Ferghana, and the like).

7. As early as the eighteenth century, following the poet Mahtum Quli, written Turkmen poetry found widespread popularity among the Turkmen tribes. In the nineteenth century, Ibrahim ("Abai") Kunanbaev, the Russophile Kazakh poet and man of letters, gave substantial impetus to the emergence of a Kazakh literary language.

8. One of the first measures in this regard was the official abolition of Persian as an administrative and state language in Bukhara, after the proclamation of the "Soviet People's Republic of Bukhara" in 1920. Even the proponents of this measure, however, did not necessarily endorse Pan-Turkic, Turkist or Turkistanist ideology, as attested by the case of the Bukharan administration's head and later high functionary of the Uzbekistan SSR, Fayzullah Khojaev (Russ. Khodzhaev), who was executed following the Moscow Trials. See F. Khojaev, *Izbrannye sochineniia* I (Tashkent, 1970), pp. 36off. There was a movement among the enlightened intellectuals ("Jadids") of the Amirate of Bukhara that looked toward the eventual institution of Persian as the lingua franca. Its most prominent proponent was the politician and man of letters Ahmad Donish, whose followers included the theologian pedagogue Domullo Ikrom. The latter founded one of the first modern schools in Bukhara in 1909, with Persian as the language of instruction. "Modern" Persian schoolbooks were also published, according to the Turkic (Tatar) pattern; two examples are *Tahzib us-sib'yan* (Samarkand, 1909/10) and *Tartil ul-Qur'on* (Bukhara, 1914) by Sadriddin Ayniy. Cf. Bert Fragner, *Sowjetmacht und Islam: die Revolution von Buchara,* in Ulrich Haarmann and Peter Bachmann, eds., *Die islamische Welt zwischen Mittelalter und Neuzeit—Festschrift für Hans Robert Roemer zum 65. Geburtstag,* Beiruter Texte und Studien 22 (Beirut, 1979), pp. 146–166.

9. In this regard see chapter 12, by R. Lorenz, in this volume.

10. The disguised multiethnic character of the new "Uzbek" nation, in good Transoxianan tradition, is clearly expressed in the chapter about the Uzbeks by Bennigsen and Wimbush, *Muslims of the Soviet Empire,* pp. 50–62, esp. pp. 57ff.

11. Tadeusz Swietochowski, *Russian Azerbaijan, 1905–1920: The Shaping of National Identity in a Muslim Community* (Cambridge, 1985). Swietochowski, in his conclusion, sums up the significance, hitherto often misunderstood, of the regional and particularist "nationalisms" among the Turkic peoples of the Soviet Union in the context of Turkic and Pan-Turkic transregional "nationisms of unification," which thus far have generally been those considered in Western research on Central Asia. Paradoxically, there have been periods in which the proponents of such regionalist tendencies have not even perceived themselves as standing in open contradiction to Turkistic theories. Swietochowski argues convincingly that there is a lack of precise historical methodology for tracing the ideological shifts and breaks among the Central Asian pre-revolutionary nationalists. In addition to Khojaev, mentioned above in note 8, prior to the revolution the enlightened men of letters Behbudi and Fitrat (who were not precisely friends of the Soviet regime) were opponents of the creation of a modern "Uzbek" language, but later they harbored complete sympathy for the creation

of a state of Turkistan. To see them—or Khojaev—exclusively as Turkistic adherents of "Turkistanism" would mean the uncritical acceptance of the official Soviet polemic of the twenties and thirties. The fact that the Communist Khojaev was executed for espousing Pan-Turkism (he was subsequently rehabilitated) does not mean that he was necessarily a Pan-Turkist in point of fact! On this subject, see Edward Allworth, *Uzbek Literary Politics* (The Hague, 1964), as well as chapter 3 by Swietochowski in this volume.

12. On Ayni recently: Jiri Bečka, *Sadriddin Ayni: Father of Modern Tajik Culture*, Instituto Universitario Orientale, Seminaro di Studi Asiatici, series minor 5 (Naples, 1980). On the development of Ayni's Tajik nationalism, see his writings, *Bukhara inqilobi ta'rikhi uchun materiyallar* (Moscow, 1926) and "Tajiklar mas'alasi," in *Mehnatlar towushi* (Samarkand, 1923/24)—both in Uzbek—as well as *Ta'rikhi amironi mangitiyai Bukhara* (Tashkent, 1923) and *Namunai adabieti tajik* (Moscow, 1926)—both of the latter in Persian/Tajik. At the time of the territorial division of Tajikistan from Uzbekistan there were heated conflicts between Uzbek opponents and defenders of the Tajik entity, which differences are usually downplayed in Soviet historiography. Detailed information is given in R. Vaidyanath, *The Formation of the Soviet Central Asian Republics* (New Delhi, 1972).

13. For details on this point, see Jiri Bečka, "Tajik Literature from the 16th Century to the Present," in Jan Rypka, ed., *History of Iranian Literature* (Dordrecht, Holland, 1968) and *Sadriddin Ayni: Father of Modern Tajik Culture;* Teresa Rakowska-Harmstone, *Russia and Nationalism in Central Asia: The Case of Tadzhikistan* (Baltimore and London, 1970), pp. 241ff.

14. "*Kommunist Tadzhikistana*, 3 January 1953," p. 2, according to Rakowska-Harmstone, *Russia and Nationalism*, p. 232.

15. The public reception of Tajik historical research plays a surprisingly large role in the intellectual and literary life of the Tajik SSR, as is seen in the popularity in his homeland of Bahodir I. Iskandarov, historian and member of the Academy (director of the "Ahmad Donish" Institute for the History of the Tajik Academy of Sciences). Another example can be seen in the considerable repercussions created by the Tajik translation of the most recent version of the standard history of Tajikistan by Babajan G. Gafurov, a professional historian and long the Party secretary (in Russian: B. G. Gafurov, *Tadzhiki* (Moscow, 1972)), with the title *Tojikon—kitobi yakum: ta'rikhi qadimtarin, qadim va asri siena* (Dushanbe, 1983) and *Tojikon—Kitobi duyum: okhirhoi asri miena va davrai nav* (Dushanbe, 1985). This translation, published over a decade after the original Russian, was considered virtually a national event in Tajikistan. In this connection it is also interesting that Sadriddin Ayni, the "father of Tajik Soviet literature," was always esteemed not only as a man of letters but as a historian as well.

16. Teresa Rakowsa-Harmstone, *Russia and Nationalism*.

17. Attitudes of this type are to be found now and then in some of Baymirza Hayit's writings; e.g., in *Turkestan zwischen Russland und China* (Amsterdam, 1971), pp. 126 ff., 186. Ahmed Zeki Velidi (Togan) formulates them explicitly in *Bügünkü Türkistan ve yaqin mazisi* (Cairo, 1929–30), pp. 67ff. Zeki Velidi's argument that the Central Asian Tajiks never spoke "correct" Persian, but rather only Persian dialects influenced by Turkic, is a futile one, since he also asserts that Persian was not only spoken as

the language of the elite, but that it had been used since ancient times by the "lower" social strata as well.

18. Ewa A. Chylinski has recently voiced such an opinion in her programmatic essay, "Social and Cultural Anthropological Research on Soviet Central Asia: A Western European Perspective," in Mark van Damme and Hendrik Boeschoten, eds., *Utrecht Papers on Central Asia: Proceedings of the First European Seminar on Central Asian Studies held at Utrecht, 16–18 December 1985*, Utrecht Turkological Series, no. 2 (Utrecht, 1987), pp. 9–19.

2. Defining the Orient: A Nineteenth-Century Russo-Tatar Polemic over Identity and Cultural Representation

Edward J. Lazzerini

The Europeans are the most civilized people of our time. Their teachers were Muslims.—Ismail Bey Gasprinskii[1]

Many write in the newspapers of the Polish question, the German question, and the Finnish question, but no one wants to recognize the birth of a *Tatar* question.—M. Mashanov[2]

At the turn of the final decade of the twentieth century, events in the Soviet Union dramatically suggest the utter failure of Communist Party (as of Imperial Russian) policy to achieve one of its longstanding goals: the shaping of a single identity for all Soviet peoples. Complex ethnic realities rooted in history have revealed their extraordinary resistance to seventy years of gross political manipulations and miscalculations; moreover, they threaten, by virtue of a rediscovered and increasingly assertive popular imagination, to destroy the integrity of the "nation" whose pretense is now patent. All along the periphery of the Soviet Union's Russian heartland—and, to a lesser degree, even within its midst—one ethnic group after another has demonstrated varying degrees of impatience with the status quo, taken steps to broaden its economic, cultural, and political autonomy from the center, and insisted in some cases on outright independence.

Much of what is manifest today, however, is reminiscent of, perhaps even a delayed conclusion to, trends unfolding a century ago during the twilight of the czarist era, when cultural awakening under early conditions of modernization began transforming many of the empire's ethnic minorities and creating the bases for separate national conscious-nesses. Looming large then and now among the country's inhabitants were the so-called Islamic peoples, overwhelmingly Turkic linguistically and Muslim by religion and historic culture, but gradually defining their identities by more localized considerations.

In the nineteenth century, Russians distinguished the Turkic peoples poorly one from the other, except for the obvious differences separating those settled into agricultural pursuits and in some numbers urbanized, and those continuing to follow the life patterns of herdsmen. Names were frequently misapplied (*Kirghiz* for *Kazakh* is a well-known example), or extended more broadly than they ought to have been (the term *Tatar* ascribed to Azerbaijanis, for instance), thereby attesting a linguistic sloppiness that reflected ethnographic ignorance to be sure, but also something of the limited respect held for these people by the Russians, who considered themselves more civilized. Of greater significance for the long-term relations between the Empire and its Turkic subjects was the overriding emphasis (with minor exceptions) placed upon the latter's attachment to Islam. However the Turkic peoples might have wished to identify themselves, most would have comfortably acceded to the central importance of Islam in their lives and would have gladly answered to the name "Muslim," even as they would have responded to other identifiers. The question of identity, however, became a subject of growing conflict between Russia and its "Orient" beginning in the second half of the nineteenth century, a conflict that produced a voluminous literature and shifting positions in a struggle for authority over colonial reality.

Sparked in large measure by his bold and provocative essays gathered under the title *Orientalism*, a substantial and often angry debate has flourished recently in reaction to Edward Said's insistence that a "whole network of European [Western] interests" has since the eighteenth century been brought to bear on the definition of "the Orient." For Said, the importance of Orientalism—that combination of academic pursuit, a style of thought, and a discourse—rests on its creation of a "body of theory and practice," a "system of knowledge about the Orient, an accepted grid for filtering through the Orient into Western consciousness." It is, following the Italian political activist, Antonio Gramsci (1891–1937), an episode of cultural hegemony at work in the wake of Western military, political, and economic domination, hegemony that presumptively authorizes the Orientalist to represent other peoples both to Westerners and to those "others" themselves.[3]

The intention here is not to engage Said over the merits of his position (one, in fact, that is quite stimulating and sufficiently useful to bring to bear on the theme of this chapter), but to address two limitations to his treatment of a subject at once marvelously complex and fascinating. The first he readily acknowledges early, and that is reliance for historical and cultural reasons on British and French sources. As he insists,

> there is a quantitative as well as a qualitative difference between the Franco-British involvement in the Orient and . . . the involvement of every other European and Atlantic power. To speak of Orientalism therefore is to speak mainly, although not exclusively, of a British and French cultural enterprise, a project whose dimensions take in such disparate realms as the imagination itself, the whole of India and the Levant, the Biblical texts and the Biblical lands, the spice trade, colonial armies and a long tradition of colonial administrators, a formidable scholarly corpus, innumerable Oriental "experts" and "hands," an Oriental professorate, a complex array of "Oriental" ideas (Oriental despotism, Oriental splendor, cruelty, sensuality), many Eastern sects, philosophies, and wisdoms domesticated for local European use—the list can be extended more or less indefinitely. My point is that Orientalism derives from a particular closeness experienced between Britain and France and the Orient, which until the early nineteenth century had really meant only India and the Bible lands.[4]

To deny the thrust of this passage insofar as it catalogs the extent of the cultural enterprise, the project that Said calls Orientalism, would be foolish; but equally unacceptable is the place he unequivocally reserves for Franco-British involvement in most of its manifestations. That France and Britain were two principal, extraordinarily active participants in the Western effort to "possess" the Orient almost goes without saying, but do not the claims for these two threaten to produce a monolithic treatment that begs for some balance, even corrective, by investigation of the Orientalism of other countries? Is there not at least one national tradition of Orientalism easily rivaling that of France and Britain in "coming to terms with the Orient . . . based on the Orient's special place in . . . [its] experience?"[5] Many would argue that there is: the Russian, with its own "particular closeness," to borrow Said's phrase, to eastern peoples and cultures. Not a few in the nineteenth century would have accepted this judgment, and might have echoed Mirza Kazem-Bek, the Russified Azerbaijani orientalist, in asking "What European state has such intimate and inherent ties with Asia and Asiatics as does Russia?"[6] If only for comparative purposes, then, the history of Russian Orientalism deserves careful synchronic and diachronic analysis going beyond the classic work of a V. V. Bartol'd.[7]

The monolithism some have detected in Said's *Orientalism* has, moreover, a second limiting feature of which he seems insufficiently aware. To be sure, his focus is on Western representations of the Orient, and he ought not to be required to write a different book; nevertheless, those representations have never operated in a vacuum or only within Western contexts, but have influenced the very cultures they claimed to describe and analyze, and not only negatively. Most significantly, they contributed typically to the emergence in many "oriental" societies of modernist movements: complex nativist efforts to come to grips with the military, political, socio-economic, and cultural consequences of Western hegemony and, in the process, confront the pleasures and discomfitures of ontological and epistemological transformation. So substantial has the influence been in some countries that David Kopf, a historian of modern India, has declared flatly that "British Orientalism gave birth to the Bengal Renaissance."[8]

Whether scholars can make the same extreme claim for Russian Orientalism remains to be seen, but evidence suggests that Russian Orientalism was a major factor in the development of modern identities for various Islamic peoples within the Russian Empire. From the mid-eighteenth to early twentieth centuries, the intellectual, academic, and practical work of Russian scholars, educators, missionaries, and officials (among them, military officers), including persons sympathetic as well as antipathetic to Islamic culture, combined to help create an environment that presented an enormous challenge to Tatars, Azerbaijanis, and subsequently Kazakh, Uzbek, and other Central Asian peoples. Out of that momentous challenge, whose genealogy is exceedingly complex, emerged several generations of Russianized Muslims who collectively established the foundations of the modernist discourse in their native cultural milieus. The list of key actors in this development is long, but the names of Abbas Kuli Aga Bakihanov (1794–1848), Mirza Fetalî Ahundov (1812–1878), Chokan Valihanov (1835–1865), Mirza Kazem-Bek (1802–1870), Shihabeddin Merjanî (1818–1889), Abdülqayyum Nasirî (1825–1902), Hasan Bey Zerdabi (1837–1907), and Ismail Bey Gasprinskii (1852–1914), figure prominently.[9] Wrestling with questions of history and culture consumed much of their attention, but as readers shall see in the following pages, it was attention focused to a large extent by the need to respond to Russian representations of their societies and cultures.

For the Russian Empire, 1881 was a fateful year. The month of March witnessed the assassination of Czar Alexander II (1855–1881) and the subsequent ascent of his son, Alexander III, to the throne of "all the Russias." For the length of the latter's reign (1881–1894), much official and semiofficial effort was devoted to undermining some of the accomplishments of the Great Reforms and restoring to the empire the unchallenged unity, centralized authority, and social stability that had seemingly characterized it prior to the reign of the Czar Liberator. Although not all that successful—restorations never really are—the effort was consequential for the illusions it provided some and the disillusionment it generated in many more.

About 1881, however, even more was fateful, although at the time scarcely anyone noticed. Two essays appeared in print that year, both moderate in tone yet principled, both aimed at Russian audiences yet from the pens of Tatars. One, by a certain Devlet-Kildeev, about whom researchers know virtually nothing save his Volga Tatar ethnic roots, was published in the imperial capital of St. Petersburg; the other, by the soon-to-be influential advocate of Islamic modernism, the Crimean Tatar Ismail Bey Gasprinskii, came off a press in the provincial town of Simferopol, once a Tatar settlement with a Tatar name (Akmescit), but by now very Russian. The one offered a justification of the Qur'ân and the teachings of the Prophet Muhammad; the other, a defense of Islam as a culture and a civilizing force. Devlet-Kildeev's *Magomet kak prorok* (Muhammad as Prophet) imparts a religious perspective and focus (its author may very well have been a mullah); Gasprinskii's *Russkoe musul'manstvo* (Russian Islam) captures the ruminations of a largely secular mind. Nevertheless, and however unintended, together they propose an Islamic world and experience decidedly different—and consciously so—from the representations insisted upon by a variety of Russian (or Russified) proponents of imperialism and colonialism. Together they respond to those representations and the colonial interests that nurtured them; together they reflect a Tatar desire for self-representation. Here is what is new and important about these essays. With their appearance a cross-cultural polemic ensued for four decades over the identity and destiny of various *inorodtsy* ("others") on the eastern borderlands of the Russian Empire, over the relationship of the Tatars to those other *inorodtsy*, and over the policies the Russian state ought to pursue to ensure not only its imperial integrity but also its own identity. In the midst of it all burned a "Tatar question." It is on the initial development of the polemic that this chapter will focus.[10]

For decades leading up to 1881, Russians had been busily constructing the southern and eastern borderlands of their empire, the edges of their own civilization inhabited mostly by Turkic peoples influenced to varying degrees by the teachings of the prophet Muhammad. A key premise—largely drawn from the imperatives of religion—of the self-reflective, and hence comforting, fiction that this construction produced was that the peoples of the world were sharply divided between the saved and the damned, the good and the bad, the civilized and the savage.[11] The longstanding concerns of the Russian Orthodox Church for the soul of the Russian Empire were heightened by the growing secularization of society and the tide of anticlericalism and irreligion sweeping it, by the national and religious friction—in part stimulated by the *glasnost'* (openness) and *perestroika* (restructuring) of the Great Reform Era—tearing at the empire's unity, and, all through the first half of the nineteenth century, by the apparent failure of missionaries to follow successfully in the footsteps of the Czar's troops.

In earlier centuries, conversions by armed force and administrative persuasion seemed to have won for the empire not just new subjects but new Christians as well, a development particularly true for Volga Tatars. Much to the chagrin of Russian churchmen and lay supporters, however, mass outbreaks of apostasy occurred in 1802–03, 1810, the 1820s, 1840s, 1850s, and finally in 1862–63 and 1865–66, as thousands of *kreshchen-nye tatary* (Christianized Tatars) returned to Islam.[12] To counter this shocking trend, elements within the Church sought to brace its proselytizing arm by establishing specialized missionary organizations (e.g., the Brotherhood of St. Gurii, with headquarters in Kazan), devising a new pedagogy for state-sponsored schools serving eastern *inorodtsy* (quickly known as the "Il'minskii system," after its founder, N. I. Il'minskii), and creating publications (e.g., *Protivo-musul'manskii sbornik* [Anti-Muslim Review]) dedicated to promulgating and disseminating the "correct" interpretation of Islam. By the mid-1870s these three projects were conjoined in pursuit of a set of tasks neatly summed up in the charter of the Brotherhood of St. Gurii: (1) to support and strengthen Orthodox converts by educating their children, publishing books in their native languages, and constructing churches; (2) to promote Christianity among Muslims and pagans; (3) to stem apostasy and error among the Orthodox; and (4) to care for the needs of the Orthodox dwelling among the *inorodtsy*.

Crucial to all of this was an appropriate representation of Islam: of its teachings, its founder, and its adherents. The starting point, however, was a critique of *magometanstvo* in its mid-nineteenth-century circumstances.[13] That the major missionary writers, who were in the forefront of this effort, focused on this theme was natural since doing so allowed them to move from evidence of specific problems, weaknesses, and inadequacies in contemporary Islam, let alone of distasteful behavior, to generalizations about the foundations of the faith and culture. Looking over the Islamic scene, they found a culture dominated by fanatical mullahs—fanaticism is by far the most common attribute they associated with Islam—who, like the blind leading the blind, fostered a view of the world so circumscribed as to encourage fatalism, intolerance, and contentment with the irrational and the crudely sensual. In the hands of such teachers, Muslims proved more inclined to ritualize their faith than study and live it (although living a religion that is represented as fundamentally flawed would hardly alter the consequences as perceived by Orthodox critics). The result is a condition, under the changing circumstances of the modern age, of backwardness in which neither philosophy nor science can flourish, in which education is reduced to the study "of that which was done long ago" and to "scholastic nicety and contrivance," in which the believer is either passively contemplative or fanatically militant, and in which the possibilities of progress are nil.

This grim appraisal of contemporary Islam in Russia and elsewhere, however, served largely as a means for the Russian critic to engage the religion's foundations—the Qur²ân and the prophet Muhammad—and subject them to sweeping examination and interpretation. The result of what became a sort of cottage industry was an extensive literature that consistently viewed the Qur²ân as a guide not along the path to wisdom but to ignorance, a source not of spiritual elevation but of decadence, and an inspiration not for amicable human relations but for hostility toward others. As a treasury of superstition, the Qur²ân could offer nothing that is civilizing except to those so savage that anything is a blessing.[14] As for Muhammad, he was this text's pitiable prophet.

And yet, Islam was considered also dangerous because of its devilish attractiveness and the untempered fanaticism it bore as a primary, dominant, and eternal characteristic. It was seen as a threat to Russia as a spiritual competitor for the allegiances of those in the southern and eastern borderlands, even as it also obstructed the "legitimate" imperial efforts to bring enlightenment and civilization to those same areas. It appeared even more threatening owing to the central role played by Tatars who, through their mullahs, ishans, and merchants, had been actively propagandizing the worst features of Islamic teachings among the long settled or still nomadic peoples of Central Asia. Viewed as impudent (derznyi), harmful (vrednyi), and cunning (khitryi), these Tatars had for decades pursued agendas that aimed not only at winning converts to their faith but establishing and solidifying their preeminence in a vast territory stretching from Kazan to the borders of China in the east and those of Turkey, Persia, Afghanistan, and northwest India in the south. Against the integrity of the Russian Empire the Tatars were accused of promoting separatism with the larger goal of achieving a Pan-Islamic ideal. For Russian critics the evidence supporting this charge abounded, and included the reluctance of Tatars to perform imperial military service as well as their inadequate respect for the emperor, allegiance to the Ottoman Sultan in his role as Caliph, inordinate desire for their own schools, and the scattered episodes of mass emigration.[15]

Mullahs, ishans, and merchants may have been a nuisance for a long time, but from the Russian Islamophobic perspective what now rendered the situation more ominous and menacing was the existence of a growing cadre of Muslims who, as has been described elsewhere, were "educated in Russian [and even European] schools, conversant with the Russian language, [and] privileged by the imperial context."[16] They posed a qualitatively different challenge as cultural crossovers, as men who bore a certain ambiguity for being "foreign yet familiar, distant yet near, self yet other";[17] who as partial insiders knew how to turn the dominant discourse against itself, or, as N. P. Ostroumov put it more bluntly, used "all the advantages of Russian culture to defend their own nationality."[18] By knowing Russian, they were not limited to speaking only to their Islamic brethren, but could, using their own and Russian presses, address Russian society directly, insinuating within it their own representation of Islam and its relationship to modern life. In this regard, they were accused of trying "to present Islam as the purest religion in the world and as promoting progress in all spheres of human endeavor."[19] Moreover, they desired to "transfer European education to the Tatars, but by no means through Russia. . . . The plan is shaped cleverly and thoroughly. . . . Drawing a curtain over Russian eyes with sham rationalism and liberalism, the Tatar intelligentsia has intensified [its effort] to create a Muslim cultural center in Russia."[20]

Beginning with the essays of Devlet-Kildeev and Gasprinskii, Tatar spokesmen strove to counter the various charges that together were seen increasingly as comprising a "Tatar problem." Like their opponents, they too began with an effort to assess the contemporary circumstances in which Islamic peoples found themselves. And like their opponents, they uncovered much with which to be dismayed and of which to be sharply critical. The more one of these men was imbued with a modernist spirit, in fact, the firmer his stance in favor of reform so fundamental as effectively to require an ontological and epistemological break with the traditional *mentalité*. Be that as it may, public admission of social, economic, political, and even moral difficulties was seldom combined with a sweeping renunciation of Islamic history or a rejection of Islam's ethical foundations. On the contrary, characteristic of Tatar polemics was a careful distinction between theory and practice (divinely inspired teaching and human application), as well as an emphasis upon Islam's historical contributions to humanity and continued relevance in the modern age. Characteristic too were appeals to reason, logical argumentation, liberal criteria for analysis and judgment (including a defense of cultural pluralism), and pleas for objectivity, all of which drew upon and played to the sensibilities and predispositions of the intellectually sympathetic within the Russian camp, while unnerving and frustrating the hostile.[21]

The fair appraisal of contemporary failings meant for Tatar polemicists a view (representation) of Islam fuller than merely picking verses of the Qurʾân out of context, as they charged their opponents with, could provide. Fanaticism admittedly characterized some Muslims, and it certainly played a role from time to time in the history of Islam, particularly in the early years when the excitement generated by religious birth ran high. But no religion has been immune to fanatical behavior on the part of its adherents. Anyone glancing at the history of humanity, argued one contributor to the debate, "will soon be convinced that fanaticism is far from being unique to Islam."[22] Neither was it fundamental, as would be revealed by a thorough reading of the Qurʾân and *hadiths* (traditions relating to what the Prophet Muhammad said and did).

Tatar polemicists likewise admitted that ignorance, reflected in the narrow range of general knowledge and the shallow depth of understanding about their own traditions, currently described many Muslims. Such ignorance was of grave concern because it impeded individual and social progress and confused not only outsiders but Muslims themselves as to the values established and promoted by the Qurʾân. These included an unequivocal commitment to education, to the study of the natural order, to scientific investigation, and to philosophical speculation. Rather than being inimical to learning, Islam had from the very beginning been supportive of its quest. The evidence to affirm this claim seemed ample, particularly the remarkable intellectual fluorescence of the ninth through twelfth centuries, a "Golden Age" during which countless scholars salvaged much of ancient Greek learning, commented and elaborated upon it, and presented the new corpus of knowledge to a Western Europe struggling to break out of its own long Dark Age.

What has hurt Islamic societies has been the failure to sustain the successes of earlier generations, owing to a kind of creeping conservatism that increasingly narrowed the scope of education to religious affairs and, even within that, to rote memorization of those dogma calculated to respect the status quo. This is not Islam's fault, Gasprinskii and others asserted, but that of shortsighted, self-centered men. The task facing

true Muslims was thus to resurrect the spirit of the "Golden Age," reform education, and rejoin the international community. In this way,
with the help of their generous Russian brothers, Muslims could once
again become contributing members of the human family.

Education to be sure, but also *sblizhenie* (rapprochement). Far from de-
siring to separate themselves from the Russian Empire, the Tatars at this
early stage wanted to be more active and productive subjects of the Czar;
far from planning to establish some Pan-Islamic utopia independent of
the empire, they hoped only to use the inspiration of a reexamined Islam
to rally Muslims to the cause of progress and a better society. For the moment at least, pragmatism, if not conviction, triumphed over unbridled
imagination.

In the representations of these early Tatar polemicists, a culture—
vital, creative, and inspiring—had flourished beyond the oriental edges
of the Russian Empire in past centuries. Rooted in the ethical precepts of
the Qur'ân, in the practice of its positive teachings, and in an openness
to Western secular learning, such a culture, they were convinced, could
thrive once again. Having a thousand years before taught Europe and
assisted Christendom in escaping its own historic limitations, Muslims
could legitimately expect Europeans to teach them now, to take their
turn as "elder brothers," and to help dispel the suffocating ignorance
engulfing the Islamic world.

Speaking from the perspective of their own budding ethnic consciousness as well as from that of a larger Islamic one, a small group of
Tatar intellectuals, some bound to traditional modes of analysis, others
to modernist assumptions, engaged defenders of a unitary Russian and
Orthodox Christian Empire in a debate over identity that began around
the middle of the nineteenth century. That debate would continue
through the revolutionary events of 1917, shifting over the intervening
decades to ever-hardening positions that made demands for independence all but inevitable not only by Tatars, but also by Bashkirs, Azerbaijanis, Kazakhs, and other Turkic peoples. In 1917 the overthrow of the
Czar and the Bolshevik seizure of power seemed to hold out the promise
of settling ethnic grievances, one way or another, in favor of the empire's minorities. However, antipathy toward nationalism harbored by
the Marxist-Leninist ideology that undergirded the Soviet experiment
proved, utlimately, to be the insurmountable obstacle preventing the
further organic development of ethnic consciousness. In the name of
internationalism and the friendship of peoples, natural inclinations were
ignored or repressed until the dramatic weakening of political restraints
in the 1980s allowed the public expression of latent ethnic sentiment

once again. Under the impetus generated by proclamations of glasnost' and perestroika, the Tatars, like other non-Russian citizens of the USSR, are struggling to reestablish links to a disrupted past that, once restored, may well carry them along paths they should have trekked seventy years ago.

Notes

1. Ismail Bey Gasprinskii, "Znanie," *Tercüman/Perevodchik*, no. 42 (October 5, 1886): 87.

2. M. Mashanov, *Istoricheskoe i sovremennoe znachenie khristianskago missionerstva sredi musul'man*, vol. 20: *Missionerskii protivomusul'manskii sbornik* (Kazan, 1894), p. 261.

3. Edward W. Said, *Orientalism* (New York: Pantheon Books, 1978), pp. 1–9 passim.

4. Ibid., p. 4.

5. Ibid., p. 1.

6. Mirza Kazem Bek, "O poiavlenii i uspekhakh vostochnoi slovesnosti v Evrope i upadke ee v Azii," *Zhurnal ministerstva narodnago prosveshcheniia*, pt. 2 (1836): 348. Note as well the central place this notion holds in many of the writings of Ismail Bey Gasprinskii, the Crimean Tatar reformer, particularly in his *Russkoe musul'manstvo: Mysli, zametki i nabliudeniia musul'manina* (Simferopol, 1881).

7. See, in addition to numerous shorter pieces, V. V. Bartol'd, "Obzor deiatel'nosti fakul'teta vostochnykh iazykov," *Akademik V. V. Bartol'd: Sochineniia* (Moscow: Izdatel'stvo "Nauka," 1977), 9:23–196; and "Istoriia izucheniia Vostoka v Evrope i Rossii," ibid., pp. 199–482. The Soviet scholar Mark Batunskii has long been engaged in just such an analysis, the results of which have appeared in numerous articles and will be contained in a formidable monograph to appear in English as (tentatively) *Russia and Her Muslim Neighbors*. Among his already published articles, see "Islam and Russian Medieval Culture," *Die Welt des Islams* 26 (1986): 1–27; "Islam i russkaya kul'tura XVIII v.," *Cahiers du monde russe et soviétique* 27 (1986); "Russian Missionary Literature on Islam," *Zeitschrift für Religions- und Geistesgeschichte* 39, no. 3 (1987): 253–66; "Muscovy and Islam: Irreconcilable Strategy, Pragmatic Tactics," *Saeculum* 39, no. 1 (1988): 63–81; and "Muscovy and Islam: In Further Quest of an Empirical and Conceptual Compromise ('The Journey Beyond Three Seas' by Afanasy Nikitin)," *Saeculum* 39, nos. 3–4 (1988): 277–93.

8. David Kopf, "Hermeneutics Versus History," *Journal of Asian Studies* 39, no. 3 (May, 1980): 501.

9. Soviet scholars have been most active in examining this development, with recent monographs providing fuller and less ideologically constrained analyses. See S. M. Mikhailova, *Kazanskii universitet i prosveshchenie narodov povolzh'ia i priural'ia* (Kazan: Izd. Kazanskogo universiteta, 1979); Ya. Abdullin, *Tatarskoe prosvetitel'stvo* (Kazan, 1975); E. M. Akhmedov, *Filosofiia azerbaidzhanskogo prosveshcheniia* (Baku: Azerbaidzhanskoe gosudarstvennoe izd., 1983); A. S. Sumbatzade, *Azerbaidzhanskaia istoriografiia XIX–XX vekov* (Baku: "Elm," 1987); and Kh. Vakhidov, *Prosvetitel'skaia ideologiia v Turkestane* (Tashkent, 1979).

10. The relevant Tatar texts for this task include: Devlet-Kildeev, *Magomet kak pro-rok* (St. Petersburg, 1881); Ismail Bey Gasprinskii, *Russkoe musul'mantsvo;* "Sud'by magometanstva," *Tercüman/Perevodchik,* no. 8 (June 10, 1883): 16; "Islam i tsivili-zatsiia," *Tercüman/Perevodchik,* no. 16 (September 16, 1883): 31–32; "Musul'manskaia tsivilizatsiia," *Tercüman/Perevodchik,* no. 22 (June 17, 1884), no. 23 (June 25, 1884), no. 24 (July 1, 1884), no. 27 (July 30, 1884), no. 32 (September 17, 1884), no. 35 (October 16, 1884), no. 40 (November 11, 1884), and no. 45 (December 18, 1884); Mirza-Alim, "Islam i magometanstvo," *Sankt-Peterburgskie vedomosti,* nos. 188, 224, 229, 239, 244, 285 (1882); Ataullah Baiazitov, *Vozrazhenie na rech' Ernesta Renana* (St. Peters-burg: Tip. A. S. Suvorina, 1883); Idem, *Otnosheniia Islama k nauke i inovertsam* (St. Petersburg: Tip. "Nur," 1887); *Islam i progress* (St. Petersburg: Tip. A. S. Suvorina, 1898); Iskander Mirza, "Russkiia shkoly dlia musul'man v Turkestane," *Vostochnoe obozrenie,* nos. 36 and 38 (1883); and Musul'manin, "Musul'manstvo i ratsionalizm," *Vostochnoe obozrenie,* no. 24 (1883).

11. Since dichotomies are seldom absolute for long, it is not surprising to find arguments made about "good savages," at least in the sense of their being childlike and hence in need of protection from the influence of fanatical Islam. See as an ex-ample, V. V. Grigoriev, *Rossiia i Vostok* (St. Petersburg, 1876), passim.

12. For information on these defections, see E. N. Voronets, *Otpadeniia inorodtsev-khristian v mokhammedanstvo* (Orel, 1876).

13. The word *magometanstvo* (Muhammedanism), widely used in Russian po-lemics against Islam and its adherents, is not merely incorrect in its identification of the religion with Muhammad (à la Christianity and Christ), but is symptomatic of the deeper Russian/Western desire to control its Oriental nemesis by reducing it to comprehensible, if distorting, terms.

14. "Only for quite primitive people (the Turks, Berbers, Negroes, and Malays) does Islam possess a civilizing power," wrote A. Krymskii, *Musul'manstvo i ego budushch-nost'* (Moscow, 1899), p. 40.

15. In order to buttress the charge of Islam's present and future danger to the en-tire Christian world, Islamophobic literature stressed that unlike Christianity, Islam was both a religious doctrine and a state system. Islam presents, therefore, not just a religious but a political problem. As M. Mashanov frankly put it, "the history of Islam becomes not so much of scientific as of practical interest." See his *Istoricheskoe i sovremennoe znachenie khristianskago missionerstva sredi musul'man,* p. 51.

16. Edward J. Lazzerini, "Ismail Bey Gasprinskii (Gasprali), the Discourse of Mod-ernism, and the Russians," *Tatars of the Crimea: Their Struggle for Survival,* ed. Edward Allworth (Durham: Duke University Press, 1988), p. 157. In early 1888, N. I. Il'minskii noted that he sensed "something new and different" among the Tatars lately. "The mass of the people, led by the parish mullahs, continue to hold orthodox views, but the intelligentsia with their affected rationalism and liberalism throw dust in the eyes of the Russian bureaucrat and intellectual." See "Izvlecheniia iz pisem' N. I. Il'minskago k N. P. Ostroumovu," *Pravoslavnyi sobiesiednik,* pt. 2 (July–August 1900), p. 51.

17. Edward J. Lazzerini, "Ismail Bey Gasprinskii," p. 157.

18. Quoted in K. E. Bendrikov, *Ocherki po istorii obrazovaniia v Turkestane (1865–1924 gody)* (Moscow: Akademiia Pedagogicheskikh Nauk RSFSR, 1960), p. 255.

19. M. A. Miropiev, *O polozhenii russkikh inorodtsev* (St. Petersburg: Sinodal'naia tipografiia, 1901), p. 47.

20. *Pis'ma N. I. Il'minskago k Ober-prokuroru Sv. Sinoda, K. P. Pobedonostsevu* (Kazan, 1895), p. 64.

21. "Among the Russian intelligentsia one notes a certain wavering with regard to the *inorodtsy* question," wrote Miropiev (*O polozhenii russkikh inorodtsev*, p. 52). Here is a decided understatement of a persistent complaint leveled not just against some members of the intelligentsia but also against officials who have proved unable to develop a consistent, firm, and "correct" policy vis-à-vis the *inorodtsy* and, as Il'minskii more bitterly expressed it, "fail[ed] to see the consequences of coddling and spoiling the Tatars." (See "Izvlecheniia iz pisem' N. I. Il'minskago," p. 52.)

22. From an article appearing in *Vostochnoe obozrenie*, no. 10 (1885), as cited in M. A. Miropiev, *O polozhenii*, p. 46.

3. Islam and the Growth of National Identity in Soviet Azerbaijan

Tadeusz Swietochowski

Azerbaijan, a land populated by a Turkic-speaking people, throughout many centuries remained within the orbit of Iran. A turning point in its history came in the early nineteenth century with the conquest of the northern part of Azerbaijan by Russia, a process that was completed by the Turkmanchai Treaty of 1828. This date marked the two fundamental facts of the Azerbaijani history in evidence ever since: the partition of the country, and the rule by a European power north of the Araxes river frontier.[1] The population of Russian Azerbaijan differed from that of the Iranian part in one essential respect: it included a comparatively large proportion of Sunni Muslims. In fact, the first, though incomplete, Russian statistics estimated that the ratio of Shi'ites to Sunnis was almost even, with a slight edge in favor of the latter. Only after midcentury, did the proportion of Sunnis markedly decrease, to stabilize at a level at which the Shi'ites of the Jafarite rite held a majority of roughly two to one.[2] The decrease in the proportional strength of the Sunni element was the effect of their migrations to Turkey, a trickle that turned into a torrent after the final suppression of Shamil's resistance by Russia in the late 1850s.

The Shi'ite-Sunni split ran deep, and the two sectarian groups represented divergent political loyalties and cultural orientations. The Shi'ites often continued their attachment to Iran, while the Sunnis gravitated toward Daghistan and, to a lesser degree, toward Turkey. The depth of the sectarian split was reflected in the nineteenth-century wars waged by Russia when the Czar was able to use Shi'ite volunteers against Turkey in 1828 and 1853–55, as well as against Shamil's *ghazavat* (holy war) in Daghistan. By contrast, the Sunnis showed signs of restiveness at the time of Russo-Ottoman conflicts and tended to support Shamil, at times arms in hand.

For all its natural proclivity to *divide et impera* policies, Russian rule in the long run became the main force in integrating, as well as the agent for change in, the traditional Azerbaijani society. One of the first consequences of the conquest was the gradual dismantling of the Azerbaijani khanates, the principalities that had formed the political structure of the country. The khanates of Ganja, Shirvan, Talysh, Baku, Karabagh, Sheki, Nakhichevan, Derbent, and Kuba disappeared, one after the other, for the most part during the 1830s and the 1840s, and the process of breaking up these traditional polities contributed to the weakening of deeply rooted local particularisms. Instead of a large number of diverse, petty principalities, uniform Russian administration was introduced, and by the late 1850s the bulk of Azerbaijan was consolidated into two *guberniias* (provinces), Baku and Elizavetpol (Ganja).[3] Jointly, they were called Eastern Transcaucasia, the term *Azerbaijan* being used only, and rather seldom, as a geographical denomination. The inhabitants of Eastern Transcaucasia called themselves "Shirvanis," and the Russians referred to them by the misnomers "Tatars" or "Caucasian Tatars."

The native effort at building a community across the lines of sectarian and regional identities came from the intelligentsia, a social group that emerged from the contact between the Islamic and European civilizations.[4] In its striving to blunt the Sunni-Shi'a antagonism, yet also inspired by the vision of modernity, the intelligentsia showed a marked inclination toward secularism. This trait, strongly visible in the founder of modern Azerbaijani literature, Mirza Fathali Akhundzadä, reputed as a skeptic, agnostic, or an outright atheist, was shared by almost all luminaries of the intelligentsia, but to a varying degree. Furthermore, for all their criticism of the theocratic traditions of Islamic civilization, they were willing to recognize the validity of the religion as the fundamental norm of the society's life. Akhunzadä wrote:

> Still, this author does not wish that people should become atheist with no religion and faith. Rather, his aim is to show that the Islamic religion is in need of reformation in accordance with our day and age. Such a thoroughgoing reformation which would be in step with the conditions of progress and civilization, . . . would moderate the despotism of Eastern monarchs, and would bring about compulsory literacy for all Muslim men and women.[5]

The intelligentsia pursued its work through the time-honored methods of building social communications and spreading education. The rise of the theater and press, as well as of the Jadidist types of schools with modernized curriculum, in turn necessitated the use of the contemporary native language at the expense of the traditional literary idioms,

Persian or classicist Azerbaijani. Generally, the intellectuals of the Sunni minority tended to be more active proponents of change, and politically more articulate, than their Shi'ite counterparts. The Baku *Akinchi* (Ploughman), the first Turkic-language newspaper in Russia, was not free of anti-Persian accents and was, in the eyes of czarist officials, pro-Ottoman enough to have it closed down in 1877, in the midst of the Russo-Turkish war. During the 1880s the Sunni-published journal *Käshkül* (Darwish bowl) was the first on record to propose the use of the term *Azerbaijani Turks* instead of *Caucasian Muslims.*[6]

While the effort of the emancipation from Persian cultural domination had some support from the Russian authorities, this was not the case with the signs of incipient Turkism and Pan-Turkism, which the regime found potentially disturbing. The two terms were closely related to each other, yet distinct: Turkism connoted the concern with ethnic identity of Turkic-speaking peoples, while Pan-Turkism dealt with the striving for their cooperation and solidarity, a goal formulated by the Crimean Tatar, Ismail Bey Gasprinskii in his slogan: *Dilde, fikirde, ishte birlik* (unity in language, thought, work). The emergence of these ethnocentric rather than religion-based programs was symptomatic of the waning of the ʿUmma group identity among the intelligentsia, and its replacement with the sense of belonging to one great nation (*qavm*) encompassing all Turkic speaking peoples and stretching from the Balkans to China.[7] The vision of this super-nation was not inherently anti-Islamic as almost all Turkic peoples were Muslims, but the idea of the *qavm* gained little acceptance among the masses. The population at large remained at the ʿUmma level of identity, and the only program that could have some popular appeal was Pan-Islamism, with its call for the unity of all Muslims of the world.

A new epoch that came with the 1905 Russian Revolution opened in Azerbaijan with the outbreak of intercommunal violence known as the "Tatar-Armenian War." The antagonism between the two ethnic groups had grown into a multifaceted historical problem. The bulk of the Armenian population in Transcaucasia were relative newcomers, who had immigrated into the region in the first half of the nineteenth century from Turkey and Iran. In comparison with the tradition-bound Azerbaijanis among whom they settled, the Armenians proved better prepared to take advantage of the opportunities arising from the development of a modern economy. As competitors in industry, commerce, professions, or government service, they usually outperformed the Muslims. Thus, in addition to its cultural-religious dimension, the Muslim-Armenian antagonism involved such aspects as the grievances of the fledgling Azer-

baijani business class beset by ruinous competition, the conflict of interests between the unskilled "Tatar" laborers and Armenian entrepreneurs
and merchants, and the animosity of the predominantly rural Muslims
toward the largely urbanized Armenians.[8]

The differences in social structure between the two communities were
reflected in the degree to which each was politically organized. Unlike
the Azerbaijanis, the Armenians produced a dynamic nationalist movement spearheaded by the Dashnaktsutiun party, which had under its
command a fighting force. The Dashnak force proved itself especially
effective against poorly organized Muslim groups when violent clashes
began from February 1905 on. The blows suffered at the hands of the
Dashnak fighting squads served as a catalyst for the consolidation of
the Muslim community in Azerbaijan. The "Tatar-Armenian War" generated for the first time the unity for a cause transcending sectarian or
local loyalties, and from then on these divisions ceased to offer a serious
impediment to political action.[9]

The post-1905 period brought the transition from cultural enlightenment and educational pursuits to political activities, which included the
formation of political parties. Of these, two that were destined to show
some longevity were: the Social-Democratic Himmät (Endeavour), 1904–
20, and Musavat (Equality), 1912–20.[10] Likewise, Pan-Turkism began to
assume a political coloring, all the more so that it found a sponsor in
the Young Turk regime that seized power in Istanbul in 1908. In this
revolutionary period, which also saw the 1906–11 constitutional crisis
in Iran, the nascent Azerbaijani national movement defined what would
amount to its long-term, supreme goal (maximum program), the unification of the two parts of Azerbaijan (Pan-Azerbaijanism) and what in
effect would be its minimum program, autonomy for northern Azerbaijan, in union with Georgia and Armenia, within the Russian state. As
for attaining the first, admittedly remote, goal, the Azerbaijani leaders
looked for help from Turkey, as for the second, apparently more realistic
one, their strategy was based on an alliance with the ephemeral Russian
democracy.[11]

These aspirations of the political elite were indicative of the growing sense of a new community, distinct not only from the ʿUmma, but
also from the qavm. The flourishing Baku press of the post-1905 years
resounded with the great debate between the proponents of the broader-
based Pan-Turkism and Pan-Islamism, on the one side, and those who
stood for regional particularism, on the other, with the latter gaining the
upper hand. As much as in the nineteenth century, the issue was "de-
Iranization" of the Azerbaijani language; now voices were raised in de-

fence against its Ottomanization.[12] The native particularism expressed itself in the notion of the *millät*, a term that originally denoted a local religious community. The leader of the Musavat party, Mammad Amin Rasulzadä, was the first on record to produce a modern definition of the term: a group linked by common language, culture, and history, as well as religion, the latter being only one of its elements. In its proper meaning, the connotation was primarily secular, and its attributes were those of a nation.[13] A secular definition of nationalism was to underlie the ideology of what was to be called Musavatism, even though Rasulzadä, on the eve of World War I, still would not go further than to refer to his compatriots as the Caucasian Turks.

Only in 1917, in the spirit of the unrestricted debate that followed the overthrow of the czardom, did Rasulzadä declare that various Turkic-speaking groups had already developed identities distinct from one another, a significant step beyond Pan-Turkism.[14] In the same year, the Musavat began to call for the turning of the Muslim-populated lands into autonomous national units within a future federal republic of Russia, and the name Azerbaijan began to appear in the party's statements.[15] With the fabric of the Russian state disintegrating apace, the idea of regional union revived, and in the spring of 1918 the Transcaucasian Federation of Azerbaijan, Armenia, and Georgia came into being. A hastily put-together structure, it not only lacked the underpinning of ethnic, religious, or cultural unity but was beset by the increasingly bitter Azerbaijani-Armenian strife. In fact, the year 1918 had been the high-water mark of intercommunal violence with its two large scale massacres: the March Days when the Dashnak forces attacked the Azerbaijanis, and the September 15 Azerbaijani revenge.[16]

After four weeks of precarious existence, the federation fell apart, and Azerbaijan proclaimed its independence (May 28), as did Georgia and Armenia. From now on, the Caucasian Muslims, Tatars, or Turks became officially Azerbaijanis, and the sense of native particularism turned into the program of the Azerbaijani nation-state.

The independent Azerbaijani Republic, which was more than autonomous but less than a fulfillment of the national maximum program, came into being accidentally, through the breakup of the Transcaucasian Federation, and remained shaky throughout the two years of its existence. The fate of the republic depended not on the outcome but rather on the continuation of the stalemate in the Russian Civil War. There could be little doubt that whichever side was to win the contest in Russia, it would do away with Azerbaijani independence. The Musavatist-dominated regime frantically searched for a foreign power that would be willing to offer its protection to Azerbaijan: first the Ottoman State, then Britain, and Italy: even union with Iran was contemplated as a round-about way to pass under the British shield. All of these efforts proved futile. Furthermore, the nationalistic, liberal Republic, ruled by the Western-oriented elite, lacked support from within, for the bulk of the population considered themselves above all Muslims, and saw little justification for a secular native rule. The opposition party, Itti-had (Union), which acted as the spokesman for grass-root conservatism, regarded Azerbaijani nationalism as splitting the unity of the Muslim world in the face of its enemy, which was to be found in the West rather than in Russia.[17]

Meanwhile, the tensions with Armenia continued, the fact that pre-cluded effective cooperation of the Transcaucasian republics in the face of common dangers. At the Versailles Peace Conference, Armenia pre-sented claims for an extensive territory, its borders to be drawn on his-torical and strategic premises, which would include parts of Azerbaijan —mountainous Karabagh, Zangezur, Jevanshir—as well the Azerbaijani-populated region in Armenia, Nakhichevan. In the disputed areas armed clashes broke out, most notably in Nakhichevan and Mountainous Kara-bagh, the area which in contrast to the former was an Armenian enclave in the Azerbaijani territory. The British occupation authorities inter-vened in the Karabagh conflict in 1919, only to find the issue intractable and left the enclave under Azerbaijani jurisdiction. As for Nakhichevan, it remained in the hands of Armenia.[18]

Yet, for all its weaknesses, the short-lived independent republic proved to be of lasting historical significance, and the present-day Soviet Azer-baijan is the successor and in many ways the continuator of the Musavatist-run state. The experience of the 1918–20 Azerbaijani nation-state was sufficiently viable to influence a major revision of the Bolshe-vik view of the nationality question among the Muslims. In 1918, the Baku Bolshevik leader, Stepan Shaumian had still referred to the very name Azerbaijan as a word of derision or ridicule, and his answer to the Musavat's claims for national autonomy was that the Bolsheviks stood not for dividing peoples, but for uniting them; that the only true distinc-tions were between classes, not ethnic or religious groups.[19] Yet within the next two years the Bolshevik party accepted the slogan "Indepen-dent Soviet Azerbaijan" and under it carried out their seizure of power in Baku in April 1920. What were the reasons for this dramatic about-face that resulted in the Bolsheviks turning into nation-makers, first in Azerbaijan, then in other Muslim parts of Russia?

Soviet Azerbaijani historians emphasize in this regard the efforts of the native Communist leaders, formerly of the Himmät party, such men as Nariman Narimanov, Sultan Majid Afandiyav, or Mohsun Israfilbakov, who, with skill and perseverance, succeeded in winning over the Bolshevik party leadership to their views.[20] If such an interpretation may well be the truth, it is not likely to be the entire truth. Within the Bolshevik councils, especially in the Transcaucasian Regional Committee, the decisions on recognition of the national status of the Azerbaijanis were the result of hesitation and lengthy debates.[21] In the end, the Bolsheviks accepted the position of the native intelligentsia rather than of the masses, and, of the considerations that tipped the scales, two appear to have been paramount.

First was the acceptance of the fact that a direct transition from a religion-based community to a socialist type of society would be impossible. In a distinctly Eurocentric view of the Bolsheviks, nationality was a necessary, intermediate stage in historical development.

A second, somewhat less theoretical consideration, subject to the expedience of the time and place, was what has been termed the *surrogate proletariat* syndrome. The native working class remained numerically weak, and even weaker in its class consciousness, their roots still deep in the traditional Islamic society of the countryside. By contrast, there was in Azerbaijan a secular-minded, active, and ambitious intelligentsia, anxious to carry out the transformation of the regional Muslim community into a nation. The intelligentsia, it could be expected, would be far quicker to win over to the Soviet cause than the masses, of whose apathy and backwardness the Bolsheviks were openly critical.

Thus, the slogan an "independent Soviet Azerbaijan," which to some sounded like a contradiction in terms or a bad joke, to others carried a coded and reassuring message. It held out the prospect of a deal between the Bolsheviks and the adherents of the Azerbaijani national movement. In fact, the surrender of the republic's parliament to Soviet authority was formalized by a document which contained, among others, two especially significant provisions: (1) "All functionaries of the governmental agencies will retain their posts, and only persons holding positions of responsibility will be replaced" and (2) "The newly formed provisional Communist government guarantees the life and property of the members of the present government and Parliament."[22]

The demise of the independent Azerbaijani Republic was bloodless, for the bulk of its army had been engaged in putting down the Armenian insurgency in Mountainous Karabagh and the wave of anti-Soviet uprisings that swept the countryside after the Communist take-over. Those uprisings were not inspired by loyalty to the fallen regime, however.

Rather, the common traits of these uprisings were slogans in defense of the Shari'a or protests against brutalities and food requisitioning. Meanwhile, as some Musavatists were being sent to prison camps in the Solovetskie Islands, others were accepting positions from the Soviet government and under its auspices took part in implementing the decades-old programs of the intelligentsia. Among these were the spread of education in general, and eradication of illiteracy in particular, a task which would entail the replacement of the Arabic alphabet by the Roman in 1926, ahead of the similar reform in Turkey. The campaign for the simplification and purification of the native literary language was carried on, as well as the search for a distinct national culture. The centerpiece of the Soviet reform program was radical secularization, which promised not only to obliterate the last vestiges of the sectarian strife, but also to sweep away cultural obstacles on the road to modernity. The process of secularization was accompanied by what Soviet historiography euphemistically calls "administrative methods," yet despite all such pressures this process has not been completed even to this day.[23] Generally, the effect of the persistent, forceful, and often brutal secularization was to weaken Islam as a religion, and few Azerbaijanis nowadays are familiar with its tenets and doctrines. At the same time, the other aspect of Islam—the way of life rooted in specific customs, traditions, and prohibitions—retained remarkable vitality. Like other Soviet Muslims, the Azerbaijanis eat no pork, drink little alcohol, retain strong kinship ties, do not marry outside of their community, and hardly ever emigrate to other, especially non-Muslim, parts of the USSR.

With the intelligentsia's active cooperation, there began to grow, north of the Araxes River, a Soviet Azerbaijani nation, no longer independent but possessed of autonomy and, what followed from it, of native bureaucracy, and the autonomy, it should be recalled, had been the most articulated aspiration of the national movement in the past.

The core of the ruling group were now the former members of the Himmät, who left their imprint on the formation of Soviet Azerbaijani nationalism. Initially, especially in the early 1920s, this tended to be an outward-looking nationalism, open toward the Turkic-speaking world outside. With Narimanov at the head of the regime, a rapprochement with Kemalist Turkey, the country with which Azerbaijan had maintained direct diplomatic relations until the formation of the Soviet Transcaucasian Federation (Zakfederatsiia), got under way in 1922.[24] One of the effects of this rapprochement was the favorable settlement, for Azerbaijan, of the territorial disputes with Armenia, an issue on which Moscow was taking into account the wishes of the Kemalist regime. Following the creation of the Zakfederatsiia, mountainous Karabagh was turned into an autonomous district (*oblast'*) (July 1923) and Nakhichevan into an autonomous republic (February 1924), both under the jurisdiction of Azerbaijan.

The rapprochement was partly the reflection of the view that both Turkey and Azerbaijan were opening an age of revolution in the Muslim East and partly the expression of the need to reinforce Azerbaijan's Turkic identity. In the spirit of friendship with Turkey, such processes as the purification of the language from foreign elements, Romanization of the alphabet, promotion of the national culture, and, above all, secularization were seen as parallel for the two countries. Characteristically, the official name for the language spoken in Azerbaijan in the 1920s and early 1930s was *Tiurkskii* (Turkic), and the same word was used with reference to the country's population.

In the next decade, with the consolidation of Stalin's rule, Azerbaijani nationalism became inward-looking, insulated from outside influences, and indifferent to the cause of Turkic or even Azerbaijani unity. This isolationist condition was greatly enhanced by the effect of Stalin's purges, which devastated the prerevolutionary intelligentsia, and, in particular, the ex-Himmätist political elite. In tune with Stalin's policy of upgrading the position of non-Russian peoples to a full-fledged nationality status, the Zakfederatsiia was dissolved, and Azerbaijan was made a constituent republic of the USSR in 1936. The adjective referring to the country's language and inhabitants now became the strictly observed term *Azerbaijani*. Because the Romanized script had made the reading of Turkish all too easy, and the learning of Russian more difficult, the alphabet was changed once again, in 1939, this time into Cyrillic.

During this same period between the wars, on the other side of the border, the newly established Iranian Pahlavi regime was applying a policy of the forceful assimilation of its Azerbaijani subjects. This policy included suppression of Azerbaijani by banning it from schools and publications, a sharp contrast to the flourishing of this language in Soviet Azerbaijan.[25] The actions of the Iranian regime indirectly strengthened the position of Baku as the beacon of the national Pan-Azerbaijani culture.

The isolationist disposition of Soviet Azerbaijani nationalism came to a sudden end with the changed circumstances of history. In 1941, upon the outbreak of the war with Germany, Soviet forces temporarily occupied northern Iran.[26] Inevitably, the Red Army's presence became a fact of political life in Iran, and the Soviets' moves reflected their thinking on that country. As had been the case in dealing with their own Muslims, the Soviets set their stakes on the nationality principle. Their apparent assumption was that national identities of the non-Persians inhabiting Iran—the Azerbaiianis, Kurds, Turkmens, Baluchis, and Arabs—would reassert themselves over sectarian or dynastic loyalties that formed the fabric of the Iranian state. During World War II the focal point of the Soviet Iranian policy was Southern Azerbaijan. Here, hosts of civilian advisers who came from Baku to assist the military occupation authorities, worked on awakening the sense of nationality among Iranian Azerbaijanis. Reversing the Pahlavi assimilationist drive, they set up Azerbaijani language schools and newspapers and organized theatrical performances, while by no means neglecting political agitation.[27] In their work for the Soviet foreign policy goals, they were also motivated by the revived spirit of Azerbaijani unity, a profound experience in the life of a generation, which was amply echoed in the literature. A new element was infused into the Soviet Azerbaijani nationalism at a time when it had already been consolidated—irredentism, which would be in evidence constantly from now on, in various degrees of intensity.

By the end of 1945 the Soviet-backed Democratic Party of Azerbaijan proclaimed in Tabriz the autonomous Azerbaijani Republic, nominally a part of Iran. Apart from self-government and land reform, the main point in the party's program was the recognition of Azerbaijani as the official language in the republic.[28]

As it turned out, the Soviets had to recognize that their ideas on Iran were premature. The issue of Iranian Azerbaijan became one of the opening skirmishes of the Cold War, and, largely under the Western powers' pressure, Soviet forces withdrew in 1946. The autonomous republic collapsed soon afterward, and the members of the Democratic Party took refuge in the Soviet Union, fleeing Iranian revenge. In Tabriz, the crowds that had just recently applauded the autonomous republic were now greeting the returning Iranian troops, and Azerbaijani students publicly burned their native-language textbooks. The mass of the population was obviously not ready even for a regional self-government so long as it smacked of separatism. Soviet attempts to loosen the ties of Southern Azerbaijan to the Iranian state backfired, and the effect was general weakening of Moscow's influence throughout Iran.[29]

South of the Araxes, a new wave of Iranization policy returned, and, in the north, the idea of Azerbaijani unity was officially shelved once again because of the requirements of Soviet diplomacy in Iran. But the hibernation of this idea was not nearly as complete as had been the case in the 1930s. Not only the genie of Pan-Azerbaijani irredentism was out of the bottle, but the efforts to put it back were not very strenuous. While Moscow maintained, on the whole, correct and at times even friendly relations with the Shah's regime, it also allowed some manifestations of Pan-Azerbaijanism on the local level of the Azerbaijani SSR. These manifestations were for some three decades limited to the Baku intellectual community, its ranks swollen by the refugees from Tabriz. Appropriately, the focal point of the Pan-Azerbaijani activity was the Union of Writers. The post-1946 spirit of Pan-Azerbaijanism gave birth to a new literary current known as "literature of longing."[30] For the most part this current expressed itself in poetry, and its standard symbol was the Araxes River, separating brothers and dividing one land. Yet, two major novels were also produced in the spirit of Azerbaijani unity and were translated into Russian, thus gaining the political approval on the USSR-wide level. One was the *Dumanli Tabriz* (Smoke-covered Tabriz), Said Faik Ordubadi, first written in 1934 and then heavily reworked for its Russian version; the other, *Gäläjäk Gün* (The Coming Day), by Mirza Ibrahimov, also revised before it came out in Russian in 1950.[31]

The same spirit appeared, and if anything on an even larger scale, in scholarship. Here, it became institutionalized in the form of special sections of institutes of the Academy of Sciences of the Azerbaijani Soviet Socialist Republic. The first of such subdivisions of the Academy was the Department of the Language and Literature of Southern Azerbaijan at the Nizami Institute of Language and Literature, established in 1976.[32]

Historians, in their writings began to use such expressions as the "bleeding wound of Turkmanchai," the "hateful yoke of the Iranian oppression," the "Iranian oriental despotism," and the "backwardness of an Iranian kingdom delaying the historical development of the Azerbaijani people." Also, the cult of the historical figures of significance for both Azerbaijans was being promoted. Among those were Shah Ismail I, Fathali Khan of Kuba, and above all Sattar Khan, the leader of the 1909 Tabriz uprising, who became the hero of the novel *Dumanli Tabriz*.[33]

Still, these manifestations of Pan-Azerbaijanism were not intended for mass consumption, even throughout Baku, and were absent from the large circulation newspapers, weekly magazines, and Russian-language media. The USSR, in its desire to remain on good terms with the Pahlavi regime, gave only a very limited imprimatur to the advocacy of the ideas of Azerbaijani unity.

The triangular relationship of the Soviet Union, Iran, and the Azerbaijani question again turned dynamic upon the victory of the Khomeini revolution in 1979. Above all, there began the penetration of ideas across the frontier, and in both directions. Of all the Soviet Muslims, the Azerbaijanis form the largest group of Shi'ites, potentially the most receptive to the message of Khomeinism beamed to them in their own language from Tabriz. The effect was stimulation of an Islamic revival, a process noticed by most observers of the local scene, although few would agree as to its extent or depth.

While the example of Iran was reanimating the benumbed religious sentiments north of the Araxes, the Soviet view of this clergy-led upheaval was that, by its very nature, it amounted to a transitory phenomenon, a prelude to further transformations no longer driven by fundamentalist fervor. Of the factors likely to influence these transformations, the principles of ethnic or national identity would be of growing importance.

As the new Iranian regime lifted the ban on the use of the native language in Azerbaijan, the first period following the revolution was marked by the proliferation of local publications. Some of these showed Soviet inspiration in their calls for linguistic, cultural, and occasionally even administrative autonomy for the ethnic minorities in Iran. By 1981, the central government in Tehran once again resorted to suppressing the Azerbaijani language publications especially those suspect of acting on behalf of Soviet interests, and in the process, of the original twelve, only one remained in existence.[34] The policy of Iranization returned, in effect, although not on the scale of the Pahlavi times.

The Soviet reaction to the general deterioration of the relations with Iran, the country where the revolution was now seen as having failed, was to authorize the circulation of the slogan "One Azerbaijan." Soviet and Iranian parts of the country were now being presented as one entity, and the unjust frontier dividing one people as destined to disappear sooner or later. If these ideas were not entirely novel, the emphasis and the scope of their presentation were. Most significantly, they remained no longer restricted to the small circulation scholarly periodicals, but were allowed in the intermediate range media—literary journals, theatrical performances, books. The Soviet Pan-Azerbaijani agitation, intensified as it has been, is still kept out of daily newspapers, especially those in Russian, a fact indicating absence of the highest degree of official endorsement.

All the same, many from among the nationalistically minded Baku intelligentsia welcomed this less than total encouragement by Moscow of the ideal of one Azerbaijan. Some see the eventual reunification as the means of reinforcing the defences against the danger of linguistic and cultural Russification, a rapidly growing concern in the age of television, urbanization, and advanced education. Although the unity of Azerbaijan would most likely be attained by the extension of the Soviet Union at the expense of Iran rather than the other way around, it would amount to the fulfillment of the old dream of national consolidation, a goal that the Ukrainians and Byelorussians have already achieved through the agency of the USSR. Moreover, Baku intellectuals view themselves as a group of power and influence in a united Azerbaijan of the future, for the intelligentsia in the south is numerically weak and lacking in national consciousness. Some have in mind an alternative that would preclude violence or invasion. Should there occur restructuring of the Iranian state on the basis of autonomy for its minorities, close relations could be developed between the two Azerbaijans, and the Araxes frontier might fade into merely an administrative line, rather than remain a psychological barrier.

While the poor Soviet-Iranian relations in the early 1980s were favorable for the resurgence of Pan-Azerbaijanism, which in turn stimulated national sentiments, few of the Baku intellectuals cherished the illusion that the "on" signal from Moscow could not at any time be switched "off," and then the idea of Azerbaijani unity would be shelved once again. As for the population at large, rather than being affected by the ebbs and flows in national aspirations, it continued in its rock-bottom identity as Muslims first and as Azerbaijanis a distant second. As such they feel themselves a part of a vibrant world civilization, whereas as a nation, and one of recent date, they are merely a small community in a remote corner of the Soviet Union, of little concern to anyone.[35]

In a broad historical perspective, Russian and then Soviet Azerbaijan followed the general stages of the evolution from the ʿUmma to a modern nation-state, noticeable in other parts of the Islamic world. The rise of a Westernized elite, the notions of secularism, the ethnocentric supra-nationalism such as Pan-Turkism or Pan-Arabism—all these phenomena had been in evidence in Azerbaijan before 1917. Then came the logical next step—small state nationalism, a condition that suited the aspirations of the elites and, one may add, of big powers, while the native masses remained indifferent or at best ambivalent.

Notes

1. For recent works on Russia's expansion south of the Caucasus, see M. Atkin, *Russia and Iran, 1780–1828* (Minneapolis, 1980). A. V. Fadeev, *Rossia i Kavkaz pervoi tretii XIX veka* (Moscow, 1960). F. Kazemzadeh, "Russian Penetration of the Caucasus," in *Russian Imperialism from Ivan the Great to the Revolution*, ed. T. Hunchak (New Brunswick, N.J., 1974), pp. 239–63.

2. For the population statistics of the period, consult Kavkazskii Statisticheskii Komitet, *Sbornik svedenii o Kavkaze* (Tiflis, 1871). See also *Obozrenie rossiiskikh vla-*

denii za Kavkazom v statisticheskom, topograficheskom i finansovom otnosheniiakh (St. Petersburg, 1836), 4:361.

3. For a detailed monograph on the administrative system of nineteenth-century Azerbaijan, see S. A. Mil'man, *Politicheskii stroi Azerbaidzhana v XIX–nachale XX vekov* (Baku, 1960).

4. On the rise of the intelligentsia, see Z. B. Qoyushov, *Azarbayjan maarifchilerinin etik qorushlari* (Baku, 1960).

5. M. F. Akhundov, *Asarlari* (Baku, 1961), 2:150. For monographic works on Akhundzadä, see N. Mammedov, *Realizm M. F. Akhundova* (Baku, 1982); Sh. F. Mamedov, *Mirovozzrenie M. F. Akhundova* (Moscow, 1962); M. Rafili, *Akhundov* (Moscow, 1959).

6. On the rise of Azerbaijani press, see A. Bennigsen and Ch. Lemercier-Quelquejay, *La presse et le mouvements nationaux chez les musulmans de Russie avant 1920* (Paris, 1960), pp. 27–30.

7. For a detailed discussion of Gasprinskii, see Alan W. Fisher, *The Crimean Tatars* (Stanford, 1978), pp. 100–106; on Pan-Turkism, see S. Zenkovsky, *Pan-Turkism and Islam in Russia* (Cambridge, Mass., 1960); J. M. Landau, *Pan-Turkism in Turkey: A Study in Irredentism* (London, 1981); *Tatars of the Crimea. Their Struggle for Survival*, ed. Edward Allworth (Durham, 1988), chaps. by Alan W. Fisher and Edward J. Lazzerini.

8. For detailed information on the economic and social structures of the two communities, see D. B. Seidzade, *Iz istorii azerbaidzhanskoi burzhuazii v nachale XX veka* (Baku, 1978); B. Ischanian, *Nationaler Bestand berufmässige Gruppierung und Gliederung der kaukasischen Völker* (Berlin, 1914); G. Pichkian, "Kapitalisticheskoe razvitie neftianoi promyshlennosti v Azerbaidzhane," in Zakavkazskii Kommunisticheskii Universitet, *Istoriia klassovoi bor'by v Zakavkazii* (Tiflis, 1930), pp. 71–122.

9. For the accounts of the communal strife see: L. Villari, *The Fire and Sword in the Caucasus* (London, 1906); J. D. Henry, *Baku: An Eventful History* (London, 1905); E. Aknouni, *Political Persecutions: Armenian Prisoners of the Caucasus* (New York, 1911); C. J. Walker, *Armenia: The Survival of a Nation* (New York, 1980), pp. 73–81.

10. On the *Himmät*, see T. Swietochowski, "The Himmät Party: Socialism and the Nationality Question in Russian Azerbaijan," *Cahiers du monde russe et soviétique* 19, nos. 1–2 (1978): 119–42. On the *Musavat*, see M. Mirza-Bala, *Milli Azerbaycan hareketi. Milli Azerbaycan Musavat Firkasinin tarihi* (Berlin, 1938). Also "Sotsial'naia sushchnost' musavatizma," in *Pervaia vsesoiuznaia konferentsiia istorikov-marksistov, trudy* (Moscow, 1930), pp. 501–20.

11. See T. Swietochowski, "National Consciousness and Political Orientations in Azerbaijan 1905–1920," in *Transcaucasia. Nationalism and Social Change*, ed. R. G. Suny (Ann Arbor, 1983), pp. 209–32.

12. See "Ana dili," in *Mollah Nasr-al-din*, no. 22, 1913.

·13. Mirza-Bala, *Milli Azerbaycan*, pp. 74–77.

14. See *Der Neue Orient* 10 (1917): 526–27; Zenkovsky, *Pan-Turkism*, pp. 146–47.

15. Mirza-bala, *Milli Azerbaycan*, pp. 85–86.

16. On the 1918 intercommunal violence, see R. G. Suny, *The Baku Commune, 1917–1918: Class and Nationality in the Russian Revolution* (Princeton, 1972), pp. 239–58; Walker, *Armenia*, pp. 260–61; F. Kazemzadeh, *The Struggle for Transcaucasia (1917–1921)* (New York, 1951), pp. 143–44. .

17. For a discussion of the Azerbaijani Republic see T. Swietochowski, *Russian Azerbaijan, 1905–1920: The Shaping of National Identity in a Muslim Community* (Cambridge, 1985), pp. 129–90.

18. For monographic works on the Mountainous Karabagh dispute, see R. Hovannisian, "The Armeno-Azerbaijani Conflict over Mountainous Karabagh," *Armenian Review*, no. 24 (Summer 1971): 3–24; A. Altstadt, "Nagorno Karabagh—Apple of Discord in the Azerbaijani SSR," *Central Asian Survey* 7, no. 4 (1988): 63–78.

19. For a discussion of the Bolshevik views on the nationality problem in Baku, see Suny, *The Baku Commune*, pp. 190–220.

20. M. S. Iskenderov, *Iz istorii bor'by Kommunisticheskoi Partii Azerbaidzhana za pobedu sovetskoi vlasti* (Baku, 1958), pp. 347–56.

21. See A. G. Karaev, *Iz nedavnogo proshlogo* (Baku, 1926), p. 54.

22. Kommunisticheskaia Partiia azerbaidzhana, Institut Istorii Partii, *Bor'ba za pobedu sotsialisticheskoi revoliutsii v Azerbaidzhane; Dokumenty i materialy*, no. 541 (Baku, 1967), pp. 461–62.

23. Akademiia Nauk Azerbaidzhanskoi SSR, Institut Istorii, *Istoriia Azerbaidzhana* (Baku 1963), vol. 3, part 1, pp. 444–45.

24. See "Mustafa Kemal und Aserbeidschan" in *Welt des Islams* 2 (1953): 274–76.

25. D. Nissman, *The Soviet Union and Iranian Azerbaijan: The Use of Nationalism for Political Penetration* (Boulder, 1987), pp. 28–29.

26. For a monographic work on Iranian Azerbaijan during World War II, see P. Homayounpour, *L'affaire d'Azerbaidjan* (Lausanne, 1967). See also E. Abrahamian, "Communism and Communalism in Iran: The Tudeh and the Firqay-i Dimukrat," *International Journal of Middle Eastern Studies* 1 (1970): 291–316.

27. For a detailed discussion of the Soviet cultural policies in Iranian Azerbaijan in the period, see Nissman, *The Soviet Union and Azerbaijan*, pp. 27–37.

28. F. S. Fatemi, *The USSR in Iran* (London 1980), p. 91. For a recent discussion of the Party, see M. M. Cheshmazar, S. J. Pishevarinin, "Azarbaijan Demokrat Partiyasinin va Azarbaijan Milli Hokumatinin jaranmasi ughrunda mubarizada rolu hagginda," in Azarbaijan SSR Elmlar Akademiyasi, *Janubi Azarbaijan tarikhi masalalari* (Baku, 1989), pp. 18–45.

29. For the evaluation of the Iranian Azerbaijan crisis, see R. Rossow, "The Battle of Azerbaijan, 1946," *Middle East Journal* 10 (1984): 199–207; see also B. Kuniholm, *The Origins of the Cold War in the Near East* (Princeton, 1980), pp. 379–97.

30. For a detailed discussion, see D. Nissman, "The Origins and Development of the Literature of 'Longing' in Azerbaijan," *Journal of Turkish Studies* 8 (1984): 199–207.

31. See Nissman, *The Soviet Union and Azerbaijan*, pp. 42–45.

32. Ibid., p. 46.

33. See *Qorkamli ingilabchi Sattar Khan*, ed. A. S. Sumbatzada (Baku, 1972).

34. Nissman, *The Soviet Union and Azerbaijan*, p. 56.

35. For a discussion of attitudes and opinions among the Azeri public on the eve of Perestroika, see T. Swietochowski, "Soviet Azerbaijan Today: The Problems of Group Identity," *Kennan Institute, Occasional Papers*, no. 211.

4. One or More Tatar Nations?

Azade-Ayşe Rorlich

The very title of this paper is an invitation into an intellectual minefield. To negotiate a safe passage through this minefield would require the elaboration of generally acceptable definitions of the concepts of nation, nationalism, and national consciousness. This is an impossible task, for the impressive volume of literature on the subject is matched only by its controversial nature. The idea of what constitutes nationhood is still in flux, despite the fact that the first prophets of national identity—Herder, Burke, Rousseau, Jefferson—projected it on the intellectual landscape of Europe over two centuries ago. There is no consensus in the scholarly community with regard to definitions of the concepts. At best, new nuances have emerged as new definitions based on modernizing or developmental models have been added to the old ones rooted in purely intellectual and political criteria. Treatment of the subject by Carlton Hayes, Alfred Cobban, E. H. Carr, and Hans Kohn fits into the traditions of intellectual history. The discussion has been vastly enriched by the works of Karl Deutsch, Elie Kedourie, Eugen Weber, Ch. Tilly, E. Gellner, and Dudley Seers (to name only a few), who have brought a social-science perspective and a focus on socio-economic change and on modernization and developmental theories to the on-going discussions regarding nationalism, national identity and the idea of nation.[1]

Accepting as an axiom the reality of a less than perfect definition of nation, this discussion will rely on Ernst B. Haas's articulation of the concept as

> a socially mobilized body of individuals, believing themselves to be united by some set of characteristics that differentiate them from outsiders, striving to create or maintain their own state. These indi-

viduals have a collective consciousness because of their sentiment of difference, or even uniqueness, which is fostered by the group's sharing of core symbols.[2]

"The socially mobilized body of individuals" who represent the focus of the present observations are the Tatars, who in 1979 numbered 6,317,468 people (see Appendix: Table 1).

The term *Tatar* refers to the descendants of the Kypchak Turkic peoples who inhabited the western wing of the Mongol empire, the ulus of Juchi; these peoples, after the disintegration of the Golden Horde, were disseminated over a vast area from the borders of Poland to the Black Sea, the Middle Volga, and the Ural Mountains. Today, major groups descending from the peoples of the Golden Horde to whom the term *Tatar* applies as a designation of ethnicity are the Volga, Crimean, Lithuanian, Siberian, Astrakhan, and Kasimov Tatars. Ethnicity is determined in this case by their distinct territory, common traditions and related dialects. The existence of an awareness of the interrelationship between themselves and their co-nationals endows these groups with the cognitive artifact of national consciousness, thus elevating them to the level of nationality.[3]

Since all these groups are endowed with the quality of nationality, which are those that qualify as nations? The argument advanced here is that only the Crimean and the Volga Tatars qualify as nations, not only because they enjoyed the reality of autonomous statehood in the past, but also because the legacy of that past legitimated their claims to extraterritorial cultural autonomy, territorial autonomy, and eventually to a brief episode of political independence in the aftermath of the 1917 revolutions.

It is in the past of the Crimean and Volga Tatars that the contention regarding the existence of two nations is rooted. Tash Timur, one of the governors of Crimea, made a first attempt at Crimean independence from the Golden Horde by minting his own coinage, but the first ruler of a Crimean Khanate, independent from the Golden Horde, was Haji Giray. The period of genuine independence (1452–1588) was followed by almost two centuries of vassalage to the Ottoman Sultan (1588–1774), then by a period of Russian protectorate (1774–1783), which culminated with its conquest by Russia in 1783.[4]

Dynastic ties were responsible for the intimate relationship between the Crimean Khanate and the Kazan Khanate, which emerged in 1445 when the fabric of the Golden Horde disintegrated. This relationship, however, was neither exclusive nor always friendly, and in neither case did it prevent the growth of a sentiment of difference, even uniqueness, despite the shared values of an Islamic *Weltanschauung*.[5] The Kazan Khanate existed as an independent political entity for 107 years. On October 15, 1552, it was conquered by Ivan IV, who launched a policy of unredeeming hostility toward its population.

The policies of the Russian state in the conquered territories of the two Khanates were aimed at assimilating the Tatars, who found themselves regarded as "aliens" (*inorodtsy*) in their own historical territories. It is not the purpose of this chapter to review or discuss those policies, but it is imperative to underline the role that they played in the emergence of a modern national consciousness among the Crimean and Volga Tatars where "the identity and the nation [were almost] created as a weapon."[6] Culture was the soil into which the seeds of the nation were first planted, and the concept of nationality was disseminated in the catalyzing climate of the Jadid movement.

Shihabeddin Merjani (1818–1889), the father of Jadidism in the Middle Volga, made a significant contribution to the shaping of Tatar national consciousness by presenting his people with their own history and by being the first to use the ethnonym "Tatar" when writing about the Volga Muslims. He urged his countrymen to call themselves Tatars, challenging them "If you are not a Tatar, an Arab, Tajik, Nogay, Chinese, Russian, French, . . . then, who are you?"[7]

A contemporary of his, Abdulqayyum Nasiri (1825–1902), enriched the reform movement by becoming the first to raise the issue of the preservation of the Tatar language, to emphasize the importance of language in shaping and maintaining one's identity, and to advocate the development of a literary language based on the vernacular of the Volga region. This language was to be free of Arabic, Persian, and Ottoman words and was to be accessible to ordinary people. The Volga vernacular became the language of literature in the pages of the calendar Nasiri published between 1871 and 1897 as a sui generis substitute for the nonexistent periodical press.[8]

Nasiri's Tatarism was not unanimously accepted. One of his most vocal critics was the father of Crimean Jadidism, Ismail Bey Gasprali (Gasprinskii), who advocated a common Turkic language for all Russian Muslims, which he promoted in the pages of *Terjuman* (1883–1914). Yet as he promoted cultural nationalism, Ismail Bey strongly believed that its development would remove the reasons for a political confrontation between the Russian government and the Muslims, and might even foster social harmony. As he said, "The *moral Russification [nravstvennoe obrusenie]* of Muslims can be achieved only by elevating their intellectual level and knowledge, and this can be accomplished only by recognizing the civic rights of the Tatar language in schools and literature."[9]

Ismail Bey's stand on the issue of language and on that of the relationship between the Muslims and the Russian state was in no way symptomatic of an imminent demise of the Crimean nation. On the contrary, it was the "soul tax" Ismail Bey paid to a past shaped by a special relationship that Crimea had enjoyed with the Ottoman empire and by a present bearing the mark of the demise of the polity in 1783. His solutions proved to be divorced from reality: the forces of Tatarism challenged Ismail Bey in his native Crimea, as well as among the Volga Tatars.

In the Crimea, Abdurreshid Mehdi advanced the idea of the "national, social, and political liberation of the Crimean Tatars." The Young Tatars around the newspaper *Vatan Hadimi* (1906–1909) proclaimed that "love of nation is love of the faith," and the members of the society Vatan (1909–1917) called for the replacement of Gasprali's Turkism with Tatarism.[10]

Among the Volga Tatars, the issue of Tatarism not only left its mark on every major development in the life of the Tatars in the decades preceding the revolutions of 1917, but shaped the interaction between cultural coalescence and political intervention in the years to come. The most vocal defender of Tatarism in the Soviet period was G. Ibragimov, who developed his thesis in an essay published in 1927, entitled "Which way will Tatar culture go?" The answers he provided reiterated a conviction he had stated in the pages of *Shura* in 1911: "We are Tatars, all we do is Tatar, and our future culture will be Tatar."[11]

Promoting a national literary language, thus, became a crucial component of the complex Jadid process of cultural innovation. It involved persistent ideological labor, creative imagination, and practical talent. Dictionaries and elementary primers, the Jadid literature and the press emerged as the most important cultural artifacts of a national tradition. If in the 1890s, Ismail Bey Gasprali, A. Osmanov, and Menulla Sabirjan's textbooks were the few textbooks available, on the eve of World War I, the number of textbooks had increased so significantly that bookstore catalogs listed them and newspapers often published reviews.[12]

Tatar intellectuals used the educational infrastructure of the Jadid school to perfect the cultural artifacts of the national tradition. They were able to do so for at least two reasons: First, the policies of the Russian government had not been conducive to their social mobilization. Second, since at the end of the nineteenth century, both the Volga and Crimea Tatars enjoyed a literacy rate higher than that of the Russians, they were better equipped to use their national school system as a vehicle for social mobilization. For a Tatar population of 100,000, there were 154 Tatar schools in the Crimea in 1867; they were attended by 5,081 students (901 girls and 4,180 boys). The comparative ratio of schools and students for Russian and Tatar inhabitants of the Crimean was:

Tatars	Russians
1 school per 649.3 people	1 school per 2,747 people
1 student per 27.9 people	1 student per 66.1 people

Thus, the Tatars, who had only 17.85 percent of the total population share, constituted 23 percent of the student population, whereas Russians, who represented 62.5 percent of the total population of the Crimea, could claim only 28.50 percent of the total student population.[13]

While between 1867 and 1914 there was no significant demographic change in the size of the Crimean Tatar population, the number of schools increased significantly as a result of the Jadid effervescence. Among the Volga Tatars, in the Kazan guberniia alone, there were 1,088 Tatar schools, of which 90 percent were Jadid.[14]

Language, religion, national culture and the memory of a "political past" were some of the core symbols that united the Volga Tatars, as they later mobilized the Crimeans at the beginning of the twentieth century. The definition of self gained a political dimension after 1905, as in both cases the concept of nation came to include a quest first for political participation and then for cultural and territorial autonomy, and even outright independence. It was during the period between 1905 and 1921 that the "organic conception of nationality" defined by G. Elley as a "contractual, inherited, historicist character of national identity" underwent a metamorphosis and reemerged as a political conception of nationality intimately linked to the notions of citizenship and popular sovereignty.[15]

The Volga Tatars' domination of the political landscape of the Muslims of Russia, their ability to press issues and advance solutions that reflected their political aspirations (the cultural vs. territorial autonomy controversy at the Muslim congresses of 1917) alienated other Muslims but indicated clearly the presence of a political ego in the equation of the nation.

The emergence of a Crimean national party, the Milli Firka, in the summer of 1917, represented the political dimension of nationalism, whereas the proclamation of a Crimean state in December 1917 seemed to have brought about the fulfillment of a national dream.[16] This Crimean state led by Chelebi Jihan—its government, parliament, and constitution—was, however, born under a falling star: the gains of the winter of 1917 were wiped out by the changing fortunes of the Civil War. At the end of that war, in a masterful act of political astuteness and tactical flexibility, Lenin set forth to implement the policy of national self-determination and thus honor the promises made when his government had been in peril. The implementation of the policy took into account the definition that Stalin had provided for a nation as "an historically evolved stable community of language, territory, economic life and psychological make-up manifested in a community of culture."[17]

On October 18, 1921, a decree of Sovnarkom announced the formation of the Crimean Autonomous Soviet Socialist Republic as an integral part of the RSFSR. Short of political independence, this decree formalized the emergence of a Crimean "nation-state"; it was the de jure affirmation of the political existence of the Crimean Tatars. The de facto realization of that state within the framework of a centralized (albeit federative) Soviet state was a much more difficult task. It fell to the generation of the Jadids led by Veli Ibrahimov to channel the unspent energies of independent nationhood into the cultural nationalism and quest for political autonomy of the 1920s that came to be known as "national communism."

The Volga Tatars traveled a similar road: on November 19, 1917, the National Assembly (Millet Mejlisi) of the Muslims of Inner Russia and Siberia proclaimed an autonomous Idil-Ural state. The crisis of the Civil War rendered impossible the implementation of this decision, yet for a moment the dream was revived on March 23, 1918, by the promise the Bolshevik leadership made to proclaim the territory of the Southern Ural and Middle Volga the Tatar-Bashkir Soviet Republic.[18]

The dream never became a reality. A large Tatar-Bashkir republic whose borders would have been too similar to the borders of the Kazan Khanate was not an acceptable political alternative for the Bolshevik leadership. Instead, two autonomous republics were born: on March 23, 1919, the Bashkir republic, and on May 27, 1920, the Tatar republic.

At first glance, there is indeed, a striking similarity in the roads the Crimean and Volga Tatars traveled to build their autonomous nations. A closer scrutiny reveals a qualitative difference in their perceptions of the political self. The Volga Tatars abandoned the ethnic criterion as a denominator for their political entity and opted instead for a territorial one. To be sure, the Idil-Ural state was the territory on which the Volga Tatars had emerged as a historical nation; they could not claim exclusivity to it, however. It is conceivable that the Volga Tatars perceived themselves as *the* heirs of the Kazan Khanate and as such had no difficulty in approaching the territorial and ethnic designations of the concept of nation as interchangeable categories. To some extent, this assumption is validated by the developments of the 1920s, when the frustrated political hopes of the national communists were channeled into a flurry of socioeconomic and cultural activities motivated by one goal, one overriding ambition: Tatarization.

The exception to these ethnocentric goals of the Tatar national communists was Mirza Sultangaliev's plan for a republic of Turan, an entity that might be called "megaTurkic." Here, too, Sultangaliev seems to have been ready to sacrifice Tatarism to Turanism, because he envisaged the Tatars as the leaders of the revolution in the East. He argued that "the Tatar working masses and the poor did not participate in the revolution but contributed to its propagation in the countries of the East."[19]

The institutional framework through which the national aspirations of the Tatars found formal scholarly expression in the 1920s was the Scientific Society of Tatarology (Nauchnoe Obshchestvo Tatarovedeniia). The journal of the society, *Vestnik Nauchnogo Obshchestva Tatarovedeniia* (1925–1930), opened its pages to discussions regarding the culture of not only the Volga Tatars but that of the Crimean, Lithuanian, and Siberian Tatars as well. These activities endowed the Volga Tatars, once again, with a leadership role in the preservation and retrieval of the heritage of the material and spiritual culture of the Tatars.[20]

In the period between 1920 and 1928, both the Crimean and Volga Tatars were caught in a cruel quid pro quo that reflected the irreconcilable gap between their understanding of autonomy and the interpretation that the government gave to it. The end of the 1920s spelled a brutal end to the aspirations of the Crimean and Volga Tatar national communists and shattered their dreams for even cultural autonomy. Not only the dreams, but those who had attempted to transform them into reality disappeared at the end of the 1920s. For having stretched the scope of their nationalist ideals and plans to limits which were incompatible with Moscow's centralizing goals, Mirza Sultangaliev, Veli Ibrahimov, and all those who adhered to their ideals were purged and then physically eliminated.[21] For its daring and political audacity, the intelligentsia of both republics were devastated, and on the eve of World War II neither the Crimean nor the Volga Tatar republics had recovered from the shock of the purges.

The war drastically altered the pattern of similarities between the two nations. It deprived the Crimeans of their historical home and stripped them of their nationality. Accused of treason "en masse," despite the fact that of a population of 300,000 only 20,000 to 30,000 had served in the "self defense" units that had aided the German occupying forces, on the night of May 18, 1944, the entire Crimean population was removed from the Crimea in a blitz-deportation conducted by the police forces under the command of Ivan Serov, First Deputy People's Commissar for Internal Affairs of the USSR. In recognition of his role in the successful completion of the operation, Serov was awarded the title "Hero of the Soviet Union" and granted the Order of Lenin. All Crimeans were deported—neither the children nor the old were spared; they all took the road of exile and soon were joined by loyal soldiers such as Commissars Ahmetov and Isaev of the Fifth Partisan Brigade, who were removed from their units and deported.[22] The abolition of the Crimean ASSR was legally articulated in the June 30, 1945, decree that transformed it into an oblast' of the RSFSR, only to be transferred to the Ukrainian SSR by a February 19, 1954, decision of the Presidium of the Supreme Soviet.

After the deportation, the main efforts of the government were directed at erasing all evidence of Crimean culture and history from the peninsula. Architectural monuments were destroyed; everything written and printed in Crimean (including Marxist literature) was burned; city and place names, in general, were changed and recast into a Slavic mold, thus putting on the map of Crimea *Kirovskoe* instead of the Islamic *Terek*, to give only one example.[23]

The question, then, emerges: Could anyone argue today that a Crimean nation still exists? Any attempt to answer this question would have to be based on the assessment of the present-day situation against the background of Ernst B. Haas's definition of nation, which was adopted as the basis for this discussion. Against all odds, the Crimean Tatars do represent a nation today, for they have endured as the required, socially mobilized body of individuals united by a set of characteristics that distinguish them from outsiders. They do strive to create their own state, and have a corporate awareness nurtured by their sense of difference or uniqueness. The group shares significant fundamental symbols.[24] Among them are a recognized sign, a flag, an anthem, an alphabet, a periodical and newspaper press published in their own language, and a body of writings.

Obviously, Haas's definition calls for a major modification here: the Crimeans today are engaged in a struggle to return to their historical homeland, not in an effort to create an independent state. The struggle for their homeland is at the center of their struggle to endure as a nation.

It unfolds under the twin banners of political activism and cultural assertiveness.

Political activism began in 1963 when Crimean community members sent delegates to Moscow to lobby for rehabilitation; it gained impetus after the September 9, 1967, decree that partially rehabilitated them and triggered the petition campaign to return to the Crimea; it acquired a new dimension with the emergence of a dissident movement marked by the tragic self-immolations of Musa Mamut and Izzet Memedaliev, and by the unbending commitment of Mustafa Jemilev to the struggle aimed at overcoming the status as "citizens of Tatar nationality formerly resident in the Crimea," which was bestowed upon the Crimeans by the 1967 decree, and at gaining the right to live in the Crimea as Crimean Tatars.[25] This aspect of the Crimean struggle is widely known, yet despite its importance and the need perhaps to reflect upon its many nuances in detail, the discussion that follows will focus only on cultural assertiveness.

Less spectacular than political activism, and deeply entrenched in the life of diaspora Crimean Tatar communities, cultural assertiveness has been the main measure of the resilience of the Crimeans as a nation. It is directed toward rescuing from extinction and passing on to the generations born in exile the core symbols of national identity that Crimean Tatars share: their language, literature, and music; their national culture and traditions; the keen awareness of the historicity of their nation.

"Our contemporary literary language is the language of the newspaper *Lenin Bayraghī*; [the language] of the literary works; [the language] of the radio broadcasts, and finally, the language of the [dance and song] ensemble 'Kaytarma,' to which we can now also add the language of the journal *Iīldīz*," wrote the Crimean literary critic and writer Alim Fetisliamov, in the pages of the journal *Iīldīz*, in 1986.[26]
In fact, his statement lists the stages of the Crimean cultural recovery that have made possible the assertiveness of the 1970s and 1980s.

The first sign of hope came ten years after the deportation, when in 1954 the government lifted the requirement that every Crimean, including the children and the old, visit the local police headquarters every other week. In 1956, Radio Tashkent began its Crimean Tatar language broadcasts, and 1957 was marked by two major developments: the Crimean Tatars living in the Tashkent area were permitted to establish their own newspaper, *Lenin Bayraghī* (Lenin's Banner), and to organize a folk dance and music ensemble named *Kaytarma*, after the national dance of the Crimeans.[27] Following a rather long hiatus, 1980 saw the publication of the literary journal *Iīldīz* (The Star), which became the latest forum available to the Crimeans for the defense of their language and retrieval of their past.

Lenin Bayraghī has been an important weapon in the struggle for the preservation and growth of the Tatar language in several ways:

1. It publishes (almost) weekly a section entitled *LUGHAT*, which is a bilingual (Russian-Tatar) dictionary. At first glance, *LUGHAT* may appear to be an effort aimed at fulfilling an internationalist task and contributing to the realization of the ultimate goal of *sliianie* through *sblizhenie*. In fact, *LUGHAT* has become a major vehicle of "Tatarization" for the generations born in exile. The February 1985 decision of the editorial board to discontinue *LUGHAT* had to be reviewed after an avalanche of letters arrived from readers who demanded its continuation. In October 1985, *LUGHAT* reclaimed its place in the pages of *Lenin Bayraghī*.

2. Once a month, it features a children's page entitled *Iīldīzchīk* (The Little Star), which fills the gap of the nonexistent children's journals. The crossword puzzles and the poems and short stories written by children belonging to literary circles such as *Yash Qalemler* (Young Pens) of Chīrchīk that are carried in the pages of *Iīldīzchīk* are meant to encourage Crimean Children to read and write in their native tongue.[28]

3. It provides wide coverage of news concerning Crimean Tatar language classes in the schools of Uzbekistan and discusses the interest in the language in general. The efforts of teachers such as Alime Batalova and Zevide Gafarova (both graduates of the Crimean Language and Literature Section of the Tashkent Nizami Pedagogical Institute), who have distinguished themselves not only in the classroom but in extracurricular activities aimed at strengthening the language skills of their students, are amply popularized in the pages of *Lenin Bayraghī*.[29]

4. It presents the contributions of scholarship, while also acquainting readers with the ongoing scholarly debates regarding the Crimean language. The article dedicated to the anniversary of the eightieth birthday of M. U. Umerov, the principal editor of the *LUGHAT* section, reveals his main contributions to the promotion of the Tatar language: a textbook, *Ana Tili* (Mother Tongue), which saw three editions between 1968 and 1983; a language curriculum for grades 3 and 4; a volume of proverbs entitled *Qaida Birlik, Anda Tirilik* (Where there is Unity, there is Vitality); as well as articles dealing with comparative Turcological Studies.[30]

Lenin Bairaghī provided ample coverage of the proceedings of the International Conference of Altaists held in Tashkent, in September 1986 and focused particularly on B. Ghafarov's paper which presented

Codex Cumanicus as a fourteenth century document preserving a vocabulary that can be considered the first dictionary of the Crimean Tatar
language.[31]

Alim Fetisliamov discussed the evolution of the written language of
the Crimeans from the language of the documents issued in medieval
Solhat (Eski Kirim) to the language of the seventeenth-century destan
Toghaibek attributed to Janmuhammed, and acknowledged the contributions of *Terjuman* to those of the *Vatan Hadimi* group around Abdurreshid Mehdi, as well as the special efforts of Shamil Toqtargaz, whose
goal was to make the vernacular the basis for the Crimean literary language.[32]

What is important to note here is not only the open support for the
Tatar language, but the very clear effort to present to readers (and to
implicitly rehabilitate) the very episode of their past history which sym-
bolized the transition to a distinct Tatar Crimean national consciousness. After all, Abdurreshid Mehdi and other Tatar youth associated
with *Vatan Hadimi* were "Tatarists" for whom "Love of nation was love
of faith."

Fetisliamov's is not an isolated voice. The title of Melish's article,
Til'ge ur"met—il'ge ur"met demektir (To honor one's language is to
honor one's land), bears a striking resemblance to the motto of the *Vatan
Hadimi* group.[33] In fact, the 1980s are witnessing a not officially sanctioned, but rather courageous rehabilitation of the nationalists shot in
the 1920s. Credit here belongs to the literary critics and literary historians. Analyzing the contemporary Crimean literature, B. G'äfarov
blamed the paucity and primitive language of some of these works on
the fact that their authors were ignorant of the pre-1930s Crimean literary heritage. He pointed to the literary contributions of writers such
as the former Milli Firka leader Osman Akchokraklī and those of the
nationalist A. Odabash (one of the signatories of the May 1916 Lausanne
Declaration of the League of Non-Russian Nationalities), with no mention of their political affiliations. In doing so, however, he reinstated
cultural figures whose names had become taboo after their purge from
the Pedagogical Institute of the Crimean ASSR in 1936 and their subsequent physical demise.[34] Most likely, their names had not instantly
disappeared from the memories of the Crimeans after 1936, because even
Veli Ibrahimov, who was a quintessentially political figure, continued to
be venerated by the Crimeans long after his execution in 1928.[35]

The deportation and the dramatic uprooting broke the continuity of
the Crimean heritage, and efforts such as those of Ghafarov aimed at retrieving it are nothing less than remarkable. Crimean writers today are

very much aware of their civic duty, of their role as the conscience and the memory of the nation. Particularly telling is a stanza from Cherkez Ali's poem entitled *Ali Agha nichiun shiir iazmaysïz* (Ali Agha Why Don't You Write Poetry Anymore?):

> Months have gone by, and years have gone by and
>   they all have tired me
> My reader became my friend and my inspiration
> Hard as it was, I threw myself into work again
> Believing that my people should never forget my land.

> *Ailar Kechti, iïllar kechti, ioruldum . . .*
> *Ok"uiïdzhïm oldï il'kham chok"rag"ïm*
> *Zor olsa da, kene ishke uruldïm,*
> *Unutmasïn, dedim, khalkïm, topragïm.*[36]

The importance given to literature in the pages of *Lenin Bayraghï* and *Iïldïz* is matched only by the attention given to Crimean folklore (musical, literary) and to old Crimean traditions and customs such as *Qashka malii*, a horse race popular in the mountain villages of the Crimea.[37] Any signs of acculturation detrimental to the preservation of Crimean identity and culture are criticized and readers are warned that national songs, instead of *meshchanskie* (petit bourgeois) [Russian] songs such as *Aravai* and *Limonchiki*, should grace happy occasions such as weddings.[38]

Neither *Lenin Bayraghï* nor *Iïldïz* publish petitions or open letters demanding a restoration of the Crimean homeland. There is, however, a very sustained campaign aimed at achieving that very goal by indirectly reiterating the injustice of the deportation in the numerous articles dedicated to war heroes in the section *Jesaret* (courage) of *Lenin Bayraghï*, which honors the memory of those who defended the Crimean and Soviet homeland with courage and valor. The obvious message of the section is that those heroes have not been forgotten, at least by their countrymen.[39]

It seems, however, that today's glasnost and perestroika can provide no hope that Soviet leader Mikhail Gorbachev can reverse the May 18, 1944, decision that changed the life of the Crimean nation. In addition to the official party pronouncements on the nationality issue, the tone of the newspaper and journal articles published in the last two years is equally discouraging. A good indicator of the fact that glasnost does not bring new hopes for the Crimeans is an article published in *Nauka i Religiia*; it restates almost with a vengeance the obliteration of Tatar presence from the Crimea. The article is dedicated to the museum of local history (*Kraevedcheskii Muzei*) housed in the former mosque of Eupatoria. It comments on the latest acquisitions illustrating the history of the Greek, Roman, and other cultures and mentions those on the history of religion and atheism. Not a single word is mentioned about the Crimean Tatars or about their culture.

Yet, despite this reality, and against the odds of deportation and uprooting, the attachment of the Crimean Tatars to their native language and heritage as reflected in their increasing cultural assertiveness seems to represent valid enough evidence to argue that Crimean Tatars have endured as a nation even if as one without a homeland.

Their struggle for a homeland seems to have found support not only among the members of the Democratic Movement but among the Tatars and the Bashkirs of Ufa, as articulated openly for the first time in a *samizdat* document dated April 13, 1977, which read: "We support the struggle of the Crimean Tatars but [our] main goal should be, in the long run, the unification of all Turkic peoples."[40]

The Volga Tatars are as concerned as the Crimeans about the endurance and growth of their national language. The "struggle for the Tatar language" is carried out not only in Tatarstan but in neighboring Bashkiria, where the Tatars—although 14.9 percent of the population, a higher share of the total population than the Bashkirs—have neither a press, nor a theater nor a Tatar section of the Writers Union. According to the samizdat material that calls attention to this reality, the seriousness of the situation is compounded by the fact that a great number of Bashkirs consider Tatar as their native language.[41]

What the samizdat document indicates is that the perception of self which Volga Tatars have is based on a definition of nation whose territory resembles more the territory of the Kazan Khanate than that of the lands comprised in present day Tatarstan. In the last two decades in particular, the Volga Tatars have directed their efforts toward restating the claim to their historical homeland by engaging in an intense effort aimed at retrieving its culture.

The journal *Kazan Utlari* (The Fires of Kazan) features a section entitled *Kulturabiz tarikhïna* (On the History of our Culture) which has been responsible for the gradual retrieval of the cultural treasures of the Volga Tatars from oblivion, whether this oblivion was the result of benign neglect or political design. There are at least two new developments which can be identified in the articles published in this section: (1) A growing interest in the small and "diaspora" Tatar groups of the

Volga Ural region, which recalls the interests of the society of Tatarology of the 1920s (2) a quiet rehabilitation of the intellectuals accused of nationalism and eliminated in the 1920s and 1930s (not unlike the Crimean case).

Kazan Utlari provides coverage of Astrakhan Tatars, Siberian Tatars, or groups such as those that settled among the Kazakhs in centuries past and, despite their isolation, preserved intact the language, the material and spiritual culture which their ancestors had brought from the native lands of Bugul'me and Belebey. Moreover, the article dedicated to those Tatars whom the Kazakhs call *"Karakalpaks"* points out that they identify themselves as Kazan Tatars and acknowledge Tatar as their native language.[42]

The significance of *Kazan Utlari*'s interest in the small and "diaspora" Tatar groups is twofold. First, the Volga Tatars seem to exhibit a perception of their nation that transcends the boundaries of their republic and comprises most of the descendants of the inhabitants of the Kazan Khanate. Second, the Volga Tatars living in the Tatar republic are assuming a leadership role in the preservation of the nation in its broadest definition when they encourage dialectological and folklore studies of "diaspora Tatars."[43]

The article dedicated to the 110th anniversary of Hadi Atlasi's birth (1876–1938) and written by the leading Volga Tatar scholars Ia. Abdullin, M. Gosmanov, and I. Tahirov amounts to the rehabilitation of this leading Tatar intellectual shot in 1938.

Hadi Atlasi was an imam in Älmät (Almet'evsk), a journalist who contributed regularly to the liberal *Yulduz,* a deputy in the Second Duma, member of the Dumachïlar faction affiliated with the Trudoviki; finally, he was a historian—the author of *Sibir tarihi* (Siberian History, 1912), *Suiumbike* (1912), and *Kazan Khanlïghï* (The Kazan Khanate, 1913). After the revolution, he was a teacher of history and German in Bugul'me (1921–1929) and a teacher of German in Kazan (1930–1938?).

The authors of the article draw upon V. V. Bartol'd's assessment of Atlasi's work as a historian and point out that although Bartol'd considered Atlasi "a Tatar patriot," he nonetheless acknowledged the fact that Atlasi objectively presented the relationship between the Kazan Khanate and the Russian state in the fifteenth and sixteenth centuries. They argue that "archival materials clearly invalidate any allegations that Hadi Atlasi was an ideologue of counterrevolutionary activities among the Tatars or a participant [in them]," and they make their strongest case for rehabilitation by emphasizing that

He comes out as an honest intellectual who was true to his people in his own way. . . . He was a representative of the bourgeois milieu and he remained one till the very end. He erred many times, he strayed away, he wavered, he deviated seriously, but in the end he accepted Soviet reality and he gave his remaining energies, experience and talent to the advancement of the Soviet School and to building the new culture.[44]

In the case of the Volga Tatars, there is one core symbol which pre-dates the Kazan Khanate period and represents an important component of their identity as a nation: the Bulgar period. A most telling redeemer of the Volga Tatar's claim to historicity and distinctiveness, the Bulgar period has occupied a special place in their efforts aimed at retrieving the rich heritage of the past. The retrieval has taken the form of linguistic, archeological, historical, folkloric and literary studies which have been enriched by novels and historical dramas such as Nurikhan Fättakh's *Kol Gali*.[45] This issue has been addressed elsewhere and is beyond the scope of the present discussion. What should be pointed out, however, is that it is difficult to identify a new development in the cultural and literary life of the Volga Tatars that ignores or is oblivious to the Bulgar period.

In May 1985, *Kazan Utlarï* inaugurated a new section entitled *Tatar-stan—tugan töbägem* (Tatarstan—my native district). The editorial that introduced the section clearly spelled out its purpose: "The task of loving, admiring, and making more beautiful the world and the mother-land, [the task] of making people happier should begin with the effort to know [one's] native district and show respect for it."[46]

The authors of the articles in this new section are the party secretaries of the districts featured in each issue. Despite the fact that the unde-clared but obvious goal of each article is to call attention to the post-1917 achievements of each district (*raion*), all of them contain "historical background" discussions of varying lengths. Some, such as N.B. Baki-rov's article on the Älki *raion*, contain information on the Bulgar period, while others make mention of the Bubi medrese and of Abdulqayyum Nasiri when they refer to the nineteenth- and early twentieth-century history of the Volga Tatars.[47]

The past—an awareness of it, respect for it, as well as a desire to make it a part of the present by keeping alive its traditions—seems to be a key issue for the endurance of the Volga and Crimean Tatars as nations.

Rising at the Congress of the Writers' Union in the spring of 1986 to defend the historical novel, which had come under heavy criticism, the Volga Tatar writer Tufan Minnulin offered perhaps the most courageous statement identifying the core symbols which nations share, thus paying tribute to the uniqueness of each people, and to their national character:

> It is impossible to write in general about a people. There exists a man, a Soviet man with a birth place and a place of permanent residence. This place he calls [his] native land. His ties with it are historical, economic, ecological, and psychological. If a human being has no feelings for the native land, he becomes a tumbleweed [*perekati-pole*].[48]

Evidence of the ties which the Crimean and Volga Tatars feel to their native lands and cultures makes it possible to conclude that these groups do represent two nations, but that as members of the broader Turkic commonwealth they are one people.

Notes

1. C. J. Hayes, *The Historical Evolution of Modern Nationalism* (New York, 1968); A. Cobban, *The Nation State and National Self-Determination* (Oxford, 1945); E. H. Carr, *Nationalism and After* (Cambridge, 1945); Hans Kohn, *The Idea of Nationalism* (New York, 1967); K. Deutsch, *Nationalism and Social Communication: An Inquiry into the Foundation of Nationality* (Cambridge, Mass., 1966); E. Kedourie, *Nationalism* (1960); E. Weber, *Peasants into Frenchmen. The Modernization of Rural France, 1870–1914* (1977); Ch. Tilly, ed., *The Formation of National States in Western Europe* (Princeton, 1975); E. Gellner, *Nations and Nationalism* (Ithaca, 1983); D. Seers, *The Political Economy of Nationalism* (New York, 1983). Also, see the following recent essays on the topic: Ernst B. Haas, "What Is Nationalism and Why Should We Study It?" *International Organization*, 40, no. 3 (1986): 707–44; Arthur N. Waldron, "Theories of Nationalism and Historical Explanation," *World Politics* 37, no. 3 (1985): 416–33; Geof Elley, "Nationalism and Social History," *Social History* 6, no. 1 (1981): 83–107.

2. Haas, "What Is Nationalism?" p. 726.

3. For a discussion of the distinction between ethnicity and nationality, see Paul Robert Magocsi, *The Shaping of a National Identity: Subcarpathian Rus', 1848–1948* (Cambridge, Mass., 1978), pp. 2, 13.

4. A. W. Fisher, *Crimean Tatars* (Stanford, 1978), pp. 1–80.

5. A. Rorlich, *The Volga Tatars* (Stanford, 1986), pp. 24–31.

6. D. Ronen, *The Quest for Self-Determination* (New Haven and London, 1979), p. 86.

7. A. Temir, "Tatar sözünün menşei hakkinda," *Kazan,* no. 3 (1971): 43.

8. A. Saadi, *Tatar ädäbiyatī tarihi* (Kazan, 1926), p. 44.

9. Ismail Bey Gasprinskii, *Russkoe Musul'manstvo*, Society for Central Asian Studies, Reprint Series No. 6 (Oxford, 1985): 60.

10. Fisher, *Crimean Tatars*, pp. 105–07.

11. A. Rorlich, *Volga Tatars*, pp. 68, 220.

12. *Zaman Kalendarï* (Orenburg, 1910), p. 39; "Livres et revues. Publications russes," *RMM*, no. 2 (1911): 403.

13. E. Markov, *Ocherki Kryma. Kartiny Krymskoi zhizni, istorii i prirody* (St. Petersburg, Moscow, 1899), p. 306.

14. Ia. Abdullin, *Tatarskaia prosvetitel'skaia mysl'* (Kazan, 1976), p. 209; "Shkol'nyi vopros v Russkom musul'manstve," *Mir Islama*, no. 2 (1913): 453–54.

15. Elley, "Nationalism and Social History," p. 85.

16. It seems that in the summer of 1917 a Crimean delegation met with the members of the Ukrainian Rada to solicit their support for the autonomy of Crimea. "Musul'mane i kievskaia Rada," *Rech*, no. 173, July 26, 1917, p. 4.

17. J. Stalin, *Marxism and the National Question*, 2d ed. (Moscow, 1936), p. 8.

18. E. B. Genkina, *Obrazovanie SSSR. Sbornik dokumentov, 1917–1924* (Moscow and Leningrad, 1949), p. 38.

19. M. Sultangaliev, "Tatary i oktiabr'skaia revoliutsiia," *Stat'i*, Society for Central Asian Studies, Reprint Series No. 1 (Oxford, 1984): 40.

20. Some samples of articles published in the journal: K. Gubaidullin and M. Gubaidullina, "Pishcha Kazanskikh Tatar," *VNOT*, no. 6: 17–49; A. Samoilovich, "K istorii krymsko-tatarskogo literaturnogo iazyka," *VNOT*, no. 7: 27–33; M. G. Khudiakov, "Tatarskaia Kazan' v risunkakh XVI stoletiia," *VNOT*, no. 9–10: 45–60; A. Rakhim, "Materialy dlia bibliografii po krymskim i Litovskim Tataram," *VNOT*, nos. 9–10: 194–200; G. Sharaf, "K voprosu o priniatii dlia tiurkskikh narodnostei latinskogo shrifta," *NVOT*, no. 5: 15–80; A. Rakhim, "Proekt sostavlenia tolkovogo slovaria Tatarskogo iazyka 100 let tomu nazad," *VNOT*, nos. 9–10: 88–104.

21. A. Bennigsen and S. E. Wimbush, *Muslim National Communism in the Soviet Union* (Chicago, 1979), pp. 42–47, 64–69, 83–89, 199.

22. Fisher, *Crimean Tatars*, pp. 165–66.

23. N. Abdülhamitoglu, *Türksüz Kirim: Yüzbinlerin Sürgünü* (Istanbul, 1974), pp. 97–98; Anne Sheehy, *The Crimean Tatars and Volga Germans: Soviet Treatment of Two National Minorities* (London, 1971), pp. 10–12; L. D. Solodovnik et al., *Istoriia mist i sil ukrainskir SSR: Krims'ka oblast'* (Kiev, 1974), p. 393.

24. Haas, "What Is Nationalism?" pp. 707–8.

25. Alan W. Fisher, "A Struggle for Survival," *Inquiry*, January 7 and 21, 1980, pp. 20–23; D. Smith, "Tatar's Fiery Suicide Told by Two Dissidents," *Los Angeles Times*, February 21, 1979, part 1, p. 20; "Kirim Gözyaşlari meclis'te," *Yeni Haber*, November 11, 1986; A. Seitmuratova, "Kirim müslümanlarïn dramïna Kulak verin," *Zaman*, November 12, 1986. On the criticism of dissent in the pages of *Lenin Bayraghï* (hereinafter *LB*), see "K'iiafetinin astarï," *LB*, June 6, 1980; Sh. Iskanderov, *LB*, April 1, 1986.

26. A. Fetisliamov, "Edebiy tilimizning shekilleshiuvinde shair ve yazï jilarïmïznïng roliu," *Iïldïz*, no. 5 (1986): 26.

27. A. Umerov, "Iïrlamak—muzïka altïnda sioilenmektir," *LB*, March 25, 1980; F. Aliev, "Muzïkamïz inkishaf iolunda," *LB*, May 22, 1980.

28. See Iïldïzchïk section on p. 3 of *LB* from December 3, 1985, February 13, March 18, April 29, May 22, August 9, 1986.

29. Alime Batalova was a teacher at the "Krupskaia" High School No. 8 of Ianïiol where more than 200 Tatar children were enrolled. Tatar language classes were taught in grades three to ten. See A. Abkeliamova, "Ana tili dersleri," *LB*, May 15, 1980; Zevide Gafarova taught at 'A. Navoi' School No. 21 in the city of Juma, where some 130–140 Tatar children learned their mother tongue and literature under her guidance. See "Ok'uv iïlï eii ekiunlendi," *LB*, June 10, 1980.

30. I. Kerimov, "Sevimli ve ur"metli oja. Til'shinas alim M. U. Umerov 80 iashïnda," *LB*, January 23, 1984.

31. I. Kandïmov and I. Kerimov's interview with Ghafarov, in *LB*, September 27, 1986.

32. A. Fetisliamov, "Edebiy tilimizning," pp. 128–30.

33. A. Melish, "Til'ge ur"met—il'ge ur"met demektir," *LB*, October 23, 1982. For other mentions of *Vatan Hadimi* and the contributions to Crimean culture of poets such as Shakirali, see "Iakub Shakirali," *LB*, April 15, 1980.

34. See Kandïmov and Kerimov's interview with Ghafarov in *LB*, September 27, 1986, and B. Ghafarov, "Belli Alim," *LB*, March 22, 1980.

35. The Crimean Narkompros was criticized in 1930 for its failure to eradicate nationalism in the Crimea. It was argued that antireligious education was inexistent in Crimean schools, in one of the Bakhchesaray schools children even composed poems and sang songs dedicated to Veli Ibrahimov. Moreover, two years after Ibrahimov's execution, his portraits still adorned the walls of the dormitories in the Kerch' Technical Institute while inspections at other technical institutes revealed the existence of mirrors which featured pictures of Mustafa Kemal, the nationalist leader of republican Turkey, on the opposite side. See Ia. Tolkanov, "O Krymskom narkomprose," *Prosveshchenie natsional'nostei*, no. 2 (1930): 75–76.

36. Cherkez-Ali, "Ali ag"a, nichiun shiir iazmaysïz?" *Iïldïz*, no. 3 (1986): 34.

37. R. Fazyl, "Ishanchlï adïm," *LB*, April 10, 1980; S. Nagaev, "Belli erbap ve edip," *LB*, March 13, 1980; "Khalk" iaratïjïlïg'ï khazinesinden," *LB*, July 15, 1986; and *LB* issues: December 10, 1985; January 18, 1986; February 20, 1986; May 6, 1986; June 14, 1986; September 30, 1986.

38. F. Sakhtara, "Bu toi meni suk"landïrdï," *LB*, September 15, 1983.

39. I. Seifullaev, "Partizanlarnïng K"anatlï iardïmjïlarï, *Iïldïz*, no. 4 (1986): 101–8. S. Nagaev, "Atesh iurek shair," *LB*, May 9, 1980; For one of the many articles on Courage, see "Dzhesaret," *LB*, September 13, 1986.

40. Kukshar (pseud.), "Zaiavlenie o pritesnenii Tatar-Bashkir (iazyk, ekonomika, religiia) s prizyvom ob ob"edinenii tiurkskikh narodov SSSR," *Arkhiv Samizdata*, no. 3085, p. 5.

41. Gruppa Tatar (anonymous), "Obrashchenie k predstaviteliam nerusskoi natsional'nosti s pros'boi podderzhki protiv rusifikatorskoi politiki Ts.K. KPSS v otnoshenii Tatar-Bashkir," *Arkhiv Samizdata*, no. 3086 (April, 1977): 7.

42. L. Arslanov, "Kämnär alar Ästerkhan karakalpaklarï?" *Kazan Utlarï* (hereinafter *KU*) no. 10 (1986): 182–87.

43. "Seber Tatarlarï äkiyatläre," *KU*, no. 10 (1986): 172–77.

44. Ia. Abdullin, M. Gosmanov, I. Tahirov, "Hadi Atlasi turïnda. Hadi Atlasinïng tuuïna 110 el," *KU,* no. 11, 1986, pp. 172–176.

45. A. Kochkina, "Idel bue bolgarlarïnda run yazuï," *KU,* no. 11 (1986): 176–79; N. Khalitov, "Kazan tatarlarï arkhitekturasïnda milli üzenchäleklär," *KU,* no. 9 (1980): 167–71; N. Fättakh, *Kol Gali, KU,* no. 9 (1983): 16–44.

46. "Tatarstan-Tugan töbägen," *KU,* no. 5 (1985): 9.

47. N. B. Bakirov, "Tufrak tugannarï bez," *KU,* no. 5 (1986): 127–31; Kh. K. Khäyretdinov, "Gölbakchada iashibez," *KU,* no. 10 (1985): 158–60; N. B. Bahramov, "Ägärjegä kilegez," *KU,* no. 6 (1986): 146–48.

48. For Minnulin's speech, see *Literaturnaia Gazeta,* July 2, 1986, p. 11.

5. Religious and National Signals in Secular Central Asian Drama

Edward Allworth

Outsiders who study relatively closed societies such as that found in the Central Asian region of the USSR believe that they can make important cultural and political judgments regarding those people. There is a widespread political assumption that from understanding the intensity in the degree of ethnic-group identity expressed by a given nationality the outsider may assess the durability, even the political viability, of such a group. That finding, in turn, may permit the analyst to apprehend an important political fact in the complex of those relating to stability and future strength of the state and government in question, so the thinking goes. In the case of dictatorial political systems, one of the more accessible avenues for such inquiry lies through the reading of artistic literature written in the language of the society to be studied.

In the field of creative writing, as well as others, the formulas of Marxism-Leninism work to obscure the actualities in Soviet nationality affairs. Public statements based upon those formulas may yield nuances of changing emphasis in policies toward the nationality question, but almost never do those declarations reveal the thinking of people and groups outside the ideologists' circle. For that reason, analysts interested in the Soviet nationality question often read imaginative literature from the USSR in order to pursue the action of plot or story. In this way they hope to find certain kinds of political expression. To some degree, this surface method of inquiry gains validity because the cultural managers in Soviet society demand that published works to a noticeable extent reflect party pronouncements.

Outside readers may also look for words, phrases, and allusions that seem to convey ideological attitudes. But public opinion as a composite of voluntary outlook drawn from a cross-section of the population on a certain date cannot be reliably ascertained from examining publications produced under the universally controlled and censored Soviet press. And, because scholars can seldom probe the Soviet mind through customary Western methods of questioning and attitude sampling, even the cursory use of literary means can sometimes, and within limits, provide an understanding of private opinion.

But Soviet literature may offer greater possibilities to the scholar who probes more deeply for ethnic meaning. Such research entails the use of a methodology and approach more literary than political. But, its findings can inform the politically oriented reader. For the present purpose, the literary genre of written drama (including comedy and serious plays) will serve as the material for this research. Several considerations make drama suitable for the investigation. Because it provides a basis for living performers to act out stories and convey moods, ideas, values, and attitudes, drama embodies action in ways alien to most prose fiction and verse. In addition, when plays combine character, visual environment, gesture (movement), facial expression, and intonation, stage works, among the literary forms, potentially possess the most enhanced capacity to convey the beliefs and standards of the personages on stage. Best of all will serve live performances of such works. Lacking that possibility, the researcher may gain many insights merely from reading the script or scenario. Thus, drama can convey the outlook of the society at large for whom the author in that sense acts as spokesman.

Drama written and performed in the Turki (later, "Uzbek") language supplies the focus and material for this inquiry into modern group identity in Central Asia. To regard study of the Turki-speaking part of the area as study of the whole region seems acceptable in this case for several reasons. Without further comparative study, a researcher cannot test the theory that Turki dramas adequately typify the plays of all Central Asia. But with respect to the matter of their ethnic group expression, the investigation takes that position. The assumption seems sound, because the southern Central Asians had previously experienced notable artistic homogeneity, despite some subregional variations. The fact that the society in that mainly non-Slavic region remains even less well-known than the people of the Soviet West further justifies the approach. Also, within the territory, the Turkistanians, as subsequent remarks will substantiate, led the way from the start in the field of indigenous modern drama. For that reason, too, nearly exclusive concentration upon recent Soviet-era Uzbek plays for this analysis should prove appropriate. The study sets out to establish the practice of group self-identification early in the twentieth century in order to compare that awareness with Uzbek ways and means of articulating group identity late in the century. And, the inquiry will go further than the main literary thesis to suggest two extra-literary representations that convey the sense of group, one concerning ethnic community and the other the role of women in Central Asian ideas of community. These observations have social and perhaps political importance as well as cultural weight. They arise especially from the characters and content of the plays reviewed.

This sampling includes several works published in the thick Tashkent literary journal, *Shärq yulduzi*, between 1980 and 1983. A few others selected at random from well-known Uzbek authors who also treat adult Central Asian life after mid-century enter into consideration. Citations from three Jadid dialogues provide bases for comparison and for recalling the indigenous beginnings of the genre in the region. Study of the Marxist-Stalinist plays prevalent throughout the period from the mid-1920s to the mid-1950s might provide useful findings but could not fit into a study of this size focused upon the more recent expression of religion and nationality in a branch of Central Asian literature.

Group awareness expresses itself directly in the new Central Asian drama through the display of obvious verbal signals and theatrical movement. Plays exhibit consciousness of nationality also indirectly by conveying the group's attitudes and revealing its beliefs and symbols. The main literary considerations important in analyzing drama as a bearer of ethnic group awareness include, above all, the artistic talent of the playwright and linguistic connection between him and his audience. Likewise, the subject matter of the play and breadth of its audience may influence the nature and extent of ethnic expression in drama.

Extraliterary factors, too, play a certain role in ethnic expression. Central Asian drama must comprehend a mixture of overlapping group identities that date back long before the inception of the region's modern indigenous theater. Since World War I, events have brought about further striking alterations in group names and ethnic territory. For the early innovators in Central Asian theater, especially Turkistan playwrights, that rapid geopolitical transformation drastically reduced the wide, heterogeneous human panorama open to them. Now, the existing union republic of Uzbekistan encloses a number of historical Central Asian towns, but by no means all of them. It complicates matters that the UzSSR also encompasses numbers of Crimean Tatars, Karakalpaks, Russians, Tajiks, and Uyghurs who contribute their own, often distinct, theatrical works to the culture of Uzbekistan. And, as late as 1979, more than fifteen percent of all Soviet Uzbeks remained dispersed outside the Uzbek SSR.[1]

These circumstances, along with the fact that Central Asians adopted modern theater fairly recently, may partly explain the uncertain nature of ethnic group identity demonstrated in some Central Asian drama. This study aims to interpret that uncertainty and to consider how literary and nonliterary factors determine the patterns of ethnic awareness expressed in today's Uzbek stage writing. This approach to literature and ethnic awareness will entail a search for ethnic-group expression in Uzbek drama and comedy concerning Central Asian life in the second half of the twentieth century.

Pre-1920 Islamic Reformist Tendencies

Before 1920 and the spread of Soviet ideology throughout Central Asia, in drama and in reality religion and group identity had displayed themselves rather differently from what an audience would come to see and hear late in the century. Two playwrights from the beginnings of formal local theater in the region represent the outlook characteristic of the time. Theirs was a period that saw expression of group identity within or through Islam. They held the idea, in a sense, of the national contained in the religious. Neither man then thought of Central Asia's components in terms of the European style of nation. Reformist (*Jadid*) literature before 1925 offered its distinctive view of religion and group identity. In the early dialogues of Abdalrauf Fitrat (1886–1938), at least one of which appeared in dramatic form on stage, the author showed no ambivalence at all regarding either religious or group identity. His large themes in *The Dispute (Munazärä)* (Istanbul 1909–10; Samarkand 1913) referred openly to the main issues involving each subject. Consistently, Mr. Fitrat spoke there about Bukhara and Bukharans as the people, the location, of his writing. Through an extended series of arguments concerning Bukhara, his two characters—a benighted Bukharan *mudarris* (seminary teacher) and an inquiring European traveler—constantly emphasize the Islamic identity of the mudarris and his country.

The author never questions the faith of the seminary teacher. Nor does the dramatist in any way demean the accomplishments of Islamic civilizations. Rather, the mudarris's undoubted pride in and overpowering ignorance of his own religion create a believable tension that sustains the entire exchange between these two characters. Through the device of revealing that nescience and its associated prejudices in the seminary teacher, the author ultimately goes beyond exposing what he considers an abysmal lack of knowledge to offer his main thesis: In educated men, including the semiliterate, any self-delusion concerning the welfare of the community (the group), and each individual's responsibility for benefiting that community, surely offends against Islam.[2] Mr. Fitrat underscores the great seriousness of that offense with many lines of ridiculous dialogue in *The Dispute*. When the conversation turns to the central problem of the Reformists' New Method (*usul-i jadid*) instruction, the Bukharan mudarris declares:

> *Mudarris:* In our opinion, the unlawfulness of this school has certainly been established. Now, isn't the effect and value of what you said [concerning the benefits from New Method schooling] nil?
> *European:* With what sort of proof has it been established?
> *Mudarris:* This school, it seems, made our children into unbelievers. The opinion has been established with this exact proof.
> *European:* I shall say—all scholars of Islam also say—that in no way at all does this school make your children into unbelievers, but makes them into perfect, well-instructed patriots [*wätänpärwär*].
> *Mudarris:* No, no, it is certain that this school is an unbeliever-maker for our children.
> *European:* Excellent! If I ask until the Judgment Day [*qiyamät*] for proof from you, you won't give an answer other than "somebody said." ...
> *Mudarris:* The Jadid school is unlawful.
> *European:* According to what evidence?
> *Mudarris:* There are a thousand proofs. The first of them is the fact that the children in this school sit on a "chair." ... That is, [according to the Muslim tradition] "If anyone makes himself resemble some certain tribe [*qäwm*], he will become one of that very tribe." ...
> To sit on a "chair" is the practice of Europeans. Therefore, if our children sit on chairs, they will become unbelievers.[3]

The *European* in this dialogue painstakingly analyzes the *Mudarris*'s argument, rejecting both the authenticity and interpretation of the supposed Muslim tradition (*hadith*—a saying attributed to the Prophet Muhammad). He dismisses the notion that chairs create unbelievers by mentioning that important Muslim leaders had sat on chairs centuries earlier. *European* uses the patient method of a teacher in bringing his pupil to understand why no one must confuse fables with true religion or genuine sayings of the Prophet. Through examining the spurious "tradition," *European* instructs his Bukharan acquaintance in the necessity to discriminate between genuine and false Muslim traditions. In another of his dialogues, Abdalrauf Fitrat educates yet a different Bukharan about the traditions authenticated by Imam Muhammad bin Ismail al-Bukhariy (d. AD 870) in al-Bukhariy's compilation entitled *Sahih-i*

Bukhariy. This time, through the voice of a Muslim visitor from Hindustan, the author relates that Imam al-Bukhariy collected 600,000 traditions, selected 9,200 of them as absolutely reliable, and found that 3,000 of those repeated each other, leaving about 6,000 different authentic traditions.[4] With those lessons presented in dramatic form, Mr. Fitrat intended to cleanse distortions of Islam from the minds and practices of nominally educated Bukharans in order to bring real Islam back to the ordinary believer without its burden of superstition. Through these two writings, the Reformist spirit around 1910 convincingly showed its faith in the religion of Muhammad and the Qur'ân. Mr. Fitrat restricted his examination into the Islam of that period within the Bukharan state's bounds. But he did not intend with this attention to religion to delimit the group identity of a particular segment of the populace. Among most indigenous Central Asians, including Turki- and Farsi-speaking Bukharans, Sunni Islam provided the broadest kind of supra-ethnic background to all local life.

Many other Reformists wrote works in this vein. Mahmud Khoja Behbudiy's best-known literary composition, *The Patricide* (*Pädärkush*) (1911), conveyed Jadid attitudes toward religion in more than one way. The author very simply dramatized a story about the wages of sin, in the Muslim understanding. Notwithstanding the startling title of his play, he focused his dialogue upon a sin of omission, rather than commission. *The Patricide* demonstrated that an individual cannot avoid responsibility for his community (simultaneously, he will not escape retribution for a failure in this respect). Specifically, Mr. Behbudiy showed that a father's failure to advance his son's education, and thus the welfare of the Turkistanian community, led directly to an irreparable disaster. The dramatist's general message: condoning the perpetuation of ignorance constitutes unpious, criminal conduct. The Prophet explicitly called upon Muslims to educate themselves by all measures and in all places at home or abroad. In this case, forces in *The Patricide* brought a retribution that destroyed the drama's family, symbol of a larger community.

Less directly, the author of *The Patricide* deals with the matter of group identity by looking at the roles of women. In *The Patricide*, the earliest Central Asian drama, its author writes at Samarkand in the Turki language, calling his play "an edifying example taken from Turkistan daily life; the first national [*milliy*] tragedy. . . ." Obviously, he held an idea of community that contrasted greatly with the European notion of nationhood. No one in the play ever mentions the word "Uzbek," but a leading character specifically refers to "Turkistan." The dramatist gives more than minor importance to the two females of the cast (played

by men at the premiere and probably at all subsequent performances).
Nonetheless, these women appear primarily by reference or implication
rather than in person. For example, Mrs. Rich, mother of the "patricide"
of the play, exists through the remarks and presence of her only son
more than on stage. Only late in the action, in the brief third act, after
the burglars murder her husband, does the audience view and hear this
female character in person, but she never appears alone. With neighbors,
she enters to see the body of the lifeless Mr. Rich lying on the floor in
the men's wing of the house. Simultaneously, she witnesses the flight
of her son, Tashmurad, from the room. The instant she recognizes him
and the dreadful situation before her, she shrieks at the "patricide," calls
him a monster, and flings herself in anguish upon the reclining corpse
of Mr. Rich. In the speech, she cries out for the police as she condemns
her son. A second and then third and final short speech spell out for
the audience the consequences for her of this awful crime: it inflicts
a double loss in denying her further role as mother and keeper of the
family hearth, and, through the arrest and certain exile to Siberia (a symbolically frozen hell), of her offspring, the chance for any future family
happiness. For the Reformist author, these domestic occurrences epito-
mized the self-inflicted damage to Turkistan from willful ignorance.

The second female character represents outside influences affecting
the Turkistan family. Through her negative potential rather than dramatic presence, she executes the duties of "the other woman" in *The
Patricide*. Liza, identified as a Christian (that is, Russian) slut, furnishes
the immediate motive for the main action in Mahmud Khoja Behbudiy's
drama. Only half-literately, she utters exactly three words on stage during the briefest of appearances in the final (fourth) short episode. "Good
ev'nun," she simpers, and "Merci," she twitters, before abruptly fleeing when the police suddenly arrive in search of the killers. But, before
entering that scene, she has already received the fifteen silver rubles that
young Mr. Rich and his cohorts committed heinous crimes to obtain.
Thus, Liza, almost without appearing, has played the destructive part of
a rival in separating young Mr. Rich from his mother. In the tragedy, she
evidently functions as the dramatic means to show the harmfulness of
outside (im)morality for the Turkistan community.[5]

Drama under the Banner of Anti-Religious Doctrine

These plays projected the Reformist ideas onto the stage. In that respect,
they were ideological forerunners of the stage works to appear under
Soviet auspices soon after 1920. With the onset of Soviet political think-

ing all over Russian Central Asia, a new ideology actively coexisted, for a time, with the previous, Muslim one. Official rejection of religion, particularly of Islam, and application of a European way of defining community caused confusion in the region that persisted under the surface of official life through the 1930s. In the plays of the two decades beginning in 1920, public life rather than private affairs dominated the stage. Prescribed "conflicts" and Marxist-Stalinist solutions to them crowded out any other thinking. Antinationalism, a form of administrative coercion, colored the entire treatment of community and group identity, to the extent that little but Stalinist dogmatism came from the mouths of characters in the plays approved for performance and publication.

Formal laws teamed with police practice to enforce antireligious doctrine in Central Asia as in the remainder of the USSR. The criminal code of the Russian Soviet Federated Socialist Republic, a model statute for the fourteen non-Russian union republics, in 1966 and at other times, defined as infractions of the laws concerning "the separation of church from state and schools from the church" any "preparation of appeals, letters, leaflets, and other documents with the aim of mass circulation or mass distribution calling for flouting the laws about religious congregations." In 1969, in the Uzbekistan Soviet Socialist [Union] Republic (UzSSR), the Council of Ministers, the executive branch of the government, again demanded from various agencies of the UzSSR vigorous action against religion. In a decree "About Strengthening Control over Observing the Laws about Religious Sects," the UzSSR Council of Ministers directed its Ministry of Internal Affairs:

> To take measures for strengthening work concerning the discovery and prevention of crimes arising from religious bases, concerning interdicting the sale and dissemination of religious literature (photocopies of sermons, extracts of the Qur'ân, tape recordings and phonograph disks with recordings of religious verses, songs, and the like), concerning interdicting the begging of able-bodied persons at houses of prayer, the activities of parasitical types from among itinerant clergy and leaders of the organizations of sects.[6]

This militant official opposition to religious activity and belief squelched positive religious expression in literature, including Central Asian drama, during the two decades that Iosif V. Stalin (1879–1953) ruled as dictator. Such police methods taught authors to seek other modes of expressing spirituality. Some of the better writers found their own ways of conveying a kind of faith unrelated to Marxist ideology.

In the late twentieth century, this spirituality carefully sought a place for itself within the framework of nationality identity, reversing the relationship between those two aspects of group identity that had prevailed during the Reformist period at the beginning of this century.

Ethnic Signs in Central Asian Plays

Each Central Asian play creates a particular esthetic and human universe. The limits of this dramatic universe may derive some external shape from obvious labeling or from topography charted in dialogue and stage direction. But, those intangible limits more faithfully follow a pattern outlined principally by general values and a sense of community. The ethnic reference material present in a dramatist's view of his group life suffuses all of them. His subliminal signals and representation of group awareness constitute the true ethnic heart of drama. Thus, altering the external (objective) recognition of ethnicity cannot be equated with the importance of changing internal (subjective) consciousness. Extraneous signs sometimes purposefully brought into drama either heighten contrasts or show similarities between outsiders and the given nationality group. Some playwrights intentionally employ foreign or artificial signals with the goal of diluting fundamental ethnic identity and distorting the configuration of the dramatic universe in the play.

The relative strength and frequency of ethnic communication stands as one measure of a play's esthetic effectiveness or artistic integrity. An author confident of his audience usually does not need to elaborate for it the ethnic identification he shares with its members. In this respect, ethnic explicitness in playwriting, unless nationality supplies the main subject of a drama, may be construed as a dramatist's lack of assurance in his connection with the audience, as irreverence toward superficial aspects of ethnic identity, or may reveal a lack of talent that forces the writer to rely upon unliterary manipulation in the playscript. At one level, drama must reach not only the semiliterate but the unthinking person. At another, it faces astute viewers or readers intolerant of dramaturgical immaturity.

Every sizable nationality bears within itself several different theatrical audiences. They decide to some extent the types of plays they want. The audience will respond most to the playwright who shows he understands it best. Generally, the broader the audience, the more obvious the content, including ethnic signals, provided by a dramatist. Playwrights hoping to reach even wider audiences, including foreigners, and anticipating the translation of their work into other languages, tend to explain Central Asian ways more than they dramatize them. These authors, too, resort to using explicit ethnic labels. But the select, well-educated city viewers require variety and originality rather than familiarity with the scenes and situations. They demand subtle inventiveness instead of stereotypes or clichés.

Degrees of subtlety, therefore, may indicate communication of ethnic group awareness in inverse proportion to the greater amount and obtrusiveness of the signals—the more blatant and superficial the ethnic signs, the less integrated and internalized the ethnic group identity. To avoid such indications altogether, if conceivable in a play, would suggest deliberate camouflage of the basic group identity. In the late twentieth century, an able dramatist will not ordinarily insert an obvious ethnic label unknowingly into his dialogue. More likely, he will employ such a tag with patriotic or ironic purpose. Unconscious employment of obvious ethnic labels in a play may typify the inexperienced or less able writer. Allowing for the factors of unartistic motivation or extraliterary contrivance, a test according to ethnic subtlety may apply generally to the study of Central Asian drama with some interesting results.

Uzbek theater offers a mid-century example of broadly popular work in the musically embellished play, "A Silken Embroidery" (Shahi sozänä), by Abdullah Qahhar (1907–1968). "A Silken Embroidery" first came out under the title "New Land" (Yängi yer) in 1949. It won a Stalin Prize after the writer revised and retitled the script in 1952, the same year the forty-seven-year-old author finally joined the Communist Party (very possibly a necessary qualification for prizewinning in his case, for party critics had subjected Mr. Qahhar to strong attacks in the late 1930s).[7]

Events in the play take place between 1947 and, in a further revision, 1958. The comedy has three acts which visually liken the map of the UzSSR to a colorful silken coverlet or wall-hanging of the sort hand-embroidered by Central Asian women for trousseaux. In Act I, the hero, Dehqanbay, first introduces the metaphor with these words: "Our Uzbekistan . . . (he sees the silken embroidery lying on the outdoor wooden cot [sori]). It's like this silk, like a silken embroidery . . . it's all full of gleaming colors." Earlier, members of the audience saw the heroine, Hafiza, singing as she worked her embroidery.[8] Neither of these early episodes involving Hafiza, Dehqanbay, and the silken embroidery appears in the 1957 Uzbek-language edition of "A Silken Embroidery." Evidently an editor, or perhaps the author, added them to a later edition in order to increase the ethnic explicitness in the play.

Besides including the embroidery as a figure of speech, the playwright supplies a profusion of incidental ethnic signs. Dehqanbay speaks about the standard Central Asian tearoom (chaykhanä) and quotes lines from the Timurid poet, Mir Ali Shir Nawaiy (1441–1501). The players cook, eat, and talk about rice, pilaw, and local meat dumplings (*chuchwärä*).[9] Two middle-aged women, mothers of the hero and heroine, utter a stream of Central Asian sayings and expressions that add local color and a display of traditional attitudes that receive little serious respect.

Love of Homeland

Specific ethnogeographical reference points in "A Silken Embroidery" consist of the Andijan and Samarkand oblast's plus the Mirzachol (Wilderness) area in Sir Darya oblast' southwest of Tashkent. A character makes one offhand mention of the Qara Qum (desert) in Turkmenistan and one reference to Moscow. Social configuration starts changing with the pending merger of the two households through the marriage of two of their younger members. It expands as far as a public farm (*kolkhoz*) in a reclamation zone that acquires this newly uniting extended family, along with many others. Secondary figures move on to jobs outside Uzbekistan. So concrete is the topography and so abundant the obvious ethnic signals that they overwhelm any deeper meaning of the composition.

This typical Central Asian play about rural life embraces an entire public farm community from the vantage point of the top administrators and the foremen directing work crews. Rural life merits attention from playwrights who find it esthetically absorbing, of course, for more than 75 percent of indigenous Central Asians lived on farms or in small villages in 1970, and over 71 percent remained there still in 1979.[10] By depicting the whole farm as a dramatic unit, such a play avoids closely focusing upon private lives experienced by individuals or larger families. The technique depersonalizes the literary treatment of people but stresses matters of authority, power and leadership. Despite the entertaining didacticism of this work, "A Silken Embroidery" may serve as a miniature version of larger public activities in Central Asia.

Two later dramas in this whole public-farm genre continue the rural concentration in a different spirit. The serious drama, "Friends (Unfounded Suspicion)" (*Dostlär* [*Orinsiz shubhä*]) (1961), includes three acts and five scenes. Internal evidence dates the play's action around 1957, but Rahmatulla Ataqoziyew Uyghun (b. 1905), its author, names neither towns nor sites that encompass most of the situation portrayed. This drama demonstrates again that the business of the public farm raises problems of leadership. Here, in a single-public-farm setting, troubles have become acute long before this action begins. Unjust actions and machinations of a *raion* [state farm] committee secretary have created chaos. The dramatist universalizes his theme by resisting the temptation to localize his farm within a particular part of Uzbekistan. Though he shuns the use of obvious methods to label the scene Uzbek, he refers to homegrown apples and pomegranates in act 1 and mentions the name of the satirical Uzbek-language humor magazine, *Mushtum*, in act 2.[11]

Those hints sufficiently alert a knowing audience to the outer limits of this dramatic horizon. Moreover, mature Central Asians cannot mistake the nature of the problem that the play deals with. The action recreates arbitrary, illegal acts of a political leader that damage the efforts of the farm and ruin the lives of many farmers before 1956. Without previous knowledge or experience of those very difficult Stalinist times, viewers might see this play mainly as empty melodrama.

"Friends" directly develops another theme that forms an undercurrent in many recent Central Asian plays, a theme that probably has particular relevance for Uzbek society. That subject concerns the powerful drive to preserve the inviolability of the specific human community. In "Friends," the defended community falls within the public farm radius. Near the main character, Haydar(jan), the author portrays a troubled marriage as a kind of metaphor for the threatened community. Qarasach and Qochqar hold their family together by sheer willpower, in spite of incompatibility and lack of true affection.

But the playwright reserves his principal attention for the whole public farm. The most terrible and most satisfying developments in the drama relate to the earlier false denunciations that led to unlawful ejection from the farm of the former farm chairman, thirty-six-year-old Haydar. Implacably, a Soviet court sentenced him to twenty years in prison. The play's entire action occurs following the innocent man's exoneration (aqlänish) and return to the community after only five years' incarceration. The reunion becomes a happy occasion for most of the farmers, who again gladly accept Haydar as chairman. Toward the close of Act III, new villainy directed against Haydar now by Qari Sulaymankhojayew, the fifty-five-year-old farm economist, is unearthed. They remove Qari from his post, and a policeman from the *raion* center arrests Qari, taking him away to face interrogation and trial.

In the play, money furnishes the motivation for this evil. Central Asian dramatists seemingly could not yet attribute any societal fault to the system of government or its underlying ideology, though both provided the opportunities for such abuses. The dialogue describes Qari as "a person alien to the public farm" (kalkhazgä yat adäm).[12] The removal from the community of that "alien" helps restore the integrity of the original human group and returns a homogeneity to the dramatic universe. These two actions (Haydar's return and Qari's expulsion) would serve no general purpose in the drama without the presence of the significant community that forms the universe on stage. Had the author elected to treat these occurrences specifically as two individuals' experiences, the play would have shifted the stress in "Friends" from public to private and deemphasized the political side of the drama.

A variant upon the theme of reestablishing the family circle comes from Otkir Räshid (b. 1915), one of the older authors encountered in this study. His two-act farm play, "As an Offspring . . ." (*Färzänd deb*) (1980) openly, rather simply, poses a Solomonic dilemma to a grown man claimed as their child by two pairs of parents, one Russian and the other Uzbek.[13] The Uzbek mother and father bore him and the adoptive Russian parents raised him. They figuratively try to tear him in two, at least psychologically and emotionally and at the end, both the Uzbek and Russian families remain fragmented. The agonizing choice between blood ties and the affectionate upbringing by foster parents also becomes a decision by the son whether to live his further life as an Uzbek or as a Russian. The traumatic personal problem, with its larger implications, fully confronts the bewildered offspring, Khaldar, as the final curtain falls. The meaning of his name, "with a birthmark," suggests that at least outwardly his physical origin remains irradicable. The playwright leaves the situation tensely unresolved, for the plot of the play, pitting one ethnic identity against another, carried too much tension in the Soviet situation to make a preference for either solution publicly acceptable.

A recent drama by Mashrab Babayew (b. 1941) again deals with farm life. His "True Friend of the Soil" (*Yer tamiri*) (1983), once more views rural existence as the management might observe it from above.[14] Just as in Uyghun's "Friends," an embattled (state) farm chairman finds himself here the target of vilification and anonymous denunciations. In addition, certain regional political figures, such as Ghafur M. Mallayew, chairman of the *raion* executive committee, attack the farm chairman publicly. Instead of suffering unjust punishment, the chairman of the farm, Begimqul J. Jabbaraw, retains the support and protection of a politician at yet a higher level, Aripaw, secretary of the *oblast'* committee. Justice appears here not as an abstract value but as the outcome of the fortunate possession of highly placed patrons. In this situation the dramatist demonstrates the traditional Central Asian view of the inseparable oneness of justice and leadership.

This confrontation allows the author to discourse upon two related ideas: unjust treatment and social inequality generate fear and apprehension in a society, by leading to concealment, lack of candor, and serious abuses; the best personnel policy is one that makes assignments on the basis of a combination of merit and local origin of employees and officials, rather than upon the practice of favoritism and conformity. An exchange between Begimqul and his protector, Aripaw, outlines the policy and suggests its ethnic implications:

> *Aripaw:* I intend to recommend you for the directorship . . . for your own state farm. . . .
> *Begimqul:* But the Director?
> *Aripaw:* We shall remove your director. Evidently he's from another räian. He will go to his own räian. . . . If we succeed in finding a man from the area for each position, our affairs will go well. We are experimenting with putting a person in every farm who came from that räian, from that farm.[15]

Playwright Babayew by inference links the group identity of the ideal leader closely with his ethnic base, for public and even state farms remain largely homogeneous in Central Asia. In effect, that passage, a reflection of Soviet policy, is saying that in most cases the ethnic origin of the leadership in Uzbek farms should correspond to the predominant nationality group in the farm population.

These plays speak, too, about the manner, behavior, and style of leadership, as well as of a group's way of life and incentives. Both "Friends" and "True Friend of the Soil" remind foremen, managers, directors, and their superiors to deal courteously and fairly with their people. Leaders are explicitly admonished to avoid damaging their authority by shouting and raising their voices. They must carry themselves with dignity. These exhortations echo those in the written record of leadership counsels as far back as the literature of greater Central Asia, including East Turkistan and Khorasan, can be traced. Wise men of the past have discussed the qualities of leaders and leadership at length. Their remarks relate to the heterogeneous civilization of Dasht-i Qipchaq (the Qipchaq Plains), Turkistan, Mawaraunnahr, and Khorasan, rather than to any single ethnic group within that great region.[16]

Mr. Babayew then refers concretely to the ethnic group awareness coincident here with the dramatic circumference of his play's world. An eighty-year-old farmer, Toqsanbay-Ata, reproves the visiting *raion* executive committee chairman, Mallayew, saying that

> Throughout his whole life an Uzbek lives in hope of a celebration [*toy*], he saves up "for a celebration." Now today, when the farmer's

goal was reached, it turns out a celebration has been organized. Someone barging in has certain duties and obligations. Especially, a big shot's arrival really will swell the attractiveness of the celebration right away! You didn't do anything. An Uzbek's custom. . . . [17]

In other words, Uzbeks know how to behave at a celebration, and the official showed himself strangely un-Uzbek. The farmers, led by their chairman, Begimqul J. Jabbaraw, as a consequence eject this outsider from the event, even though he seems by origin a Central Asian and functions as a regional communist leader. (Earlier, farm director Begimqul J. Jabbaraw, in a remonstrance, had directly called Mr. Mallayew "no communist.") In the final scene, Mallayew fails completely the significant tests of hospitality, generosity, and conviviality expected of an Uzbek leader at a moment of great family (community) importance, a *toy* for circumcision of a son or marriage of an offspring. The farmers refuse to allow Mallayew to spoil the happy celebration, and, besides demanding that he leave, they depose him, in a sense, for he loses his authority altogether in their eyes. This action by the ordinary farmers on stage gives an additional intimation that townspeople such as the *raion* politician cannot quite qualify as true Uzbeks and that the popular will affects local political arrangements.

That climactic scene develops at the end of the play's six titled episodes, none of which is labeled or numbered as an act or part. It comes following many statements from the hero, Begimqul J. Jabbaraw, and others, to the effect that they believe in courtesy, justice, fairness, and truth: "Now there really is justice, there really is truth" (*Ädalät bar-ku, äkhir. Häqiqät bar-ku!*).[18] Such expressions of values, ethics, and attitudes toward leaders seem thoroughly appropriate in this literary work. It emulates the form and spirit of the medieval Central Asian fictional (though not then dramatic) dialogue tradition. The author himself calls his work not a play but a "dispute" (*Munazärä*), echoing the revival early in this century by Abdalrauf Fitrat of the form traditionally presented in conversational style.[19] The dialogue in "True Friend of the Soil" remains remarkably unideological. The labor ethic prevails but seems natural under the circumstances. Speeches include a few remarks about how a good communist should behave, but the audience also hears various figures use expressions like "thank God," "praise God" (*Khudagä shukur*), "if God wills" (*Khuda khahläsä*), and the like.[20]

Unlike Mr. Fitrat, with his first dialogues, cited earlier in this inquiry, in which women played no active part, Mashrab Babayew attempts to incorporate the human female in "True Friend of the Soil." When hero

Begimqul J. Jabbaraw obtained his education in an institute five years before the present action, he studied along with Zeba (the name also means
"beautiful, well-proportioned"), referred to in the play as "a city girl."
The two quote love poetry by Azerbaijanian and Uzbek poets (Fuzuli
and Mirtemir) to one another but seldom see each other. The interest
shown this woman by the male lead blossoms not into happy romance
but serves as the basis for a denunciation by the villain, Mallayew. He
falsely accuses the hero of living disreputably, of summoning his lover
(oynäsh) from Tashkent for lascivious purposes and spending a whole
day, but not the evening, with her in Samarkand.[21] This slander makes
up a part of the charge laid against the hero by his adversaries.

The hero's interaction with another woman, a fellow worker on the
farm and long-time acquaintance, illustrates a cold precept of leadership
style. Once the hero becomes the director of the state public farm, his
old friend, Huriyewa (notice the Slavic ending, -ewa), chairman of the
village council, a local political post, tells him she can no longer call him
Begimqul-uka, "Little Brother Begimqul," because now he has become
her boss. And in return he must refer to her (in Russian, but not Central Asian, style) by first name and patronymic, rather than some earlier,
more familiar form he must have used for her.[22] The presence of these
two women in the play adds an oddly wry flavor to the life of the main
male lead, giving the impression of futility and lack of personal meaning
to relations between the sexes. These female characters lack the significant function of centering the family and community that they might
have performed. As a result, members of the state public farm cohere
in this drama because of their sense of traditional behavior rather than
through the pull of a family nucleus.

In the later plays relating to contemporary Central Asian life, the
Uzbek woman sometimes resides at the center of that community. In
addition to forming and anchoring the family, she plays a crucial role in
the plays and therefore in the universe of the community represented by
them. In this respect, Central Asian drama has moved far from its initial
days in the second decade of the twentieth century. Serious Uzbek dramas regarding contemporary Central Asian life—all evidently originate
from Tashkent—seemed in the second half of the twentieth century to
edge most women away from the decisive center of stage action. But
females in the ten newer stage works studied here usually revealed themselves, their attitudes, and their feelings much more openly than their
predecessors in the early Turkistan Jadid dramas created by Mahmud
Khoja Behbudiy and his followers.

The man's world of the public farm presented in Uyghun's "Friends" and Mashrab Babayew's "True Friend of the Soil," for example, relegates women to the periphery of the plays. In them, no woman motivates or carries out the action. Nevertheless, the new women on stage usually appear equal to the male characters in intelligence, education, or status. But in none of these plays do they set the stage for what will ensue or determine the outcome of a plot. Rather, they significantly remain the objects rather than directors of attention. In that position as object, eight times out of ten, women nevertheless prove indispensable to the stories in the dramas.

Whether "True Friend of the Soil" can become gripping drama will depend partly upon the staging and performance. The composition be-longs in the category of stage works presenting obvious ethnic labels, though it is written by an able dramatist. He reveals openly didactic aims and perhaps no strong intention to entertain his audience with the problems he puts forward. The simplicity of the dialogue, the persis-tent return to a device of both figurative and physical wrestling (equally with trying people and situations), and the black and white complica-tions showing no gray between them, unclearly identify the expected audience. "True Friend of the Soil" does not seem to aim at a restricted, well-educated audience. At the same time, its wordy, abstract dialogue might not appeal to the broadest range of viewers. Nevertheless, as lit-erature, it is instructive reading that contributes usefully to a discussion about religion and group identity in rural Central Asia.

Modern Drama As Mirror of Urban Society

City life also receives serious attention repeatedly in the new dramas. In contrast to the public farm plays, urban dramas seldom, perhaps never, restrict themselves to the public arena. They look at the personal life of a few characters. Psychological growth, change, or peculiarity, as a consequence, may occasionally find expression in them. It follows that these plays may not define their fictional territory so exactly as the pub-lic farm plays did. The limits of the intellectual or urban environment remain more elusive, with one puzzling exception. The populous UzSSR claims thirteen sizable towns, but the plays in this sampling select just one as a setting.[23]

Lines in "Faith" (*Iman*) (1960), by Izzat Sultan (b. 1910), an unhumorous play in two parts, mention Tashkent Radio, Tashkent Railroad Station, Tashkent water, and Uzbekistan workers. The dramatist specifies the location for the play as the environs of Tashkent, to which the characters make repeated reference merely as "the City." All of the main personages in "Faith" work there as scholars, administrators, or students, and may reside there. Some plan and describe trips to Moscow. Others angrily turn off foreign radio broadcasts that annoy them. With these specific allusions, the location becomes unambiguous and the time contemporary.[24]

On one level of meaning, Mr. Sultan selected the title of his stage work and devised the plot of "Faith" as a kind of long play on words. The dialogue spells out the lack of belief or faith of the leading figure in the traditional religion of Central Asia. The action hinges rather melodramatically upon the purloining of a manuscript left unpublished by a deceased medical researcher. The hero of the drama, honest Dr. Yoldash Kamilaw, while personifying perfect virtue, behaves like a stiffly righteous elder. Two other men, Dr. Kamilaw's own son, Arif, a junior medical man who plagiarizes the stolen manuscript, and Naim Sanjaraw, who makes the work available to Arif, embody evil. A family member recovers the manuscript just before the plagiarizer can present the work as his own dissertation, thus preserving the family's honor. This represents a method of protecting the community, for that action symbolizes not only a defense of the group's honor but a rejection of others' ideas, perhaps alien, embodied in the stolen manuscript.

In this case, the home of Dr. Kamilaw supplies the effective circumference enclosing this urban scene. It houses a small extended family that includes the senior Kamilaw, a widower, his young daughter, Azada, a thirty-two-year-old son, Arif, the son's wife, as well as seventy-five-year-old Risalat, Dr. Kamilaw's mother-in-law. Close by, but not dwelling within the household, an older daughter who directs a research institute, plays a strong role in facing the ethical dilemma. That dramatic universe extends by assertion, but not dramatically, to the Tashkent medical research institute in which the main *dramatis personae* (*ishtirak etuwchilär*) participate as members or students. Monologues by the paragon, Dr. Kamilaw, about "faith," "honor," "morals and ethics," the sacred calling of the "intelligentsia," and the like, fill the lines. More basically, the drama concerns the sanctity of the home, and, by analogy, the homeland (*wätän, yurt*), to which subject the dialogue specifically turns.[25] According to dramatist Izzat Sultan, these revered places cannot endure the existence within them of dishonorable (*benamus*) members, whatever their formal kinship. Thus, the author's script purges them of membership in the group, although the status and ties of son and husband link with the family the principal exile, Arif Kamilaw. Strong ties of another sort connect Naim Sanjaraw, the manuscript thief, with Dr. Kamilaw, with whom Mr. Sanjaraw studied as a schoolmate and worked as a lifelong colleague in the medical institute and elsewhere.

The playwright seems to feel a weakness in this indictment of Arif

Kamilaw, the plagiarizer. To damn him further, Mr. Sultan adds a hint of matricide as well as symbolic patricide by suggesting that the younger Kamilaw committed two serious acts: someone accuses him of having failed to medicate his own mother properly when she fell ill and died; in the present situation, he raises his fist hostilely against his father. The elder Kamilaw offers an almost irrelevant, feeble explanation for his son's serious character flaw by speaking briefly about a lust for money and influence.[26] The family somehow holds his transgression against the older evil-doer, Naim Sanjaraw, for he arouses such antipathy among the Kamilaws that, un-Central Asian-like, the family discourteously ejects him from the house and threatens him with dismissal from the medical institute as well.[27] Dr. Kamilaw and his older daughter, Aysha, promise court action against the culprits, openly declaring them "alien" (beganä) to family and to scholarly community. As the play presents the situation, the father, rather than administering compassionate correction, sternly disowns and banishes his son from the family. A redemption that might have healed the break in the family circle never appealed to the hero. In a reversal of the behavior recommended over the ages to ideal Central Asian leaders, he meant to punish, rather than forgive. The dialogue emphasizes that contrast when Dr. Kamilaw banishes his son, Arif, in a florid speech that says, in effect: "Never darken my door again!" (Shundäy färzänd mengä keräk emäs! Mening oghlim yoq. Mening oghlim olgän!).[28]

The language of another urban drama, "The Saw," (Ärrä) (1970), by Abduqahhar Ibrahimaw (b. 1939), sounds more natural, reproducing the ring of actual speech, with its unpredictable twists and spontaneity. "The Saw" resembles "Faith" superficially—in subject and structure. Two acts set in contemporary Tashkent show the audience a medical institute professor—a family dynast—interacting mostly with kin and neighbors in his own home. Like Dr. Kamilaw in "Faith," he dominates the immediate surroundings and people, but not with impeccable virtue. He employs more mundane methods of guiding every relationship according to a quid pro quo (Uzbek: aldi-berdi). "The Saw," unlike "Faith," reveals development and change of character. In Mr. Sultan's "Faith," Dr. Kamilaw remains the same man from the beginning to the end of the play. Ultimately, he reveals an implacability toward those he has ostracized that only reinforces the image of his cold inflexibility, his unsusceptibility to human feelings of kinship.

Dr. Murad Mansuraw, the cutting edge of "The Saw," finally comes to terms with himself. He changes as the result of a benevolent act on the part of two wholly disinterested (beghäräz) people who neither think of themselves as especially generous nor understand the transactional motives of a man like Dr. Mansuraw. He regards what he calls love as a practical bargain between two parties, happiness an arrangement for mutual benefit and marriage without advantage as undesirable.[29] Playwright Abduqahhar Ibrahimaw achieves growth in the characters of his play through the use of gentle surprise. From outside the interdependent structure of his senior hero's array of barterers, the dramatist, near the finale, introduces a young couple. They demolish Dr. Mansuraw's whole system of obligatory reciprocity. A knock at the yard gate, insistently shut during the play by Dr. Mansuraw, announces the unheralded entrance of a young man and woman. The man who enters rather poetically remarks that "the wind of affection flew us here . . . the two of us made serious vows to one another [to marry in the coming September]." Dr. Mansuraw's son, Batir, responds: "Wonderful, wonderful." The girl from Wadil, Ma'fura, explains enigmatically: "How we suddenly got here, we don't even know ourselves. We became engaged, and we truly didn't know where we were going or with whom we were going to share our joy. Finally, we turned out to have come right here."[30]

But, something that happened much earlier stirred up part of the "wind of affection" that wafted the couple specifically to Dr. Mansuraw's closed gate. The young male visitor briefly relates how he had recently gone home to Denaw (in southern Uzbekistan) and learned that a retired herdsman there had long prayed for Dr. Mansuraw's welfare. Ten years earlier a car had accidentally struck down the herdsman while he was on a visit to Tashkent. Dr. Mansuraw rushed the seriously injured man to the hospital in his private automobile. The elder herdsman, Qadir-baba sent greetings to his savior through this young man (the name Qadir means "powerful" and by extension "Almighty God"; popular religious usage attaches the epithet "-baba" to the names of saints).

The student pair, after conveying that astonishing message, at once, in the truly deferential Central Asian manner, asks permission to depart. Dr. Mansuraw, amazed, too, by this behavior, slightly and very slowly begins to understand that they have dropped in only to share their own love with a professor (the young man is a student in his medical research institute, although Dr. Mansuraw appears oblivious of it), and to relay the distant herdsman's respect to the doctor. No single individual had ever before come to the Mansuraw house without a request or petition. Dr. Mansuraw's son, portrayed up to that moment as a sullen, guitar-strumming loafer, also learns a lesson of personal unselfishness. The family's seventeen-year-old only child shows amazement that these two students seek no reward. His final speech finishes all dialogue aptly with a young person's half-articulate, sudden insight: "This is something else!" (*Mänä bu bashqä qäp!*).[31]

On one plane of meaning, the great old quality of Central Asian generosity replaces bureaucratic exchange of favors as the prevailing value in that household. On an even higher level, the drama achieves a mystical tone that conveys a most modern expression of spirituality. In the dialogue, the dramatist emphasizes the importance of personal names by allowing Dr. Mansuraw's thirty-seven-year-old wife, Halida, embittered over what she construes as her husband's unrelenting megalomania, to announce to the family that she will take back her maiden name and strike Mansuraw off her personal records.[32] The first name of the main character, Murad (desired, wished), hints at a more elevated source than even generosity for all benefaction. The drama conveys it through the unexpected, mysterious arrival of two unknown, quiet emissaries of goodheartedness (Näbi, the young man's name, means in Muslim religious terms, "God's messenger," "apostle," or "prophet"). Thus, Mr. Ibrahimaw ends his play hopefully, but seriously on a new note, not with the family catastrophe that threatened, but with the imminent likelihood of transformation in the lives of all Mansuraw family members. In attitude, they appear now to draw closer together. The little group will enlarge itself with the coming of the first new baby in many years to Mrs. Mansuraw and by extending the family to include Dr. Mansuraw's brother, heretofore alienated from him, and brother's wife and children. Happy community promises to replace former incompatibility.

Among the plays studied in this review, "The Saw" offers the most subtle but striking treatment of spirituality in recent Uzbek-language drama. It does not arise from the almost ironic portrayal of blind faith by an old visitor who recites the "Fatihä" (prayers from the beginning of the Qur'ân), nor from the unthinking utterance of expressions like "thank God" (*Khudagä shukur*).[33] Mr. Ibrahimaw's working with religiously significant personal names hardly constitutes a hidden piety, though it may titillate Central Asian audiences bored with ordinary playwriting and hungry for meaning. Rather, this drama communicates an intellectual urge for greater range in life, for grappling with ethical and moral absolutes on a grand scale from high to low rather than following limited, obvious ideological guidelines. "The Saw" shows realism when it demonstrates that inner human lives are interesting because they have extraordinary complexity. In transmitting that idea, the play conveys a subtle reality of contemporary life.

Much more explicitly in every respect, Ghulam Alimaw Shuhrat (b. 1918) writes in "My Big Girl" (*Anä qizim*) (1982) a three-act, seven-scene musical drama, about drawing the ethnic universe together with itself.

The drama tells about the immigration to Uzbekistan from Kashghar, Eastern Turkistan, People's Republic of China, of an Uzbek woman and her niece. The niece believes the older woman to be her mother. Events occur in Tashkent during the late 1950s. Speeches and songs glorify the topic of homeland (*wätän*), of native soil (*anä tuprak*), and lament the life lived in an alien land (*yat olkä*).[34] Young men and women peopling this play work as applied artists in a Tashkent china factory. They earnestly face the assignment of creating fresh designs that "constantly glow with our own nationality spirit [*milliy ruh*]." This demanding task differs, for example, from writing a play for one's own ethnic group, for, the heroine declares: "Someone from another ethnic group who takes our product into his hand must recognize instantly the fact that it is Uzbek. . . ."[35] What constitutes a truly Uzbek design she does not describe, but the hero asserts that "creating and preserving the nationality spirit and knowing how to display the special trait [*khaslik*] for yourself to a degree that will not become distasteful to others . . . demands great art and keenness."[36] The distaste he mentions undoubtedly refers to artistic expression that might assert Uzbekhood too prominently or distinctly. Central Asian drama rarely attempts in this way to get to the esthetic heart of art or design of a nationality.

"My Big Girl" opens, according to stage directions, in "One of the old-style households; two houses, one veranda; fruit trees in the courtyard; an outdoor wooden cot [*sori*] under it."[37] By the time of the closing lines of the last scene, the hero, Ikhlas, dismisses that same traditional household as an alien enclave. Speaking to heroine, Charas, and her aunt/mother, he declares: "Well, let's go, we'll leave this foreign land [*ghurbät-khanä*]."[38] He takes them away from the old family house to a new place to live with his own mother and sister, thus bolstering the family. This makes their migration from Kashghar a change from emigranthood, which the dramatist equates with orphancy. The dialogue and action characterize the shift out of the old Tashkent neighborhood as a change from past ways to present.[39] "My Big Girl," like the other plays, concerns itself with restoring and strengthening community. That preoccupation, so noticeable in these serious Uzbek dramas, extends amusingly into comedy, as well.

Tradition vs. Modernity as Theme on the Uzbek Stage

From the first lines in the musical comedy, "Diversion before the Wedding Celebration" (*Toydän aldin tamashä*) (1982), playwright Jumaniyaz Jabbaraw (b. 1930) propels his characters briskly through the process of arranging a marriage for the 27-year-old student, Ilham. The hero's entire family, old and young, and his friends, devote energy to keeping this man in the community's fold. At the outset, his father's sister urges Ilham in rhyme: "My dear boy, be fair, and don't be obstinate, / When will you let it light on your hand, the bird of the fortunate?" That is, when will you get married and settle down? [40]

The mother of Ilham and parents of a twenty-three-year-old prospective bride (relatively old for marriage by traditional Central Asian custom), Feruza, take the usual path of bringing the two together. The elders cannot, of course, force this educated urban pair to get married. The play's main action concerns the stratagems that Ilham and Feruza adopt to please the parents, maintain social decorum, and yet permit themselves to find their own, personally selected mates. The preferred partner of each works or will get a job far away from the parental base of these two. This light comedy uses all the situations of matchmaking amidst benevolent family relations to press one issue. It makes the point that the younger members of a community today insistently expand the limits of their universe, thereby simultaneously enlarging the horizon of their older generation. This argument becomes unmistakable when Feruza's parents disagree over the acceptability of Ergash, the suitor whom she favors:

Subhanqul: You say that's the one who's going off to the Qarshi plains after finishing up the irrigation project? He's impossible. We'd be completely separated from our daughter, in that case.
Sayqalkhan [Subhanqul's wife]: Why would we turn out to be completely separated? Clan will be joined to clan, the tribe of relatives will grow; what's wrong with that? [*elqä el qoshilädi, qärindash-uruqh artädi, yamanmi?*] [41]

The prospective bridegroom, Ilham, initially meets his real beloved while away studying in the Lenin Library in Moscow. His academic advisor invites Ilham to his living quarters and introduces him to someone: "Your Uzbekistan countrywoman, an aviatrix" (*Ozbekistanlik yurtda-shing, uchuwchi qiz*). [42] Some good-hearted intrigues become a harmless way of persuading both Feruza's parents and Ilham's mother to choose their offspring's preferred partners in place of other candidates. This reassures the elders that the young people respect their wishes, that the home place will remain where they live, and that the young generation will not settle beyond the horizon. Mr. Jabbaraw's treatment of the family circle thus resembles considerably the version offered thirty years earlier by Abdullah Qahhar in "A Silken Embroidery." Both plays hold the extended family together, but hint that the younger members of it some of the time may escape the immediate community, without damaging it. Rather than emulating Mr. Qahhar's more declamatory style, Mr. Jabbaraw displays mild humor in "A Diversion before the Wedding Celebration." It results largely from the benign treatment of the familiar Central Asian marriage market and the skillful deception the dramatist creates for the young couples to practice.

The theme of matchmaking motivates another recent play. "May the Nuptials be Blessed" (*Toylär mubaräk*) (1981), in two acts, four scenes, by Otkir Hashimaw (b. 1941), takes its title from the popular wedding song of the same name, but there the resemblance to tradition ends. The author exhibits outlandish wit and striking language to achieve imaginative theatricality. The play develops mainly in an urban institute, with suitable excursions to a restaurant and to the apartment of a key personage. Emphatically contemporary, the playwright wastes no time or effort creating a plot that tries to make either a believable love match or a forced arrangement. He makes the voices in this stage piece sound as strident as those in the previous play spoke gently. Discarding conventional techniques and situations, Mr. Hashimaw writes an outrageously laughable, irreverent mockery of standard marriage rituals, but succeeds also in removing the scent of propaganda.

In the farce, a contest rapidly evolves between Kimya Khala, waitress and karate-proficient aunt/chaperone of the girl, Madina, and a pair of wild male matchmakers. Nematilla and Latifjan serve as staff members and friends in the section of an institute headed by lovestruck Mominjan Qabulaw. They proceed to secure an engagement between Madina and Mominjan, in spite of a vigorous physical defense of her niece by the guardian that leaves the matchmakers black and blue.

Each ethnic reference to locality by the dramatist, rather than obtruding or stopping the dialogue irrelevantly, enhances the humorous action. Tashkent Railroad Station becomes the site of Mominjan's instant infatuation with Madina. Dialogue between the male matchmakers and their client comically brings up the matter of paying the outlawed but flourishing custom of tendering the Central Asian bride price (*qälin*):

Latifjan: First of all, you will pay the bride price.
Mominjan: A lie! Bride price has completely ceased to exist.
Nematilla: Milk money [*sut puli* or *sut häqi*] has replaced it. That ...
Latifjan: You will pay! ...
Mominjan (suddenly shouting): I don't believe it! It's a lie! Madina is not that kind. Madina won't sell herself.

> *Nematilla:* Maybe Madina isn't the type, but have you seen her
> aunt? . . . a real dragon; this is the Dragon![43]

Further ethnic whimsies arise late in scene two, during Madina's conversation about ethnic food with the manager of the restaurant where
her aunt Kimya has worked for 30 years:

> *Madina:* . . . Listen, a dish called Beef Stroganoff [*befstragän*] took a
> man's name, I guess. I sort of learned this recently.
> *Nariman* (stepping out of the kitchen): Yes, indeed, Madinakhan! A
> man named Beef Stroganoff invented Beef Stroganoff. . . .
> *Madina:* . . . All the same, no sort of dish matches our own pilaw.
> Pilaw is a totally unique dish, in fact. It's tasty, especially when
> someone else cooks it (she quietly opens the apartment door, slips
> out).
> *Nariman* (comes out of the kitchen again): Uhuh. What do you mean
> to say, Madinakhan? Pilaw was invented exactly 1231 years ago.
> They say that when Alexander the Great came to Uzbekistan, he
> ate pilaw, apparently; so there really was such a dish in the world,
> evidently. Why don't you laugh, Madinakhan! . . .[44]

The dramatist weaves further references into a ridiculous exchange
between Madina's aunt and the matchmakers. They negotiate over the
girl's dowry (*sep*), which, they declare, must not affront the "important"
bridegroom whom they represent. Kimya Khala brings out satins, vel-
vets, quilted coverlets and pillows that, she says, she sewed with her own
hand. Intending to wear down the Aunt's resistance, the matchmakers
promptly rip open some and reject them scornfully, claiming that they
are made of second-rate cotton. They demand something better from the
distraught Aunt:

> *Latifjan:* . . . You will cover a quilt with caracul.
> *Nematilla:* First-rate Astrakhan!
> *Latifjan:* That's right, it must be first-rate Astrakhan!
> *Kimya Khala:* What? A single fur coat costs one and a half thousand
> alone, you know. Where will I get enough caracul for a quilt? Why,
> it will take the skins off a whole flock!
> *Nematilla:* What's the alternative, dear lady! Caracul is plentiful in
> Uzbekistan. You'll stuff it with goose down.[45]

The dialogue produces not only extravagant statements but Tashkent
dialectism (*yuruwdinq* for standard *yurib edinq*) and a great many more
Russian borrowings than most of the other plays analyzed in this study.

These Russian terms repeatedly create irony or amusing effect in the half-grammatical mispronunciations of Kimya Khala, the waitress. Confused by the matchmakers' relentless intimidation tactics, she cries in Uzbek: "Suddenly I'm completely [*säpsem* for the Russian *sovsem*] mixed up." Several times she insists "I'm an up-to-date woman" (*men sawremeniy khatinmän*), slightly distorting the sound of the Russian adjective she borrowed for "up-to-date."[46] The author repeatedly inserts foreign words both to add humor and convey Kimya Khala's milieu and cultural level. At the same time, his writing technique stresses Uzbek language identity by supplying some foreign linguistic context that contrasts with the native tongue.

The Upshot: Bases for Ethnic Communication via Drama

The terms "ethnic awareness" or "nationality consciousness" probably do not properly describe the subtle messages in this native speech. Language can transmit a rush of ethnic material to the people of the mother tongue without ever touching an overt signal. Familiar expressions and idioms abound in much Central Asian drama. These serve to communicate the hardly liminal signals most significant in authenticating the play's dramatic identity. Most listeners "hear" such messages unconsciously.

Like common sayings and phraseology, the old primary Central Asian values—justice, generosity, responsibility, and the like—recur in nearly every play late in this half-century, just as they did at the beginning of it. Some of the most compelling dramas explore the application of those values to new times. That newer attention to them contrasts with what authors could give in playwriting of the 1950s and 1960s. In those two decades much of the theater saw priority given in Soviet Central Asia to traits such as energy, optimism, dauntlessness, obedience, and self-denial. Mr. Ibrahimaw's "The Saw" in a sense projects one extended dissertation regarding both the personal and social destructiveness of selfishness. It gives an affirmation of the power of true generosity. Mr. Babayew's "True Friend of the Soil" runs on perhaps too didactically about injustice. Even so, the drama does carry the weight of the traditional Central Asian value system for an impressive distance. The newer comedies discover fresh conceptions of happiness and love. They contrast with the plays of the 1950s and 1960s, which notably reflected acute social tension in a dangerous environment. They showed public ostracism, expulsion from the human community, even trial and imprisonment of innocent persons. Later plays written by a new generation not only disregard such trouble, but seem to have dropped the obligatory political advisor, usually Russian, noticeably present earlier in both serious drama and domestic comedy like "The Heart's Secrets" (*Yuräk sirläri*) (1953), by Bahram Rahmanaw (1915–1961).[47] That disappearance of an outsider from the script restores an essential symmetry to the Uzbek milieu in the dramas. In "The Heart's Secrets," Mr. Rahmanaw develops an urban story of impending separation and divorce resulting from severe misunderstanding. He saves the disintegrating marriage by reconciling the two educated partners. This keeps the family intact, if not happy, a combination of conditions noticed in other dramas among those surveyed here.

This slowly narrowing view of Central Asian life begins to shift attention from large-scale, whole institutions. It moves to closer scrutiny of individuals and motivation of smaller scope. This raises implications for the entire society, beyond the immediate dramatic scene. In that respect, some new drama takes on aspects of universality found in the work of the world's past great dramatists. On the broadest scale, the new Central Asian playwrights appear to advance the conception of modernity, as they see it. Within that liberating idea a contemporary expression of spirituality takes a place. The stage works give meaning to private life and to self-reliance in ways not encountered in Uzbek plays of decades earlier than the late 1960s. These creative currents go beyond a purely idealistic approach to life and endeavor to reach the essence of Central Asian existence in its everyday domestic manifestations. Elements of surprise, change of character, and mysteriousness that make good theater have enlivened several recent plays, notably those by some newer playwrights, Mr. Ibrahimaw, Mr. Hashimaw, and Mr. Jabbaraw, studied here.

For the inquiry into nationality consciousness, a difference in chronology of composition and in the age of the dramatist acquires some extraliterary significance in the study of this drama. Age and chronology may have less effect than comparisons between serious and comic plays, for humor enjoys the wider audience. In the writing, the cleavage between country and town settings have the most importance. Whether intended or not, rural scenes shown by most playwrights in Central Asia accommodate uncomplicated people and situations. These literary choices contribute to a more obvious handling of ethnic identity. Degrees of subtlety in ethnic signals, of course, depend upon much more than physical setting and a playwright's precise age and era. The more impersonal the subject matter in a play, the greater the likelihood that it will lend itself to obvious ethnic expression. And, seriousness associates less with large numbers of ethnic signals than does comedy.

Perhaps even more than breadth of subject or audience, the artistic talent of a dramatist determines the subtlety of ethnic communication. The gifted author selects more carefully than others the ethnic signs for his work. The dramatist's decisions carry weight, for the nature of even the most obvious ethnic signals seldom confines them, separately, to one nationality identity. They require configuration before they identify. A tearoom (*chaykhanä*) can be found under that name amongst several different nationalities. Ethnic food gives some local identity, but a traveler may eat similar dishes across Central Asia, including Kazakstan, Afghanistan, and Eastern Turkistan. Reflections of the traditional values appear everywhere in Central Asian life and its theater. For the audience of outsiders, these features also symbolize Uzbek life but do not, uniquely or individually, define it. Nevertheless, when such signals flash on the scene in a local play performed in Uzbek in Uzbekistan, for an Uzbek audience they serve to prompt agreement upon group identity. Depending upon the composition of that audience, the same recognition may come from subtle hints quietly given in more personal plays by talented authors.

Perhaps the most significant expression common to the Uzbek-language plays already discussed emerges in the configurations of what this essay refers to as the dramatic universe. Those families, farms, or institutes each constitute small segments of society that suggest a miniature. As allegory, they seem to represent their entire nationality. Key people within the plays exhibit earnest concern, bordering upon panic, in fixing attention on metabolic processes especially crucial to the body of the nationality. That they do not give equal scrutiny to religious unity results from official proscription more than literary preference. So, with their entrances and exits the dramas emphasize merger, exile, disability, reunion, emigration, ejection, and reconnection. These motions function not so much as personal problems but as social and ethnic events. The action depicted in these plays never projects beyond what now generally constitute Uzbekistan's borders, but the idea of home country may reach farther. Speeches mentioning Calcutta, Kashghar, Moscow, or other distant places merely add exoticism while defining by exclusion the outer reaches of an Uzbek homeland. That homeland vaguely resembles the limits of Central Asia.

This pattern of uneasiness over potential alienation from the world on stage that symbolizes the ethnic community persists throughout a good

percentage of these contemporary plays. That leads to more than a sup-
position that the uncertainties displayed in this manner emanate from
deep, possibly unconscious anxiety over the cohesion of the nationality
group itself, and regarding the future of its fundamental identity.

Notes

1. The author presented a much earlier version of this article to a symposium concerning literature and Central Asian nationality held in the Gorky Institute for World
Literature, Moscow, in 1985. The author also acknowledges with gratitude an invitation to membership in the Institute for Advanced Studies, The Hebrew University of
Jerusalem, which allowed the time needed during spring 1987 to make extensive re-
visions to that first draft. For simplicity, the text of the essay gives names of dramatists
and their stage personages without diacritical markings, but footnote references trans-
literate authors' names from the original sources employing the transliteration system
published in Edward Allworth, *Nationalities of the Soviet East: Publications and
Writing Systems* (New York: Columbia University Press, 1971), pp. 375–78; *Naselenie
SSSR. Po dannym Vsesoiuznoi perepisi naseleniia 1979 qoda* (Moscow: Izdatel'stvo
Politicheskoi Literatury, 1980), pp. 27–30.

2. Fiträt, *Hindistandä bir färängi ilä bukharali bir mudärrisning bir nichä
mäs'älälär häm usul-i jädidä khususidä qilgan munazäräsi* trans. to Turki from Farsi
by Hajji Mu'in ibn Shukrullä Sämärqändiy (Tashkent: Turkistan Kitabkhanäsi. Tipo-
Litografiia V. M. Il'ina, 1913).

3. Fiträt, *Hindistandä bir färängi ilä bukharali bir mudärris . . .* , pp. 23–27.

4. Abd-ur-Rauf, *Razskazy indiiskago puteshestvennika (Bukhara kak ona est'*
trans. from Farsi/Tajik by A. N. Kondrat'eva (Samarkand: Izdanie Makhmud-Khoja
Bekbudi. Tipo-lit. T-va B. Gazarov i K. Sliianov, 1913), p. 87.

5. Mähmud Khojä Behbudiy, *Pädärkush, yakhud oqumagan balaning hali* (Samarkand: Tipo-Litografiia T-va B. Gazarov i K. Sliianov, 1913), pp. 13–16; "The Patricide,"
trans. Edward Allworth, *Ural-Altaic Yearbook*, no. 58 (1986): 72, 83, 91–2.

6. *Ugolovnyi kodeks RSFSR* (Moscow: "Iuridicheskaia Literatura," 1978), p. 169;
"Ob usilenii kontrolia za vypolneniem zakonodatel'stva o religioznykh kul'takh—
Postanovlenie Soveta Ministrov Uzbekskoi SSR ot 7 fevralia 1969 g. No. 65," *Za-
konodatel'stvo o religioznykh kul'takh (Sbornik materialov i dokumentov)*, 2d ed.
(Moscow: "Iuridicheskaia Literatura," 1971), p. 158.

7. *Sawet Ozbekistanininq yazuwchiläri* (Tashkent: OzSSR Däwlät Bädiiy Ädäbiyat
Näshriyati, 1959), pp. 167–68; "Kakhkhar, Abdulla," *Bol'shaia sovetskaia entsiklo-
pediia*, 2d ed. (n.p.: Gosudarstvennoe Nauchnoe Izdatel'stvo, 1953), 20:408; Edward
Allworth, *Uzbek Literary Politics* (Leiden: Mouton and Company, 1964), p. 234.

8. Äbdullä Qähhar, *Tänlängän äsärlär* (Tashkent: OzSSR Däwlät Bädiiy Ädäbiyat
Näshriyati, 1957), 1:285–56; Abdulla Kakhar, "Silk suzanei," *Soviet Literature*, no. 8
(1958): 45–46, 53, 98.

9. Äbdullä Qähhar, *Tänlängän äsärlär*, pp. 329–30; Abdulla Kakhar, "Silk suzanei,"
pp. 44, 78.

10. V. I. Kozlov, *Natsional'nosti SSSR. Etnodemograficheskii obzor* (Moscow: "Finansy i Statistika," 1982), p. 100; *Itogi Vsesoiuznoi perepisi naseleniia 1970 goda* (Moscow: "Statistika," 1973), 4:202–08, 223–29, 284–88, 295–97; *Naselenie SSSR . . . ,* p. 9.

11. Uyghun, "Dostlär (Orinsiz shubhä)," in Uyghun, *Äsärlär* (Tashkent: Ghäfur Ghulam namidägi Ädäbiyat wä Sän"ät Näshriyati, 1978), 5:170–72, 187.

12. Ibid., pp. 199–200, 216.

13. Otkir Räshid, "Färzänd deb . . . ," *Shärq yulduzi,* no. 9 (1980): 216–17.

14. Mäshräb Babayew, "Yer tamiri," *Shärq yulduzi,* no. 3 (1983): 96–116.

15. Ibid., p. 102.

16. Yusuf Khas Hajib, *Qutadqhu biliq,* trans. to Uzbek by Käyum Kärimaw (Tashkent: Ozbekistan SSR "Fän" Näshriyati, 1971); Käykawus, *Qabus-namä,* 2d ed., trans. Agähiy (Tashkent: "Oqituwchi" Näshriyati, 1968); 'Alishir Nawa'i, *Mahbub al-qulub,* ed. A. N. Kononov (Moscow-Leningrad: Izdatel'stvo Akademii Nauk SSSR, 1948); *Täwarikh-i quzidä—Nusrät-namä,* ed. A. M. Akramaw (Tashkent: Ozbekistan SSR "Fän" Näshriyati, 1967).

17. Babayew, "Yer tamiri," p. 116.

18. Ibid., p. 107.

19. Ibid., p. 96.

20. Ibid., pp. 107, 109.

21. Ibid., pp. 95, 110–11.

22. Ibid., p. 105.

23. *Naselenie . . . ,* pp. 11–15.

24. Izzät Sultan, "Iman," *Äsärlär* (Tashkent: Ghäfur Ghulam namidägi Ädäbiyat wä Sän"ät Näshriyati, 1971), pp. 155–208.

25. Ibid., p. 193.

26. Ibid., pp. 200–6.

27. Ibid., pp. 185–86.

28. Ibid., p. 199.

29. Äbduqähhar Ibrahimaw, "Ärrä," *Birinchi bosä. Ärrä. P'esälär* (Tashkent: Ghäfur Ghulam namidägi Ädäbiyat wä Sän"ät Näshriyati, 1978), pp. 71–73.

30. Ibid., p. 132.

31. Ibid., p. 135.

32. Ibid., p. 73–74.

33. Ibid., pp. 77, 82.

34. Shuhrät, "Anä qizim," *Shärq yulduzi,* no. 6 (1982): 101–2.

35. Ibid., pp. 112–13.

36. Ibid., p. 104.

37. Ibid., p. 99.

38. Ibid., p. 127.

39. Ibid., p. 104.

40. Jumäniyaz Jäbbaraw, "Toydän aldin tamashä," *Shärq yulduzi,* no. 1 (1982): 111.

41. Ibid., p. 126.

42. Ibid., p. 123.

43. Otkir Häshimaw, "Toylär mubaräk," *Shärq yulduzi,* no. 5 (1981): 132, 134, 151.

44. Ibid., p. 140.

45. Ibid., p. 157.

46. Ibid., p. 151.

47. Bähram Rähmanaw, "Yuräk sirläri," in Rähmanaw, *P'esälär* (Tashkent: OzSSR Däwlät Bädiiy Ädäbiyat Näshriyati, 1957), pp. 116, 168.

6. Primordial Ethnicity or Modern Nationalism: The Case of Yugoslavia's Muslims, Reconsidered

Sabrina Petra Ramet

I

One of the longest standing debates in social science has been that which has divided students of ethnicity over the issue of modernization. On the one side are the tribalists, who emphasize that the ethnonational consciousness of a self-defined group is historically rooted and believe that processes of racial and cultural homogenization associated with the broader phenomenon of modernization promote the gradual breakdown of ethnic boundaries within states and ultimately encourage the spread of global culture and the disappearance of "tribal" languages (this might include such examples as Catalan, Sorb, Romansch, and perhaps also Welsh, Macedonian, and Estonian). In this view, ethnocentrism is negatively correlated with the degree of interaction, and multiethnic societies are supposed to be less ethnocentric than ethnically homogeneous societies. There are two chief variants of this approach represented by the functionalists (assimilationists) and the Marxists.[1]

On the other side stand those who view the French Revolution as the incunabulum of modern nationalism, whether of *patrie* or nation, and who see modernization as having a variable effect on group consciousness. In this view, sometimes called "pluralism," modernization may cause certain groups to fuse, but it may also cause others to split and new ones to arise. Often it strengthens the group consciousness of a traditional ethnic group. Racial and cultural homogenization are seen as not necessarily entailing the demolition of group boundaries. The former processes, pluralist theorists argue, may influence intergroup tensions and thus reinforce ethnocentrism. Thus, according to this vein of thought, ethnocentrism may be positively correlated with the degree of group interaction, and multiethnic societies are apt to be more ethnocentric (or at least more overtly ethnocentric) than ethnically homogeneous societies, because subordinated or excluded groups are encountered on a recurrent basis. The independent variable is seen as cultural threat rather than homogenization per se. Thus, insofar as increased interaction produces increased cultural threat, ethnic groups in a multiethnic society will tend to display more heightened group consciousness, which manifests itself in ethnocentric behavior. Thus, the expectations of this second school are the exact reverse of those of the first school.[2]

The classic statement of the tribalist position was given by Clifford Geertz in his essay, "The Integrative Revolution—Primordial Sentiments and Civil Politics in the New States," in which he argued that nationalism is an epiphenomenon of tribal passions, which will fade as modernization proceeds and contacts with other groups increase.[3] This same assumption marks the theories of Marx and Engels, for whom communist modernization ineluctably entailed the withering away of ethnic and linguistic boundaries and communist centralization and resocialization represented propulsive forces toward social and ethnic homogenization.[4]

By contrast, the pluralists argue that, even if a group manipulates tribal and traditional symbols and exploits myths of primordial origin, its boundaries and specific cultural coloration may have been only recently defined. Crawford Young specifically countered Geertz with the following rebuttal:

> Contemporary cultural pluralism is not usefully viewed as a resurgence of "primordial" sentiments. . . . The basic units of contemporary cultural conflict, themselves fluid and shifting, are often entirely novel entities, in other instances substantially altered and transformed, in most cases redefined versions of cultural groups.[5]

For this second school of thought, ethnic group boundaries are fluid, subject to historical pressures, and influenced by the contours of specific conflict situations.

Partial syntheses of the two approaches have been worked out by Chong-Do Hah and Jeffrey Martin, Cynthia Enloe, and Harold Isaacs. Chong-Do Hah and Martin used the concept of relative deprivation (perceived group exploitation or deprivation) to link modernization and nationalism and argued that modernization both reinforces group integration and promotes intergroup conflict. But their conclusion, that "modernization generates nationalism indirectly by integrating groups at the societal level, and directly by causing relative deprivation,"[6] puts them de facto in agreement with the pluralists, who exclude the rapid erosion of ethnicity by modernization. Enloe's study is founded on a modern view of nationalism but concludes that, while ethnic identity and nationalism may be heightened by modernization in the short run, in the long run traditional cultures and identities are vulnerable to dilution and effacement by modernization.[7] Finally, in a complete reversal of Enloe's position, Isaacs believes that the assumption of tribal ethnogenesis need not lead one to expect modernization to erode ethnic consciousness, and he reconciles the tribal view with the expectation that "tribal separatenesses are here to stay."[8]

The choice between these two approaches is not politically innocent. On the contrary, those who view modernization as erosive of ethnic loyalties—whether they link ethnicity to "primordial" sentiment or view it as a creature of industrialization (hence the Marxist formula, "bourgeois nationalism")—outline theories which may reinforce the policies of established regimes hostile to ethnic divisiveness. By the same token, those who wish to promote separatism among peoples with distinct characteristics and splinter multiethnic societies into homogeneous fragments are apt to stress the "modernity" of nationalism. The Marxist disposition to follow Stalin in treating nationality as a product of "common language, territory, economic life, and psychological make-up,"[9] reflects not merely an analytic understanding of nationality in terms of dynamic and manipulative factors, but an outline of the prerequisites for ethnic homogenization. It follows from the Stalinist definition—used by Soviet ideologists until Gorbachev's accession to power[10]—that when different peoples inhabiting contiguous lands come to participate in a common political and economic life, adopt the same language and culture, and acquire similar psychological dispositions, they in fact *become a single nation*. It also follows that if nationality is analyzed in terms of specific residues of the past, then the path to "modernization" lies in the annihilation of those residues. Posed in this fashion, opposition to ethnic homogenization appears as a nostalgia for the past.

For the purposes of this chapter, a simpler definition will be employed. *Ethnic group* is defined here as a group of people who believe that they constitute a primary cultural unity and who believe that they have common cultural interests. *Nation* is defined as an "ethnic group that seeks to advance its interests through organized political action." The word *people* will be used interchangeably with the word *nation* in this chapter. *Nationality* is the sum of those cultural attributes which are taken to give definition to a group of people, i.e., to constitute their claim to an identity. And, finally, *cultural* will be used to mean the contributions of a particular people to the sum of human knowledge and experience, including language, religion and morals, symbology and myths, folklore, art, music, literature, history, and science. The fact that nations have almost without exception been associated with a common territory is inessential to an understanding of nationality, in that territorial cohabitation constitutes only a necessary condition for the creation of a culture but is not in itself a sufficient condition for the development of a unified national culture (witness polyglot Transylvania and the south Tyrol), let alone a part of nationality itself (as Marxists seem to think).

The continued agonizing over the identity of Yugoslavia's Muslim population is played against the background of the unresolved controversy over whether the Muslims are "primordially" Croats (or Serbs) or a "modern" nation, and whether the relationship of the Islamic religion to Muslim ethnic consciousness (assuming this exists) is that of a historical residue to its primordial and evanescent product or that of antecedent progenitor to an identity with an autonomy of its own. These are the questions which this chapter will address.

II

This study concerns itself exclusively with that segment of the population of Bosnia-Herzegovina which, since 1968, has been defined by the regime as "ethnic Muslims." Excluded from the discussion, thus, are those Turks, Albanians, and Gypsies who live in Yugoslavia, as well as Macedonians (and others) of Islamic belief. In the 1981 census, some 2,000,034 persons—three quarters of them in Bosnia-Herzegovina—registered themselves as "ethnic Muslims," accounting for 8.9 percent of the total population of Yugoslavia, and representing the third largest group in the federation, after the Serbs and Croats.[11]

(From a religious standpoint, however, the analyst must reckon with some 3.8 million confessional Muslims. Aside from those listed as "ethnic Muslims," essentially all Turks, most Albanians, a minority of Macedonians, and also some Gypsies, Croats, Serbs, and Montenegrins accept Islam. These groups live primarily in Bosnia-Herzegovina, or in Kosovo, the Sandžak of Novi Pazar, Macedonia, and Montenegro. Most of Yugoslavia's confessional Muslims, thus, live in the southern half of the country.)

The official recognition of the Muslims as a nation dates only from 1968, when the regime decided to accept Islamic *culture* as the basis for nationhood. In spite of that, the League of Communists of Yugoslavia (LCY) has never fully acknowledged the linkage between Islamic *culture* and Islamic *religion*, in this connection. For the LCY, Muslim nationality had nothing to do with Islamic religion. In this respect, the LCY's perspective was distinctly Western and reflected a tendency to generalize from Western experience and Marxist principles. Muslims themselves view the relationship somewhat differently. "Islamic culture," according to British Muslim Gai Eaton, "is neither more nor less than an aspect of the religion; there is no secular culture whatsoever. Moreover, the community is still essentially a religious community, and to quit the religion is to leave the community."[12] By contrast, the LCY insisted that a secular Muslim culture existed in Bosnia-Herzegovina, and accordingly, every interference on the part of clergy in political and ethnic questions risked condemnation as a "politicization of religion" or "clero-nationalism." And for most of Yugoslavia's communist era (1945–1990), nationalism was considered the most dangerous foe.

The roots of Bosnian Muslim ethnicity may be traced as far back as the seventeenth century, when at least some Bosnian Muslims (for example, Muhamed Hevaji Uskufi and the early Bosnian journalist Mehmed Šaćir Kurtćehajić) viewed themselves as Slavs. Later, many Slavophone Muslims outside Bosnia-Herzegovina, starting with the Sandžak of Novi Pazar, viewed themselves as Bosnians and called their language Bosnian, even if their derivation from native Bosnian blood could not be proven. And by the nineteenth century, the culturally influential Franciscans of Bosnia were referring to the language as "Bosnian."[13] In the course of the nineteenth century, two competing "national ideologies" were introduced in Bosnia-Herzegovina. Among Catholics, there were attempts to link Bosnian national identity with Catholicism and to stimulate a national awakening on the basis of that linkage. These attempts came to naught.[14] Among politically conscious Muslims, on the other hand, there was a growing dissatisfaction with geographically based identity, and while the concept of "Bosnianness" served, during Ottoman times, to distinguish persons so designated from "Turks," it was less useful after 1878 in providing a primary cultural defense against Serbs and Croats.

Benjamin von Kállay, who served as governor of Bosnia-Herzegovina from 1882 to 1903, in the service of the Habsburgs, believed that the stimulation of a Bosnian consciousness could serve as a foil to the spread of Serbian nationalism and therefore welcomed the creation in 1897 of an Islamic Reading Society (Kiraethana), which aimed at stirring a Muslim cultural revival. But while Kállay's promotion of a separate Bosnian national identity won some adherents, especially among the intellectuals, it did not appeal to most of the population,[15] and even among intellectuals there were frequent instances of identity confusion or opportunism.

Even so, it is significant that the Muslims of Bosnia-Herzegovina, at least in part because they felt culturally threatened by Catholic Habsburg rule, created a number of political parties in the era of Habsburg occupation, including the Muslim National Organization (1906) and the United Muslim Organization (1911), and in 1905, the Muslim cultural society Gajret (in Arabic, *ghäyrät*: zeal, energy) established an Islamic printing press in Sarajevo.

III

Controversies about the Muslims of Bosnia-Herzegovina are more than a century old. The different theories put forth have different conceptual starting points and entail different assumptions about the nature of ethnogenesis and nation-building. The anterior analytical choice is between "exclusivist" theories which hold that Bosnia's Muslims are "really" members of some other nationality group ("tribalist" theories, thus), and "pluralist" theory, which holds that new nationality groups may arise as a result of ethnic mixing and other processes.

Among the Bosnian Muslims themselves, there have been three "exclusivist" theories: those who view themselves as Croats and believe that all Bosnian Muslims are "ethnogenetically" Croats; those who, in the past at least, viewed themselves as Serbs and identified all Bosnian Muslims as Serbs; and those who have rejected these identities and hold, as did the Yugoslav communist regime, that Bosnia's Muslims have acquired a unique identity and, regardless of their origins, can no longer be equated with either Croats or Serbs. Thus, in addressing the complex question of the ethnicity of the Bosnian Muslims and the modernity of that ethnicity, scholars must recognize the fact that the people of Bosnia themselves are divided (i.e., some are Serbs, some are Croats, and some are ethnic Muslims), and, hence, that any "exclusivist" theory must first of all either repudiate the subjective self-perceptions of some of the group members, or construe these avowals as self-serving lies made under duress.

Of the three exclusivist theories, the Serbophile theory is probably the oldest, since Serbian exclusivism antedates Croatian exclusivism. As early as 1836, the Serbian linguistic reformer Vuk Karadžić, in an essay entitled "Srbi svi i svuda" [Serbs, all and everywhere], argued that only the Serbian name was truly national and concluded that not only were the Muslims of Bosnia Serbs, but Croats themselves were only Catholic Serbs. By the 1870s, Serbian nationalists were claiming Bosnia up to the Vrbas River as part of Great Serbia and they maintained, in consonance with Karadžić, that *all* of Bosnia's inhabitants were Serbs. A native Muslim, Dervišbeg Ljubović, author of a brochure, *O stanju Bosne i Hercegovine* (1895), wanted Serbia to annex both Bosnia-Herzegovina and Montenegro, and considered all inhabitants of Bosnia-Herzegovina, including Catholics, to be Serbs.[16] Indeed, the peasant revolt in Bosnia-Herzegovina of 1875–1876 saw calls for union with Serbia, and in the summer of 1877, there was formed an ephemeral Bosnian government with a pro-Serbian orientation.[17]

The Serbophile tendency also penetrated into the thinking of Serbian Social Democrats of the nineteenth century, and Svetozar Marković, for instance, could describe Bosnia as "a country where the Serbian nation is divided into three faiths."[18] Similarly, Dimitrije Tucović referred to the inhabitants of Bosnia as "the largest, purest and most capable part of the Serbian people."[19] This same tendency reappeared in the writings of the Yugoslav communists, such as Sima Marković, the first general secretary of the party, who favored the assimilation of the entire population to the "Serbo-Croatian" nation, and Marxist theoretician, Veselin Masleša, who, in an essay written in 1942, argued that while Bosnia's Muslims possessed some distinguishing characteristics, it would be most sensible to view them as a religious group, although their nationality remained Serbian.[20]

During the late 1950s and early 1960s, the heyday of Aleksandar Ranković's influence as head of the Yugoslav secret police, Bosnia was treated as a Serbian backyard, and Serbian appointments for governmental and party slots far outnumbered Croatian and Muslim appointments. The firing of Ranković in July 1966, however, made possible a reconsideration of the regime's policy toward Muslims and, after 1968, their situation improved tangibly, at least in the short run.

Advocates of the Serbophile theory have looked for "primordial" sources for their claims. V. Glušac offered support here, in describing the old Bosnian Church (twelfth to fifteenth centuries), whose adherents may have provided indigenous converts to Islam, as an autocephalous Orthodox Church.[21] In a related vein, Olive Lodge treated Bosnia's Muslims as descendants of the heretical Bogomil cult, and she identified them as ethnic Serbs of a "Protestant" persuasion, allowing for some admixture of Osmanli Turks.[22] The infrequency with which Serbophiles actually cite "primordial" evidence suggests a paucity of supportive data (a troubling consideration, given their assumption that primordial evidence is appropriate). After the accession to power of the communist party, the preferred approach (of communist Serbophiles) was to stress the dynamism, rather than the constancy, of national identity and to emphasize the susceptibility of nationalism to effacement through modernization. For them, group consciousness based on religion is seen as being more vulnerable to the effects of secularization and unlikely to make the transition from ethno-cultural particularity to national identity. Thus, the Fifth Conference of the KPY (Zagreb, November 1940) resolved that "Muslims have not forged a nation, but [are] an ethnic group."[23] Moreover, those communists partial to "integral Yugoslavism," that is, to the idea that a unified Yugoslav people would be created under the conditions of communist modernization, continued up to the Eighth Party Congress of 1964 and even afterward to resist Muslim national assertion, calling it reactionary and antimodern.

By contrast, the Croatophile theory, which construes the Bosnian Muslims as ethnogenetically Croats, has a marked preference for "primordial" arguments, though Croatophiles do not fail to insist as well that the Muslims remain animated by Croatian nationalism. In particular, advocates of this theory trace indigenous Muslims to the mass conversions to Islam that occurred after the Ottoman conquest in 1463, claiming that most of the adherents of gnostic Bogomilism in Bosnia, and likewise of the Bosnian Church, were ethnic Croats. They sometimes add that Ottoman discrimination against Catholicism persuaded some Catholic Croats to convert to Orthodoxy, thus in the course of generations, producing "Serbian" families. Ivo Pilar, a prominent Croatian nationalist during World War I, even tried to use racial characteristics to "prove" that the Muslims were ethnic Croats.[24]

Although Fr. Filip Laštrić (1700–1783) had viewed Bosnia and Croatia as parts of a single nation, which he preferred to designate by the latter term (i.e., *Croatia*),[25] it was only in the late nineteenth century, as Croatian exclusivism gathered strength, that Croats began to insist that Bosnia was Croatian territory. An early work in this vein was Petriniensis's *Bosnien und das kroatische Staatsrecht* (Zagreb, 1898). Ante Starčević, founder of the Croatian Party of Right, viewed Bosnia as the Croatian heartland. The Croatian Peasant Party created by Stjepan Radić likewise refused to foreswear Bosnia, despite the political activity in interwar Yugoslavia of the Yugoslav Muslim Organization, and party chief Vladko Maček himself once described the Bosnian Muslims as "the purest part of the Croatian nation, by origin, by history, and by dialect."[26] Bosnia also occupied an important place in the conceptions of Ante Pavelić's nationalist Ustasha, the Croatian fascists who collaborated with Hitler during World War II. Mile Budak, an Ustasha disciple, echoed Maček in describing the Bosnians as "the purest, least tainted Croats," and denied that the Serbs had ever settled in Bosnia at all, attributing the Orthodox presence there entirely to Croatian conversions which the Ustasha proposed to reverse.[27] The annexation of Bosnia-Herzegovina to the so-called Independent State of Croatia established by the *Ustasha* was the natural consequence of this aspiration.

It is revealing that in the postwar period, there have been few advocates of the Croatophile theory speaking out within Croatia. Some— such as Zagreb's Archbishop, Franjo Cardinal Kuharić,[28] and Split's now retired Archbishop, Frane Franić[29]—are to be found within the ranks of the Catholic Church hierarchy. Likewise both Ivan Mužić, in his *Razmatranje o povijesti Hrvata* (Split, 1967), and Većeslav Holjevac, in his *Hrvati izvan domovine* (Zagreb, 1967), describe Bosnian Muslims as "Croats of the Islamic faith." Among Croatian emigres, as well, assertion of this claim to Bosnia appears to be a constant and central feature. For instance, Franciscan Fr. Dominik Mandić has argued this case in books published in Rome and Buenos Aires. The émigré journal, *Republika Hrvatska* (published in Buenos Aires), treats it as all but self-evident that Bosnian Muslims are ethnic Croats, stating that, "in the eyes of Croats, Bosnia differs from other Croatian provinces only in certain specific respects, as the result of long and deep development under Turkish rule. But the development of the religious and cultural specificity of Bosnia is nothing stronger than the specificity, for example, of Dalmatia."[30] For *Nova Hrvatska*, another Croatian émigré periodical (published in London), the Muslim reawakening in Bosnia is strictly religious and, despite the regime's claims, lacks any specific nationalist component. But when Husein Djoza, Hilmo Neimarlja, and others were fired in late 1979 from the editorship of the Islamic newspaper, *Preporod*, for alleged Pan-Islamic proclivities,[31] *Nova Hrvatska* claimed that they had been animated by pro-Croatian sentiment.[32]

The Croatophiles reject the concept of the dynamism of ethnic boundaries and insist on the stability of the Croatian national community, racially conceived. While there has at times been a tendency to assert Muslim distinctiveness over Serbian and Croatian claims and to hold that today's Muslims are simply the descendants of Turks and other Muslim immigrants with little Slavic admixture,[33] the official policy adopted by the League of Communists of Yugoslavia (LCY) stressed the indigenous and Slavic character of the Bosnian Muslims and emphasized the cultural component over the racial, arguing that complex processes of conversion and immigration mixed together people of different ethnic origins. And if it may be granted that constant anti-Bogomil agitation from both Catholics and Orthodox prior to 1463 disposed the Bogomils to accept Islam, the followers of other confessions also followed their example.[34]

An early advocate of Bosnian Muslim national identity wrote, in a work first published in 1929:

> We have a healthy basis for a specific national thought just as much as the Serbs and Croats, and what appear to be national communities are, in reality, both in form and in ideological content, both foreign and inaccessible, because they actually represent their own religious communities.[35]

If Serbs wanted to champion Orthodoxy and Croatian Catholicism, they could not also lay claim to Bosnia's Muslims. By 1938, Yugoslav Marxist theoretician Edvard Kardelj had conceded the "ethnic particularity" of the Muslims, a point reaffirmed at the Zagreb party conference in 1940 and by Rodoljub Čolaković in a party brochure in 1943.[36] In the course of discussions of the first constitution (January 1946), however, there remained some confusion over their status, as reflected in Čolaković's comment that they remained "in large part [an] as yet nationally undetermined Slavic ethnic group."[37] As a result, the LCY treated Muslims strictly as a confessional group in both the 1948 and 1953 censuses, and only in 1961 allowed them to register as an "ethnic" group.[38] Since 1968, they have been treated as a "national" group on a par with Serbs, Croats, et al.

Thus, unlike the Serbophiles and Croatophiles, and, for that matter, in a fashion distinct from the Turkophiles, the LCY has in fact conceded a prominent role for religion in the formation of ethnic identity, even if Yugoslav communists have been apt to divorce religion from nationalism. Sociologist Ruža Petrović, in a 1968 article, found that,

> Religion was a factor for ethnic differentiation not merely in the case of the Muslims, but also among our other nationalities. And not merely in the past but even today for a large number of people, especially those living in ethnically and religiously heterogeneous districts, religion is a synonym for nationality.[39]

But, if the LCY seems slightly closer to the Turkophiles on this point, it diverges from them when it comes to the question of modernity as a source of national feeling, and of the susceptibility of national identity to effacement under conditions of modernization. For Marxists, "primordial" considerations like religion may create complexities, but nationalism per se can only be traced to the development of capital-intensive, free

Table 6.1 Theories about the Ethnicity of Bosnian Muslims

	Tribalists					Pluralists
	Neo-tribalists		Marxists			
	Serbian nation-alists	Croatian nation-alists	Turkophile Islam-icists	Serbophile Commu-nists	LCY	
Ethnicity is "old" + = yes − = no	+	+	+	+	+	−
Modernity as source of national feeling + = nationalism is dynamic − = national feeling is a fixed racial given	−	−	−	+	+	+
Religion as a source of ethnicity + = important − = not important	−	−	(−)	−	(+)	+
Susceptibility of ethnicity to effacement through modernization + = susceptible − = not necessarily	−	−	−	+	(+)	−
Normative assessment of nationalism + = positive − = negative 0 = neutral	+	+	+	(−)	−	0

enterprise economies ("capitalism") and to the development of pluralist ("bourgeois") political ideas. Hence, "nationalism in our conditions is one of those reactionary ideological factors which leads backward, closes off socialist perspectives, obstructs the formation of socialist conscious-ness and cripples . . . socialist activity."[40]

Like other partisans of the first school, Yugoslav Marxists believed until recently that multiethnic societies are apt to see declining de-grees of ethnocentrism, though obviously, in their view, this was only because of the steady advance of socialism. Still, within that frame-work, the Yugoslav communists often felt confident enough, in the Tito era (1945–1980), to claim that, "in principle—that is to say as a prob-lem of an oppressed people and of hegemony—the national question has been decisively resolved in new Yugoslavia."[41] And a number of writers have written of the development of a Yugoslav patriotism and a drawing together of nations (spajanje naroda).[42]

The theoretical differences between these different approaches to the question of the ethnicity of the Muslims are shown in table 6.1. From the table it is apparent that all tribalists view ethnicity as "old" and yet tend to downplay the importance of religion for the formation of national con-sciousness. Even the Turkophiles base their argument chiefly on racial and kinship factors. Nor are the Marxists willing to concede that reli-gion can be a source of ethnic identity; the LCY's official position is that Muslim ethnicity and Islam are separate phenomena linked only by "culture" and that to conflate them is to be guilty of clericalism and the subversion of religion for political purposes. The Serbophile commu-nists, in addition, could not concede place of honor to religion without endangering their tenet that the Muslims are Serbs. Despite its official position, though, the LCY in fact does derive Muslim ethnicity from Islam in the sense in which the Muslims themselves understand it, i.e., as an all-encompassing way of life.

Marxists differ from other tribalists on other questions, however, in-cluding the normative assessment of nationalism. While the sundry nationalists identified here simply as "neo-tribalists" are consistently positively oriented toward nationalism, Marxists view nationalism as inimical to their system and minatory to the preservation of a unified Yugoslavia. Only the pluralists appear capable of neutrality on this issue.

IV

It is rather striking that all the tribalists party to the Yugoslav debate take as their starting point the Ottoman invasion and the fate of the Bogomils. They assume thereby that the ethnicity of Bosnia's Islamic population is ultimately a racial question whose answer lies buried in the fifteenth century. Even the LCY, which tactfully endorsed all three theories of Muslim ethnogenesis and which in other ways came the closest to finding a new empirical basis for judgment, contributed by its very endorsement to the perpetuation of that interpretive fallacy (viz., that the ethnicity of Bosnia's Islamic population is ultimately a racial question).

At the same time, it would be pointless to go to the other extreme and attempt to address the question of the relationships among religion, nationalism, and modernization by focusing exclusively on postwar Bosnian developments. If the national feeling of a people (or nation) is to be probed and its modernity and religious component assessed, it would be most useful to examine the context in which that people became politically conscious and active. Thus, rather than focusing on the Bogomil issue and racial questions of ethnogenesis, this essay will adopt a pluralist perspective and focus on the rise of Muslim group consciousness during the period of the Austrian occupation of Bosnia (1878–1918), sketching out, at the same time, some of the major issues in the contemporary period.

As Cynthia Enloe notes, "there are few multireligious ethnic groups and their relative scarcity suggests that religion is the root of ethnic differentiation or that religious distinctiveness is a key to ethnic saliency."[43] Religious customs, behavioral codes, concepts of self, dietary and dress codes, and group symbology all contribute to the development of a cultural and ethnic distinctiveness that transcends narrow confessionality.[44] But it may well be, as Enloe suggests, that "[religious] resources are most valuable for ethnic groups only in the earliest stages of communal political development."[45] For the Bosnian Muslims, communal political development began with the movement for religious and educational autonomy under Austro-Hungarian rule and expanded into a full-fledged political party, the Yugoslav Muslim Organization, during the interwar period.

Prior to the Austrian occupation of Bosnia, the Muslims led a privileged but politically unconscious life. Linked with the Ottomans by religion, dress, and political fidelity, the Bosnian Muslims commonly referred to themselves as "Turčini." This did not preclude the development of a regional identity, a sense of "Bosnianness," however, and the indigenous population, including that of Herzegovina, referred to itself most often as "Bosniaks."[46] Bosnian Muslims enjoyed a number of prerogatives not open to Bosnian Christians in Ottoman times, including the right to own land, to serve in the Ottoman state apparatus, to wear green, and to ride horses. Ninety-five percent of the serfs (kmetovi) were Christians, and Muslims dominated Bosnia's cities. Understandably, while Bosnia's Serbs repeatedly rose up in revolt against the Turks, with the Catholics occasionally taking part, the Muslims never did.[47]

The roots of the Bosnian cultural movement may be traced to the creation of the Vilayet Printing Company in 1866 and the inception of a series of newspapers: *Bosanski vjesnik* (1866–1867), *Bosna* (1866–1878), *Sarajevski cvjetnik* (1866–1972), and *Neretva* (1876). But it was the Austro-Hungarian occupation itself that more directly sparked a new consciousness. This occurred in the first place because local Muslims drew up literally hundreds of petitions in the first five years of Austrian rule in an effort to safeguard their religious interests and secondly because the Austrian authorities, and particularly longtime provincial governor Benjamin von Kállay (1882–1903), sought to stimulate a Bosnian consciousness as a foil to Serbian nationalism. Out of these petitions grew the Muslim autonomy movement, which sought religious autonomy and autonomy of *waqf* (*vakuf* in Serbo-Croatian; "religious property" in English). This immediately involved questions of education and farmlands. With the removal of ex-Mufti Ali Fehmi Džabica and his coterie from a position of leadership and their replacement by influential landowners headed by Alibeg Firdus, the movement assumed a political character. Its goals included autonomy for the districts, recognition of civil liberties (Bosnia was governed by military law), freedom of the press, abolition of censorship, and mass participation in district elections.[48] But, even if it soon embraced such goals, the incunabulum of Muslim political consciousness was distinctly religious.

The Muslims were also mobilized to political action by class interests. Though the peasant uprising of 1875 in Bosnia had been occasioned by resentment at the system of landholding and the large estates, the Austrian authorities initially made little effort to correct this situation, since the Muslim landowners were politically dominant and agreed to maintain the Ottoman land regulations of 1859, which favored the landowners. When the Austrians eventually proposed a land reform, the Muslim landlords resisted and a major dispute over constitutional provisions regarding property rights ensued in 1907–1908. Inevitably, the Muslim opposition began to cite Shariat regulations in its dispute with the Austrian regime—a tactic rejected out of hand by the Austrians,[49] but symptomatic of a tendency among Muslim leaders to translate class and cultural interests into religious terms.

In the 1890s, the Serbian and Croatian nationalist movements both endeavored to woo Muslim intellectuals and to absorb the Muslim community. Mujaga Komadina, a wealthy Mostar Muslim, concluded that Muslims would lose their distinctive culture unless they organized; the result was the creation of the Kiraethana reading society in 1897 to promote Muslim cultural revival. Government officials enthusiastically endorsed the move as a means of combatting Serbian national ideology. (Among the members of Kiraethana's first executive committee was Mehmed Spaho, later president of the Yugoslav Muslim Organization.) By early 1900, Kiraethana no longer appeared so innocent and was dissolved by the Austrians for its alleged role in stimulating unrest in the Muslim community. By September 1900, the Muslim community was sufficiently politicized to discuss seriously the feasibility of the establishment of an Islamic bank, and, later that year, Muslims drew up a proposed autonomy statute and presented it to Kállay.[50]

Yet, it is also from this period that the chronic ethnic confusion among Bosnian Muslims must be dated. In one of the earliest examples, Mostar landlord Šerif Arnautović promoted Croatian national identity for Bosnian Muslims in articles he wrote for Croatian newspapers in the early 1890s; in 1898, after the Austrians twice refused to promote him, he defected to the Serbs and began to promote Serbian nationalism.[51] Suljag Salihagić, on the other hand, had most of his life viewed himself as a Serb but in later years came to regard himself as a "Bosnian Muslim" and, in a brochure published in Banja Luka in 1940, wrote that "we Muslims have had and have our own name."[52] Bosnian literary figure, Musa Ćazim Ćatić, began life too as a "Serb," but later declared himself a "Bosniak," and ended his life as a "Croat."[53] Ethnic "conversion" became commonplace among Muslims, and even "the greatest protagonists of Serbian national identity among the Muslims, Avdo Hasanbegović, Hasan Rebac, Hamid Kukić, and others [had] declared themselves Croats in early youth."[54] Ironically, Croatian sentiment was stronger among Muslims during the interwar years than it had been during the Habsburg occupation, which was favorably disposed toward the development of Croatian-Muslim links. Even so, Croatian nationalist penetration was by and large restricted to the Muslim intelligentsia and, of course, there were oscillations.[55]

Various cultural societies, clubs, and presses were founded by Bosnian Muslims in the early years of the century, especially between 1906 and 1908. Turkophiles, led by Džemaladus Čaušević (later Reis-ul-ulema, i.e., head of Bosnia's Islamic community), promoted the use of Arabic for the Croatian language.[56] And while some Muslims, especially those educated in Vienna and Zagreb, cooperated actively with the Austrians and inclined toward Croatian culture, in 1903, Muslim Serbophiles created the Gajret cultural society specifically to promote Serbian identity among Muslims and to draw them into contact with Serbia; indeed, after 1929, Gajret was officially redesignated the "Serbian Muslim Cultural Society."

The waxing courtship between Serbs and Muslims at this time seems to have been motivated both by the Muslim landlords' belief that co-operation with the Serbian national movement might help to safeguard their landed estates for the future, and by Muslim fears of Catholic prose-lytization, astutely manipulated by the Serbs.[57] In late 1898 and early 1899, Austro-Hungarian authorities received reports that Gligorije Jefta-nović and other Sarajevo Serbs were making efforts to contact leading Bosnian Muslims with an eye to overt Serb-Muslim cooperation. While on a visit to Istanbul, Jeftanović even suggested that the governor of an autonomous Bosnia (within a Serbian kingdom) could be a vizier of the Islamic faith. Meanwhile, the regime's efforts to draw the Catho-lic and Muslim populations closer produced a backlash among Muslim radicals whose writings acquired an anti-Croatian tone by the end of the nineteenth century, with some even accusing the regime outright of attempting to "Croatize" the Muslims.[58] Muslims connected with the Serbian nationalist organ, *Srbobran*, now wrote that Serbian conscious-ness was developing among Muslims, and that it was rooted in hatred of the Croats. At a meeting held in Nova Gradiška, November 17–18, 1900, Muslim oppositionists accepted the draft of an agreement, proposed by certain Serbs, for common action toward the goal of Bosnian autonomy, with the exception of those paragraphs that designated the official lan-guage (which the Muslims called "Bosnian") as "Serbian," which stated that it be written exclusively in Cyrillic and which called for an agrarian reform. The anti-Catholic thrust of the document is clear from its posi-tion that all non-native Bosnian Catholic clergy should be expelled from Bosnia, leaving the Franciscans intact, but threatening Sarajevo Arch-bishop Stadler with expulsion.[59]

While Gajret espoused the view that Muslims were Serbs who lacked ethnic consciousness, and thus even "anational" Serbs,[60] rival organiza-tions with diverse national lines were created. In 1908, Ademaga Mešić set up the Muslim Progressive Party which had a Croatian orienta-tion, and opened a paper, *Muslimanska svijest*, though by 1910, this party (which was renamed the Muslim Independent Party) rejected both Croatian and Serbian national identification for Muslims. On the other hand, the Mostar periodical, *Biser* (1912–1914 and 1918), despite its Pan-Islamic coloration, nonetheless described "Croatia" as the homeland and had a Croatian nationalist bias. A direct rival to Gajret did not emerge until 1924 when the Narodna uzdanica Society was established. Although it was widely viewed as a "Croatian Muslim" organization, Narodna uzdanica actually had little connection with Croatian nation-alism and its strongest support came from adherents of Spaho's Yugo-slav Muslim Organization (YMO).[61] But on July 27, 1941, at the behest of the Ustasha, Narodna uzdanica was redesignated the "Croatian Muslim Cultural Society."

Throughout the Habsburg period and the early years after World War I, a sense of confessional-group interest was articulated and developed among the Muslim political and cultural elite. Although the Muslims displayed considerable confusion, or perhaps opportunism, ethnically, they never compromised their Islamic religious interests, and their flirtation with both the Croatian and Serbian national movements never dulled their consciousness of their distinctive religio-cultural heritage. The conclusion which some Muslims drew was aptly summed up by a leading Muslim writer in 1925:

> To identify oneself nationally means at the same time not to be a Muslim, because Islam is not the religion of Serbs and Croats, nor of mankind in general. . . . To be a Muslim and to feel national at one and the same time is not possible. Islam takes precedence over nationality.[62]

Hence, in contradiction of tribalist and Marxist theories, group consciousness was developing, during an era of modernization, on the basis of religious and cultural interests, mediated by relative deprivation and perceived cultural threat. This brief account also makes it clear that Bosnian Muslims did not start out with racially given certainties: on the contrary, in many instances, ethnic identity was planted or changed by the conscious activity of politically motivated cultural societies. This likewise stands in confutation of tribalist theories.

V

Although the YMO, the dominant political force in the interwar Muslim community, edged toward the conviction that the Bosnian Muslims constituted a distinct *ethnic* category, it has been said that, as a whole, the Bosnian Muslims tended to view the YMO as a *religious* party and to vote for it out of confessional loyalty.[63] The solidarity which developed between Muslims and Croats in the 1920s may have been derived from their common perception that neither enjoyed favorable conditions for economic development when compared to the Serbs. Certainly, despite the subsequent cooperation of YMO leaders with the Croatian Ustasha during the Second World War, most Bosnian Muslims rejected Croatia's annexation of Bosnia.[64] And though some Muslims joined the Ustasha's S. S. Handžar (Dagger) Brigade, or cooperated in other ways, a group of Muslim clergy and businessmen showed their displeasure with Ustasha

Croatia in 1942 when they sent Hitler a letter, imploring him to create an independent Bosnian state separate from Croatia.

Given the varied positions adopted by leading Muslim figures over the years on the subject of nationality, it is understandable that the Yugoslav communists were perplexed about how to deal with the group. Up until 1968, the party consensus was probably best summed up by Mladen Čaldarević when he wrote in 1963 that "Muslims of the same derivation as Serbs and Croats . . . in large part do not feel Serbian or Croatian today, but consider themselves a particular ethno-historical, or most often even a religious group."[65]

There is a certain irony in the fact that it is precisely the LCY, which chastises "bourgeois" theories of nationality for overemphasizing the linguistic and cultural components of ethnicity and for underestimating the materialist basis in the division of labor,[66] which in 1968 accorded full national status to a group whose chief distinguishing feature was not its position in the division of labor but its religion and culture.

Clearly, the LCY's theoretical position up to 1968 regarding the Muslims was anomalous, in that this was the only group in the country whose nationality was not defined—and that in a country that made nationality the foundation of its federalism and of a wide-ranging system of proportional representation. In view of the latter, both the Bosnian party generally and the Muslims specifically stood to gain from the proclamation of Muslim nationality. On the other hand, there were signs of resistance to this among Croats and Serbs, and it was not until 1971 that the Croatian and Serbian party organizations recognized the Muslims' new status.[67]

Nation was defined above, for the purposes of this chapter, as "a group of people who believe that they constitute a primary cultural unity, who also believe that they have common cultural interests, and who seek to advance their common interests through organized political action." The argument that has been set forth is that the Bosnian Muslims gradually became more "national" in the wake of the Austrian occupation of 1878, that the development of their national consciousness was sparked by relative deprivation and the perception of cultural threat, and that this process is even now not complete, giving rise to different convictions among the Muslims themselves. Two caveats should be registered here. First, while the evolution of Bosnian Muslim consciousness shares some common features with the development of the Serbian and Croatian national identities, Bosnian Muslim consciousness differs at the same time from each of Serbian and Croatian national consciousness in the weight given to the religious element, in the lesser weight given to language as a badge of group identity, and in the tendency of Muslims to view non-Slav Muslims, rather than non-Muslim Slavs, as their closest kin outside Yugoslavia. Second, processes of nation-building may be reversible, at least in cases where the process is not yet complete.

The proclamation of Muslim nationality seems to have catalyzed ferment among the Bosnian Muslim community. As early as 1970, certain Muslims were trying to have "Bosanski" (Bosnian) declared a distinct linguistic variant on a par with "Srpski" (Serbian) and "Hrvatski" (Croatian).[68] Shortly thereafter, Muslim nationalists began agitating to have Bosnia declared a "Muslim Republic" in the same way that Serbia was declared the "Republic of the Serbs" and Macedonia the "Republic of the Macedonians." This, however, would have deleted mention of Croats and Serbs as additional claimants to a Bosnian "homeland" and was therefore rejected by the party.[69] After 1973—and most especially during the voluble pro-Arab agitation by Bosnian Muslims during the October War between Israel and certain Arab states[70]—warnings about the dangers of Pan-Islamic and Muslim nationalism became a regular feature in the Yugoslav press, both during the Tito era and in the years immediately thereafter.

The LCY charged the Muslim community with "a particular escalation of attempts to politicize the religious communities" and to "take Islam not as a religion (and only as a religion) but to make of it also a political ideology."[71] But religion cannot be "made" political; it is political in its very soul. For,

> Religion is not merely a set of beliefs about a "world beyond" but also, and perhaps more importantly, a set of beliefs about how the present world—its laws, its authority, its hierarchical relations—should be organized. Liturgy and ritual, valued by participants for the feelings of rapture and spirituality they impart, serve another function, clearly more important from the organizational point of view, viz., that of communal reaffirmation of the authority of ecclesiastical leaders. The breadth of that authority may be narrow, limited essentially to social behavior (morality), or it may extend to prescriptions about attire, culture (as in the proscription of certain kinds of music), civil codes, and political behavior.[72]

The LCY also charged that some Muslims wrongly identified Islam and Muslim national identity and promoted a religio-nationalism that was contrary to LCY ideology.[73] Yet insofar as religion endeavors to define and explain human existence and construes its definitions as dogma, i.e., as *absolutely* valid, and insofar as religions have historically arisen within the context of particular communities having particular needs, the identification of religion and nationalism is organic and natural. Indeed, Marx himself saw the erosion of both under communism as going in tandem.

Is LCY concern justified? Perhaps in part; it is certainly intelligible. A lengthy Islamic pamphlet first written in 1970 and widely distributed in several languages affirms precisely this identification of religion and politics which is anathema to the LCY. This "Islamic Declaration," which later figured as the central piece of evidence in a trial of 13 Muslim "counterrevolutionaries" in the summer of 1983, challenges communist rule head-on:

> Islamic society without an Islamic government is incomplete and impotent; an Islamic government without an Islamic society is either a utopia or a tyranny.
>
> A Muslim, on the whole, does not exist as an individual. If he [or she] wants to live and exist as a Muslim, [she or] he must create an environment, a community, a social order. [She or] he must change the world or he/[she] . . . will be changed. *History does not know of a single truly Islamic movement which was not simultaneously a political movement.* This is because Islam is a religion, but at the same time it is also a philosophy, a morality, a social order, a style, an atmosphere—in a word, a comprehensive way of life. *It is impossible to believe in Islam and yet work to earn a living, amuse oneself, and govern in a non-Islamic way.*[74]

This pamphlet thus pushes Islamic consciousness to its "logical" conclusion: if Muslim identity is defined by Islam, then the nation cannot be restricted to a mere branch of that community, but must embrace the whole. Hence, for the author of the "Islamic Declaration," "Bosnian Muslimness" would seem to be a "counterfeit nation," but cut off from its own past, and the authentic political goals of Muslims can only be to create a unified Islamic state stretching from Morocco to Indonesia, in which all aspects of family and social life are governed by Islamic principles.[75]

VI

Hence, it is quite clear, all in all, that the self-consciousness of the Bosnian Muslims had been stirred earlier, in Habsburg times. And this was further reinforced by the activity, in the interwar period, of the YMO. This political party, like most in interwar Yugoslavia, catered to a specific constituency—in this case, the Muslims. The YMO repeatedly rejected notions that Muslims might accept either Serbian or Croatian national identity, and throughout the 1920s, there was a growth in Muslim consciousness, as evinced in tendencies of Muslim adherents of Serbian and Croatian political parties to insist on measures to safeguard their special interests and specifically tendencies to set up expressly "Muslim" branches within those parties.[76] And therefore, the recognition of the Muslims as a nation figured not merely as a political calculation but was specifically a reaction to this rising self-awareness. The LCY hoped to define Muslim nationalism and contain it within a Marxist framework. But this recognition sparked controversy. First of all, the Macedonian party displayed nervousness as early as 1970 lest Islamic Macedonians suddenly declare themselves "ethnic Muslims." Some conservatives sought to impose a "solution" under which only residents of Bosnia-Herzegovina would have been allowed, in the 1971 census, to register as "ethnic Muslims."[77] Although this solution was not accepted, the incident showed the difficulties entailed in adopting this approach.

Second, there were accusations during the censuses of 1971 and 1981 that non-Albanian Muslims in Kosovo and the western part of Macedonia (where the majority of the local population is Albanian) were being pressured to declare themselves "Albanian." And after both censuses, it was claimed that the number of "ethnic Muslims" or "Albanians" had been overestimated or underestimated.

Third, there has long been a tendency for the Islamic ulema and also the mouthpiece of the Islamic community, *Preporod* (published in Sarajevo), to present themselves as the advocates and defenders of the interests of their community. In June 1970, for example, *Preporod* argued forcefully for the need to establish specific Muslim *cultural* institutions, within which Muslims could develop an autonomous social and cultural life, separate from other Yugoslavs.[78] Some Muslims have proposed the establishment of a Matica muslimanska, after the model of Matica hrvatska, the Croatian literary society suppressed by Tito in December 1971.

In a more blatant interference in political affairs, the Islamic Council of Bosnia-Herzegovina, Croatia and Slovenia tried, in the wake of the disputed census of 1981, to carry out its own tally of Muslims. The clerics were sharply reprimanded by the authorities and quickly dropped this project.[79]

And fourth, the sundry controversies about the "real" nationality of Muslims—explored in the early sections of this chapter—are far from dead. In the context of the political debates of 1989–90, when various polemicists have urged a revision of the boundaries separating the republics, this dispute could spell the difference between an enlarged Croatia, an enlarged Serbia, and the maintenance of the territorial status quo.[80]

The nervousness of the communist leaders who inherited Tito's legacy was therefore understandable. This nervousness led directly to the above-mentioned decision, in 1983, to "set an example" by arresting Ali Izetbegović—author of the aforementioned "Islamic Declaration"—and twelve other Muslim clerics and lay persons. They were sentenced to some ninety years in jail, all told. Bosnian law professor Fuad Muhić explained the regime's point of view:

> The fundamental meaning of the "Islamic Declaration" consists in its total politicization. . . . "Our goal is the Islamicization of the Muslims, our solution is to believe and to fight"—so declare the champions of this Declaration. . . . Between Islamic believers and non-Islamic societies and political institutions no reconciliation is allowed and no coexistence.[80]

This charge betrayed the regime's apprehension that Islamic institutions might become more important vehicles for mobilizing and organizing political viewpoints among Bosnian Muslims.

In February 1987, three more Muslims were arrested: Fadil Fadilpašić, Munib Zahiragić, and Ibrahim Avdić. The nature of the case against them was first mooted in the Sarajevo daily, *Oslobodjenje,* which claimed that Fadilpašić had established contact with "hostile émigrés" in Turkey in 1983 and obtained a copy of the Islamic Declaration from them. Zahiragić, *Oslobodjenje* alleged, had advocated recourse to violence and terrorism in order to set up an Islamic state in Bosnia. They were put on trial on May 18 on charges of "spreading hostile propaganda" and convicted on June 5. Their sentences ranged from two to five years in prison.[81]

Not surprisingly, Ali Izetbegović's request to be permitted to publish a book entitled *Islam between East and West* was disapproved by the authorities. The decision was handed down by the Bosnian Committee for Education, Science, Culture, and Physical Culture on March 24, 1987.[82] Eventually, in late 1988, all of those incarcerated for Muslim nationalism would be released as part of a more general amnesty.

But in the context of the increasingly fluid politics of 1989–90, the Muslim question assumed new saliency. Amid renewed claims that ethnic Muslims are an artificial construct, designed for political reasons, Bosnian party president Nijaz Durakovic issued a statement reprimanding advocates of that position.[83] Meanwhile, Croatian economist Branko

Horvat, who has increasingly assumed the role of political pundit, suggested abandonment of the term *Muslim* in the ethnic sense, which he
described as "a most unfortunate choice," and suggested instead that
Bosnia's Muslims be allowed, in the 1991 census, to declare themselves
"Bosnians." The name *Muslim*, he argued, led to ideas of an Islamic
Republic, and inflamed interethnic tensions in the republic of Bosnia-
Herzegovina.[84] Horvat's admonition has been little heeded, however, and
instead, this most recent period has seen the appearance of Bosnian
political parties whose appeal is specifically to Muslim ethnic and religious concerns. This gives the lie to arguments that Bosnia's Muslims
should be seen uniformly as either Croats or Serbs.

VII

Today in Bosnia-Herzegovina, there are Muslims who consider themselves primarily "Muslim Croats," those who consider themselves "Muslim Serbs," those who consider themselves "Bosnian Muslims" (i.e.,
"Muslims in the ethnic sense"), and those who, in the spirit of the
"Islamic Declaration," see themselves simply as "Muslims." In addition,
there are those Muslims who in the 1981 census declared themselves
"Yugoslavs." This already complex picture is made more so by the presence of persons like Fuad Muhić, who describe themselves as "atheist
Muslims," and who thereby completely divorce religion from nationality.

This confusion of identities accords far better with "pluralist" theories, which are prepared to trace it all the way back to the origins of the
group, than with "tribalist" theories, which are inclined to interpret such
confusion as evidence of erosion. The persistence and even escalation of
nationalist exclusivism and ethnocentrism since 1878 is likewise consistent with "pluralist" theory but is inexplicable within the confines
of "tribalist" theory. And, as noted earlier, the retention of central symbols of loyalty and authority is compatible with either theory. To brand
an identity "primordial" only because its chief resources are religious
is both to view religion narrowly and to exclude religion from modernity—a fallacious proposition. Yet, as Enloe cautions, the very fact that
religious resources appear to be most useful in the early stages of the
development of communal-ethnic identity, suggests that

> ethnic groups will inevitably outgrow their dependence on reli-
> gious resources. Or, if they do not, then they risk deflation of their
> political potential and even their capacity to survive as a distinct

group. Ironically, when the religiously-derived symbols, values, institutions are critical elements in a group's distinctiveness vis-à-vis other groups, the secularization apparently necessary for continued development may result in a collapse of the ethnic boundaries it was intended to preserve.[85]

Religion and ethnicity are mutable aspects of individual and collective identity, and hence their relationship is mutable over time. The politicization of either or both is likewise mutable. And hence, the meanings assigned to various parts of the equation must necessarily change over time.

Notes

This is a revised synthesis of the chapter which appeared in the German edition of this book and of the author's earlier article, "Primordial Ethnicity or Modern Nationalism: The Case of Yugoslavia's Muslims," which was originally published in *Nationalities Papers* 13, no. 2 (Fall 1985). This version is also scheduled for publication in a forthcoming issue of *South Slav Journal*.

   1. Examples of tribalist/assimilationist literature include: Peter M. Blau and Otis Dudley Duncan, *The American Occupational Structure* (New York: John Wiley, 1967), p. 429; Karl W. Deutsch, "Social Mobilization and Political Development," in *Political Modernization*, ed. Claude E. Welsh, Jr. (Belmont, Calif.: Duxbury Press, 1971), pp. 167–68; Clifford Geertz, ed., *Old Societies and New States* (Glencoe, Ill.: Free Press, 1965); William Fielding Ogburn, "Social Change and Race Relations," in *Race Relations*, ed. Jitsuichi Masuoka and Preston Valien (Chapel Hill, N.C.: University of North Carolina Press, 1961), pp. 204–6; Robert Ezra Park, *Race and Culture* (Glencoe, Ill.: Free Press, 1950), pp. 204–8; Edward B. Reuter, "Race and Culture," in *An Outline of the Principles of Sociology*, ed. Robert E. Park (New York: Barnes & Noble, 1939), pp. 209–10; Boyd C. Shafer, *Nationalism and Internationalism: Belonging in Human Experience* (Malabor, Fla.: Robert E. Krieger Publ. Co., 1982), pp. 130–32; and Brian K. Taylor, "Culture: Whence, Whither and Why?" in *The Future of Cultural Minorities*, ed. Antony E. Alcock, Brian K. Taylor, and John M. Welton (London: Macmillan, 1979).

   2. Examples of pluralist literature include: Walker Connor, "Nation-Building or Nation-Destroying?" *World Politics* 24, no. 3 (April 1972); Walker Connor, "The Politics of Ethnonationalism," *Journal of International Affairs* 27, no. 1 (1973); Milton M. daSilva, "Modernization and Ethnic Conflict: The Case of the Basques," *Comparative Politics* 7, no. 2 (January 1975): 228; Hans Kohn, *The Idea of Nationalism* (Toronto: Collier Books, 1969); Alvin Rabushka and Kenneth A. Shepsle, *Politics in Plural Societies* (Columbus, Ohio: Charles E. Merrill, 1972); Teresa Rakowska-Harmstone, "The Dialectics of Nationalism in the USSR," *Problems of Communism* 23, no. 3 (May–June 1974): 1–2, 9–15; Jeffrey A. Ross, "The State, Public Policy and Polarization: The Dialectic of Ethnic Mobilization and Ethnonationalism" (Paper presented at the

Meeting of the American Political Science Association, New York, September 3–6, 1981); Richard A. Schermerhorn, *Comparative Ethnic Relations* (New York: Random House, 1970), pp. xii, 57–58, and *passim*; William L. Yancey, Eugene P. Ericksen, and Richard N. Juliani, "Emergent Ethnicity: A Review and Reformulation," in *Understanding Minority-Dominant Relations*, ed. F. James David (Arlington, Ill.: AHM Publ. Corp., 1979); Crawford Young, *The Politics of Cultural Pluralism* (Madison, Wisc.: University of Wisconsin Press, 1976); Crawford Young, "The Temple of Ethnicity," *World Politics* 35, no. 4 (July 1983); and *Ethnicity*, ed. Nathan Glazer and Daniel P. Moynihan (Cambridge, Mass.: Harvard University Press, 1975).

3. See Geertz, *Old Societies*.

4. See Horace B. Davis, "Nations, Colonies and Social Classes: The Position of Marx and Engels," *Science and Society* 24, no. 1 (Winter 1965); and Joseph A. Petrus, "Marx and Engels on the National Question," in *Journal of Politics* 33, no. 3 (August 1971).

5. Young, *Politics of Cultural Pluralism*, p. 34.

6. Chong-Do Hah and Jeffrey Martin, "Toward a Synthesis of Conflict and Integration Theories of Nationalism," *World Politics* 27, no. 3 (April 1975): 385.

7. Cynthia H. Enloe, *Ethnic Conflict and Political Development* (Boston: Little, Brown, 1973). See also Gary K. Bertsch, "The Revival of Nationalisms," *Problems of Communism* 22, no. 6 (November–December 1973): 7–8.

8. Harold R. Isaacs, "Nationality: 'End of the Road'?" *Foreign Affairs* 53, no. 3 (April 1975): 447.

9. Joseph Stalin, *Marxism and the National-Colonial Question* (San Francisco: Proletarian Publishers, 1975), p. 2.

10. Boris Meissner, "Nationalitätenfrage und Sowjetideologie," *Europäische Rundschau* 7, no. 4 (Fall 1979): 81; and Paul Goble, "Ethnic Politics in the USSR," *Problems of Communism* 38, no. 4 (July–August 1989).

11. *Statistički kalendar Jugoslavije 1982* (Belgrade: Savezni zavod za statistiku, February 1982), p. 37; and Slobodan Stanković, "Danger of Pan-Islamism in Yugoslavia?" *Radio Free Europe Research* (August 26, 1982): 3.

12. Gai Eaton, *Islam and the Destiny of Man* (London: George Allen & Unwin, 1985), p. 15, quoted in S. Enders Wimbush, "The Muslim Ferment in Soviet Central Asia," *Global Affairs* 2, no. 3 (Summer 1987): 111.

13. Muhamed Hadžijahić, *Od tradicije do identiteta: Geneza nacionalnog pitanja bosanskih muslimana* (Sarajevo: Svjetlost, 1974), pp. 8, 22, 25.

14. Ibid., p. 35.

15. Barbara Jelavich, *History of the Balkans*, vol. 2: *Twentieth Century* (New York: Cambridge University Press, 1983), p. 62.

16. Kasim Suljević, *Nacionalnost Muslimana* (Rijeka: Otokar Keršovani, 1981), pp. 120–21; and Hadžijahić, *Od tradicije*, pp. 35, 167–68.

17. Nikola Babić, "Od ideje o autonomiji do socijalističke republike Bosne i Hercegovine," in *Nacionalni odnosi danas*, ed. Milan Petrović and Kasim Suljević (Sarajevo: Univerzal, 1971), pp. 159–74.

18. Quoted in Suljević, *Nacionalnost*, p. 123.

19. Quoted in ibid., p. 129.

20. Veselin Masleša, "Muslimansko pitanje", *Vojno-politički pregled*, no. 7 (1942),

summarized in Atif Purivatra, *Nacionalni i politički razvitak muslimana* (Sarajevo: Svjetlost, 1970), p. 117.

21. John V. A. Fine, Jr., *The Bosnian Church: A New Interpretation* (Boulder, Colo.: East European Monographs, 1975), p. 1.

22. Olive Lodge, *Peasant Life in Yugoslavia* (London: Seeley, Service, 1919), p. 180.

23. Quoted in Purivatra, *Nacionalni i politički*, p. 57.

24. Ivo Pilar, *Die Südslawische Frage und der Weltkrieg* (Vienna: Manzsche K.U.K. Hof-, Verlags-, u. Universitäts-Buchhandlung, 1918), pp. 170–213, esp. pp. 170, 192, 195, 209.

25. In his *Epitome vetustatum provinciae Bosniensis* (1765), cited in Hadžijahić, *Od tradicije*, p. 32.

26. Quoted in Babić, "Od ideje o autonomiji," p. 174.

27. Mile Budak, *Hrvatski narod u borbi za samostalnu i nezavisnu hrvatsku drzavu* (1934), quoted in Fikreta Jelić-Butić, "Bosna i Hercegovina u koncepciji stvaranja Nezavisne Države Hrvatske," *Pregled* (Sarajevo) 61, no. 12 (December 1971): 665.

28. AKSA (December 4, 1981).

29. Frane Franić, "Muslimani i katolici," *Crkva u svijetu* no. 5 (1967), cited in Purivatra, *Nacionalni i politički*, pp. 21–22.

30. "Stvaranje novog narodnog identiteta," *Republika Hrvatska* (Buenos Aires) 34, no. 145 (June 1984), p. 60. See also "Prikrevana obrana Jugoslavije," *Republika Hrvatska* 34, no. 144 (April 1984): 60–62; and "Muslimanska narodnost ili jugoslavenska pokušni balon?" *Republika Hrvatska* 34, no. 145 (June 1984).

31. See Fuad Muhić, "Islamske institucije i nacionalizam," in *Socijalizam* 22, no. 11 (November 1979).

32. *Nova Hrvatska* (London), May 8, 1983, p. 11.

33. Cited in Purivatra, *Nacionalni i politički*, p. 9.

34. Peter F. Sugar, *Industrialization of Bosnia-Herzegovina, 1878–1918* (Seattle: University of Washington Press, 1963), p. 14.

35. Husag Čišić, *Bosansko-hercegovački Muslimani i bosanska autonomija* (1929; 2nd ed., 1940), quoted in Hadžijahić, *Od tradicije*, p. 38.

36. Purivatra, *Nacionalni i politički*, pp. 54, 57, 118.

37. Rodoljub Čolaković, *Izabrani govori i članci* (Sarajevo: Svjetlost, 1960), quoted in Purivatra, *Nacionalni i politički*, p. 122.

38. "Staat und Nationalität in Jugoslawien," *Wissenschaftlicher Dienst Südosteuropa* 19, no. 8 (August 1970): 113–14.

39. Ruža Petrović, "Etno-biološka homogenizacija jugoslovenskog društva," *Sociologija*, no. 2 (1968): 5–6.

40. Franc Šetinc, *Misao i djelo Edvarda Kardelja*, trans. from Slovenian into Croatian by Ivan Brajdić (Zagreb: Globus, 1979), p. 101.

41. Ibid., p. 100; and Djordje Uskoković, "Pokušaj sociološkog objašnjenja nacionalnog i nacionalističkog," *Gledišta* 17, no. 5 (May 1976): 514.

42. Šetinc, *Misao*, p. 53; Milan M. Miladinović, "Pojam i suština jugoslovenskog patriotizma danas," *Obeležja* 7, no. 6 (November–December 1977): 1153, 1165–1166; and Mihailo Mitić, "Razmatranja o smislu jugoslovenstva," in *Federalizam i nacionalno pitanje* (Belgrade: Savez udruženja za političke nauke Jugoslavije, 1971), p. 230.

43. Cynthia H. Enloe, "Religion and Ethnicity," in *Ethnic Diversity and Conflict in Eastern Europe*, ed. Peter F. Sugar (Santa Barbara, Calif.: ABC-Clio, 1980), p. 359.

44. Enloe, "Religion and Ethnicity," p. 364; and James A. Christenson et al., "Value Orientations of Organized Religious Groups," *Sociology and Social Research* 68, no. 2 (January 1984): 195. See also Arnold Dashefsky, "And the Search Goes On: The Meaning of Religio-Ethnic Identity and Identification," in *Sociological Analysis* 33, no. 4 (Winter 1972): 239–41.

45. Enloe, "Religion and Ethnicity," p. 366.

46. Hadžijahić, *Od tradicije*, pp. 18–20.

47. Ibid., pp. 108–109, 111.

48. Nusret Šehić, "Neka pitanja agrarnih odnosa u politici muslimanskog autonomnog pokreta," *Prilozi* (Sarajevo) 13, no. 13 (1977): 133–34.

49. Jelavich, *History of the Balkans*, vol. 2 (1983), p. 61; and Sehic, "Neka pitanja," pp. 137, 140.

50. For a more detailed examination of these developments, see Robert J. Donia, *Islam under the Double Eagle: The Muslims of Bosnia and Hercegovina, 1878–1914* (Boulder, Colo.: East European Monographs, 1981), pp. 101–40.

51. Donia, *Islam*, p. 107.

52. Quoted in Hadžihaić, *Od tradicije*, p. 39.

53. Ibid., p. 164.

54. Quoted in ibid., p. 144.

55. Ibid., pp. 207–09, 219.

56. Ibid., pp. 129–30.

57. Dževad Juzbašić, "Pokušaj stvaranja političkog Saveza izmedju vodjstva srpskog i muslimanskog autonomnog pokreta u Bosni i Hercegovini," *Prilozi* 14, nos. 14–15 (1978): 145, 149.

58. Ibid., pp. 158, 164–65.

59. Ibid., pp. 170–71.

60. Ibrahim Kemura, "Kongres Muslimana intelektualaca u Sarajevu 1928. Godine," *Prilozi* 16, no. 17 (1980), pp. 176–77.

61. Hadžijahić, *Od tradicije*, p. 141.

62. Osman Nuri-beg Firdus, "O nacionalnom opredjeljenju bosansko-hercegovačkih Muslimana," *Nova Evropa* (April 1925), quoted in Hadžijahić, *Od tradicije*, p. 74.

63. Atif Purivatra, *Jugoslavenska muslimanska organizacija* (Sarajevo: Svjetlost, 1974), pp. 540, 544.

64. Purivatra, *Jugoslavenska muslimanska*, p. 558.

65. Mladen Čaldarević, *Socijalistička Republika Bosna i Hercegovina* (Sarajevo: Svjetlost, 1963), quoted in Purivatra, *Nacionalni i politički*, p. 21.

66. Dušan Dragosavac, "O nekim aspektima medjunacionalnih odnosa," in *Udruženi rad i medjunacionalni odnosi*, ed. Milenko Marković and Dušan Janjić (Belgrade: Komunist, 1978), p. 125.

67. Zachary T. Irwin, "The Islamic Revival and the Muslims of Bosnia-Hercegovina," *East European Quarterly* 17, no. 4 (January 1984): 445.

68. *Borba* (April 26, 1970), p. 5.

69. For a more detailed discussion of this issue, see Sabrina Petra Ramet, *Nation-*

alism and Federalism in Yugoslavia, 1962–1990, 2nd ed. (Bloomington, Ind.: Indiana University Press, forthcoming), chapter 9.

70. For criticism of the Muslims' stand on the Arab-Israeli war of 1973 see *Oslobodjenje* (December 5, 1973), p. 6 (December 6, 1973), p. 4, and (December 7, 1973), p. 6.

71. *Ibid.* (October 29, 1982), p. 3, trans. in Joint Publications Research Service (JPRS), *East Europe Report*, No. 82626 (January 12, 1983), p. 91.

72. Pedro Ramet, "The Interplay of Religious Policy and Nationalities Policy in the Soviet Union and Eastern Europe," in *Religion and Nationalism in Soviet and East European Politics*, ed. Pedro Ramet, revised and expanded ed. (Durham, N.C.: Duke University Press, 1989), p. 3.

73. Tanjug (April 14, 1983), trans. in Foreign Broadcast Information Service (FBIS), *Daily Report* (Eastern Europe), April 15, 1983.

74. Alija Izetbegović, "The Islamic Declaration," *South Slav Journal* 6, no. 1 (Spring 1983): 67 (emphasis in original).

75. Ibid., pp. 58, 61.

76. Purivatra, *Jugoslavenska muslimanska*, pp. 558–65.

77. Details in Ramet, *Nationalism and Federalism*, chapter 8.

78. *Preporod* (June 15, 1970), trans. into German under the title "Bosnien und Herzegowina—ein 'Jugoslawien im kleinen,'" *Osteuropa* 22, no. 12 (December 1972): A856.

79. Mushtak Parker, *Muslims in Yugoslavia: the Quest for Justice* (Toronto: Croatian Islamic Centre, 1986), p. 14.

80. Fuad Muhić, "O muslimanskem nacionalizmu," *Teorija in praksa* nos. 1–2 (Ljubljana, 1984), trans. into German under the title "Der Islam in Jugoslawien," *Osteuropa* 35, nos. 7–8 (July–August 1985): A435–A436.

81. *Oslobodjenje* (April 10, 1987), cited in *Keston News Service*, no. 274 (April 30, 1987), p. 15; *Vjesnik* (June 6, 1987), p. 12; and *Keston News Service*, no. 278 (June 25, 1987), p. 4.

82. Interview, Belgrade, July 1987.

83. *Danas*, no. 394 (September 5, 1989), p. 33.

84. *Večerniji list* (Zagreb, September 4, 1989), p. 5.

85. Enloe, "Religion and Ethnicity," p. 366.

Part II *Policies toward Muslims*

7. Czarist Policy toward the Muslims of the Russian Empire

Andreas Kappeler

At the beginning of the twentieth century, the Russian Empire (aside from the protectorates of Bukhara and Khiva, declared independent according to international law) included more than 14 million Muslims: more than eleven percent of the total population.[1] Central Asian lands, where about half of the Russian Muslims lived, had been under Russian rule for only a few decades, but Russia had a long, uninterrupted tradition of connections with the Islamic world, in contrast to most Western European colonial powers. Because this thousand-year-old legacy was also important for the policies of Russia toward the Muslims of the Empire during the late czarist period, what follows will refer back to earlier historical periods. It will only sketch some lines of development and formulate a few theses.[2]

The first Muslims with whom the Rus were in contact as neighbors over the course of centuries were the Bulgars of the Volga. According to the oldest Eastern Slavic chronicle, almost exactly a thousand years ago Prince Vladimir refused to accept their beliefs, because Islam forbade the enjoyment of alcohol: "Rusi est' vesel'e pit'e, ne mozhem bes togo byti" (The Rus love to drink: we cannot be without this").[3] Even after the conversion of the Kievan empire to Orthodox Christianity, some connections—primarily commercial ones—were maintained with the Bulgars of the Volga. It is certain that this first direct contact with Islam consisted of a basically peaceful relationship with settled Muslims who were on the same economic and cultural level as the Eastern Slavs.[4]

The conquest of Russia (and Volga Bulgaria) by the Mongols, as well as the subsequent conversion of the Golden Horde to Islam in the fourteenth century, altered substantially connections with the Muslim world. Now, the Orthodox Rus found themselves under the domination of Muslim nomads of the steppe. Sources from that time, like most Russian histories of the nineteenth and twentieth centuries, characterize the relationship of the Eastern Slavs to the Tatars as a continual conflict between believers and heathen. More recent Western research, in contrast, emphasizes the pragmatic cooperation of the Eastern Slavic princes and the Orthodox Church with the khans of the Golden Horde; Eastern Slavic sources, devoted to an exclusively Christian world view, were naturally silent for the most part about such cooperation.[5]

Such a revisionist interpretation of the Tatar yoke is part of a broader trend in research to free the relationship between Christendom and Islam—in the Byzantine Empire, in Spain and in southeastern Europe— of the ballast of ideologies of national religion, rather than giving a biased portrayal of the heroic defense of the Occident against unbelievers.[6] Ambivalence of connections with the Islamic world; gaps between ideological conflict and pragmatic policy: such—so runs the argument in this essay—are the characteristics of Russian policy toward the Muslims up to the twentieth century.

When the Golden Horde disintegrated in the fifteenth century, the initiative passed to Russia. As one of the legacies of the great empire, in the sixteenth century the Moscow government initiated the "Gathering of the lands of the Golden Horde," just as it carried out the "Gathering of the lands of Rus" to the west. In both processes of expansion, Moscow applied with success the method of winning over partisans of foreign elites. So it was that numerous Muslim Tatars from the concurrent neighboring empires entered the service of the Moscow princes: from the Khanate of Kazan, Astrakhan, Siberia, and the Crimea, as well as from the Nogai Hordes. They were furnished with properties, in return for which they had to serve as cavalry in the Moscow armies. Members of the Tatar aristocracy were recognized as being essentially peers and, particularly where the Chinggisids were concerned, were accepted into honorable positions among the nobility of Moscow. The barrier of belief, of course, blocked the way to complete cooptation, however.[7] The "gathering of the lands of the Golden Horde" was a driving force in Russian policy toward the steppe and toward Islamic states in later periods as well.

The conquest of the Khanate of Kazan in the middle of the sixteenth century constituted a turning point in the relations between Russia and the Islamic world. This was the first time a sovereign Muslim state had come under Russian rule. Thus, the relationship that had held since the thirteenth/fourteenth centuries was overturned, and policy toward the Muslims also changed. The resistance of the Tatars was broken with force; many were slain. Members of the elite were deported into the western regions of Russia and forcibly baptized, and Muslims were exiled from Kazan to the countryside or to outlying areas of cities.[8]

With the strong opposition movements vanquished and the Moscow regime apparently secure with regard to the khanates of Kazan and Astrakhan, the government of Ivan IV nevertheless returned to a pragmatic policy toward the Muslims. Flexibility and cautious reserve served the primary goals of securing the reign and of utilizing personal and economic resources better than did repression. Moscow worked together with the loyal Muslim upper class; guaranteed its tenure of land, its privileges and functions in local administration; and integrated it into the upper stratum of the czar's regime that performed military duty. Because of the paucity of Russian nobility, Moscow had to depend on the service of foreign elites to secure and administer newly won territories. In addition, it made use of the specific abilities of these elites: in the case of the Tatars, first their military and later their commercial capacities. The status quo was also guaranteed to the other social groups of both khanates, which also meant broad tolerance with regard to Islam. The Muslims were not the equals of Orthodox Christians in all respects, however. The conversion of Christians to Islam was therefore strictly forbidden.

On the whole, *pragmatic flexibility* was nevertheless the guiding principle for Moscow policy, not only toward the Volga Tatars but generally toward the Muslims and other ethnic minorities of the empire in the sixteenth and seventeenth centuries. This thesis diverges from most recent presentations, and treatment of its arguments may be found elsewhere.[9] Two examples will suffice for illustration here.

The first is that of the Tatar Khanate of Kasimov, established on the Oka in the mid-fifteenth century as a vassal of Moscow and maintained as an autonomous Muslim enclave in the heartland of Greater Russia until the second half of the seventeenth century. Its Islamic culture was conserved, along with its mosques and the socio-political organization of the Mongol era. The Chinggisid Muslim rulers of Kasimov remained— at least according to the theory of service registers—the highest-ranking subjects of the Muscovite rulers.[10]

The second example is even more fundamental in nature. The loyal Tatar upper class of the Khanate of Kazan and other regions in the eastern part of the Muscovite empire were not only able to retain their rights of ownership of land, but engaged Russian peasants as labor on their land. Thus, throughout the seventeenth century, tens of thousands of Russians lived as dependent peasants on Tatar lands, with the official approval of the authorities: Orthodox peasants were bondsmen of Muslim landowners. Such a subjection of believers to unbelieving masters would have been unthinkable elsewhere in Europe; it gains even greater significance by the fact that, in the converse situation, Russian landowners were forbidden to bring Muslim peasants under their control. Until the emancipation of the serfs in 1861, there were virtually no Muslim bondsmen of Orthodox masters. In this respect, then, the Muscovite regime discriminated against Christian Russians vis-à-vis Tatar Muslims.[11]

Orthodoxy opposed this pragmatic policy, with its broad concessions to the unbelieving Tatars. Representatives of the church thus would occasionally plead for an active policy of missionary activity among the Muslims. It thus appears to have been representatives of the church like Makarii or Sil'vestr, with their considerable political influence, who carried out the aggressive policies of the mid-sixteenth century: the destruction of the mosques of besieged Kazan, the subsequent acts of force and compulsory baptism.[12]

Shortly afterward, however, as the opposition in the conquered Khanate of Kazan reached greater proportions, the orientation changed. In the instructions of the czar to the newly appointed archbishop Gurii in 1555, the principles of a foresightful state policy of missionary activity were formulated: "He shall baptize those Tatars who seek baptism voluntarily, but without the use of force."[13] In a missive to the Nogai Horde from 1563, the Muscovite government—not without foreign policy intentions—supplied a further theological basis for the policy of tolerance toward Islam: "There are people who say, 'Belief is the enemy of (other) beliefs. Therefore Christian rulers annihilate the Muslims.' But it is written for us in the Christian scriptures that it is never permissible to convert anyone to our faith by force. For whoever will hold a belief, he should believe in that belief. God will judge in the Hereafter who has the true belief and who has the false. Human beings have no say in this. Among us, in our land, many people of the Muslim religion serve us, and they live according to their belief."[14]

The cautious policy of Christianization had few successes and was dispensed with in the 1560s. For more than a century, the Orthodox Church gave up missionary activity among the Muslims of the empire almost altogether, since it had been unable to prevail against the autocratic rulers. The government held to its own priorities: the maintenance of rule over the population of border regions and the use of their human and economic resources were more important than the conversion of those of other faiths. An ideology based on belief in the czar and on dynastic and imperial consciousness served the fusion of the multiethnic and multireligious empire better than did Orthodoxy.[15] The French traveler Philippe Avril summarized this dominance of politics over ideology at the end of the seventeenth century as follows: "Ils ne regarderont la Religion que comme un moyen propre à faire reussir leur politique, ainsi qu'ils ont toujours fait, et qu'ils ne voudront pas faire céder leur politique aux interêts de la Religion" (They will regard religion only as a suitable means of bringing their policies to fruition, and they will not wish to sacrifice their policies to the interests of religion).[16]

This does not mean that Moscow was not interested in the political-administrative, economic, social, and cultural-religious integration of the Muslims. On the one hand, it was believed that such integration would take place automatically, so to speak; on the other, experience had taught that an aggressive policy of integration provoked opposition, jeopardizing Russian rule. A careful policy that did not discriminate against the Muslims in principle, seemed to be conducive to gradual integration.

This pragmatic and flexible policy of government was not infrequently contradicted by administrative practices in the regions, however. In the Russian provinces, corruption, extortion, and arbitrary practices were the order of the day, and this held true for the Muslim population as well, due especially to linguistic and religious barriers. This discrepancy between centrally formulated policy and the praxis in effect in the regions is also worth bearing in mind with regard to subsequent periods.

Russian policy toward the Muslims of the empire began to change at the end of the seventeenth century, and the first half of the eighteenth century brought the first systematic and direct offensive of the Russian government against Muslim elites and Islamic values.[17] In 1713 the Muslim nobility was finally faced with the alternative of being baptized or relinquishing their lands to Orthodox peasants. Some Tatars converted to Christianity and gradually rose in the Russian nobility; most remained faithful to Islam and were consequently demoted to the rank of specialty workers in the Admiralty, were put in the new category of state peasants, and were subject to poll tax just like Muslim peasants.

A direct attack on Islam ensued in the 1740s. The policy of Christianization—carried out by various means, including force, discrimination, and economic incentives—met with great success among animists, but not among Muslims. The destruction of numerous mosques and other repressive measures that marked the high point of intolerance unleashed powerful opposition, ranging from the flight of thousands of Tatars toward the southeast to armed uprisings, first in the so-called Holy War of 1755 and then in the Pugachev Uprising of 1773–75, waged primarily by Tatars and Bashkirs.

The switch from a pragmatic policy to an intolerant policy of force under Peter the Great and his female successors cannot be attributed to the influence of the church, which had lost political influence by that time. Behind the change stood, instead, new goals of westernization and of leveling and systematizing Russia's complex socio-cultural relationships. Received rights and traditions, those of the Muslims of Russia among them, appeared to stand in the way of the modernization of the empire: a regularized and unified state was supposed to have a unified faith as well.

These ideas overtook Petrine Russia from the West, with early absolutism and Western intolerance toward the non-Christian world serving as models. Time and time again Western visitors to Russia, among them Gottfried Wilhelm von Leibniz, were surprised by the tolerance toward believers of other faiths and suggested that they be converted. Now, Russian thinkers, such as Ivan Pososhkov, took up these ideas and proposed Catholic missionary activity as a model for the Russian government: "If we look at its efforts, must we not be ashamed of ourselves?" Although many heathen in distant lands had been converted, it was said, the Russians had never succeeded in spreading the word of God in their own empire.[18] Moscow's traditional tolerance thus appeared to be an element of backwardness in comparison to the West.

The evident failure of an aggressive policy vis-à-vis Islam led to a new 180-degree shift beginning in 1755. Under the impetus of the Bashkir and Tatar uprisings, and perhaps also under the influence of the ideals of enlightened absolutism, the regime of Catherine II returned to a pragmatic and flexible policy. It proclaimed tolerance toward the Muslims, repealed the discriminatory edicts of the first half of the century, and created a "Spiritual Council" responsible for Islam, which offered broad opportunities for religious development and, at the same time, was to serve as an instrument of control over mosques and religious schools.

Like preceding regimes, that of Catherine II cooperated with representatives of the Tatar-Muslim elite, the small group of rehabilitated nobility and especially with representatives of the declassé upper stratum, which had found a new sphere of activity in commerce and manufacturing, as well as with the clergy. Tatar merchants and mullahs, traditionally in close relationships with Central Asia, were to serve as instruments of the economic and political penetration of Russia into the steppes and oases of Central Asia.[19]

This new policy of cooperation, formulated in reciprocation with the gradual annexation of the Crimea, held sway into the second half of the nineteenth century and achieved its desired objectives. On the other hand, however, this policy also led to a renaissance of Tatar-Islamic culture, to the consolidation of a Tatar economic middle class and, thus, to the rise of the Tatar nationalist movement. Tatar influence on the Muslims of the plains, especially on the Kazakhs, also had a dual aspect: the Tatars intensified the role of Islam and of Tatar culture, and thus also laid the foundation for later political and cultural movements.

In the eighteenth and nineteenth centuries, Russia continued to carry out the "Gathering of the Lands of the Golden Horde" with success and extended its influence to new regions inhabited by Muslims. After many centuries of both inimical and peaceful contact with the plains people, the Russian Empire finally brought the plains under its control and gradually annexed the regions of the Bashkirs, Crimean Tatars, and Kazakhs.[20] A military conflict with Persia brought the Muslims of Transcaucasia under Russian domination, while the Muslim mountain people of the northern Caucasus were only to be subjugated after a colonial war of several decades.[21]

Colonial expeditions to Central Asia were organized in the second half of the nineteenth century, bringing old centers of high Islamic culture, such as Samarkand and Tashkent, under Russian rule.[22] In most cases the Muslims put up embittered resistance to the Russian expansion; this was especially true of the plains nomads and mountain people who lived in confederations on the basis of clans or families. The greatest losses, including those through emigration, were incurred by the Circassians.[23]

The question arises as to whether the pattern of Islamic politics, as it had developed among the Kazan Tatars since the sixteenth century, was transferred at this time to other Muslim groups under different circumstances. Although it would be possible to give an affirmative answer at least in part, there was no unified Russian policy toward all Muslims. The political, social, and cultural contingencies and traditions in separate regions were too diverse, as were the circumstances of their conquest and annexation by Russia. In addition to these factors, other changes took place in the course of the nineteenth century.

On the whole, however, policies toward the Muslims who had been subjugated since the eighteenth century show numerous parallels to Moscow's traditional patterns of pragmatic flexibility. When rule was secured, and when the new subjects appeared to be loyal, the status quo was guaranteed in local administration, taxation systems, social organization, and in matters of land tenure. The privileges of the Muslim upper class were retained; the regime and regional authorities worked together with loyal Islamic elites. Considerable tolerance was exercised toward Islam, and missionary activity and even Russification remained very distant goals. The traditional policy of pragmatic flexibility was manifested in the incorporation of the Crimean Tatars and the Muslims of Trans-caucasia in the Russian Empire. The loyal elites retained their privileges and their property and were coopted as Muslims into the nobility of the empire.

While the Crimean Tatars and the Muslims of Transcaucasia exhibited a social structure and high culture that could be equated with those of Russia, relations with the nomadic and mountain people, who had a social order and way of life quite divergent from the Russian model, proved to be more complex. Here, too, the main features—tolerance and the guarantee of the existing situation in the local district—remained, but the Russian administration intervened more strongly in the socio-political system of the nomads, especially where Eastern Slavic colonization was at issue. In fact, Russia sought to collaborate with clan leaders: their cooptation into the imperial nobility, however, was rarely in question, if at all. This policy stood in contrast to the willing acceptance of Tatar nomads in earlier centuries.

The Muslims of the oases and river valleys of Central Asia were the last to be subjugated; with regard to them, too, the old lines of Russian policy were only partially followed. Although the elite was settled and socially stratified and possessed an old high culture, it was no longer co-opted into the nobility as the nobility of Transcaucasia continued to be. In other regions as well, substantial changes in policy became apparent during the second half of the nineteenth century. There was a set of new factors that had an impact on Russian policy toward the Muslims of the empire.

1. One problem that took on greater significance in the course of the eighteenth and nineteenth centuries was the "Land Conflict" between the Muslims and Eastern Slavs who had immigrated. There had already been disputes over arable land in the former Khanate of Kazan, but the holdings of the Tatars and other non-Russians were to some extent secured until the time when the main wave of Russian colonization passed through the middle Volga and broke on the fertile regions of the southeast. Here the Russian settlers clashed with the steppe nomads, and ceaseless conflicts broke out over the fertile northern borderlands of the steppe, which had particular importance as summer pastures for nomadic herding economy.

It was especially the Bashkirs in the southern Urals who were drawn into conflict, not only by Russian settlers but by Muslim colonists from the middle Volga; their pastureland was desired for cultivation but also as location and surroundings for the new mining centers. The Bashkirs' land was no longer secured by the regime as it had been under the Muscovite Empire, and the disputes constituted an important factor in the Bashkir uprisings that took place throughout the eighteenth century.

The Crimean Tatars had been incorporated into the Russian Empire on relatively favorable terms, but they experienced the pressure of colonization in the course of the nineteenth century, too. Great landowners and foreign colonists pressed the Crimean Tatars into the inner region of the peninsula. The Tatars' economy went into decline; many emigrated to the Ottoman Empire, and the Crimean Tatars were reduced to a minority in the area they had settled.[24]

The scenario was repeated during the nineteenth century among the Kazakh and Kirghiz nomads, when their pastureland was gradually reduced, despite repeated insurrections. At the end of the nineteenth and beginning of the twentieth centuries, conflicts became very dramatic as Eastern Slavic colonization increased vigorously toward southern Siberia and the northern Kirghiz steppes, that is, into northern Kazakhstan. Violent disputes over land broke out between settlers and nomads, reaching their peak in the great uprising of the Kazakhs and Kirghiz in 1916.[25] The conflict over land was not primarily one between Russia and Islam, but was rather part of a secular clash between expansionist agriculture and nomadic cattle-breeders. This fact is supported by the above-mentioned disputes between Muslim colonists (Tatars) and Muslim nomads (Bashkirs).

2. Old Russia had respected the Muslims and steppe nomads, with whom it had had close ties since the beginning of its history, basically as peers, albeit as heretical members of other high cultures. In addition to this respect, credit was given to the governmental organization of the Mongols and Tatars, who had dominated Russia from the thirteenth to fifteenth centuries.

From the eighteenth century onward, as mentioned, pressure on the Muslims and nomads increased, with the influence of Western ideas providing decisive impetus. With their gradual westernization, the educated Russian elite adopted an attitude of "Eurocentric superiority" toward the Asians. The Russians saw themselves more and more as bearers of culture; as the representatives of an advanced Europe that was to bring—with force, if necessary—the blessings of civilization to the barbaric Mohammedans and progressive agriculture to the primitive nomads. In addition, there was new racial prejudice, also derived from the West. The conception of Russia's "civilizing mission" in Asia was pervasive not only among reactionary nationalists, but also among radicals oriented toward European ideas of progress.[26] Such colonialist ideologies became more and more predominant during the second half of the nineteenth century, under the additional influence of international politics in the age of imperialism, and they came to affect policy toward the Muslims as well, especially in the incorporation of Central Asia into the Russian Empire.

The objective of the policies was no longer the gradual integration of the Muslims, supported by flexible methods, but segregation. Colonial rule, bearing resemblances to the British model, upheld the arrangements prevailing in local administration, social organization, culture and religion even more markedly than had the policies of Moscow. The protection of traditional relationships seemed to be the best means toward maintaining Russian rule.[27] The policy of segregation and non-interference went to such lengths that the old Muslim realms of Bukhara and Khiva remained formally independent protectorates; foreign policy considerations also played a role here.[28] The segregated Muslims were officially declared to be second-class citizens. The legal category of *inorodtsy* ("allogenous," i.e., of a separate race), created for the peoples of Siberia, was applied to the Muslims of Kazakhstan and Central Asia but not, however, to the Muslims of Transcaucasia, the Volga-Ural region and the Crimea. The status of *inorodtsy* encompassed all groups that the Russian regime considered to be so removed from the patterns of Russian social organization that they could not be integrated into them. The *inorodtsy* received a peculiar status with diminished rights, but also with privileges such as exemption from military service, as well as with special rights regarding self-government and religion.[29] Discrimination and segregation both contributed to the conservation of cultural and ethnic identity among the Muslims affected.

3. The interdependence of the Muslim policies with Russian foreign affairs was actually not a new factor, but had gained in significance during the nineteenth century. Most notable in this regard were relations with the Ottoman Empire, which had stood forth as the defender of the Muslims of the Russian Empire since the sixteenth century. The interactions between domestic and foreign policy were especially striking in the case of the Crimean Tatars, who had been vassals of the sultan prior to the Russian conquest. Their fate was at issue time and time again during the continual Russo-Turkish wars. One result was the repeated waves of Tatars emigrating to the Ottoman Empire, peaking in the years during the Crimean War and just afterward, as well as the mass migrations of Circassians into various regions of the Ottoman Empire.[30]

Foreign policy considerations were also a factor in policy toward the Muslims of Transcaucasia, in which England and France were involved, along with Iran and the Ottoman Empire. Strategic considerations, first and foremost the rivalry with England, ultimately played a great role in Russian Central Asia policy, and they also affected policy toward Muslims. The demarcation of boundaries in the south divided up an old and vast terrain populated by Muslims and cast into doubt the future relationships of the Muslims living under Russian rule with the Muslims of Persia, Afghanistan, and Chinese East Turkistan.[31]

4. In this context, traditional factors of economic influence should be mentioned once again, for they became increasingly important during the age of modernization and industrialization. In the eighteenth century there was the matter of exploitation of the mineral resources in the Bashkir lands. In the second half of the nineteenth century and the beginning of the twentieth, the picture came to be dominated by the petroleum of Baku and the forced cultivation of cotton, which was supposed to free the Russian textile industry from dependence on foreign imports. With regard to economic policy, railway construction is to be mentioned along with the advancement of cotton production that inclined toward a monoculture. The effect of these policies on the society and economy of the Muslims of Central Asia can generally be equated with the economic consequences of Western European colonialism.[32]

5. Just as during the reign of Peter the Great, Russia's new efforts toward modernization during the second half of the nineteenth century were linked with inclinations toward unification and the leveling of social classes, seeking to sweep away special privileges as obstacles in the path of progress. The Orthodox Church no longer played a primary political role, but, once again, the faith could be proselytized among the Muslims of the empire, in connection with the ideology of disseminating European civilization.

Apostasy of baptized Tatars to Islam was one reason for the new attempts at religious and cultural integration. The proselytization program called "Il'minskii" (after its promoter, Nikolai A. Il'minskii) implemented more flexible techniques than had previously been the case. Christian instruction in native-language schools was believed to further the Christianization—and ultimately the Russification—of Russia's Muslims. The new missionary program, "national in form, Orthodox in content," had certain successes, especially among the Tatars, but the inorodtsy of Central Asia and the Caucasus, as mentioned, were effectively unintegratable.[33]

6. The new attempts at integration were also connected with the rise of nationalism in the Russian Empire. Extreme nationalists actually combated Il'minskii's reforms because they considered the Russian language, rather than religion, to be the means of integration, and thus

only approved of Russian-speaking schools. Il'minskii's missionary program also conflicted with the regime's policy of segregation in Central Asia. It is clear that, once again, there could be no question of a unified and consistent policy toward the Muslims and toward nationalities in general.

Russian nationalism, taking hold of the society of the czardom more and compensation was sought in the East. The new Russian nationalism imposed pervasive restrictions on the society, journalism and pub-Muslims. Russian self-confidence suffered continual blows in the West, and compensation was sought in the east. The new Russian nationalism imposed pervasive restrictions on the society, journalism and public opinion, and had no substantial influence on Russian policy toward the Muslims. The autocratic state remained mistrustful of nationalism, as of other social movements. Until the end of the czardom, Russian nationalism did not become a guiding ideology of the state; rather, it was pre-nationalistic and supranational ideas that were decisive for the regime.[34] Nevertheless, modern Russian nationalism affected Muslims in that counterideologies and movements for reform and protest emerged in its wake.

To summarize briefly, an initial qualification must be made: this overview of Russian policy toward the Muslims of the empire has a one-sided perspective. It observes the interrelationships primarily from the perspective of the central government. Much would seem different from the perspective of the affected Muslims. This is not only true because of the above-mentioned discrepancy between theory and praxis: the Russian administration was a foreign rule of nonbelievers, brought about through conquest. This was also the case during the long spans of time when this foreign rule did not have so repressive a character; during times, at least, when Muslims did not put up resistance to it.

There can be no discussion of unified Russian policy toward the Muslims; rather, there were numerous variations and interruptions, both over time and in geography. Nevertheless, it is possible to propose the thesis that the decisive model, at least in the premodern period, that is, until the mid-nineteenth century, remained that which developed in the Middle Ages. Disparity between aggressive ideology and pragmatic policy led to intermittent deviations from the basic flexible line. Despite such verges toward a repressive policy, and despite stringent measures of force at times when subjects' loyalty was in question, the regime always returned to the pragmatic policy, for it served the priorities of economic exploitation and the maintenance of power better than did aggressive intolerance, which provoked opposition. Thus it was not without reason that an enlightened liberal like Nikolai Turgenev should observe that, "among all the parts of the world, it is only in Russia that both these religions [by which are meant Christianity and Islam] live side by side in peaceful, if not wholly free, relationships."[35]

It is more difficult to answer the question as to whether this premodern model was substantially altered from the middle of the nineteenth century onward, under the influence of new factors that have already been mentioned: the colonialist feeling of superiority, industrialization, imperialism, and nationalism. The new ideologies that took hold in broad sectors of Russian society called the traditional policy toward the Muslims into question. The autocracy, whose power had gradually eroded, had to consider this to a certain extent. Even at this point, however—such is the thesis here—ideology did not determine policy. Basically, the czar's regime adhered to the traditional pragmatic patterns in its Muslim policy as in its nationality policy generally. Only in this manner could this multiethnic empire, with its Great Russian minority, be held together. Ambivalence between aggressive ideology and pragmatic policy, as well as the thousand-year-old tradition of interaction with the Muslim world, were part of the inheritance that the new Soviet regime received from czarism.

Notes

1. *Obshchii svod po imperii rezul'tatov razrabotki dannykh pervoi vseobshchei perepisi naseleniia, proizvedennoi 28 ianvaria 1897 goda,* vol. 1 (St. Petersburg, 1905), pp. 250–51.

2. On Russian nationality policy in general, cf. Boris Nolde, *La formation de l'Empire russe. Etudes, notes et documents,* vol. 1–2 (Paris, 1952/53); Georg von Rauch, *Russland: Staatliche Einheit und nationale Vielfalt,* Föderalistische Kräfte und Ideen in der russischen Geschichte (Munich, 1953); Marc Raeff, "Patterns of Imperial Policy toward the Nationalities," in *Soviet Nationality Problems,* ed. Edward Allworth (New York, 1971), pp. 22–42; S. Frederick Starr, "Tsarist Government: The Imperial Dimension," in *Soviet Nationality Problems and Practices,* ed. Jeremy R. Azrael (New York, 1978), pp. 3–38; Andreas Kappeler, "Historische Voraussetzungen der Nationalitätenproblems im russischen Vielvölkerreich," *Geschichte und Gesellschaft* 8 (1982): 159–83.

On czarist policy toward the Muslims of Russia specifically: Alexandre Bennigsen, "The Muslims of European Russia and the Caucasus," in *Russia and Asia: Essays on the Influence of Russia on the Asian Peoples,* ed. Wayne S. Vucinich (Stanford, 1972), pp. 135–66, esp. pp. 135–52; Alexandre Bennigsen and Chantal Quelquejay, *Les mouvements nationaux chez les musulmans de Russie. Le "sultangalievisme" au Tatarstan* (Paris/La Haye, 1960), pp. 21–41; Alexandre Bennigsen and Chantal Lemercier-Quelquejay, *Les musulmans oubliés. L'islam en U.R.S.S. aujourd'hui* (Paris, 1981), pp.

9–42; Hans-Heinrich Nolte, *Religiöse Toleranz in Russland 1600–1725* (Göttingen, 1969); Edward Lazzerini, "Muslims in Russia and The Soviet Union," in *The Modern Encyclopedia of Russian and Soviet History*, ed. Joseph L. Wieczynski, vol. 24 (Gulf Breeze, Fla., 1981), pp. 4–17.

3. *Polnoe sobranie russkikh letopisei*, vol. 1: *Lavrent'evskaia letopis'*, part 1: "Povest' vremennykh let," Izd. 2-e (Leningrad, 1926), col. 85 (reprint Munich, 1977).

4. Cf. Andreas Kappeler, *Russlands erste Nationalitäten. Das Zarenreich und die Völker der Mittleren Wolga vom 16. bis 19. Jahrhundert* (Köln/Wien, 1982), pp. 23–31. Mark Batunsky has recently described the spiritual relationship between Kievan Rus and Islam as an extremely negative one, without venturing into the field of the pragmatic interrelationships: "Islam and Russian Medieval Culture," *Die Welt des Islam* 26 (1986): 1–27.

5. On this subject, most convincingly, see Charles J. Halperin, *Russia and the Golden Horde: The Mongol Impact on Medieval Russian History* (Bloomington, 1985).

6. Cf. Charles J. Halperin, "The Ideology of Silence: Prejudice and Pragmatism on the Medieval Religious Frontier," *Comparative Studies in Society and History* 26 (1984), pp. 442–66.

7. Cf. Andreas Kappeler, "Ethnische Minderheiten im alten Russland (14.–16. Jahrhundert): Regierungspolitik und Funktionen," *Forschungen zur osteuropäischen Geschichte* 38 (1986); 131–51, esp. 141–42; Kappeler, *Russlands erste Nationalitäten*, 49–55.

8. On this subject and in general for Russian policy toward the Volga Tatars during the sixteenth to nineteenth centuries, cf. Kappeler, *Russlands erste Nationalitäten*, passim.

9. Contrary intepretations in Bennigsen, "Muslims," pp. 137–41; Bennigsen and Quelquejay, *Les mouvements nationaux*, pp. 23–25; Lazzerini, "Muslims," Azade-Ayşe Rorlich, *The Volga Tatars. A Profile in national Resilience* (Stanford, 1986), pp. 37–39.

10. Cf. Nolte, *Religiöse Toleranz*, pp. 61–62; Kappeler, *Russlands erste Nationalitäten*, pp. 53–54, 213, 219, 246.

11. Cf. Kappeler, *Russlands erste Nationalitäten*, pp. 165–66, 210, 213, 217–18 (with documentation).

12. Andreas Kappeler, "Die Moskauer Nationalitätenpolitik unter Ivan IV," *Russian History* 14 (1987): 263–82.

13. *Akty, sobrannie v bibliotekakh i arkhivakh Rossiiskoi Imperii Arkheografi-cheskoiu Ekspeditsiiu Akademii Nauk,*. vol. 1, no. 241, pp. 259–60. A presentation that diverges substantially from that offered here with regard to the interpretation of the Russian missionary activity is offered by Chantal Lemercier-Quelquejay: "Les missions orthodoxes en pays musulmans de Moyenne- et Basse-Volga," *Cahiers du monde russe et soviètique* 8 (1967): 369–403, esp. pp. 371–82.

14. *Prodolzhenie Drevnei Rossiiskoi Vivliofiki*, Chast X. (St. Petersburg, 1795; repr., 1970), pp. 318–19.

15. Cf. Andreas Kappeler, "Nationalismus im russischen Vielvölkerreich?" in *Nationalismus in vorindustrieller Zeit*, ed. Otto Dann (Munich, 1986), pp. 83–99.

16. Philippe Avril, *Voyage en divers Etats d'Europe et d'Asie, entrepris pour découvrir un nouveau chemin à la Chine* (Paris, 1692), p. 156.

17. Cf. also the following: Nolte, *Religiöse Toleranz*, pp. 82–89; Lemercier, "Les missions orthodoxes," pp. 382–92; Kappeler, *Russlands erste Nationalitäten*, pp. 245–321.

18. I. T. Pososhkov, *Zaveshchanie otecheskoe* (St. Petersburg, 1893), pp. 320–28.

19. Alan W. Fisher, "Enlightened Despotism and Islam under Catherine II," *Slavic Review* 27 (1968): 542–53; Serge A. Zenkovsky, "A Century of Tatar Revival," *The American Slavic and East European Review* 12 (1953): 303–18.

20. Cf. Nolte, *Religiöse Toleranz*, vol. 1, pp. 192–273; vol. 2, pp. 115–95; Alton S. Donelly, *The Russian Conquest of Bashkiria, 1552–1740: A Case Study in Imperialism* (New Haven, 1969), pp. 139–74; Alan Fisher, *The Crimean Tatars* (Stanford, 1978), pp. 58–93; Bennigsen, "Muslims," pp. 147–51; Serge A. Zenkovsky, *Pan-Turkism and Islam in Russia* (Cambridge, Mass., 1960), pp. 56–71; Martha Brill Olcott, *The Kazakhs* (Stanford, 1987), pp. 28–53.

21. Cf. Muriel Atkin, *Russia and Iran 1780–1828* (Minneapolis, 1980); Tadeusz Swietochowski, *Russian Azerbaijan, 1905–1920. The Shaping of National Identity in a Muslim Community* (Cambridge, 1985), pp. 4–17; Firuz Kazemzadeh, "Russian Penetration of the Caucasus," in *Russian Imperialism from Ivan the Great to the Revolution,* ed. Taras Hunczak (New Brunswick, N.J., 1974), pp. 3239–63; Paul B. Henze, "Fire and Sword in the Caucasus: The Nineteenth-Century Resistance of the north Caucasian Mountaineers," *Central Asian Survey* 2, no. 1 (1983): pp. 5–44.

22. To list a few works amidst the wealth of literature: Richard A. Pierce, *Russian Central Asia, 1867–1917. A Study in Colonial Rule* (Berkeley, 1960); *Central Asia: A Century of Russian Rule,* ed. Edward Allworth (New York/London, 1967).

23. Paul B. Henze, "Circassia in the Nineteenth Century, The Futile Fight for Freedom," in *Turco-Tatar Past, Soviet Present: Studies Presented to Alexandre Bennigsen,* ed. Ch. Lemercier-Quelquejay, et al. (Paris, Louvain, 1986), pp. 243–73.

24. Fisher, *Tatars*, pp. 92–93.

25. Cf. George J. Demko, *The Russian Colonization of Kazakhstan 1896–1916* (Bloomington/The Hague, 1969); Olcott, *Kazakhs*, pp. 57–126.

26. Cf. Otto Hoetzsch, *Russland in Asien. Geschichte einer Expansion* (Stuttgart, 1966), pp. 128–36; Nicholas V. Riasanovsky, "Asia Through Russian Eyes," in *Russia and Asia,* ed. Vucinich, pp. 3–29; Dietrich Geyer, *Der russische Imperialismus. Studien über den Zusammenhang von innerer und auswärtiger Politik 1860–1914* (Gottingen, 1977), pp. 72–74; Seymour Becker, "The Muslim East in Nineteenth-Century Russian Popular Historiography," *Central Asian Survey* 5, no. 3/4 (1986): pp. 25–47.

27. For other works on Russian policy toward the Muslims of Central Asia, in addition to works cited in n. 22 see: Hélène Carrère d'Encausse, "La politique culturelle du pouvoir tsariste au Turkestan (1867–1917)," *Cahiers du monde russe et soviètique* 3 (1962): 374–407; Serge A. Zenkovsky, "Kulturkampf in Pre-Revolutionary Central Asia," *The American Slavic and East European Review* 14 (1955): 15–41.

28. Cf. Seymour Becker, *Russia's Protectorates in Central Asia: Bukhara and Khiva 1865–1924* (Cambridge, Mass., 1968).

29. There has been no investigation concerning the legal and social category of the *inorodtsy.*

30. Alan W. Fisher, "Emigration of Muslims from the Russian Empire in the Years

after the Crimean War," *Jahrbücher für Geschichte Osteuropas* 35 (1987), pp. 356–71.

31. Cf. *Soviet Asian Ethnic Frontiers,* ed. William O. McCagg, Jr., and Brian D. Silver (New York, 1979).

32. An instructive example is the discussion in Soviet historiography in which one trend stresses the economic motivation of Russian policy in Central Asia and the other, the strategic; cf. Geyer, *Imperialismus,* pp. 74–77; Lowell R. Tillett, "Russian Imperialism and Colonialism," in *Windows on the Russian Past: Essays on Soviet Historiography since Stalin,* ed. Samuel H. Baron and Nancy W. Heer (Columbus, Ohio, 1977), pp. 105–21.

33. Stephen J. Blank, "National Education, Church and State in Tsarist Nationality Policy: The Il'minskii System," *Canadian-American Slavic Studies* 17 (1983): 466–86; Isabelle Kreindler, "Nikolai Il'minskii and Language Planning in Nineteenth Century Russia," *International Journal of the Sociology of Language* 22 (1979): 5–26; Jean Saussay, "Il'minskii et la politique de russification des Tatars 1865–1891," *Cahiers du monde russe et soviètique* 8 (1967): 404–26.

34. Cf. Hans Rogger, "Nationalism and the State: A Russian Dilemma," *Comparative Studies in Society and History* 4 (1961/62): 253–64.

35. N. Tourgeneff, *La Russie et les Russes* (Paris, 1947), 2:311.

8. Soviet Policy toward Islam

Hans Bräker

Any consideration of Soviet policy regarding Islam must take into account the interdependence of foreign and domestic Soviet affairs. The analysis at hand will focus particularly on domestic issues, while recognizing that inquiry into foreign policy is essential to thorough understanding of the question of Islam. The reader should, however, keep the international context in mind.

Criteria for Framing the Problem of Islam

At the outset, there must be an explanation of the several criteria on which the investigation of the problem is to be based.

Political and Religious Aspects of Islam: Shari'a and 'Umma

The basic theological principles of Islam with regard to religion and politics cannot be overlooked.[1] These are reflected not only in the characteristics shared by Judaism and Christianity but, more significantly, in the divergent features of these three great world religions:

Islam, like Judaism and Christianity, is a monotheistic religion. Its texts and precepts proclaim a common origin with those two faiths, but it claims to embody the final and absolute truth, as revealed by God to the Prophet Muhammad, and to him alone. From an Islamic perspective, Judaism and Christianity represent earlier stages in the history of the revelation of God's truth. In this sense, these older faiths are tolerated and even offered protection. Moses and Jesus, however, are seen as prophets to whom God revealed only parts of the truth.

From the Muslim's perspective, therefore, it is only Islam that calls for the unconditional yielding of humanity to God's will, which principle is expressed in the name of the faith, which means "submission." Islam's political outlook derives from this precept: the demand for absolute and unconditional submission of the human being to God's will is expressed in the Shariʿa, which derives both from the Qurʾân—the record of God's truth as revealed to the Prophet—and from the Sunna (from Arabic, meaning "tradition"), the record of the Prophet's utterances and actions as well as of his silent approval of what was said or done in his presence (hadith).

For Muslims, the Shariʿa embodies the totality of all the norms; all "provisions and demands" of Allah. It regulates the life of every human being, down to very small details. In addition to specifying the forms of ritual and worship, the Shariʿa sets forth all political, social, and (in the narrowest sense) legal requirements for the individual. It thus reflects the whole Islamic world view; it is the most express manifestation of the Muslim way of life, in which legal/political norms and the norms of religion are inseparable. Because of this way of thinking, it may be unusually difficult—if not impossible—for the non-Muslim Western reader to find any consistently reliable system in Islamic law.

The lives of all Muslims are determined by the complex structure of the Shariʿa. To put it in other terms, Islam regards everything in life as being within the province of religion. In Islam, there is no distance from the world, nor any denial of it: Islam is as concerned with worldly things as it is with the afterlife. As a consequence, the Qurʾân and the Sunna are not just religious texts; they are also the primary—the sole—sources for law and justice. Because of the fact that, in Islam, the spiritual and earthly realms are so inextricably linked as to be identical, this faith differs fundamentally from other monotheistic world religions. Martin Luther's teachings about the realms of the earthly and the divine, for example, would be completely unimaginable in Islam.

The claim of Islam to possession of absolute truth is ultimately both root and motive force for evangelistic thinking, leading as it does to the idea that God's absolute truth must be carried out in the world by any means necessary. Jihad, the struggle (which may or may not involve war) against unbelievers, is seen as serving God, and one who participates in it may hope thereby to enter Paradise.

These Islamic precepts go far toward explaining the unprecedented expansion of Islam. The faith was initially transmitted by Arabs, whose fiery ardor spread Allah's revelation through North Africa to the Atlantic and through Persia and Central Asia to China, only some hundred years after the Prophet's death. This was the creation of the ʿUmma: the worldwide community of Muslims that, according to the Qur'ân, is the perfect community envisioned in God's plan of creation and redemption. Subsequently, it was the people of the missionary areas, especially the Turkic people of Central Asia, who added the more distant regions of the Indian subcontinent, southwestern Asia and the Balkans to the 'Umma.

Islam: The Soviet Union's Largest Foreign Religion

Framed by this general and roughly outlined background, the analysis of Soviet domestic policy toward Islam must take as its starting-point the fact that there are nearly fifty million Muslims within the borders of the Soviet Union.[2] To a great extent, these Muslims are from Turkic (Azerbaijanis, Turkmens, Uzbeks, Kirghiz, Kazaks, and others) and Iranian (particularly Tajik) groups who live in the Caucasus-Transcaucasus and Central Asia. Their territories have belonged to Russia politically since the end of the nineteenth century and to the Soviet Union beginning in 1917. Since the Soviet Union's foundation, Islam has been far and away its largest "foreign" religion.[3]

The Transregional Islamic Question

Islam's socio-political nature meant that the political integration of these Muslims into the Russian Empire would have to involve their separation from other Turko-Persian Islamic cultural regions. Because of this necessity, the Islamic Question in the Caucasus-Transcaucasus and Central Asia is one that cannot be contained within the borders of the republics involved, nor within the borders of the Soviet Union, whether along its southern borders with Turkey, Iran, and Afghanistan or along that with China. For the most part, these borders were drawn up in treaties between Russia and England, with the objective of establishing and securing their respective power interests in Central Asia. The borders created under these circumstances divide ethnic groups, clans and even families. This state of affairs is at the root of the primary problems of Islam in the Soviet Union.[4]

From these historical circumstances, it follows that the religious/Islamic consciousness of Caucasian-Transcaucasian and Central Asian people was considerably strengthened through nationalism. It was through their common confession of Islam that they became aware of their own ethnic similarities, as well as the differences between themselves and ethnic Russians and, for those who lived near the Chinese border, the Han Chinese.

As a consequence of these emergent senses of identity, the consciousness of the ʿUmma among the Muslims of the Soviet-Chinese region became more distinct. Of course, they had never doubted their place in the
ʿUmma, but they had been generally unaffected by the problems faced by
Muslims living in the original nucleus area of Islam, as, conversely, Arabic Muslims had been generally unaware of the problems of their north-
ernmost coreligionists and were little interested in them. Most crucial
for the development of Muslim society in the Caucasus-Transcaucasus
and Central Asia had been, first, their religious, ethnic, and political
bonds among themselves; then their relations with "brother" peoples
and tribes in East Turkistan (Xinjiang Province of China), Afghanistan,
and Iran; and, finally, their traditional ethnic, religious, and historical/
political relations with the Turks of modern-day Turkey.

The Problem of Sources for Assessing Moscow's Islamic Policy

For seventy years, Islam in the Soviet Union has experienced considerable political and ideological assault from the state and from the Communist Party.[5] Despite these aggressive policies, it has remained for
Moscow a dangerous, unquantified factor; during recent years, Islam has
become a substantial problem for Soviet leadership.

There are numerous difficulties involved in the assessment of Soviet
policies toward Islam. First, the only materials are central (in Russian)
and regional (Russian or Turkic) literature, the language of most of which
is official or even officious. To the extent that a position on Islam is expressed, it is in the form of critical statements that always reflect the
official Moscow line of thinking. Any investigation, therefore, must be
based on extracting the development and status of Islam in the Soviet
Union from what is said about it in this literature.

Interdisciplinary Research on Islam for the Soviet Union

From what has been said above, it should be clear that the "instrument
of Sovietology" alone will not suffice for the full investigation of the
problems of Islam and Turkic people in the USSR. The application of
Sovietological principles runs up against serious methodological blocks.
This realization should not cast doubt on the usefulness of Sovietological work. Experience until now, however, shows that this type of
research has as its main goal the formulation of principles having to do
with the theories and concrete religious and international policies of
the Soviet administration. Such works are invaluable. If they are to bear

fruit, however, there must be close collaboration with the contributions of Orientalist researchers who are concentrating on contemporary issues in Central Asia.

The Structure and Character of Islam in the Soviet Union

From a formal perspective, the profile of Islam in the Soviet Union can be compared with that of Islam in the 'Umma as a whole. In both cases about 90 percent of Muslims are Sunni and the remaining 10 percent, Shi'ite. In Soviet literature these two groups are generally grouped together and termed "official" or "institutionalized" Islam.

Just as in the case in most of the missionary or expansion regions of South Asia (the Indian subcontinent) and Southeast Asia (especially Malaysia and Indonesia), however, it was Sufism that provided the strongest impetus for the spread of Islam in Central Asia, and particularly for its enduring rootedness in the Caucasus-Transcaucasus, Turkistan, and Xinjiang. The forms of Sufism—that is to say, mystical Islam, that have had particular influence in the areas relevant to the discussion here have been the Naqshbandi order and (especially in the Caucasus) the Qadiriya Brotherhood. In accordance with its nature, Sufism can only be "grasped" with great difficulty, if at all, for it is generally not institutionalized. In Soviet terminology, it is thus described as "Parallel Islam" and, occasionally, even as "illegal" Islam.[6]

It was principally the mystic brotherhoods that brought Islam to the most remote regions of the Caucasus-Transcaucasus, Central Asia, and Xinjiang. It was these brotherhoods that put up resistance, initially to Russian expansion in these areas, then to Czarist advances with their associated Russification policies and, finally, to Moscow's policy of Sovietization after 1917.[7] This resistance repeatedly called into serious question the Russian, and then the Soviet, presence in these regions. This is the origin of what can now be described as the Soviet "trauma of Islam."

The distinctive feature of Islam in the Soviet Union has thus never been its breakdown into "confessions," as has been the case in the Arabic-speaking part of the 'Umma, but rather the collective struggle of all its subgroups against the unbeliever, the *kafir*. Sufism here has always provided the dynamism for this struggle, as it does today. This trait is unique to Islam in the Soviet Union.

Securing Possession of Central Asia; Islamic Resistance

From the Soviet perspective, there were two politically active, or even militant, groups that were primary sources of Islamic resistance to Moscow's systematic Sovietization program in Central Asia and in the Caucasus-Transcaucasus, as had been the case for resistance against the czarist Russification program prior to 1917. The Special Deputy for Semirechiye Affairs, Georgi Safarov, speaking at the Tenth Congress of the RKP(b), characterized these two groups as the "conservatives," or "traditionalists," as opposed to the "progressive" or "modernist" camp.[8]

According to Safarov, the "conservatives" not only denied every nationality; they regarded themselves as a Muslim "nation" that subsumed every other nationality. As such, they identified themselves as an integral part of the worldwide 'Umma. The "progressives," in contrast, propounded a chauvinistic Muslim nationalism; one that they believed could even gain a foothold within the Communist Party. The objective of these progressives, from the Soviet perspective (and here there must be a perception of threat to the emerging state), was the creation of an independent national-Communist state in Central Asia that would be a seed and a center for an International of Colonial Peoples. As such, it would not focus on the Muslim 'Umma, but it would also have very few, if any, ties to Moscow and the Communist International.

Because of the dangers they posed for the realization of the "Federation of the USSR," proclaimed by Lenin in December 1922, both of these Islamic movements were vigorously combatted.[9] By the beginning of the 1930s, they were more or less defeated, and their leaders were cut off from their constituencies. The clerical representatives of the "conservatives" were sent into exile; in 1941–42, however, many of them had to be returned, in connection with the shift in Soviet Islamic policy.[10] The leaders of the "faction" that Safarov had termed "progressive" were eliminated, or even killed. One notable defender of the idea of national Communism, the "atheist Muslim" Mirsaid Sultangaliev, disappeared from the political scene and then was executed during the purges of the 1930s.[11]

As Safarov's comments demonstrate, directly after the October 1917 Revolution, Soviet leaders began to recognize the direct link between the issues of nationalities and the question of Islam: they saw clearly the great dangers posed by the resistance of both Islamic "factions" to their policies. For Moscow, however, the securing of the territories of the Caucasus-Transcaucasus and Central Asia that the czarist regime had annexed was a top priority. The status of these territories seemed particularly threatened by centrifugal political efforts like those of Sultan-galiev.

Fears of this type are indirectly reflected in the "Message to Working Muslims in Russia and the Orient," signed by V. I. Lenin and Joseph V. Stalin and published in December 1917.[12] A passage from this document states:

> Muslims of Russia, Tatars of the Volga region and the Crimea, Kir-ghiz and Sarts of Siberia and Turkistan, Turks and Tatars of Trans-caucasia, Chechen and mountain people of the Caucasus! You whose mosques and houses of worship have been destroyed; whose be-liefs and customs have been trampled by the czars and the Russian oppressors! From this time onward, your creed and customs, your national and cultural institutions are declared free and unassailable. Go on with your national life free and unhindered. It is your right. Know that your rights, like the rights of all peoples of Russia, will be protected with the full power of the Revolution and its agencies, the councils of worker, soldier and farmer deputies. . . .[13]

Orientation of Soviet Islamic Policy toward the Russian Orthodox Church

The question of Islam was initially considered to be a religious prob-lem of minor domestic concern for the Soviet leadership. Moscow's primary—if not its only—ideological and religio-political concern was the Russian Orthodox Church. This was an institution of considerable political importance up to the October 1917 Revolution on account of the Church's extensive identification with the state as well as the deep roots of Christianity among the Russian population.

The importance of this reciprocal relationship for the new Soviet leadership can only be judged in connection with its historical dimen-sion, particularly the equation of "Orthodox" with "Russian."[14] This identity was originally a deep and powerful impulse arising from medi-eval Russian self-assertion against Asiatic and Mongolian conquerors. After the fall of Constantinople, the center of the Eastern Church— the "Second Rome"—in 1453 to the Muslim Turks, the court clergy as well as to the princes of Moscow began to proclaim that the Russian people and its rulers were the sole and divinely ordained guardians of the true faith and Moscow, "the Third Eternal Rome," was the one center of Christianity. Prophesies in the Bible, as in Matthew 21:43 in which it is promised that "God's realm will be taken from you and given to a nation producing the fruits of it," could so be transformed from a transcendental call for penitence into a domestic political statement and could be a basis of the claim to universality by the Moscow czar and his patriarchs.

The cult of the "Orthodox Third Rome" surrounded the growing Moscow Empire with a glory only to be compared to the empire cult of oriental cultures. With this state "ideology" it was no doubt a question of the deepest inner penetration of a total Christian sense of responsibility as well as the desire for global domination. These factors help to explain the identification of the Russian Orthodox Church with the state's colonial expansionist aspirations, in particular the annexation by the Russian state of such "heathen" areas as Central Asia. This far-reaching identification of state and Russian Orthodox Church, or rather state and Holy Empire, was what promoted, on the one hand, a strictly hierarchical institutionalization inside the Orthodoxy and, on the other, simultaneously bound it very tightly to the state.

Therefore, if any spiritual force stood in the way of the execution of the Marxist-Leninist-atheist system after 1917, it had to be the Russian Orthodox Church. By contrast, Islam as well as the other "foreign" religions in the Soviet Union, such as Buddhism, for example,[15] were viewed to some extent as "quantités negligeables." The Moscow leadership consequently aligned the constitution and codification of its policies on religion in accordance with the institution of the Russian Orthodox Church, as well as the theology and the spiritual manifestations of Eastern, or Orthodox, Christianity. The result was a religious policy that operated on two levels. The first was the state's religious legislation, whose foundation was the decree of 23 January 1918, "On the separation of church from state and of school from church," directed principally toward divesting the Orthodox church's institutional influence.[16]

The express goal of the Communist Party's aggressive atheist policies, on the other hand, was—and still is—the "extinction of religious consciousness." This religious policy, oriented toward the Russian Orthodox Church, was the sole basis of the policy of the Soviet state and Party leadership toward Islam as well, and has remained so until today.[17] It was therefore doomed to pass by Islam: to miss its stated goals and fail to achieve its objective, or even to be counterproductive. The reason for the inevitability of the policy's failure was this: in contrast to other monotheistic religions, Islam, even in the Soviet Union, never developed institutionalized "church" structures of importance approaching those of the Orthodox Church. The Prophet Muhammad had founded a religion which remained without almost any framework, so that questions about clerical hierarchy and jurisdiction had never played a central role in Islam. Islam had never mandated institutionalized congregations or religious communities, nor church offices; the presence of mosques as places of worship was never indispensable for the practice of Islam.

The actual binding force for Muslims has always been not a "church" institution or organization, but rather a community of believers: the ʿUmma. And the only framework regulating the life of this community—the relationships between its individuals as well as those with non-Islamic communities (to "nonbelievers")—are the Qurʾân and the Sunna. The Qurʾân demands believers' commitment to just five practical commandments, known as "pillars." The first, the article of faith, is summed up in one sentence, the *shahadda:* "There is no god but Allah, and Muhammad is His messenger." The second commandment is the profession of this creed, among other recitations, five times daily in prayer (*salat*); the third commandment is the giving of alms (*zakat*); the fourth is the fast of Ramadan (*sawm*); and the last is pilgrimage to Mecca (*hajj*).

As a consequence, the Communist Party's policy of promoting atheism had more difficult problems to overcome than the state's religious legislation could solve. There were no clear criteria to determine the policy's success, prospects for which consequently became linked to the perception that the "extinction of religious consciousness" was not to be obtained through legislation but rather, if at all, through a very long process involving some higher "quality."

The Stages of Soviet Policies Regarding Islam

The details of Soviet policies concerning religion in the Caucasus-Transcaucasus and in Central Asia must be considered and evaluated against a background only the salient features of which have been depicted here. These policies were implemented in three stages: the first, from the October 1917 Revolution until approximately 1928; the second, from that time until about 1942, and the third continuing on until today. The developments in these phases will be outlined here, prior to a description of the effect on Islam of Moscow's policies and Islam's reaction.

Integration of the Canonical Right and Transfer
of Religious Establishments to State Control

In this initial stage, in the midst of general legislation on religion, all important laws—still in effect—were adopted that shaped policy regarding Islam. However, their implementation turned out to be impossible under the conditions existing in the Caucasus-Transcaucasus and Central Asia at this time. This may be illustrated here with two important examples: first, the "integration" of canonical law into the new Soviet laws and, second, the nationalization of the "religious foundations"—the *waqf* properties.

As early as 1918, Soviet legal interpretation, or rather legal order—to the extent that it had taken a concrete form at that time—was declared binding, as was Soviet jurisdiction over all Islamic regions within the RSFSR's domain. Theoretically, this remedy was tantamount to the elimination of Islamic canonical law: the Shari'a itself and the Shari'a courts, which amounted to the elimination of the administration of justice through the Islamic canonical law. In 1922, however, the Shari'a courts had to be permitted once again; their immediate elimination was found, in practice, to be impossible. In 1923, however, a "Society of Shari'a Courts" was founded, with the goal of finding the "correct interpretation" of canonical law in terms of Marxist-Leninist legal norms. Appropriately enough, the Society was under Soviet leadership.

When even this mechanism for "integration" proved fruitless, the Shari'a Courts were deprived of a financial base.[18] In this case—the second example for the central topic here—it was a question of nationalizing the religious foundations supported by land, also known as *waqf* property. Even in Russia, *waqf* properties provided financial support not only for the Shari'a Courts but also for mosques and religious schools (*madrasas*), as well as for numerous other public welfare and cultural facilities in Islamic communities.

Waqf property had been nationalized in 1918, and the availability of spiritual establishments was eliminated. In the middle of 1922, this remedy was not actually juristically countermanded, but it was de facto overlooked, primarily because the existence of the religious schools had been deprived of its foundation. The state could not abolish the religious schools, however, as long as there were no secular schools to replace them. For this reason, permission was granted for the foundation of Muslim "Educational Societies," which received the right to maintain *waqf* estates. From the beginning there was absolutely no doubt that this was only a temporary concession to Islam. In 1928—the end of the phase of "New Economic Policy" (NEP)—the Moscow government considered the problem solved, and the nationalization of *waqf* estates automatically went into effect.[19]

The remedies described above show that the relatively "soft treatment" in the legislative implementation of Islamic policies from im-

mediately after the October 1917 Revolution until 1927–28 was motivated solely by pragmatic considerations. The implementation, like the
creation of the NEP itself, was only intended to accommodate the political necessities for consolidating Soviet control during the first phase
after October 1917.

Such remedies, however, although they might temporarily infringe on
Islamic institutions, could not challenge their existence substantially
and in the long term. Leaders in Moscow were either unaware of this fact
or simply ignored it. They did not see—to return to the problem of *waqf*
property—that the *zakat* (voluntary payment of a certain percentage of
one's income as decreed by the Qur'ân) was another important source
of stability for Islamic communities in the Caucasus-Transcaucasus and
Central Asia, as it was throughout the Muslim 'Umma. In most Islamic
states founded after the end of the colonial period, such as Pakistan,
the tax laws were structured taking *zakat* requisitions into consideration. For Muslim minorities in non-Muslim countries, this payment
was often the only means for financing the numerous duties imposed on
the believer by the Qur'ân, Sunna and Shari'a. Soviet publications of the
1930s reflect Moscow's considerable uneasiness toward this "nuisance"
payment, because it circumvented practically all state control.

Religious Criticism, Atheistic Propaganda

The matter of atheistic policies of the Communist Party was ultimately
no different. In contrast to the legislative approach toward Islam, the
Party had consistently advocated atheism since the October 1917 Revolution, without yielding to considerations of what was realistically possible. This promotion of atheism, however, took on its aggressive character only with the beginning of Stalin's dictatorship, which marks the
beginning of the second stage in the Soviet Union's policy regarding
Islam. To an extent, the promotion of atheism became integrated into
legislation of the uncompromising policy toward Islam that was pursued
after 1928.

It is impossible, in this short chapter, to go into the details of this
policy. It is more important to look for the consequences it had on the
Islamic peoples in the Soviet Union and on the practice of their beliefs.
One of its most important consequences can be seen in the Soviet Muslims' "retreat" from the upkeep of their traditions, their rituals and their
habits; in their practice nothing has changed up to this day.

The party and state leadership thought it recognized in this—as a
result of their politics of "extinction of religious consciousness"—defi-

nite indications of a gradual dampening of the population's devotion to Islam, which they had initially categorized as a "remnant of religious consciousness" and then as merely an expression of folk beliefs.

Whether this corresponded to the true assessment of the situation in the Caucasus-Transcaucasus and in Central Asia, or whether it reflects an opportunistic evaluation of Moscow's policy on Islam, can be left here unanswered. In any case, Russian leaders persecuted and even physically abused the Muslims for their adherence to their traditions and for their preservation of their customs; ultimately, however, they had to tolerate the Muslims' beliefs, however grudgingly.

What these leaders evidently failed to recognize was that these beliefs and social patterns were not an expression of folk beliefs, but rather one of the adherence to religious standards that apply unconditionally to all Muslims in the 'Umma. For example, until recently it was continually determined that almost all Muslims were circumcizing their sons, that the celebration of Ramadan was being observed, that weddings by Islamic ritual were common, and that burials in Muslim cemeteries were, as always, more a rule than an exception. Leaders in Moscow, most significantly, did not realize that these religious practices were acquiring particular religious and political significance for the Muslims living in an atheist environment.

Only in the late 1960s did warnings appear against a rigidly Marxist-Leninist interpretation of Islamic practices as "relics." For example, in 1966 a prominent orientalist and Islamicist felt compelled to point out: "Investigations of the degree of religious conviction among the population show that the percentage of believers in the republics in the Soviet East is considerably higher than those in other Soviet republics." Soviet experts finally had to admit that they possessed "only insufficient knowledge of the number of modern Muslim followers, of their spiritual world, of their psyche," and that they had thus far treated "the particular characteristics of Islam's ideology"—if at all—with irresponsible dilettantism. In short, they paid "as little attention to Islam . . . as to some insignificant sect."[20]

In April 1978, the same Soviet Islamicist criticized the Islamic faith: no "modernization," apparently, could "change the reactionary, inhuman nature . . . of the Islamic religion." He stated, further, that through the practice "of traditions, customs and rituals" Islam led "to separation and isolation . . . ; to the reinforcement of national isolation, and to obstruction of progress in building friendship among the Soviet peoples."[21]

Pragmatic Modification of Islamic Policies

During the first year of the war against Germany, at the latest, leaders in Moscow must have realized that the ideological determinism of the Marxist-Leninist doctrine on religion and nationality would hinder any realistic estimation of Islam's religio-political content and the recognition of the nature of the Islam and nationality problems in the Soviet Union.

With the establishment of the "Spiritual Council of Muslims" in 1941–42 in Tashkent, Baku, Buinaksk, and Ufa, already mentioned in another connection, the third stage of Moscow's policy on Islam began. In this stage, all hands in the Islamic republics were to be mobilized in the struggle against the Third Reich in this critical stage of World War II. At this stage, however, there are also distinct indications of errors and omissions in Moscow's Islam policy as well as certain limited concessions toward Islam.

Moscow felt itself forced to accommodate the true situation in the Caucasian-Transcaucasian and Central Asian republics. But, at the same time, it turned out that Soviet leadership was determined to treat the newly created Spiritual Councils as instruments of its revised Islam policy and to tolerate them only as such. The councils were to be instruments that would carry out a policy of pragmatic, limited and, above all, regulated tolerance toward Islam. This objective of regulation became particularly evident with the establishment of a central "Committee for Religious Matters of the Ministry of the USSR" as the highest supervisory organization.

This plan did not work out. For one thing the development of Islam started by this policy proved to be irreversible after the end of the war; a return to the prewar policies was no longer possible. In addition, the spiritual leaders who were allowed to return from banishment or exile to head the four Spiritual Councils did not behave according to the expectations of state and Party leaders: they did not become obsequious instruments for carrying out their policy toward Islam.[22]

As a result, the next step taken by Soviet leadership was consistent with Soviet religious doctrine and with the Islam policy that was based on that doctrine. The atheistic policy was significantly intensified to achieve "the permanent extinction of the vestiges of religious consciousness," the expression always used in bureaucratic language. This policy was supplemented and strengthened by massive social, educational, and economic development measures in the Islamic republics. These measures were aimed at the permanent and irreversible integration of the

Islamic ethnic groups from the Caucasus-Transcaucasus and Central Asia into Soviet society and into the Marxist-Leninist system.

Through the 1970s, Soviet leadership actually appeared to be convinced that its policy on Islam had made decisive progress toward the integration of the peoples of the Caucasus-Transcaucasus and Central Asia. They were able to point to the positive results of their extensive economic development program in the region. This program had enabled the populations of both regions, which at the time of the October 1917 Revolution were still isolated and economically backward, to make a great leap into modernity after the end of World War II. The population, 95 percent of whom were illiterate during the time of the czars, had attained a substantial level of education, primarily because of a comprehensive system of education. Of course, there was a large and growing economic gap between these two regions and the republics to the north and west. Nevertheless, the average standard of living in the Islamic republics in the Soviet Union is comparatively higher than in neighboring Turkey, Iran, and Afghanistan.

In addition, leaders in Moscow had felt certain that its "power infrastructure" in these areas was gaining in stability. For many years, every non-Russian leader had been subordinate to a Russian. Soviet leaders could also point out that the deviations of Turkic peoples or Muslims from the organized Soviet world not only did not exist and that one could even discern a positive attitude toward the politics of the Soviet state and party leadership in all statements by higher Muslim clergy in the USSR.

The central government's perception of stability, however, derived from the fact that dissidence tended to be invisible. Until recently, signs of anti-Soviet movements that had nationality or Islam as their rallying-points were no more detectable than expressions of displeasure by Soviet Muslims whose views were shared by dissident groups in any other part of the Soviet Union.

Islamic Revival: A New Dimension of Confrontation

Soviet leaders failed to recognize, or to acknowledge, that, disguised by the "retreat" of Islam to its traditions (as discussed above), a new, forward-looking form of Islam had grown up almost imperceptibly. This form of Islam might be called "modernized," but not in the sense applied by the Muslim ʿUmma to one particular branch of the "Islamic Revival Movement."[23] Rather, this "modern" and distinctly Soviet development consisted of the pragmatic and highly flexible adaptation on the part of the predominantly Muslim republics to the rigid conditions imposed by the central Soviet administration.

By mid-1978 Moscow leaders were confronted by a completely new Islamic situation in the Caucasus-Transcaucasus and Central Asia. They were forced to acknowledge that their expectations, which had been based on educational and economic reforms, had been erroneous. Their development policies had indeed led to a noticeable improvement of the level of growth and education of the Muslims, but the result had been a heightened consciousness of distinction among the Muslims of the Caucasus-Transcaucasus and Central Asia rather than their integration into Soviet society.

Moscow found itself confronted by a completely new self-assessment of the so-called "official Islam" ("institutionalized Islam"): it did not declare absolute antagonism to Soviet ideology as in the 1920s and the 1930s; instead it attributed the teachings of socialism, not to Marx, Engels, and Lenin, but to the Prophet Muhammad. This new expression of Islam no longer questioned the Soviet system as such; but instead of acknowledging the bases of Communist ideology in the writings of Marx, Engels, and Lenin, it proclaimed that these same ideas derived from the will of Allah as revealed to the Prophet Muhammad. In this way of thinking, Karl Marx, with his great knowledge of history, was said also to have been inspired by the Qur'ân. "I admire the genius of the Prophet," asserted a participant at a conference of Muslims in Tashkent in September 1970, "who announced the principles of Socialism. I am happy that a large number of the socialist principles are nothing other than the realization of the Revelation bestowed on Muhammad."

Growing Self-Confidence

The consequences of this Islamic revival will be presented here in terms of three important areas. They are interdependent and therefore difficult to distinguish.

The first topic has been alluded to in the quotation above: the espousal of "socialist-Islamic" principles indicates the intention to detach socialism from its materialistic nineteenth-century origins and to attribute it to much older ones: to Islam itself. The goal of this or other comparable arguments is not difficult to recognize: Islam should be freed of the "taint" with which it was imbued by religious criticism and atheist propaganda: the claim that it is obsolete, antisocial, and therefore hinders the progress of humanity. As an example, the periodical *Muslims of the Soviet East* includes a statement to the effect that the conceptual roots of true democracy can be found in the Qur'ân.[24] Elsewhere it is argued that everything said today about friendship and brotherhood was advocated by Muhammad.[25]

Attitudes like these demonstrate the importance, for clergy and Muslim intellectuals, of presenting Islam as a creative as well as a flexible belief system. They try to characterize it as a religion that has always promoted social and cultural progress, rather than hindering it. This noteworthy argument amounts to the revival of the thesis that Islam and Communism are definitely reconcilable. This approach shaped the fundamental and trendsetting article, "Islam," in the first edition of the Bol'shaia Sovetskaia Entsiklopediia, presenting an interpretation of the Qur'ân and Sunna that is both creative and diplomatically skilled, all the more because the article is not from a Muslim but a Soviet pen.[26]

Another aspect of the Islamic revival is the increasing sense among Muslim Turkic people that their culture is distinct from Russian/European culture. This emerging cultural identity rests on the awareness of a great past with unique traditions. There has been a rediscovery of the history of the Turkic and Iranian people in this area, whose greatness is said to have been reached through the dynamic force of Islam. In this new view, the inheritors of this cultural tradition have the potential for making a significant impact on the future development of the domains of the 'Umma, but also on the cultures outside it in Asia and Europe.

Furthermore, this new self-definition includes the proposal that there is a continuous, highly refined, and living literary tradition that has transmitted the history and achievements of the Turkic and Iranian people in the Caucasus-Transcaucasus and Central Asia. There is also an awareness that Bukhara and Samarkand, as well as Shahrisabz, Khiva, Khokand, and Termez, were among the major scientific, cultural, and political centers of Central Asia, and of the world, from the eighth and ninth centuries. There is a growing conviction that Uzbeks, Kazaks, Kirghiz, Turkmens, Bashkirs, and Tajiks are the inheritors of a culture that gave the world such great men as al-Ferghani, al-Termezi, al-Biruni, Avicenna (Ibn Sina), al-Farabi, al-Bukhari, and al-Khwarazmi, to name only a few important theologians, poets, doctors, and scientists. As Muslims of the Soviet East repeatedly points out, the teachings of these thinkers still hold wisdom for today.[27]

This re-evaluation of the history and tradition of Turkic people also contains a plea for acceptance within the 'Umma. This desire becomes apparent in the introductory speech of the Tashkent Spiritual Council's chairman, Mufti Ziyauddin Babakhan, in September 1979 at the opening of a preliminary symposium in the festivities for the beginning of the fifteenth century A.H. (in 1980 A.D.). "In our country the system has changed, the social relations have been changed, a new type of state and a new social order have come about," explained Babakhan, "but the Muslim faith continues and flourishes, and, what is more, its prestige is growing. . . . The Muslims of the Soviet East [are] an inseparable part of the 'Umma, . . . all Muslims are one body . . . when a part of it suffers from a disease, the pain can be felt throughout the body."[28]

The third area to be discussed here follows from the issues just described. It concerns the growing political self-assurance of the Islamic Turkic people. This confidence is based on the conviction that their unique history is not confined to the past; it was not even cut off in the Soviet period, but continues through the present. Because the generations of previous centuries were capable of making important contributions to Islamic thought—in both science and culture—it must follow that present and future generations will be capable of accomplishments that will advance the whole Islamic world.

Part of what reinforces this attitude is the fact that Soviet leaders, in keeping with their policies for the developing world, consider the Muslims of the Caucasus-Transcaucasus and Central Asia to have superior technical knowledge and abilities—compared to other countries in the Near and Middle East—that makes them particularly useful emissaries to other Islamic countries.[29] The Muslims use this interesting interpretation as a basis for their own mission in developing countries; that mission, however, is still largely determined by Moscow's foreign policy objectives.

This concept points to a prevalent belief among the Islamic peoples in the Soviet Union: that they are the most highly qualified Muslims in the Islamic world. As a consequence, they see themselves as responsible for assisting the rest of the 'Umma by sharing their technical and professional knowledge, so that their co-religionists may reach a similar level of competence. Far from damaging their faith, this conviction has confirmed and deepened Muslim identity. To be at all successful in its foreign policy, Moscow must not only tolerate their activities in the Islamic countries as "Muslim ambassadors" of an advanced technology, but must even encourage them. This is another positively "schizophrenic" result of Moscow's Islam policy in the Caucasus and in Central Asia, which had set out "to extinguish religious consciousness." Ironically, the policy appears to have had the opposite result.

Moscow's Reaction to Islamic "Modernization"

Moscow's reaction to the results of Islam's efforts to modernize itself, to remove its image of backwardness and remoteness from life, is instructive. It may be illustrated here with some examples of official opinions toward nationality problems and journalistic pronouncements on the "modernization efforts" within Islam.

The theses of the Central Committee of the CPSU for the fiftieth anniversary of the founding of the USSR in December 1972 reveal a certain disillusionment with the concrete development in the Islamic republics.[30] In the beginning of the theses it was stated that differences and conflicts among the peoples in the Soviet Union had disappeared and in their place the "Soviet race" had arisen, characterized by the "Soviet patriotism" of the "Soviet individual." Further on, however, the theses called for the "unconditional struggle against tendencies of nationalistic demarcation and exclusion; against glorification of the past and the suppression of class struggle in the history of the races; against customs and habits that hinder the Communist agenda."

In his report to the Twenty-sixth Party Congress in February 1981, Leonid I. Brezhnev stated once again that relations among the nationalities—over one-hundred—in the Soviet Union were "brotherly and friendly" and explained that there were "today . . . no longer any backward ethnical border regions."[31] On the other hand, he also expressed sharp criticism of "chauvinism, nationalism and nationalistic deviation" and said it was the Party's "sacrosanct duty" to "educate the people in the spirit of Soviet patriotism and of Soviet internationalism, to further a spirit of pride in belonging to the Soviet Union."

Fifteen months later, however, in December 1982, Yuri V. Andropov sounded different notes in a speech on the sixtieth anniversary of the founding of the USSR.[32] Like Mr. Brezhnev, he stated that the nationality problems inherited from the presocialist age had been resolved "successfully, permanently and irrevocably" through Soviet rule and that "a new historical community" had been created. And he, too, discussed this subject in terms of "negative manifestations," "national arrogance or presumption," and "disrespect for other nations and peoples."

However, in contrast to First Secretary Brezhnev, he added the statement that "it would be wrong to consider [these manifestations] as being only vestiges of the past." Mr. Andropov differed from all his predecessors in that he ultimately framed his evaluation of the nationality problem in historical-philosophical terms: "Life shows," he determined, "that the economic and cultural progress of all nations and peoples is accompanied by the growth of their national self-consciousness. This is a orderly and objective process."

It seems that First Secretary Andropov's remarks on the nationality question in the USSR were alluding to the unresolved problems of nationality and Islam in the Caucasus-Transcaucasus and Central Asia. The potentially explosive power of Islam in the Soviet Union derives from the ethnic identity of the Turkic and Iranian peoples in the Caucasus-Transcaucasus and Central Asia as well as from their religious convictions. Islam's "revival" after World War II can be traced in large degree to Moscow's ignorance of the strength of these identities.

Credit is due to Mr. Andropov, however, to the extent that he, in contrast to all his predecessors, gestured toward the actual situation in his remarks and pointed out—if only indirectly—mistakes of the Party and state leadership in carrying out nationality policies. The attempt to diffuse this reality with the disarming assertion that the "growing national consciousness" of the ethnic groups was a totally normal occurrence in the history of all races displays the inability of the Soviet leadership to deal with immediate political problems.

First Secretary Mikhail Gorbachev's speech on 22 November 1986 was unequivocal in its statements that Soviet leadership would make no concessions in issues of religion and nationality, at least as far as the Islamic ethnic groups were concerned. In his speech he called for "a decisive and unconditional struggle against religious manifestations; a strengthening of the political enlightenment of the masses and of the atheist propaganda" and went on to explain that "even the smallest discrepancy between word and action is unacceptable." He was directing his words not only toward the assembled Party functionaries but also, implicitly, toward the "ideologists of Islam," who were not present. It was definitely no coincidence that this unusually hard-line speech was delivered in Tashkent.[33]

Until the late 1970s, publications in the Soviet Union were oriented toward "revealing" the "true meaning of modern Islam." They sought to prove the absurdity of the notion of a direct link between Islam and the national identity of the Turkic peoples; it was to be regarded as a creation of fantasy. Soviet leaders had always denounced such assertions as that linking Islam and national identity as one of Islam's weaknesses, stating that Muslim spiritual leaders were deluded in their efforts to convince believers that Central Asians had contributed to the progress of Islamic civilization. In addition, the Soviet line asserted, it was absurd for "religious propaganda" to claim that outstanding Central Asians had made the development of Islam into a national religion.

Arguments like these indicate resignation, frustration, and even helplessness. These attitudes may not be immediately apparent, but the fact that they underlie official rhetoric foreshadows the gradual realization that Islam retained extraordinary vitality, counter to all official expectations and prognoses. It became evident that Islam had managed to survive and even to thrive, without losing hold on its basic tenets, by adapting to Soviet conditions. It would seem that, today, the fabric of Soviet policy on Islam is completely in tatters, as a result of the ideological inertia that has prevailed in other dimensions of the discussion of spiritual and political phenomena. In this regard, it is worth noting that the period of the shift in the Soviet evaluation of Islam's efforts to "modernize" itself roughly parallels that of the events in Iran and Afghanistan: the late 1970s and early 1980s.

A. Akhmedov's book *Sotsial'naia doktrina Islama* (1982) is one example of this evident shift in outlook in Soviet literature.[34] It is particularly Akhmedov's discussion of the issue of "modernization" in Islam that indicates this new orientation,[35] which will no doubt play an increasing role in the years to come.[36]

In contrast to earlier literature, Akhmedov's work no longer disparages the "modernization of Islam" as a "tactical move" of the Islamic clergy that will merely postpone the permanent "bankruptcy" of Islam. Rather, he credits the Muslims with appropriating the ideals of scientific socialism—after a long learning process—because they recognized their own ideals in them. According to Akhmedov, the Muslims have finally realized that, in spite of the distance they keep from ISTOMAT (Historical Materialism) and DIAMAT (Dialectical Materialism), they have always been part of the efforts of the Soviet citizens to complete the great social, national, and human tasks at hand in the Soviet Union. In the Caucasus-Transcaucasus and Central Asia, he states, this recognition has also kindled the "modernization" process, which is no longer just a matter of updating Muslims' social and ethnic values, but now affects all areas of Islamic doctrines and practices.

It is also important to note that Akhmedov's words in no way imply that, with the "adoption" of the "ideals" of Soviet socialism, Soviet Muslims are giving up their Islamic values and thus their Islamic identity. Nor does he claim that the Muslims are about to integrate themselves into Soviet society, whose ultimate goal is the creation of a *homo sovieticus*.

Implications of Policy on Islam for Foreign Affairs

Since foreign policy considerations have not been treated in this analysis, it is difficult to judge whether or not arguments like Akhmedov's suggest the beginnings of a new orientation in Moscow's attitude toward

Islam in the Soviet Union. A set of assumptions with regard to this topic were indicated at the beginning of this work, but there are two other circumstances that need to be added.[37] First, Islam in the Soviet Union knows no national boundaries; second, aggressive czarist policies in the Soviet East have been perpetuated in Soviet Middle Eastern policy since 1917.

One basis for these policies was the czarist military advance, initially in the Transcaucasian region (up until the mid-nineteenth century) and then, until the end of the nineteenth century into Central Asia; that is, to the current border of the Soviet Union with Afghanistan and Iran. Another basis was the so-called Convention of St. Petersburg (1907), during which Persia/Iran was split up into zones of influence by Russia and England.

Founded on these factors, Soviet policies on the Middle East have been carried out in four stages. The first was that of "Friendship Treaties," concluded with Persia (26 February 1921), Afghanistan (28 February 1921) and Turkey (16 March 1921). These treaties secured all the territories that Russia held in Central Asia prior to the events of 1917. All these agreements were drawn up in virtually the same way, with the exception of that with Persia. This treaty included two appended articles (the fifth and sixth), to the effect that the Soviet Union would have the right to intervene in case of any threat to Persia from a third power. Since the drawing up of this treaty, it has been absolutely clear that Persia/Iran is the focal point of Soviet policy in the Middle East. Incidentally, both of these articles were renounced unilaterally on 10 November 1979 by Ayatollah Ruhullah al-Musavi Khumayni (Khomeini) and by then-president Abu'l-Hasan Bani-Sadr.[38] In the second phase of the development of Soviet policy on the Middle East, these "Friendship Treaties" were expanded, as early as the late 1920s and early 1930s, to become pacts of neutrality and nonaggression, and, in the case of Persia, a commercial treaty. (The agreement with Turkey, however, dissolved when that country refused to renew its treaty of friendship with its northern neighbor.) After World War II, particularly in the 1960s and early 1970s, the Soviet Union was able further to strengthen its relations with Iran and Afghanistan through a diverse system of economic development and military agreements, marking the third stage of policy-making.

In the fourth phase, beginning in the early 1970s, the Soviet Union further extended and consolidated its influence and economic-political status in the Near and Middle East through "flanking" treaties of friendship and cooperation with Egypt (May 1971; annulled by Egypt in March

1976), India (August 1971), with Iraq (April 1972), Afghanistan (December 1978—a modification and extension of the treaty of 1921 by pledge of assistance in emergencies) and with Syria (October 1980).

This process of development emphasizes the fact that Soviet policy regarding the Middle East has been determined by objectives involving power politics, in addition to economic ones. It also indicates that the ideological viewpoints that are formulated in foreign policy doctrine (for instance, Revolutionary, Development, and Alliance Theory), played at most a superficial role, in the conception of this policy. And, finally, it follows that such ideological catchwords as "state of national democracy," "state of noncapitalistic orientation," or "state of socialistic orientation" are, at best, applicable as indices of internal developments in the so-called developing countries.

This short overview demonstrates, finally, that the issue of Islam was not a criterion for Soviet leadership in the conceptual planning or execution of Near and Middle East policy. Moscow either failed to recognize, disregarded or consciously ignored the crucial significance of Islam for policy, until the Communist overthrow of Nur Muhammad Taraki in Afghanistan in April 1978 and the ensuing resistance against the Kabul regime by the Mujaheddin, based in Iran and Pakistan, and, finally, until the overthrow of Iran's Pahlavi Shah regime.

Even months after the Islamic revolutionary upheaval in Iran, Soviet leadership described these events in terms of their "democratic and anti-imperialistic character," referring to them in terms of "an action in which industrial workers, other laborers from the city and country, the national bourgeoisie, intellectuals, the youth, a considerable portion of the state machinery and several religious figures" were participating. In addition, shortly before the Soviet invasion of Afghanistan, Moscow's leaders officially determined that although the "opposition movement led by Ayatollah Khomeini" was "superficially" religious, it was an essentially socio-political manifestation.

Such disregard for both the religious and the political ramifications of Islam in Near and Middle East policy was deleterious to Soviet policy, exclusively based as it was on considerations of power politics and economics, in the region as a whole. After being built up with great intellectual and material effort following the October 1917 Revolution and systematically extended after World War II with a series of treaties, these policies were effectively neutralized, if not paralyzed. Soviet foreign policy activities were greatly hindered and may even have proven counterproductive.

If the Soviet Union had wanted to avoid further weakening of its position, it should have thoroughly reconsidered this system of treaties and re-initiated it on new foundations as promptly as possible. One prerequisite for such policy change, however, was a fundamental change in its attitude toward Islam. Considering the politically explosive nature of Islam and of the ethnic minorities within its own borders, there were considerable, if not insurmountable, difficulties.

The most important barrier for the Soviet Union's Near and Middle East policies has always been the multilayered nature of Islam within its own borders. Whether the Soviet leadership could have broken down this barrier depended upon its willingness to compromise one of the taboos of Marxist-Leninist doctrine: that against religion.

Notes

1. Literature on Islam and the development of the Islamic world is so extensive that this note only refers to a recently published handbook containing an extensive bibliography for each contribution: *Der Islam in der Gegenwart* (Munich, 1984).

2. For a discussion of this figure from the Soviet point of view, see also H. Bräker, "Die Islam-Frage als Problem der sowjetischen Religions- und Minderheitenpolitik," *Sowjetunion 1980/81: Ereignisse, Probleme, Perspektiven* (Munich and Vienna, 1981), pp. 79–80.

3. For evaluation of Islam in the Soviet Union, see A. Bennigsen and S. E. Wimbush, *Muslims of the Soviet Empire: A Guide*, foreword by Hans Bräker (London, 1986). This work is part of a large research undertaking directed by the author and financially supported by the Volkswagenwerk Foundation.

4. On this topic, among others, see Hans Bräker, "Die Stellung des Islams und des islamischen Rechts in der Sowjetunion und in der Volksrepublik China," in *Der Islam in der Gegenwart*, ed. Werner Ende and Udo Steinbach (Munich, 1984), pp. 248–74; "Nationality Dynamics in Sino-Soviet Relations," in *Soviet Nationalities in Strategic Perspective*, ed. Alexandre Bennigsen and S. E. Wimbush (London and Sidney, 1985), pp. 101–57.

5. See the detailed, still current book by Walter Kolarz on Soviet religion policies up until the beginning of the 1960s: *Die Religionen der Sowjetunion: Überleben in Anpassung und Widerstand* (Freiburg, 1963), especially pp. 396–442. In addition, see *Religion and the Soviet State: A Dilemma of Power*, ed. M. Hayward and W. C. Fletcher (London, 1969), especially pp. 187–98. On current Islamic problems: Alexandre Bennigsen and Chantal Lemercier-Quelquejay, *Islam in the Soviet Union* (New York, 1967); Geoffrey Wheeler, *Modern History of Soviet Central Asia* (New York and London, 1964); Hans Bräker, *Kommunismus und Weltreligionen Asiens: Kommunismus und Islam*, 2 vols. (Tübingen, 1969–71).

6. See the comprehensive portrayal (complete with documents) of Sufism in the Soviet Union by Alexandre Bennigsen and Chantal Lemercier-Quelquejay, *Le soufi et le commissaire: Les confréries musulmanes en URSS* (Paris, 1987). For a general history of Sufism, see Annemarie Schimmel, *Mystische Dimensionen des Islams: Die*

Geschichte des Sufismus (Cologne, 1985); this work, however, does not treat Sufism in the Soviet Union.

7. See the contributions by Uwe Halbach and Richard Lorenz in this volume. The resistance movements before and after 1917 have so far received relatively little treatment. In recent years, however, there has been an increasing interest in this area. Up until now the research results have been published mainly in the magazine *Central Asian Survey* (*CAS*), issued by the Society for Central Asian Studies at Oxford. Several articles from this journal are worthy of note: Paul B. Henze, "Fire and Sword in the Caucasus: The Nineteenth Century Resistance of the North Caucasian Mountaineers," *CAS* 2 (1983): 5–44; Marie Broxup, "The Basmachi," *CAS* 2/1 (1983): 57–81; Glenda Fraser, "Basmachi," *CAS* 6/1 and 6/2 (1987); H. Aymen de Lageard, "The Revolt of the Basmachi According to Red Army Journals (1920–1922)," *CAS* 6/3 (1987): 1–35.

8. His speech at the Tenth Party Congress of the RKP (b) in *Desiatyi s'ezd RKP (b), Mart 1921 goda, Stenograficheskii otchet* (Moscow, 1963), pp. 189–201.

9. See Boris Meissner, "Entstehung, Fortentwicklung, und ideologische Grundlagen des sowjetischen Bundesstaates," in *Bundesstaat und Nationalitätenrecht in der Sowjetunion*, ed. F. Chr. Schroeder and Boris Meissner (Berlin, 1974), pp. 9–68.

10. Among these are all the heads (*muftis*) of the four "Spiritual Councils" of Muslims, created in 1941–42 in Baku, Buinaksk (now Makhachkala), Ufa, and Tashkent. Ali Zada (Baku) was to suffer extensive persecution before his appointment because of his religious activity and was sent into exile; Gebekov (Buinaksk) spent fourteen years in prison and in exile before his appointment to the position; Rasulaiev (Ufa) was repeatedly imprisoned for his religious activity and was ultimately brought back from exile. The best known of these spiritual leaders, Babakhan (Tashkent), who was only recently replaced by his son and has since died, had to be brought back from exile in order to take up his duties in Tashkent.

11. For the national communist movement, see mainly Alexandre Bennigsen and S. E. Wimbush, *Muslim National Communism in the Soviet Union* (Chicago, 1979) (with short biographies of the leading representatives). On Sultangaliev in particular, see Alexandre Bennigsen and Chantal Lemercier-Quelquejay, *Sultan Galiev: Le père de la révolution tiers-mondiste* (Paris, 1986).

12. Original text in *Sobranie ukazov, rasporiazhenii raboche-krest'ianskogo pravitel'stva*, no. 7 (19 December 1917): appendix 2.

13. Quoted here from the German translation in Baymirza Hayit, *Sowjetische Orientpolitik am Beispiel Turkestans* (Cologne and Berlin, 1962), pp. 45ff.

14. See Hildegard Schaeder, *Moskau das Dritte Rom* (Darmstadt, 1963).

15. Hans Bräker: "Buddhism in the Soviet Union: Annihilation or Survival?" *Religion in Communist Lands* 11, no. 1 (1983): 36–48.

16. Documents concerning Soviet religious legislation (translated into German) can be found in O. Luchterhand, *Die Religionsgesetzgebung in der Sowjetunion* (Berlin, 1978).

17. See the section in this chapter entitled "The Stages of Soviet Policies Regarding Islam."

18. For the development of Islamic law in Russia and in the Soviet Union, see the article "Shariat," *Bol'shaia Sovetskaia Entsiklopediia* 64 (Moscow, 1934), pp. 852–55.

19. For the development of the institution of *waqf* property in prerevolutionary Russia, see the article "Vakuf," *Entsiklopedicheskii Slovar'* (St. Petersburg, 1891), 5:390 (with numerous references), and "Vakuf," *Bol'shaia Entsiklopediia* (St. Petersburg, 1902), 4:315 D (with references). For the Soviet assessment: N. Fioletov, "Vakufnoe pravo," *Bol'shaia Sovetskaia Entsiklopediia* (Moscow, 1927), 8:608, and "Vakuf," *Bol'shaia Sovetskaia Entsiklopediia* (Moscow, 1951), 6:550.

20. N. M. Vagabov, "Bol'she vnimaniia sovetskomu islamovedeniiu," *Voprosy filosofii* 12 (1966).

21. N. M. Vagabov, article in *Izvestiia Severo-Kavkazkogo Nauchnogo Tsentra Vysshei Shkoly* 4 (1978).

22. See note 10 for a discussion of the creation of the "Spiritual Councils" and the persecution of their leaders.

23. See F. Steppat, "Islam und Politik," in *Islam: Herausforderung an Ost und West,* ed. G. Schult (Altenburg, Germany, 1981), pp. 182–95, and Hans Bräker, "The Islamic Renewal Movement and the Power Shift in the Near/Middle East and Central Asia," in *Passé Turco-Tatar, Présent Soviétique: Etudes offertes à Alexandre Bennigsen,* ed. Chantal Lemercier-Quelquejay et al. (Paris, 1986).

24. *Muslims of the Soviet East* is the only official periodical of the "Spiritual Councils" for Muslims in the Soviet Union. It is published in Uzbek, Arabic, Dari, and Farsi, as well as in English and French, but not in Russian.

25. See, for example, the editorial "Holy Qur'ân and Hijrat," *Muslims of the Soviet East* 2 (1980): 2.

26. Evgenii Beliaev, "Islam," in *Bol'shaia Sovetskaia Entsiklopediia* (Moscow, 1935), which also gives extensive references for both Russian and non-Russian literature).

27. See the following article of Babakhan's, the mufti from Tashkent: "Ibn Sina: Great Thinker and Philosopher," *Muslims of the Soviet East* 2 (1980): 3.

28. *Muslims of the Soviet East* 4 (1979). On this symposium, see also the report of the correspondent from the *Neue Zürcher Zeitung,* 23–34 September 1979, "Sowjet-Islam auf dem langen Marsch. Strategie der Anpassung an den atheistischen Staat." The Soviet press reported on the symposium, which Muslim representatives from more than thirty countries attended only briefly, if at all. *Literaturnaia gazeta,* no. 39 (1979), for example, reported a brief interview with Mufti Babakhan.

29. *Muslims of the Soviet East* 4 (1979).

30. Published as: "O podgotovke k 60-letiiu obrazovaniia Soiuza Sovetskikh Sotsialisticheskikh Respublik," *Pravda,* 22 December 1982.

31. Wording of the account in *Pravda,* 24 February 1981. There is no doubt that this criticism "incensed" Muslim minorities, particularly, for in another passage of the account the "uneasiness" toward Islam was described in the following manner: "We Communists respect the religious beliefs of the people who believe in Islam. . . . The most important concern remains the question of the objectives of these forces who are preaching one solution or another. It is possible that the struggle for liberation will be waged in the name of Islam: the experiences of history attest to this fact. But Islamic solutions can also cause a reaction leading to counterrevolutionary rebellions. The outcome ultimately depends on the real content of one movement or another."

32. *Pravda,* 22 December 1982.

33. Quoted here from the extensive report in *Pravda Vostoka,* 25 November 1986;

the complete text of the speech has never been published, evidently. A lengthy article on the subject of "Atheism and Culture" appeared in *Pravda* on 16 January, 1987, only a few weeks after Gorbachev's speech in Tashkent. The content of the article gives reason to infer that the necessity for Soviet Party leadership's reinforcement of policies of atheism politics came, for the most part, from Islamic problems in the Caucasus-Transcaucasus and Central Asia. The article takes a strong stand against the so-called ideologists of Islam and makes a general proposal for the safeguarding of the atheist education mandate as set forth in the resolution of the XXVIIth Party Congress.

34. A. Akhmedov, *Sotsial'naia doktrina Islama* (Moscow, 1982).

35. Akhmedov, *Sotsial'naia doktrina*, pp. 114–21, 124–32.

36. This expectation has been emphatically confirmed by the development in the Soviet Union up to the end of 1988. See Hans Bräker, "Moskaus orientalische Frage: Gorbatschow vor der Zerreissprobe?" *Osteuropa* 9 (1988): 783–96.

37. The basis for this judgment can be found in earlier works by the Hans Bräker on the foreign policy dimension of Islamic problems in the Soviet Union, of which only a few will be mentioned here: "Religionsproblematik und Nationalitätenpolitik. Zur sowjetischen Zentralasienpolitik und ihrem aussenpolitischen Aspekt," in Schroeder and Meissner, *Bundesstaat*, pp. 113–129; "Die langfristigen Interessen der Sowjetunion in der Region Mittelost und die Islamfrage in Zentralasien," in *Die sowjetische Intervention in Afghanistan*, ed. H. Vogel (Baden-Baden, 1980), pp. 15–66; "Die Sowjetunion und der Mittlere Osten: Politik im Spannungsfeld strategischer Zielsetzungen und Islam-Frage," *Aus Politik und Zeitgeschichte* 17–18 (1982): pp. 5–62; "The Implications of the Islamic Question for Soviet Domestic and Foreign Policy," *CAS* 2/1 (1983): 111–28; "Aussereuropäische Regionen im gegenwärtigen Stadium des Ost-West-Konflikts: Islamische Welt," in *Die neueren Entwicklungen des Ost-West-Konflikts*, ed. W. Link (Cologne, Berlin, and Munich, 1984), pp. 135–143.

38. See the detailed study of Hans Bräker, "Zwei Jahre nach der Machtübernahme Khomeinys: Zwischenbilanz der sowjetischen Iran-Politik," *Aktuelle Analysen des Bundesinstituts für ostwissenschaftliche und internationale Studien* 5 (1981).

9. The Status of Muslims in the Federative Systems of the Soviet Union and Yugoslavia

The Federative Framework

The Basic Concept

In the Western democratic world, federalism developed organically as a result of several historical factors. Communist federalism, in contrast, is the result of a conscious political decision from above, made relatively late, by the party in power, and for the sole purpose of solving the nationality question in a multiethnic state.

Although Vladimir I. Lenin proclaimed the right of the self-determination of peoples, the Bolsheviks originally thought that such a right could only be realized by proposing a harsh alternative: participation in a unified Soviet Russian state (the Bolsheviks' preference, of course) or secession and formation of a separate national state. After the October 1917 Revolution, however, the Bolsheviks, who had traditionally taken a unitarian, antifederalist stance, accepted the view that the self-determination of peoples could be realized even in the framework of a federal state.

Behind this decision was Lenin, for whom the extent of the nationality question became so clear between April and June of 1917 that he made a complete shift in policy.[1] The final decision was reached by the edict of the Council of People's Commissars, 17/4 December 1917. This edict offered the Ukraine the choice of separating from Russia or entering into negotiations with the Russian Republic concerning "their federal or other similar relationships."[2] With this decision, it became clear that the Austro-Marxist concept of cultural autonomy and of a "people" as an association of individuals had been dismissed. As both Lenin and

Joseph V. Stalin had insisted for some time, the nationality problem now rested exclusively on the territorial principle. Other issues, however, remained open.

Among the unresolved questions was that of the legal structure of federalism itself. While the concept of federalism is conventionally associated with federally united states, for the Communists it was not—and still is not—so clear. Considerable differences of opinion arose between Lenin and Stalin on this point. These differences came to light in June 1920 and then again in 1922, during the preparations for the founding of the Soviet Union.[3]

Stalin was a resolute opponent of federation, maintaining that national/territorial autonomy in the framework of a unified state was entirely sufficient. In theory, such a view would be associated with regionalism. In the Russian Republic's Constitution of 10 July 1918, this concept formed the basis of the vision of the Russian Soviet state as a "Federative Republic." Yet this constitution actually established the newly created Soviet state as a centralized one: Article 11 envisioned only the possibility that regional Soviets might unite on a national basis to form "autonomous regional unions" (avtonomnye oblastnye soiuzy), which would belong to the republic "according to the principle of federation." The authors of this constitution thus worked under the assumption that the Russian Soviet state should include all of the domains of the former Russian Empire.

Events took a different course, however. Within the territory of the Russian Soviet Federative Socialist Republic (RSFSR), a number of nominally autonomous entities emerged, but the Soviet republics of Belorussia, the Ukraine, and those of Transcaucasia positioned themselves outside the RSFSR. Soon, treaties bound these republics, as they did the RSFSR, to the federal state of the Soviet Union. In this manner, the ideas of Lenin, who acknowledged the validity of various types of federation, were put into effect. In March 1921, to Stalin's dismay, the Tenth Congress of the Communist Party, granted equal legitimacy to forms of regional autonomy that had hitherto been labeled simply as the "Bashkir" or "Ukrainian" types. These types reflected the political reality of the Soviet Union, created between 1922 and 1924.[4]

For a time, the Soviet concept of federalism even embraced a third variant that was oriented toward confederation. This variant was created with the federal treaty that was drawn up among the three Transcaucasian republics on 12 March 1922, but it disappeared as the relationship of these states was transformed from a "federative association" into a "federative republic," as dictated by the Transcaucasian Constitution of 13 December 1922.

As a result of the early years of Soviet rule, various "federative" regional entities emerged. Their disparate forms of legal status were brought under complete control by Stalin's Soviet Constitution of 1936. In this constitution, the "union republic" holds the highest status, as a member state within the federal state; below this level there are different degrees of regional autonomy, all existing as parts of a unified state belonging to the federation. At the Soviet Union's inception, there were primarily "autonomous republics" and "autonomous regions." The "national district" was first introduced in 1925 as the lowest level, appearing on a broader scale in 1930, and received the designation of "autonomous district" in 1977.

From the beginning, however, the differentiation between Soviet federalism and Soviet autonomy was so blurred as to be nonexistent because of the principle of "democratic centralism," which ultimately only accommodated a centralized pseudofederalism. This is the only way to understand the otherwise contradictory characterization of the Soviet Union, in Article 70, Section 1 of the Union Constitution of 1977, as a "multinational unified and federal state" (*edinoe soiuznoe mnogonatsional'noe gosudarstvo*).

The federative solution to the national question came as a late insight for the Yugoslav Communists as well, but at the time of their rise to power, this proposal was virtually uncontested.[5] Yugoslavia's Communist Party was originally founded as a unitary body, and it was only after the creation of the Soviet Union as a federal state that the Yugoslav Communist Party, under massive pressure from the Comintern, adopted a radical change of course, suddenly endorsing the dissolution of the unified Yugoslav state into separate nation-states.[6] When the Comintern reviewed its platform six years later, with the consequence of releasing the Yugoslav Communists from external pressure, the Fourth Party Conference reverted to the idea of a unified state. Such a concept, however, was far less attractive to the Croats and Slovenes than it was for the Serbs, so domestic conflict was not put to rest.

The final resolution in favor of the transformation of Yugoslavia into a federated state based on the nationality principle was made on 29 November 1943 in Bosnian Jajce, during the second session of the Anti-Fascist Council for the Popular Liberation of Yugoslavia (AVNO), which had been formed the year before by some of Marshal Tito's partisans.[7] It was also ratified by the Tito-Subasic Agreement of 1 November 1944; on 29 November of that year, the Constituent Assembly proclaimed the "Federative People's Republic of Yugoslavia," whose constitution was passed on 31 January 1946.

In its original conception, the Yugoslav federal state, with its six republics and two autonomous regions, represented a patent imitation of Stalinist pseudofederalism. After the break with Moscow, however, decentralization of the state structure proceeded swiftly, gaining momentum with the constitutions of 1953 and 1963, as well as with the constitutional amendments of 1967, 1968, and 1971. In the constitution of 1974, the process of decentralization was brought to a tentative conclusion.

In the process of territorial decentralization (federalization), both of the autonomous provinces were involved to such a degree that, ultimately, they gained status comparable to that of a republic. Moreover, the gradual consolidation of workers' self-management was used as a means to pursue functional decentralization, with results that were highly questionable. Overall, the federative system underwent such profound changes that there is justification for the occasional comments heard today of a shift of the system toward a confederation.[8]

The Nationality Principle

According to the Communist perspective, the federative solution to the nationality question is supposed to derive from the people's right to self-determination, and it should be in strict alignment with the nationality principle. The question of which criteria are to be used to determine a group's status as a "people" is left unanswered, however. As a consequence, the candidate who seeks a piece of the federative pie—as in the case of the "Muslim peoples" who constitute seventeen percent of the Soviet population and eighteen percent of Yugoslavia's—faces a difficult ordeal.

Stalin's concept of *nation* admits only language, territory, economics and culture as grounds for a community's claim to identity; religion is not included.[9] This concept is not very helpful for a society that has no national literary language and that may be characterized by mixed and scattered settlements, diverse socio-economic structures, as well as a diffuse and multilayered sense of religious, cultural, and ethnic identity whose reference point is both above and beneath the level of nation. Consequently, in putting federation into practice, the Communists were guided by political considerations, rather than by the principle of nationality or any other ideological assertion.

During the first years of Soviet rule, the Bolsheviks seemed generally inclined to accept the religiously based and transnational communal identity of the Muslim ʿUmma. Consequently, just four weeks after the October 1917 Revolution, the Council of People's Commissars issued an exhortation to "all working Muslims of Russia and the East," in order to win them over.[10] It became evident that this acknowledgement was linked, at the very least, to the goal of political domination when, in February of 1918, the massacre of Khokand was carried out. Further evidence of this intention was given during the Civil War of 1918–20, with the annihilation of the Muslim political organizations that had shown themselves to be more or less cooperative, such as the Bashrevkom in Bashkiria, the Alash Orda of the Kazakh plains, the Musawat, as well as other Muslim parties in the Caucasus, and the Milli Firka in the Crimea.

The same happened to the multiregional "Pan-Russian Muslim Movement," which had been undermined with the help of the Pan-Islamic Communist Mulla Nur Vakhitov.[11] When, in June 1918, Vakhitov initiated the formation of a Bolshevik party for Muslims (Rossiiskaia Partiia Kommunistov/b/ Musul'man) that would have its own Central Committee, Moscow center's initiative of physical liquidation, using the Czechoslovak Legion, began almost immediately.

The incorporation of the Muslim Communists in the Party took place in November 1918, with the official transformation of the Vakhitov Party into the "Central Bureau of the Communist Organizations of the RKP(b)," which was changed in March 1919 to the "Central Bureau of the Communist Organizations of the People of the East," with a dilution of the Muslim constituency. When the area of its jurisdiction was extended to non-Muslims, the Central Bureau was ranked with the subsidiary regional bodies of the Central Party Leadership that existed for separate Islamically dominated territories, such as the Transcaucasian Bureau and, later, the Central Asian Bureau, as well as the Caucasian Bureau, founded in April 1920.

As they worked to develop the federative system of the Soviet Union, the Bolsheviks began more and more to ignore the Muslims' sense of community—partly by discovering new "peoples" continually—not only because they sought to rule through Party mandates, but also because of their growing fear of the incalculable consequences of Pan-Islamic power, even though it might profess a Communist ideology.[12]

When the Volga-Ural settlement region of the Kazan Tatars was redivided along "national" lines, the political goal using federative structures to atomize the Muslim world became apparent for the first time. Initially, the Moscow leaders seemed inclined to comply with the desire of all Muslim groups for the establishment of a unified Greater Tataria, where the Volga Tatars, who were not clearly distinct from the Bashkirs, would also have a federative homeland. In March 1918, the People's Commissariat for Nationality Affairs decreed the establishment of a Tatar-Bashkir Republic, but the Civil War cut short the enactment of this resolution.[13]

Once the Bolshevik center had resumed full power, by March 1920, it had changed its mind, amidst the pressures of the Pan-Turkic and Pan-Islamic struggles for autonomy, and wrote "Divide et impera" on its flag. Against the will of the people affected by the decision, separate republics were created for the Tatars and the Bashkirs.[14] In Transcaucasia, the creation of an Azerbaijani state was already presumed to be an eventual reality and was thus unproblematic. Here, the leaders in Moscow were most concerned to apply federation as a device to perpetuate tensions among the various Transcaucasian peoples. In accordance with this goal, after their defeat by the Red Army, the Azerbaijanis, Armenians, and Georgians, who bore considerable animosity toward each other, were forced under the common roof of a Transcaucasian Federation, which was finally abolished in 1936.

Two Muslim thorns pierced the Christian flesh of Georgia and Armenia when, in July 1921, an Ajar Republic was established for Georgian Muslims on the former territory of Batum, and, in the area of Nakhichevan, entirely surrounded by Armenia, an autonomous region was established for the Azerbaijanis. The latter was given the rank of "Soviet Socialist Republic" when it was made an exclave of the Azerbaijan SSR, at the end of 1923. These events were not only brought about by the Bolsheviks, but also by Turkey, especially, who had wrested from Soviet authorities the promise of autonomy for their co-religionists in Batum and Nakhichevan in the treaties of Moscow and Kars.[15] On the other hand, in July 1923 the autonomous region of Nagorno-Karabakh was created as an enclave for Armenians within the boundaries of the Azerbaijan SSR. This region was not connected to the Armenian SSR, although the geography of the region would have allowed it.

In the Northern Caucasus, with its geographic as well as ethno-linguistic fragmentation, differences between clans were exaggerated to the level of national ones in order to divide and weaken highly virulent resistance forces. The new divisions also differed substantially from the czarist administrative divisions of the Caucasian governorship in that, in January 1921, an Autonomous Republic of Dagestan was created from the Region of Dagestan, and an Autonomous Mountain Republic (Gorskaya Respublika) was created out of the Terek Region. During the following years, this mountain republic was successively broken up into its "national" components, and it was finally dissolved in July 1924.

In this process—considering what was technically possible—the territorial unification of ethnic dissimilarities seems to have been as much an objective as was the severing of bonds between ethnic commonalities. Thus, the Caucasian Kabardins were joined to the Turkic Balkars, and the Caucasian Circassians with the Turkic Karachay, in their respective autonomous regions. The Circassian Adygei received their own autonomous region. The Chechen and the Ingush, despite their close linguistic ties and similar social structures, received separate autonomous regions, which were finally united in 1934. The Iranian Ossetin clans, only partially Islamicized, were separated into neighboring regions, despite the fact that there would have been no technical reason not to unite the northern Ossetic region, in the RSFSR, with the southern one, in Georgia. The Abkhaz of the Czarist district of Sukhumi, who are partially Muslim but belong ethnically to the Circassian, gained the status of a republic as part of Georgia,[16] yet they had shown strong inclinations to join a Northern Caucasian state, and were dissatisfied living among the Georgians, who had become a majority.[17]

The final and decisive blow to Islamic unity fell in the area of Central Asia and Siberia, the home of some two-thirds of all Soviet Muslims, whose resistance was only broken by the Bolsheviks at the end of the 1920s. The major factor was the so-called "establishment of national boundaries" (razmezhevanie), in 1924–25.[18] Prior to that time, the Czarist administrative boundaries had been left essentially unchanged, since, in the boundaries of the RSFSR the General Steppe Government of Turkestan became the Kirghizistan ASSR and, outside of the RSFSR, the Emirate of Bukhara and the Khanate of Khiva, now known as the Soviet Socialist Republics of Bukhara and Khwarazm, continued to be treated as Russian protectorates. The new objective, however, was the destruction of all transnational Islamic/Pan-Turkic loyalties, as well as subnational loyalties to clan, tribe, and territory.

In accordance with this plan, six "peoples" were invented, and all were granted separate regional entities, differing in status. The Uzbeks and Turkmens each received a Union Republic right away. The Tajiks and Kazakhs were allocated autonomous provinces: the Tajiks, within the Uzbek SSR, and the Kazakhs, within the RSFSR. In 1929 and 1936, respectively, these were given the higher status of Union Republics. The Kirghiz had to begin with an autonomous region, but subsequently gained the status of Autonomous Republic (1927) and then Union Republic (1936). The Karakalpaks achieved a more modest gain: they began with an autonomous region, which first came under the authority of the Kazakh ASSR and then, in 1930, came directly under the RSFSR's administration. In 1932 it was raised to the rank of Autonomous Republic and then, in 1936, was transferred to the Uzbek SSR.

The Autonomous Region of Gorno-Badakhshan, within the boundaries of the Tajik Republic, became the seventh entity, and with its establishment the nationality principle could no longer hold. No appropriate national designation could be found for the Iranian tribes of "Mountain Tajiks" and "Pamir Peoples" living there. The one common feature that would most readily serve to link them—their adherence to the Ismaili branch of Islam—was not taken into consideration, for understandable reasons. The accomplishments of the new regional divisions measured rather modestly against their own standard of the nationality principle: according to the results of the 1939 census, Uzbeks had never constituted even two-thirds of the population of the "nationally homogenous" Uzbek SSR, and in the Karakalpak ASSR, the eponymous nation only constituted one third of the total population.[19]

In short, the goals of territorial reorganization, which were expected to alter community identity, met with limited success in the Muslim lands of the Soviet Union. Subnational tribal and clan identities were weakened in many ways, but these loyalties are still alive among the Kazakhs, Kirghiz, Karakalpaks, Turkmens, and most of the Northern Caucasians. Expert observers are in general agreement that the supranational identity of the Muslim ʿUmma is just as strong as it was in the past and even overlays the officially favored national sentiments of the middle level.[20]

In the case of the Yugoslav Communists, there was never a self-interested instrumentalization of the nationality principle that hurt the Muslims. Rather, there were, and still are, other difficulties that obstructed full inclusion of the Muslims in the federative system. The Soviet Union saw itself, in principle, as a completely multiethnic state; moreover, no significant political weight was accorded to the distinction—based on group size as well as the Stalinist concept of nation—between "nations" (natsii) and "peoples" (narodnosti). But Yugoslavia sought a different model, since it wished to become a southern Slavic state. Consequently, the republic status was reserved for the southern Slavic nation-states (narody). Other groups were designated "national minorities" (natsionalne manjine) until 1963; subsequently they were called "nationalities" or "peoples" (narodnosti), and, in accordance with this concept of statehood, they could only claim the lower levels of autonomy.

This was the case for the two identifiably "Muslim" groups, the Albanians and the Turks. Because the Turks were so few in number, they had virtually no hope of achieving a "federative" region for themselves. The Albanians' situation was different, for they had always been more numerous than the Montenegrins and, at the end of the 1960s, surpassed the Macedonians in population. An autonomous region was established for them within the boundaries of the Serbian Republic, although it was not theirs in name: its official designation of "Kosovo-Metohija" did not conform to the nationality principle, but bespoke the Albanian-Serbian terrain. This autonomous region gained the designation of Autonomous Province in 1963, thus becoming equal in status to Vojvodina. Then, because of the anti-Serbian demonstrations, the Serbian part of its designation was dropped in 1969. Although the Albanian and Muslim character of the Autonomous Province of Kosovo is now more marked than ever before, and although the status of "province" is now much closer to that of "republic," it is maintained, on the basis of the constitutional principle, that Kosovo is a lower-ranking multiethnic entity.[21]

Bosnia-Herzegovina is generally regarded as the one truly Muslim republic. When the Yugoslav federation was created, there could be no serious doubt that the status of member-state should be granted to this culturally mixed region that had a distinct historical development, and where at least a third of the Serbian and Croatian population belonged to the Muslim faith. To establish such a state on the basis of the nationality principle would be meaningless; moreover, no single group of people could be found whose identity could define such a state.

In effect, the decision ultimately was determined by the lack of political alternatives: there was no more possibility of assigning this region to Croatia (as had been the case in the Greater Croatian Ustasha-State) than there was of incorporating it in Serbia. The possibility of dividing the region between these two republics also had to be rejected, since that situation would have posed considerable danger to the political stability of Yugoslavia.[22]

During the initial search for a "state nation" of Bosnia-Herzegovina it became apparent that there was only one solution, if not an especially satisfying one: the southern Slavic Muslims would have to be counted as a Yugoslav "state-nation." There was vigorous dispute over whether such a measure could be accepted, and there is still some debate about it today, although there has been a substantial breakthrough in the discussions since the fall of Ranković, the Secret Service chief, in July 1966.

The first official recognition of a Muslim nation appeared in the census of 1961, which introduced the category of "Muslim in an ethnic sense." In the subsequent censuses of 1971 and 1981, this recognition has been retained in the category, "Muslim in the sense of nationality." The primary function of this designation is to provide a collective identity for those Muslims who do not wish to be considered as Serbs, Croatians, or as any other particular people, and who are also not interested in the supraregional and multiethnic catch-all term of "Yugoslav," which has been offered since 1953.

This possibility for collective identification seems most suited to the needs of the diffuse community feeling of the Bosnian Muslims, and may even give this group an increasingly strong profile.[23] Still, it can scarcely be asserted that Bosnia-Herzegovina is a Muslim national region, since the Muslims' constituency of 40 percent of the population is not much greater than that of the Serbs (32 percent), and there is also a considerable Croatian minority (18.4 percent) in the region. In order to do justice to these facts, the republican authors of the 1974 constitution abandoned any national characterization of the region, choosing instead to represent the Muslims, Serbs and Croatians as "the peoples of Bosnia-Herzegovina."[24]

The Territorial Principle

In the federative system, the definition of states is based on regions rather than groups of people. The nation, or nationality, stands at the midpoint of the spectrum as a territorial community, rather than being considered as the association of a particular group of people. The consequences of this concept are twofold. The first is that groups of people who are not conceded a national region, whether because of their settlement patterns or for any other reason, are stripped of their rights when a federative solution is adopted for the nationality question.

Among the larger Muslim groups in the Soviet Union, the Uyghurs, in particular, have found themselves in such a position. The situation of the Tatars is not much better. In fact, the Autonomous Crimean Republic was regarded as existing for the Crimean Tatars, even though they were always a minority there, but it was dissolved in 1944. In 1920, the Tatar Autonomous Republic, centered in Kazan, was so narrowly delimited that a great proportion of the Volga Tatars who lived in the Volga-Ural area were left outside its boundaries. Today about 29 percent of the Volga Tatars, and only about 26 percent of all Soviet Tatars, live in the Tatar ASSR.[25] The case of the Tatars, who live in wide-ranging diaspora, reveals the limited effectiveness of the nationality principle, which can only offer rights to people who live in compact settlements. In Yugoslavia, it is the Turkic minority who have fallen through the sieve of the territorial principle.

The second consequence involves the ethnic composition of national regions. Rights that are linked to territorial autonomy can only benefit the "eponymous nation" if that group actually constitutes a majority in its region. If it does not, "foreign" groups in the region can gain these rights by virtue of their majority.

A look at the nineteen regional entities of the Soviet Union that can be regarded as "Muslim" according to their eponymous nation or their district designation, makes it apparent that Muslims constitute an absolute majority in five republics (Azerbaijan, Kirghizia, Tajikistan, Turkmenia and Uzbekistan), five autonomous republics (Chechen-Ingushia, Dagestan, Kabardin-Balkaria, Karakalpakia and Nakhichevan) and in the Autonomous Region of Gorno-Badakhshan (cf. Appendix Table 2).[26] In the Union Republic of Kazakhstan, as well as in three autonomous republics (Ajaria, Bashkiria, Tataria) and in the Karachay-Cherkess Autonomous Region, the percentage of the Muslim population ranges between 40 and 49 percent, and Russians greatly outnumber the eponymous nations in Kazakhstan and in the Karachay-Cherkess region.

Other groups constitute such small minorities in their autonomous regions that they have no prospects at all: the Adygei, for example, are only 21.2 percent of their region's population, as against a Russian majority of 70.4 percent. Among the semi-Muslim people of the Caucasus, the minority position of the Abkhaz in their autonomous republic, with only 16.8 percent of the population, is even worse. The Ossetes have two national regions, of which only the Severo-Ossetin ASSR, to the north, could be regarded as a "Muslim" republic, since the Ossetes in the Iugo-Ossetin Autonomous Oblast are nearly all Christian. In Severo-Ossetia, moreover, although Ossetes constitute about half of the population, only about half of that number is Muslim, so that even this cannot be termed a Muslim republic.

There are two regional entities of Yugoslavia that were conceived on a multiethnic basis and have no eponymous nations, but, in point of fact, they serve as territorial reference-points for Muslim groups (cf. Appendix Table 3). Of these two, it is the province of Kosovo that is more characteristically Muslim, and it is becoming more strongly so with time. With a population comprising about 77.5 percent of Albanians in 1981, and about 80 percent religious Muslims, this area can be said to be a truly Muslim one. In the higher-ranking Republic of Bosnia-Herzegovina, on the other hand, although ethnic and religious Muslims make up about 40 percent of the population, they are the largest group; nevertheless, because of the principle of majority, this status does not suffice to grant them the exclusive jurisdiction that was intended for the republic.

The inherent structural flaws of the territorial principle should be compensated by measures to protect minorities, on an individual or group basis, so groups who have been ignored or mistreated in the federative system can be ensured due protection. Such protection of minorities is virtually nonexistent in the Soviet Union, but relations in Yugoslavia do not give cause for complaint.[27] In the South Slavic state, adequate measures for minority protection have been taken, for example, in the establishment of the right to native languages—including Albanian and Turkish, which are virtually national languages—in education and administration, the latter of which has been more thoroughly developed through communal statutory rights.[28]

Party Supremacy

The federative principle applies above all to the organization of states, and thus is involved in only part of the political system. Because, in all Communist countries, the Communist Party supersedes the state, decentralization of state powers can be altered at any time by the centrally organized Party.

This is the situation in the Soviet Union. The Bolsheviks never gave serious consideration to the possibility of decentralizing the Party. The Eighth Party Congress, in March 1919, had vetoed federalization of the Party.[29] Moreover, the Communist Party Statute of 1925, rendered necessary in the process of the Soviet Union's creation, stated unequivocally, in Article 32, that the Party organizations of the national republics and regions held the same rank as other regional organizations, and were thus unconditionally subordinate to the Central Committee of the CPSU(b). This relationship also still applies to the union republic Party organizations that use the title of "Communist Party" only symbolically. The pseudo-federalism of the state is thus dominated by the Party's centralism, whereby the coordination of the national regions and their subordination to Central Party leadership are jointly secured.

The Communist Party in Yugoslavia, in contrast, which was renamed an "Alliance" in 1952, has been somewhat drawn into the process of federalization.[30] With the changes in statute of 1969 and 1974, the separate republic and provincial associations have retained such a degree of power that they constitute a model "Federal Party," even in their organizational structures. A set of statutes, issued in 1978 and 1982, that sought to strengthen the Central Party, failed to alter the degree of decentralized power. In contrast to the case of state structure, the organizational principle of "democratic centralism" has not entirely disappeared, but it has been so weakened that there can be no doubt about the decentralizing of the whole political system.

The Status of the "Muslim" Regional Entities in the Federative System

Political and Administrative Jurisdiction

One of the fundamental principles of federation and regional autonomy involves the assignment of definite state functions to member states and autonomous regional entities. The complex issues of administrative structures in federative systems is of utmost relevance to Yugoslav politics, but space does not permit proper treatment of this important subject in this chapter.[31] The best that can be done is to give a partial answer to the question of whether, and to what extent, the political and administrative functions of "Muslim" regions have been—or will be—used to reinforce ethno-religious characteristics. In so far as the allocation of rights in the Soviet Union and Yugoslavia does reflect distinctively Muslim features in various regions, a negative answer can be anticipated. Nevertheless, these special characteristics have been reinforced in order to counter Islam.

Abolition of regional Islamic legal systems. The Soviet Union and Yugoslavia are among the few countries where the whole "prerevolutionary" legal system was abolished in a single act following the Communist takeover.[32] This mandate for abolition consequently invalidated, at a single blow, all of Islamic law, whether pertaining to individuals, families, inheritance, or courts. Until this time, all Muslim non-Russians (*inorodtsy*) in the Russian Empire, and all Muslims of Bosnia-Herzegovina in the Kingdom of Yugoslavia, had known that they had the option of recourse to the jurisdiction of Islamic law, even if they did not regard its authority as absolute.[33] The complex realities of the legal systems persisted after the revolutionary mandate, however. Legal practices that were deeply rooted in Islamic culture, as well as tribal practices based on custom, compelled the Communists to make short-term compromises.

In Soviet Russia, after the October 1917 Revolution, despite the fact that the prohibition of religious marriage ceremonies applied to Islamic regions, in the Muslim stronghold of Turkistan, the Islamic Shari'a and customary law ('*adat*) remained in effect for another ten years.[34] This re-

gional legal system was upheld by the legislative authority of the Turkistan ASSR, which was invested with an unusual degree of power for a
mere autonomous republic. When state relations were legislated after
the ending of the Civil War, in 1920, the RSFSR received only jurisdiction over foreign and military affairs, as well as over foreign trade, so
that Turkistan retained its jurisdiction over all other legal matters.[35] In
1922, legislators in Turkistan recognized the legitimacy of the Shariʿa
courts, subject to supervision by the state.[36] All Muslims and Kazakhs
living in Turkistan thus had the right to choose Islamic jurisdiction,[37]
while their fellow tribesmen in what was then the Kirgizistan ASSR had
no such prerogative.[38]

The domain of the Shariʿa was defined as extending to minor civil
and criminal disputes, as well as to all family and inheritance disputes
that did not involve real property, provided also that these involved old
marriage contracts drawn up according to Islamic law. In every case,
all parties had to accept the Islamic procedure. In effect, for all matters
treated by Islamic law, Muslims in Turkistan could choose between two
parallel legal systems. This opportunity for choice, however, was forcibly
restricted after the territorial partition (razmezhevanie), through political and administrative measures, and it was completely eliminated in
the course of the 1927 campaign for the emancipation of women.[39]

In Yugoslavia application of the Shariʿa was abolished by the mandate of 1946 concerning "prerevolutionary" law,[40] but the problems of
judging cases involving marriages contracted prior to that time persisted
in various regions for some time.[41] Federalism generally played a secondary role in this regard, particularly when marital and family law, in
1946–47, and inheritance law, in 1955, were unified on a statewide and
secular basis. At this time, the republics played a minimal role in legislation, although they might occasionally be involved. Thus, for example,
Islamic law stipulates that a husband must provide his wife a contracted
sum or portion of goods (mahr) if he divorces her, but this practice was
forbidden by Serbian law in 1950.[42]

With the decentralization of legislative authority in the beginning of
the 1970s, however, the legal organization of the federal state underwent profound changes. According to the Constitution of 1974, republics
and provinces have exclusive jurisdiction over family and inheritance
laws. Examination of the regulations for federative regional bodies that
were passed in the mid-1970s, reveals considerable degree of variation,
particularly with regard to divorce law. This allows for a distinction between "conservative" and "progressive" member-states, although it does
not recognize any specifically Muslim elements.

Anti-Islamic penal legislation. The aspects of family and inheritance law just described were temporary and are only of historical interest today. Legislation of penal codes in both states, in contrast, continues to demonstrate federative characteristics that are specifically directed against Islamic marriage practices.

In the Soviet Union, despite constitutionally ordained jurisdiction,[43] federative practices became an integral part of penal law from the very beginning, so that the Union regulates the General Part in a "basic statute" (1924, 1958) and, in special laws, regulates political and military penal law (1927, 1958), as well as certain other areas of penal law, on occasion. The union republics, however, have their own penal codes. According to this constitutional practice, anti-Islamic penal legislation became primarily the affair of the union republics. On 16 July 1923, Azerbaijan took the first step in an amendment of its penal code that established penalties for polygamy, marriage to a minor, coercion of a woman to marry, as well as purchase or abduction of a woman for marriage.[44] In October 1924, the RSFSR drew up similar penal legislation,[45] and Georgia and Abkhazia followed suit in 1925.[46] Similar legislation was also eventually passed in Armenia, as well as in the Central Asian regions that had gained the jurisdiction of penal legislation when they were elevated to the rank of union republics. The current Soviet penal codes were passed in 1959–1961.

The explicitly anti-Islamic penalties mentioned above are only found in the codes of the five Central Asian republics, the three Transcaucasian republics and the RSFSR.[47] There is a noteworthy difference with respect to their place within the system of penal codes. In the eight non-Russian republics, these penalties are set forth in various clauses as pertaining to crimes against persons, the political rights of citizens, or against public law and order. In the penal code of the RSFSR, however, these are treated in the penultimate Chapter XI, under the heading "Crimes Involving Vestiges of Local Customs." The reason for this variation in systems, which was characteristic of penal codes during the 1920s, is that the actions in question were not subject to penalty everywhere in the republic, but only in those "autonomous republics, autonomous regions and other areas" where they were regarded as "vestiges of local customs" (Article 236 Penal Code RSFSR 1960).

In contrast to the Penal Code Amendment of 1924, which specified these republics and regions by name,[48] it is no longer possible to deduce from the Penal Code, nor from any other legal code, in exactly which areas of the RSFSR these criminal penalties apply. There can be no doubt, however, that Islamic regions are meant. In line with this assumption, the Supreme Court of the RSFSR repealed a sentence of the Kemerovo regional court that was issued for an uxoricide's bigamy (Article 235 Penal Code RSFSR). The accused was acquitted on the basis of the assertion that polygamy was not a local custom of Kemerov.[49] The guilty party could not take much solace in this acquittal, however, for he was subsequently sentenced to death for murder.

Local anti-Islamic penal law is still very much in effect, since bride purchase (*kalym*), contracted marriages, and similar customs are still practiced in the Muslim regions of the Soviet Union. As late as 1969, the Supreme Court of the RSFSR saw fit to pass a resolution of principle regarding juridical policy in cases of violations perpetrated in accordance with vestiges of local custom.[50] One offense that was not considered worth mentioning, however, was that of "refusing pardon in the arbitration of reconciliation of blood feud."[51] It can thus be inferred that, even among the North Caucasian tribes, the old fondness for blood feuds had died out.

In Yugoslavia, penal sanctions on a regional basis were first applied in 1950–51, in order to enforce the banning of the veil for women, and the federation retained jurisdiction over the establishment of criminal penalties until 1971.[52] According to Article 281, Number 12 of the 1974 Constitution, this jurisdiction is now limited to the General Part and to other specific areas of penal legislation. When the republics and provinces passed their penal codes in 1977, no move was made to establish specifically anti-Islamic legislation.[53] The only exception is the penal code of Kosovo, with its mention of an instance not cited anywhere else: forcing a woman to marry becomes subject to a more severe penalty when she is a minor.[54]

Religious legislation. It may be presumed that distinctively Muslim legal features that originate in federative systems lie in the domain of religious law, which has been included in the jurisdiction of the union republics from the Soviet Union's inception. In Yugoslavia, the republics were given jurisdiction over religious law in 1971. Investigation of the religious law of Muslim regions—in so far as the inadequate documentation allows—generally reveals only insignificant discrepancies, and these are only of historical interest.[55] The most interesting of these discrepancies are those involving the system of pious endowments (*waqf*) that are characteristic of the Islamic legal system.

A specialist has correctly observed[56] that the *waqf* system was theoretically abolished in Soviet Russia by the "Separation Decree" of 23 January 1918,[57] which denied the ownership capacity of religious societies (Article 12), declaring their property to belong to the people (Article

13).[58] In 1922, however, the *waqf* system was re-authorized for the madrasahs and mosques of the Turkistan ASSR, under the jurisdiction of a
joint mosque-state administration.[59] The first Turkistanian *waqf* decree,
in 1922, still left the question of property ownership open,[60] but the
second such decree, in 1923, already designated endowment property as
"social and state propoerty of the native inhabitants of the Republic of
Turkistan."[61] The third of these decrees, in Uzbekistan in 1925, is said
to have explicitly designated all bequests as "state property."[62] The cor-
responding legal acts of the Turkmenistan SSR, in 1926 and 1928, are
emphatic in their assertions that religious associations are not corporate
bodies, nor do they have the right to own property, and that, by virtue
of these facts, they may only use nationalized religious property when
no monetary exchange is involved.[63] Disregarding technicalities of legal
terminology, the entire system of religious endowments was effectively
brought under government control in Central Asia during the latter part
of the 1920s, so that the status of Muslim religious societies under civil
law no longer differed from that of any other church or religious group.

In Yugoslavia, in contrast, *waqf* property, although considerably diminished since 1945, continues to play a certain role.[64] Religious societies have never lost their status as corporate bodies there,[65] and all of
the constitutions have stated expressly that they may even own real
estate (at this writing, Article 174, Paragraph 6, Constitution of 1974).
Although no express mention is made in the previous Federal Law on
the legal status of religious societies of 27 March 1953, nor in the republic laws that took its place in 1976–77, religious societies clearly have
some autonomous jurisdiction in matters involving property law.[66] In
any case, the broad legal framework of the *waqf* system has always been
established in the statutes of the Islamic Society in Yugoslavia (1947,
1959, 1969),[67] which, in turn, refer to the precepts and the spirit of the
Shari'a for specific details.[68]

Linguistic and Cultural Autonomy

Linguistic and cultural autonomy are perhaps the most important freedoms that a federative system grants, in varying degrees, to its member
states and other regional entities. Among the essential elements of these
types of autonomy are: the use of the native language in education and
administration, conservation of culture, and the existence of the member
states' identity. With regard to the coordination of the federative regional
entities, linguistic and cultural autonomy is the key to maintaining the
sense of national identity. It is difficult, however, to define these types

of autonomy legally, because the degree to which they can be standardized is necessarily limited. The Soviet Union, especially, has lagged far behind, even in terms of possible standardization, so that its true extent can only be inferred from detailed analysis of power structures and administrative practices, the possibility of which, in turn, is restricted by obvious difficulties. In the Soviet Union, appropriate regulation only exists with regard to the language of public administration; in Yugoslavia, however, the entire complex of linguistic functions, including those of administration, judicial systems and education, is subjected to a very detailed—even obscure—code of laws. The reader is referred to other treatments of this problem;[68] the present discussion will focus on a few fundamental issues that have particular bearing on the Muslims' situation.[69]

In the Soviet Union, territorial linguistic autonomy has a double effect on Muslim people. On the one hand, the setting of territorial "national boundaries" was accompanied by that of linguistic boundaries, with the intention of destroying the unity of the Muslim world. The Muslims can be divided into three main linguistic groups.[70] Among the population of Central Asia, Transcaucasia and the Volga-Ural area, the largest language group by far is that of the Turkic-speakers, constituting about 85 percent. The remaining 15 percent is divided about equally between the Caucasians in the North Caucasus and the Iranian Tajiks in the southeastern part of Central Asia.

At the Soviet Union's inception, there were noticeable differences between the languages of the Caucasian tribes, one of which, the Avars, had developed a semiliterary language in the eighteenth century. The Tajiks used classical Persian as their literary language, but among the Mountain Tajiks numerous dialects were in use in everyday speech. The linguistic homogeneity of the Turkic people was, in contrast, quite striking. The literary language used in Central Asia was Chaghatay; in the Caucasus, Azerbaijani; and, in the Volga-Ural region, Kazan-Tatar. After the nineteenth century, Kazakh was added to this list. In the Pan-Islamic movement, both before and after the October 1917 Revolution, there was a strong impetus to establish Kazan-Tatar as the lingua franca of the Muslim people.[71] In order to counter this development of yet another potential basis for Islamic unity, in the process of federalization in the 1920s, the Bolsheviks followed a policy of creating a separate national language (and in the case of Dagestan, ten of them) for each national region.

Toward this end, it was intended that separate dialects should effectively become literary languages. Time has proved these efforts fruitless, however: experts in the field report that there are fewer differences between Turkic dialects now than there were sixty years ago.[72] On the other hand, the second aspect of linguistic autonomy—its function as a defense against Russification—has developed remarkable effectiveness. Soviet statistics on the correlation between ethnic and linguistic identity show that over 95 percent of the Muslims throughout the Soviet Union have retained their linguistic identity, and 98 to 99 percent of them have retained it in their regional areas.[73] Although there is generally a distinct difference in status between the union republics and the lower-ranking autonomous regions, which offer fewer opportunities for national education, this difference appears to have much less effect on Muslims.[74]

One exception to this rule, however, is the case of the Tatars and Bashkirs. The Tatars' situation confirms the potential of territorial linguistic autonomy to defend linguistic identity. According to the data of the 1979 census, 97.7 percent of the Tatars living in the Tatar ASSR regard Tatar as their mother tongue, in contrast to 81.8 percent of the Tatars in the diaspora.[75] Since three-quarters of all Tatars live outside the Tatar ASSR, the proportion of those throughout the Soviet Union who claim Tatar as their mother tongue is only 85.9.

Soviet statistics give a misleading picture with regard to the Bashkirs, suggesting that there are fewer within the Bashkir ASSR who identify Bashkir as their mother tongue (64.4 percent) than there are outside it (72.6 percent).[76] This apparent paradox results from the Soviet policy of elevating the Bashkir idiom to the level of a national language. Even today a large number of the Bashkirs who have settled among the Tatars in the Volga-Ural region state that Bashkir is their mother tongue.[77]

In Yugoslavia, linguistic autonomy plays an especially important role for the group identity of the Albanians and Turks. In these cases, that identity is probably much more national than Muslim/transnational. Albanian is the Albanians' official language and language of education by the authority of the constitution in Kosovo, while in Montenegro and Macedonia it serves that function on a municipal basis, just as Turkish does as the language of the Turks in Macedonia and Kosovo. The basic right of the individual to speak in the mother tongue follows from these community rights.

It is particularly important that Albanians have the opportunity to study in their native language at the University of Priština, as well as at the Alaundin Medrese, and that instruction at the Isabeg Medrese in Skopje, which opened in 1984, instruction is supposed to be in Turkish.[78] There is, of course, rather less significance in the linguistic autonomy of the state people of Muslims in Bosnia-Herzegovina, where the official language, according to the constitution (Article 4, Clause 1, Constitution of Bosnia-Herzegovina), is "the Serbocroatian, or Croatioserbian, language, with Ijekavian pronunciation." From the point of view of linguistic studies, the situation in this republic is particularly interesting, however, for developments there seem to be tending toward the elimination of the differences between Serbian and Croatian in the creation of a standard language for Bosnia-Herzegovina.[79]

Opportunities for Participation at the State Level

The federative system not only creates a division of authority between the larger state and its members on a regional basis; it also ensures that the regions have the potential to influence the decision-making process on the state level. In this context, constitutional law and constitutional practice in the Soviet Union and in Yugoslavia differ fundamentally.

In the Soviet Union, the provisions of constitutional law involve a representative system within the constitutional bodies of the Union. This system is most developed in the highest constitutional authority, which also has the least say: the Supreme Soviet of the USSR. The Supreme Soviet's second chamber, the Soviet of Nationalities, is organized according to the nationality principle. In every national region, a set number of deputies are "elected" on the basis of federative rank. Article 110, Section 3 of the Union Constitution of 1977 stipulates that thirty-two deputies are to be elected in each Union republic; eleven in each autonomous republic, five in each autonomous region and one in each autonomous district.

According to this rule, of the total of 750 deputies in the Soviet of Nationalities, there are 295 deputies who are from the seventeen nominally "Muslim" regions (317 if the semi-Muslim autonomous republics of Abkhazia and Severo-Ossetia are included) and 220 deputies from the eleven regions having a Muslim majority.

In the more important constitutional bodies, such as the Presidium of the Supreme Soviet, in the Council of Ministers and in the Supreme Court of the USSR, only the union republics are represented, with one representative each. As a rule, this representative is the head of a similar republic agency.[80] In the most important state agency, the Presidium of the Council of Ministers, there is no constitutional requirement for representation, similar to the case in all the central Party bodies. Finally, the union republics probably still retain—as a relic of the early Soviet treaty federation—Permanent Representations at the Council of Ministers of the USSR in Moscow.[81]

With regard to the relationship between the autonomous republics and their respective union republics, this outline of the representational system applies unconditionally only outside the RSFSR.[82] In the RSFSR, on the other hand, which comprises the largest number of autonomous republics, these are only represented in the Presidium of the Supreme Soviet of the RSFSR, but not in the Council of Ministers or the Supreme Court.

In the framework of the constitution, however, these federative opportunities for participation do not play a very large role. There are good reasons for the assertion that the central decision-making process is influenced by regional struggles over allocations, particularly economic and financial ones,[83] in which the Muslim republics (Central Asia and Azerbaijan), as the least economically developed republics,[84] are forced into a supplicant role. No accurate assessment can be made, however, of the degree to which constitutionally institutionalized mechanisms of influence are applied in this regard. A good example is the project, now shelved, for diversion of the great Siberian rivers to Central Asia, which received strong support from Party leaders during the Leonid I. Brezhnev Era. Although they promoted this cause publicly, they did so outside of federal institutions and protocol.[85]

In Yugoslavia, federative entities have participated in the central political decision-making process since the reforms of the late 1960s and early 1970s, according to the principles of parity and rotation. The decisive point here is that these principles apply equally to the state and to the Party. The parity principle appears in a number of variations in appointments in state and party agencies.[86] Normally it implies a graduated parity, in the sense of "equal representation of the republics" and "appropriate representation of the provinces," with the ratio of participation of republics and provinces varying from between three to two and two to one.

In the domain of the state, this applies unconditionally to the legislative bodies (the two chambers of the Federal Assembly) and for the judiciary (the Federal Constitutional Court and the Federal Court). For the executive branch, however, there is the limitation that only elected members of the Federal Executive Council—but not its appointed federal secretaries, who preside over the department—must be appointed in a ratio of two to one. In the formation of the highest party bodies, it is not only territorial organizations that are given consideration, but the army as well, which may be ranked along with provincial organizations

(Central Committee, Statutes Commission, Supervisory Commission) or with a smaller constituency (Party Presidium, Party Conference).[87] In the state's most important governing agency, the State Presidium, the provinces attained full parity in 1974: every republic and provincial assembly elects a member.

The rotation principle has played a stronger role since the death of Marshal Tito, the state and party head: the chair of the state and the party presidium now changes every year.[88] In this system, every republic and province has a turn every eight years. An Albanian from Kosovo has headed the Party Presidium for a year (A. Šukrija, 1984–85), and another has headed the state presidency for the same length of time (S. Hasani, 1986–87). Bosnia-Herzegovina has twice provided the Party Presidium with its chairman (1978–79, 1986–87), and has provided one head of state (1980–81), but none of its representatives has been Muslim.

In the highest state and party bodies, decisions are reached by a (qualified) majority rule. The Council of Republics and Provinces is one exception, where all decisions must be made unanimously. This council is by far the more important of the two chambers of the Federal Assembly, since it has sole jurisdiction over matters of economic law. Each assembly sends twelve and eight delegates, respectively, to the Council of Republics and Provinces. These delegates present themselves and vote as a single body, in the more advanced phases of the legislative process. Moreover, the passage of most bills by the Council of Republics and Provinces requires the agreement of all of the republics and provinces, which means that each regional body has, in effect, the power to veto any bill.

In order to prevent the complete impasse in the decision-making process that would be possible in such a system, Article 301 of the 1974 Federal Constitution sets forth detailed procedures resolving legislative crises.[89] Between 1974 and 1983, the State Presidium was forced on ten occasions to take "emergency measures" under this constitutional guideline. Regional bodies can use another brake, in addition to the veto, however: the enforcement regulations issued by the Federal Executive Council for certain laws of the Council of Republics and Provinces require the consent of the appropriate republic and provincial organizations.

The possibilities for participation outlined here suggest that Yugoslavian regional organizations do not merely exercise great influence over the federal government, but have overtaken it. The federation has indeed become a joint sovereignty of the republics and provinces. Under these circumstances, it is scarcely surprising that, in the political decision-making process in Yugoslavia during the past twenty years, the interaction of new sets of institutional and procedural arrangements has created a "cooperative federalism."[90] The struggle for balance and compromise of interests has not occurred only in the Council of Republics and Provinces, and in the subcommittees of the Federal Assembly. It has also been evident in the numerous boards that are not expressly designated in the constitution, as well as in the permanent commissions of the Federal Executive Council, the special interest committees and the federal social councils.

The impetus for this detailed process of political decisionmaking, for which the expression "harmonizing of stances" (*usaglašavanje stavova*) has been adopted, has been provided by the Federal Executive Council. Aside from the army, this Council is the organization that is most representative of the interests of the Yugoslav state. There is no suggestion, however, of any state-wide organization for Muslim interests.

Sabrina Petra Ramet, who has done exhaustive research on the federative decision-making systems, has produced convincing arguments for the application of the term *balance of power system* to describe Yugoslavian politics, with their characteristic ad hoc coalitions of republics and provinces.[91] The tendency of "Muslim" regions to form coalitions is no exception to this observation. Bosnia-Herzegovina and Kosovo have split into opposing camps under some circumstances, but on other occasions they have acted in concert.[92]

Recently, allocation of scarce economic resources has been the root cause in all federal disputes, whether directly or indirectly. Because of this situation, the economic weakness of the South may result in the formation of an interest group of local organizations in that region, but such a development is not inevitable and depends on the various interests involved. In any case, it is economic concerns, rather than religious or cultural interests, that are pushing the "Muslim" regions to form alliances under certain circumstances.[93] The controversy over the ethnic identity of the Macedonian Muslims, which came to a head in 1971, is one of the few exceptions to this rule.[94] In this case, Bosnia-Herzegovina and Kosovo, as well as Serbia, formed an alliance against the efforts of the Macedonian Party leadership (which was supported by Croatia) to designate Macedonian-speaking Muslims as Macedonian people. The unity of the stances of both sides, however, was fractured along the lines of ethnic identities of their regional constituents.

In conclusion, it would appear that both earlier and contemporary findings are too disparate to allow general statements to be made regarding the significance of federalism for Muslims. This holds true for relationships in the Soviet Union and Yugoslavia on the whole, as well as for the separate regions in both of these federal states. Federative structures constitute only one dimension of ethno-religious and socio-political realities. Their larger significance can only be evaluated through study of the overall picture.

Notes

1. Precisely when this shift in policy occurred is a point of debate even among Soviet scholars. See the evidence provided by Boris Meissner, "Entstehung, Fortentwicklung, und ideologische Grundlagen des sowjetischen Bundesstaates," in *Bundesstaat und Nationalitätenrecht in der Sowjetunion*, ed. F.-Ch. Schroeder and B. Meissner (Berlin, 1974), pp. 9ff., 14ff.

2. *Sobranie Uzakonenii RSFSR*, no. 6 (1917): Article 90, which has been published many times in various volumes. See, for example, *Istoriia Sovetskoi Konstitutsii*, ed. S. S. Studenikin (Moscow, 1957), p. 74; *Obrazovanie i razvitie SSSR kak soiuznogo gosudarstva*, ed. V. I. Vasil'ev and P. P. Gureev (Moscow, 1972), p. 33.

3. On this point, see R. Pipes, *The Formation of the Soviet Union*, rev. ed. (Cambridge, Mass., 1964), pp. 269ff.; Meissner, "Entstehung," pp. 24ff., 30ff.

4. Item II/5 of the resolution of 15 March 1921, "On the Current Tasks of the Party in the Nationality Question," in *Istoriia*, ed. Studenikin, p. 276; *KPSS v rezoliutsiakh i resheniakh s"ezdov, konferentsii i plenumov TsK*, 8th ed., (Moscow, 1970), 2:250–51.

5. On this development, see P. Ramet, *Nationalism and Federalism in Yugoslavia 1963–1983* (Bloomington, Ind., 1984), pp. 48ff.

6. Resolution "On the Economic and Political Situation of Yugoslavia and the Role of the KPY"; text in *Nacionalno pitanje u djelima klasika marksizma i u dokumentima i praksi kpj/skj* (Zagreb, 1978), p. 240; also cited in G. Vlačić, *KPJ i nacionalno pitanje u Jugoslaviji, 1919–1929* (Zagreb, 1974), p. 137; Ramet, *Nationalism*, p. 52. The formation of the states of Croatia, Montenegro, Serbia, and Slovenia was provided for; the state of Macedonia, on the other hand, was to have been created out of territories lying in both Yugoslavia and Bulgaria. The areas of Yugoslavia that had been settled predominantly by Hungarians and Albanians were to be transferred to the current state.

7. Resolution "on the organization of Yugoslavia according to the federative principle" of 29 November 1943; text in L. Geršković, *Historija narodne vlasti* (Belgrade, 1954), pp. 257–58.

8. F. Mayer, in *Südosteuropa-Handbuch—I: Jugoslawien*, ed. K.-D. Grothusen (Göttingen, 1975), p. 57; Ramet, *Nationalism*, p. 80.

9. J. V. Stalin, *Natsional'nyi vopros i sotsial-demokratiia, Prosveshchenie*, no. 3 (1913): 54; see *Der Marxismus und die nationale und koloniale Frage* (East Berlin, 1952), p. 32: "The nation is a stable community, having a historical evolution, comprising people who share a common language, territory, mode of economic life, as well as a distinctive psychology, which is manifest in cultural life."

10. Appeal of the Council of the People's Commissars of 20 November/3 December 1917, to "all working Muslims of Russia and the East," *Sobranie Uzakonenii RSFSR*, no. 6 (1917): Appendix 2; text in *Istoriia*, ed. Studenikin, pp. 66ff.; *Obrazovanie*, ed. Vasil'ev and Gureev, pp. 7ff.

11. See A. Bennigsen and C. Lemercier-Quelquejay, *Les mouvements nationaux chez les musulmans de Russie* (Paris, 1960), pp. 112ff., 126ff.; Pipes, *Formation*, pp. 155ff.; A. Bennigsen and S. Wimbush, *Muslim National Communism in the Soviet Union* (Chicago, 1979), pp. 59ff.

12. Evidence for this underlying motivation can be seen in Item III/1 of the Resolution of the Tenth Party Congress, cited *Istoriia*, above, which item lists 22 different Muslim groups. By comparison with the very basic list of peoples in the "call to Muslims" cited above, a remarkable increase in the number of Muslim groups would appear to have taken place in just over three years (between November/December 1917 and March 1921). The only groups that are mentioned in both lists are the Crimean and Volga Tatars and the Kirgiz, but in 1921 the Bashkirs are mentioned together with the Tatars. In 1924, the Soviet officials began to use the term *Azerbaijanians* for the people formerly known as *Turks of Transcaucasia*, in an attempt to curb Pan-Turkist inclinations. Among the diverse North Caucasian peoples, it was only the Chechen who received official mention in 1917: the widely-used general term *mountain people* (*gortsi*) was regarded as sufficient designation for all other groups. In the Nationalities Resolution, however, no fewer than twelve North Caucasian groups are listed. The general term, *Sarts of Siberia and Turkistan*, moreover, was broken down into the following groups: Tajiks, Turkmens, Uzbeks, Bukharans, and Khivans. The latter two of these groups only had a brief existence, ending in 1924/25.

13. Documentation is given by O. I. Chistiakov, *Stanovlenie Rossiiskoi Federatsii* (Moscow, 1966), pp. 107–8; Bennigsen and Lemercier-Quelquejay, *Les mouvements*, p. 121.

14. See W. Kolarz, *Die Nationalitätenpolitik der Sowjetunion* (Frankfurt am Main, 1956), pp. 44–45, 55–56; Pipes, *Formation*, pp. 161ff.; Bennigsen and Lemercier-Quelquejay, *Les mouvements*, pp. 141ff.

15. In Article 2 of this treaty between the RSFSR and Turkey of 16 March 1921, as well as in Article 6 of the friendship treaty made on 13 October 1921 between the Armenian, Azerbaijanian and Georgian SSRs, on the one hand, and Turkey on the other, Georgia was given sovereignty over Batum, and the population was assured of autonomy in affairs of local administration as well as the exercise of religious rights. In Article 3 of that first treaty, and in Article 5 of the second pact, Nakhichevan was put under the protection of Azerbaijan. The texts of these agreements can be found in: *Dokumenty vneshnei politiki SSSR*, vol. 3 (Moscow, 1959), pp. 597ff., and vol. 4 (1960), pp. 420ff. On the steps taken in 1923 to incorporate Nakhichevan as a state into Azerbaijan, see I. G. Tarigpeima, *Istoriia gosudarstva i prava Azerbaidzhanskoi SSR* (Baku, 1973), pp. 277ff.

16. After the Bolshevik occupation, an Abkhazian SSR was proclaimed, and this republic concluded a federal treaty with Georgia on 16 December 1921. This treaty was officially effective until 19 February 1931, at which time Abkhazia was incorporated into the Georgian SSR as an autonomous republic. See Ia. V. Putkaradze, *Natsional'naia gosudarstvennost' soiuznykh respublik*, ed. D. L. Zlatopol'ski (Moscow, 1968), p. 258, n. 2.

17. In the constitution-making process of 1977–78, there were incidences of anti-Georgian unrest as well as protests by Abkhazian intellectuals, who prevailed upon the Moscow authorities to send I. V. Kapitonov, the Central Committee Secretary, who had jurisdiction over affairs of Party organization, to Georgia and then to Abkhazia, to

smooth out the conflicts at their origin. Kapitonov agreed that some of the grievances were justified, but he rejected the demand that Abkhazia be transferred out of the Georgian SSR into the RSFSR.

18. See B. Hayit, *Turkestan im XX. Jahrhundert* (Darmstadt, 1956), pp. 223ff.

19. V. I. Kozlov, *Natsional'nosti SSSR*, 2d edition (Moscow, 1982), pp. 121–22.

20. A particularly noteworthy work treating the diverse senses of community identity among Soviet Muslim groups is the brilliant and concise analysis of A. Bennigsen and C. Lermercier-Quelquejay, *Les musulmans oubliés* (Paris, 1981), pp. 276ff. See also E. E. Bacon, *Central Asians under Russian Rule* (Ithaca, N.Y., 1966), pp. 202ff; H. Carrère d'Encausse, *Risse im Roten Imperium* (Wien, 1979), pp. 242ff.; A. Bennigsen, "Soviet Muslims and the World of Islam," *Problems of Communism*, no. 3 (1980), pp. 38ff.; E. A. Chylinski, "Islam in Soviet Central Asia: Ethnicity and Religion," in *Soviet Central Asia: Continuity and Change*, ed. E. A. Chylinski (Esbjerg, 1984), pp. 41ff.; G. Simon, *Das nationale Bewusstsein der Nichtrussen in der Sowjetunion*, Bundesinstitut für ostwissenschaftliche und internationale Studien/ Köln, Report No. 47/ 1986, pp. 27ff.

21. Article 1 of the Kosovo Constitution of 27 February 1974 does not provide for the assignment of the province to any particular group of people. Instead, it states that the Albanians, Muslims, Serbs, Turks, Montenegrins (listed in Serbian alphabetical order), as well as others, should have equal rights within it. Article 2 discusses the subject of groups and nationalities in Kosovo, but it does not name them. The text is in *Ustav SFRJ, ustavi socijalistickih republika i pokrajina* (Belgrade, 1974), pp. 675ff.

22. On this and the following point, see Ramet, *Nationalism*, pp. 145ff.

23. V. Meier, "Bosnien und seine Muslime," *Südosteuropa-Mitteilungen* 1 (1986): 12ff.

24. Preamble, Introduction and Articles 1–3 of the Constitution of the Socialist Republic of Bosnia-Herzegovina, 25 February 1974. Text in *Ustav SFRJ*, pp. 91ff.

25. In Soviet statistics, the Tatars are now considered to be a unified group. According to the census of 1979, 1,641,000 of the 6,317,000 Soviet Tatars were living in the Tatar ASSR. The number of Volga Tatars is probably around 5.6 or 5.7 million. The Crimean Tatars, numbering approximately four hundred thousand constitute the next larger group, followed by the Siberian Tatars (approximately 150 thousand). Bennigsen and Lemercier-Quelquejay, *Les musulmans*, pp. 134ff. and 171–72, give further information on this point.

26. See the detailed summary given by Bennigsen and Lemercier-Quelquejay, *Les musulmans*, pp. 87ff.

27. See G. Brunner, "Minderheitschutz in Osteuropa," *Jahrbuch für Ostrecht* 25 (1984): 9ff., 30ff., as well as his "Die Rechtstellung ethnischer Minderheiten in Südosteuropa," *Südosteuropa* (1986): 235ff., 253ff.

28. There are various types of constitutional provisions for the protection of minorities. The Constitution of Montenegro includes a set of special provisions for the Albanians (Articles 174–79). The Constitution of Macedonia makes clear the concept that is both a nation-state of the Macedonian people and a state of the Albanian and Turkish nationalities (Article 1, Section 1), whose equality of rights is set forth in a particular chapter (Articles 177–83). In the Constitution of Kosovo there are a number of provisions which deal specifically with the Turkish minority (Articles 5, 217: Section 2, 218: Section 1, and 236: Section 1) and which govern the details of

the "Law of the Establishment of Equality of Languages and Scripts in the Socialist Autonomous Province of Kosovo" of 28 December 1977 (*Službeni list Socialisticke Autonomne Pokrajine Kosovo*, no. 48/1977). The texts of these constitutions can be found in *Ustav SFRJ.*

29. Item 5 of the resolution of 22 March 1919, "On Organizational Questions," published in *KPSS v rezoliutsiiakh*, 2:73–74.

30. On this complex process of development prior to 1972, see O. N. Haberl, *Parteiorganisation und nationale Frage in Jugoslavien* (Berlin, 1976); A. Carter, *Democratic Reform in Yugoslavia: The Changing Role of the Party* (London, 1982). On the period after 1972, see S. Stankovic, *Titos Erbe* (Munich, 1981).

31. There is no satisfactorily comprehensive work in any Western language on the relationship of administrative structures to federative systems in Yugoslavia. The best references are found in the Yugoslav contributions to the 1984 German-Yugoslav Legal Conference that was dedicated to the problem of federalism: *Probleme des Föderalismus* (Tübingen, 1985). On the jurisdictions of the Soviet Union republics, see the careful study—which was published, however, prior to the Union Constitution of 1977 currently in effect—of H.-J. Uibopuu, *Die Völkerrechtssubjektivität der Unionsrepubliken der UdSSR* (Vienna, 1975), especially pp. 128ff. and 228ff. A summary of the current legal situation can be found in the commentary to Articles 73, 82, and 86 in *Handbuch der Sowjetverfassung*, ed. M. Fincke (Berlin, 1983).

32. In Soviet Russia the first three judiciary decrees cleared the way for this radical change, which was made final with Article 22 of the RSFSR Law of the People's Courts, 30 November 1918 (*Sobranie Zakonov RSFSR*, no. 85, Article 889). This law contains a note that prohibits courts from applying laws of the old regime. In Yugoslavia the change took place with the decree of the AVNOJ-Presidium of 3 February 1945 (*Službeni list*, no. 4/1945) and the law of October 1946, "On the Invalidity of the Laws Issued Before 6 April 1941 and During the Occupation" (*Službeni list*, 1, no. 86/1946).

33. For details see H.-J. Kornrumpf, "Scheriat und Christlicher Staat: Die Muslime in Bosnien und in den europäischen Nachfolgstaaten des Osmanischen Reiches," *Saeculum* (1984): 17ff.

34. As far as legal technicalities are concerned, this took place through the Turkestanian administration's resolution to amend Article 22 of the RSFSR law discussed in note 2, above. The amendment stated that, at the request of both parties in a dispute, the People's Courts could apply Islamic law as long as it did not run counter to the spirit of the laws following from the October 1917 Revolution; see *Istoriia sovetskogo gosudarstva i prava Uzbekistana*, vol. 1, ed. Kh. S. Sulaimanova and A. I. Ishanov (Tashkent, 1960), p. 501.

35. Article 3 of the Decree of the All-Russian Central Executive Committee of 11 April 1921, "On the Establishment of the Turkistanian Soviet Socialist Republic" (*Sobranie Uzakonenii RSFSR*, no. 32 [1921]: Article 173); text in *Istoriia*, ed. Studenikin, pp. 282–83.

36. Decree of the Central Executive Committee and the Council of the People's Commissars of the Turkistanian ASSR of 23 December 1922, "On the Status of the Jurisdiction of Qadis and Beys." Abstracts of this text can be found in P. V. Gidulianov, *Otdelenie tserkvi ot gosudarstva v S.S.S.R.*, 3d edition (Moscow, 1926), pp. 516–17.

37. Decree of the Council of People's Commissars of the Turkistanian ASSR of

6 January 1923, "On the Jurisdiction of Beys in the Fergana Region"; text in Gidulianov, *Otdelenie*, p. 517.

38. In that region, by 1921 the jurisdiction of the *aksakal*s had been forbidden by a circular issued by the People's Commissariat for Justice of the Kirgizistan ASSR; see *Istoriia gosudarstva i prava sovetskogo Kazakhstana*, vol. 1, ed. S. Z. Zimanov and M. A. Binder (Alma-Ata, 1961), pp. 438–39.

39. According to evidence in *Istoriia*, ed. Studenikin, the number of Shariʿa courts decreased from 350 to 72 in the course of the year 1924 (vol. 1, p. 506), and by 1927 they had practically disappeared (vol. 2, 1963, p. 83). Other figures, derived from Soviet sources, and which do not contradict the observation of this trend, are cited by Hayit, *Turkestan*, p. 306 and W. Kolarz, *Die Religionen in der Sowjetunion* (Freiburg, 1963), p. 408.

40. B. Spuler in *Osteuropa-Handbuch: Jugoslawien*, ed. W. Markert (Cologne, 1954), p. 186.

41. See M. Begović, "Les vestiges du droit musulman dans le droit yougoslave," *Jugoslavenska Revija za Medjunarodno Pravo* (1956): 125ff.

42. Begovic, *Les vestiges*, p. 127; A. G. Chloros, *Yugoslav Civil Law* (Oxford, 1970), p. 93.

43. Article 1 (o) of the Union Constitution of 1924 limited the power of the Union to the basic principles of penal law of the Union Constitution of 1924. Article 14 (u) of the Constitution of 1936 reauthorized extensive legal jurisdiction for the union, but a constitutional amendment of 11 February 1957 limited its power once again to jurisdiction in the basic principles. In Article 73, Item 4, of the now-effective Constitution of 1977, penal law is no longer specifically mentioned; instead, general terms grant the Union legislation of basic principles.

44. V. S. Prokhorov in *Kurs sovetskogo ugolovnogo prava*, vol. 5, ed. N. A. Beliaev (Leningrad, 1981), pp. 222–23; *Istoriia gosudarstva i prava Azerbaidzhanskoi SSR (1920–1934 gg.)* (Baku, 1973), pp. 327–28, 382–83.

45. Resolution of the All-Russian Central Executive Committee and the Council of People's Commissars of the RSFSR of 16 October 1924 (*Sobranie Uzakonenii RSFSR*, no. 79 [1924]: Article 787).

46. Prokhorov, *Kurs*, pp. 223–24.

47. For an extensive treatment of the current legal situation, see Prokhorov, *Kurs*, pp. 225ff.

48. The places listed are the Bashkir, Buryat-Mongol, Kirgizistan and Turkistan autonomous republics, as well as the Adygei, Kabardin-Balkar, Kalmyk, Karachay-Cherkess, and Oirot autonomous regions: Prokhorov, *Kurs*, p. 223. It is worth noting that there is no mention of the Tatar ASSR (because mention was unnecessary?) or the Dagestan ASSR (because mention was too risky?).

49. Judgment of the Penal College of the Supreme Court of the RSFSR of 23 August 1974 (*Biulleten' Verkhovnogo Suda RSFSR* 2 [1975]: 12–13).

50. Plenary resolution of 19 March 1969; text in *Sbornik postanovlenii plenuma Verkhovnogo Suda RSFSR 1961–1977* (Moscow, 1978), pp. 222ff.

51. The arbitration of reconciliation is governed by a resolution of the All-Russian Central Executive Committee and the Council of People's Commissars of the RSFSR of 5 November 1928, "On the Arbitration of Reconciliation in the Struggle against the

Custom of Blood Revenge" (*Sobranie Uzakonenii RSFSR*, no. 41, Article 927). Evidence that this legal standard is still in effect can be found in the following sources, among others: Prokhorov, *Kurs*, pp. 253–54; V. V. Shubin in *Kommentarii k Ugolovnomu Kodeksu RSFSR*, ed. Iu. D. Severin (Moscow, 1980), note 3 to Article 231. It is also worth noting that, according to the penal codes of the RSFSR and the Central Asian union republics, the concept of blood revenge serves as a criterion to qualify premeditated slaying as murder.

52. Spuler, *Osteuropa*, p. 187; V. Strika, "La comunità religiosa islamica della Jugoslavia," *Oriente Moderno* (1967): 1ff., 44.

53. The authority of the provinces follows from the Serbian Constitution of 25 February 1974, which includes a catalog of legal matters that can be arbitrated on a uniform basis throughout the republic. Penal legislation is not mentioned, so that, according to the general understanding of the legal systems, it pertains to the legislative authority of the provinces.

54. Penal law of the Socialist Autonomous Province of Kosovo of 29 June 1977 (*Službeni list Socijalisticke Autonomne Pokrajina Kosovo*, no. 20/1977); text in *Zbirka krivicnih zakona*, 2d ed. (Belgrade, 1977), pp. 627ff.

55. Legal acts pertaining to the historical situation can be found in the following texts: Gidulianov, *Otdelenie*; N. Orleanskii, *Zakon o religioznykh ob"edineniiakh* (Moscow, 1930); *Zakonodatel'stvo o religioznykh kul'takh*, 2d ed., ed. V. A. Kuroedov, (Moscow, 1971), pp. 83ff. Further remarks, scanty in other respects, can be found in O. Luchterhandt, *Die Religionsgesetzgebung der Sowjetunion* (Berlin, 1978), pp. 42ff.; Iu. A. Rozenbaum, *Sovetskoe gosudarstvo i tserkov'* (Moscow, 1985), pp. 38ff. An understanding of current religious law in the union republics can be extracted from the legal compilation, "Svod Zakonov," in so far as the appropriate vol. 1 has been published (to date, for Azerbaijan and Tajikistan). References to source materials appear in Rozenbaum, *Sovetskoe*, pp. 49–50, note 75.

56. Kolarz, *Religionen*, p. 407.

57. On the various types of *waqf* in Central Asia, see I. M. Matley, "Agricultural Development," in *Central Asia: A Century of Russian Rule*, ed. E. Allworth (New York, 1967), p. 279.

58. Decree of the Council of People's Commissars of the RSFSR, 23 January 1918, "On the Separation of the Church from the State and the Schools from the Church" (*Sobranie Uzakonenii RSFSR*, no. 18 [1918]: Article 263). The text can be found in German in Luchterhand, *Religionsgesetzgebung*, pp. 105ff., among other places.

59. Decree of the Republic of Turkistan, 20 June 1922, "On the Returning of Waqfs to the Madrasas and Mosques"; text in Guidulianov, *Otdelenie*, pp. 278.

60. Decree of the Central Executive Committee of the Republic of Turkistan, 28 December 1922, "On Waqfs"; text in Giduljanov, *Otdelenie*, pp. 279–80.

61. Waqf-Decree of 22 October 1923; reference in *Istoriia*, ed. Studenikin, vol. 2, pp. 243–44.

62. Waqf-Decree of 19 December 1925; reference in *Istoriia*, ed. Studenikin, vol. 2, p. 83.

63. Instruction of the People's Commissariat for Domestic Affairs and the People's Commissariat of Justice, 16 January 1926, "On the Procedure of Registering Religious Communities" (items 9 and 12); Instruction of the Central Administration at the

212 Policies toward Muslims

Council of People's Commissars, 29 April/3 October 1928 (items 3 and 9); texts in Orleanskii, *Zakon*, pp. 207ff., especially 210ff.

64. B. Spuler, "Vom Feldzeugmeister zum Schauprozess. Die Lage der Muslime in Jugoslawien," *Glaube in der 2. Welt*, no. 1 (1986): 25ff., 29. On the development until the mid-1960s, see the thorough work of Strika, *Comunità*, pp. 28ff.

65. D. Pavic and F. Duic, *Prava na nekretninama* (Zagreb, 1972), pp. 36, 88.

66. In the "Muslim" regions the following laws concerning the legal status of religious communities are in effect: 1. Bosnia-Herzegovina: Law of 15 December 1976 (*Službeni list Socijalisticke Republika Bosne i Hercegovine*, no. 36/1976); 2. Kosovo: several provisions of the Serbian Law of 27 October 1977 (*Službeni glasnik Socijalisticke Republike Srbije*, no. 44/1977) and the Law of Kosovo of 5 May 1977, amending the latter (*Službeni list Socijalisticke Autonomne Pokrajine Kosova*, no. 10/1977).

67. Strika, *Comunità*, pp. 24, 25; M. Begović, "Vakuf," *Enciclopedia Jugoslavije* (Zagreb, 1971), 8:450.

68. Brunner, *Minderheitschutz*, pp. 30ff., 38ff.; Brunner, *Rechtsstellung*, pp. 251–52, 254ff.; Brunner, "Die Rechtslage der Minderheiten nach sowjetischem Verfassungsrecht," in *Die Minderheiten in der Sowjetunion und das Völkerrecht. Nationalitäten- und Regionalprobleme in Osteuropa*, ed. G. Brunner and A. Kagedan (Cologne, 1988), 2:23ff., 31ff.

69. Currently, this occurs in Articles 6 and 7 of the State of 5 November 1969 (*Glasnik Vrkovnog Islamog Starješinstva u SFRJ* 1970, pp. 105ff.).

70. An overview in tabular form for the Muslim languages can be found in A. Bennigsen and M. Broxup, *The Islamic Threat to the Soviet State* (London, 1983), pp. 156ff.

71. A Bennigsen and S. E. Wimbush, *Muslim National Communism in the Soviet Union* (Chicago, 1979), p. 88.

72. Bennigsen and Lemercier-Quelquejay, *Les musulmans*, p. 281.

73. On this point, see, among others, Carrère d'Encausse, *Risse*, pp. 179ff.; H. L. Krag, "The Language Situation in Central Asia," in Chylinski, *Islam*, pp. 57ff., 60ff.

74. Brunner, *Die Rechtslage*, pp. 37–38, which gives further references.

75. Kozlov, *Natsional'nosti*, pp. 240–41.

76. Ibid.

77. Bennigsen and Lemercier-Quelquejay, *Les musulmans*, p. 141.

78. Spuler, *Vom Feldzeugmeister*, pp. 29–30; A. Popović, *L'Islam balkanique* (Berlin, 1986), p. 351.

79. J. Matešić, "Über die Sprachbenennung bei den Kroaten, Serben, Montenegrinern und Musulmanen," *Südosteuropäische-Mitteilungen* (1987): 29ff., 34.

80. The Union Constitution dictates this set-up for the chairmen of the Councils of Ministers (Article 129, Section 2) and for the presidents of the Supreme Courts (Article 153, Section 2) of the union republics. With regard to the Presidium of the Supreme Soviet of the USSR, Article 120 only stipulates that 15 deputies of the chairman must come from the various republics. This is in accordance with the constitutional practice of having these deputies be the chairmen of the presidia of the supreme soviets of the republics.

81. Some time ago, P. J. Potichnyj, "Permanent Representations (*Postpredstva*) of Union Republics in Moscow," in *Politics and Participation under Communist Rule*, ed. P. J. Potichnyj and S. Zacek (New York, 1983), pp. 50ff., drew attention to this

fact. They overestimated, however, the significance of permanent representations. His most important source of evidence is an essay by M. A. Krokhotin, "Postoiannye Predstavitel'stva—organ sviazi Sovetov Ministrov Soiuznykh Respublik s Sovetom Ministrov SSSR," *Sovetskoe Gosudarstvo i Pravo* 11 (1968): 90ff.

82. This is not the case for the supreme soviets, because they only consist of one chamber in the union republics.

83. J. F. Hough and M. Fainsod, *How the Soviet Union is Governed* (Cambridge, Mass., 1979), pp. 511ff.; A. Nove, *Das sowjetische Wirtschaftssystem* (Baden-Baden, 1980), p. 74.

84. J. A. Dellenbrant, "Regional Policy and Regional Development in Soviet Central Asia," in Chylinski, *Islam*, pp. 119ff., 123–24.

85. As the following may have done during the Twenty-Fourth Party Congress of the Communist Party in February 1981: D. A. Kunaev, from Kazakhstan (*Pravda*, 25 February 1981); Sh. R. Rashidov from Uzbekistan (*Pravda*, 27 February 1981) and M. G. Gapurov from Turkmenia (*Pravda*, 27 February 1981).

86. On the most significant details, see R. K. Furtak, "Elemente kooperativer Konfliktregelung in Jugoslawien," *Sowjetsystem und Ostrecht. Festschrift für B. Meissner* (Berlin, 1985), pp. 327ff., 332ff.

87. About two-thirds of the delegates are elected by lower Party organizations in proportion to the size of their membership. It is only the other third that is formed according to the rule of graded parity, with a ratio of 6:4:3.

88. By virtue of his office as state and party president, respectively, Marshal Tito was the chairman of both governing bodies until his death in May 1980. In October 1978, however, the Party Presidium issued rules of procedure instituting the office of a chairman who was to lead the sessions in Tito's absence.

89. *NIN* of 6 May 1984.

90. See the study by S. L. Burg, "Decision-Making in Yugoslavia," *Problems of Communism* 3 (1980): 1ff., 15ff.; Burg, *Conflict and Cohesion in Socialist Yugoslavia* (Princeton, N.J., 1982). See also Furtak, *Elemente*, particularly pp. 237ff.

91. Ramet, *Nationalism*.

92. Ramet, *Nationalism*. On pp. 237ff. there is a listing in tabular form describing the development of coalitions in situations of conflict.

93. An interesting example of this impetus is seen in the coalitions that formed in 1980 in the course of debate over the Fifth Amendment to the Constitution of 1974. The subject of the new legislation was the term of office of the chairman and the members of the Federal Executive Council. Bosnia-Herzegovina, Kosovo and Montenegro argued for the shortest possible term of office and, in consequence, for a weakening of the central administration. The opinion expressed by Burg, *Conflict*, p. 334, and Furtak, *Elemente*, p. 342, that a weakened Federal Executive Council improved the chances of the underdeveloped southern regions through negotiations regarding allocations of finances, cannot be dismissed.

94. See Ramet, *Nationalism*, pp. 149ff.

10. Yugoslavia's Communists and the Bosnian Muslims

Wolfgang Höpken

The Problem of a Muslim Nation

In the latest census in 1981, about two million citizens—8.5 percent of the total population of Yugoslavia—described themselves as belonging to the Muslim nation. By far the greatest number live in the member republic of Bosnia-Herzegovina, where the Muslims, with 38 percent, constitute a plurality of the population.[1] The term *Muslim*, however, inevitably causes confusion. In Yugoslav usage, it has semantically dual character, designating both religious confession and ethnic affiliation with one of the six Yugoslav "peoples" or the other.[2] This seems contradictory to the foreign observer, and even in scholarly literature it has occasionally given rise to misconceptions as to the number and ethnic status of the Muslims. But even in view of the intra-Yugoslav discussion, the claim of Muslim historian Atif Purivatra is deceiving, when he states that in being misunderstood only by foreigners, but posing "no difficulties" inside Yugoslavia, the Muslim nation is a factually accepted concept and a phenomenon theoretically consistent with nationalism.[3] Although the Muslim nation—and in the following we will only consider its character as an ethnic national group[4]—has had guaranteed rights in the constitution of Bosnia-Herzegovina since 1963 and although it also has been tolerated politically by the Central Committee of the Communist Party of Bosnia-Herzegovina since 1968, the existence of a Muslim nation is politically and theoretically controversial. In spite of attempts by Muslim historians, sociologists, and politicians to create an historical and theoretical foundation for this, the youngest of all Yugoslav nations, there is no shortage of voices even inside Yugoslavia who see the Muslim nation as no more than a politically expedient hybrid. In Serbia and Croatia—albeit mainly in dissident or semidissident intellectual circles—the upgrading of Muslims to a nation has again and again been called into question[5] or openly rejected as *ismišljeni narod*— a "made-up" people.[6]

Political calculations of these various positions and national interests of their representatives aside, the manner in which the Muslim nation was more or less called into being by a party decision begs the question of its historical and theoretical legitimation. The Macedonian nation is a parallel case, and the question asked there has to be put to the Muslim nation as well: did the nation grow out of the peoples' awareness of communality, of shared social and cultural values, or is it, in the final analysis, merely an artificial creation?[7]

Until now, historical scholarship has paid little—and in the case of Yugoslav literature sometimes inadequate—attention to this question.[8] If the theme is addressed in Yugoslavia at all, it is done almost exclusively by Muslim historians, who may turn up valuable details in their research, but who on the whole frequently fall prey to distortions in their perspective. The paradigm of Muslim nation-building developed by them may be summed up as follows:

1. The Muslim nation looks back on a continuous history beginning in the pre-Islamic Bosnian Middle Ages. Above all the Bogomils, members of the Bosnian Church, developed a special anti-Orthodox and anti-papal territorial and religious consciousness, which might be considered the nucleus of the later Muslim nation-building.

2. The Bogomil heresy fostered the Islamization of the ruling class and of broad sections of the populace after the Ottoman conquest of 1463 and created a religiously and culturally separatist consciousness during the Ottoman reign. After the Ottomans lost the Balkans, this consciousness grew stronger in the contest with the ethnically and religiously alien Austro-Hungarian monarchy and consolidated into a feeling of national identity.

3. The resistance of feudal social structures and the dominance of religious hierarchies hindered formation of a modern secular national ideology, but on the whole, Muslim nation-building followed a course similar to that of Serbs and Croatians, albeit with a time lag.[9]

The main objection against this version of Muslim nation-building— given here in a very condensed form—is that it foreshortens the premodern history of the Muslims teleologically and deterministically into a prehistory of nation-building in socialist Yugoslavia. In particular, the thesis of the Bogomils as the "ethnic essence" of the Muslim nation has been refuted as historically unfounded and as a thinly veiled attempt to construct for the Muslims a continuity from the Middle Ages similar to that of the Serbs and Croatians.[10] The representation of the Muslims in the late stages of the Ottoman empire was criticized for overinterpreting a consciousness of regional identity as a "national awakening."[11] Far from being accorded status as character-forming movements, such stirrings were at best considered valid during the rule of Austria-Hungary over Bosnia after 1878.[12]

It would be a mistake, however, to exclude the possibility of confessionally grounded, genuine Muslim nation-building from the highly profiled canon of Western European paradigms of nation-building. There simply needs to be some skepticism about the credibility of the concepts offered by Yugoslav (Muslim) historians.

Even in Central Europe, equating the rise of "modern nations" with the structural changes of the "double revolution" in the late eighteenth and early nineteenth centuries is no longer satisfactory, but had to be supplemented by the concept of "premodern nationalism."[13] For Southeastern Europe, it is no less true than for Central Europe, that "modern nations began to form under premodern conditions, and in doing so they drew on elements that cannot be considered entirely as relics, but must be recognized as important in the nation-forming process."[14] In this context, the role of the Church has been pointed out, in Serbia and Rumania for instance, where the "confessional nation" is recognizable as an early stage on the way to a modern political community.[15] Contrary to the position of Ranke, who held that Islam—unlike the Christian Church— contributed nothing to the emerging national consciousness in Southeastern Europe, the first question about Muslims should be whether there is empirical evidence that a nation was formed from a confessional community and was later overlaid by secularism.[16] The answer to this question can only be obtained by including the Muslims in comparative research into nation-building in Southeastern Europe and is beyond the scope of this essay.

In the period following 1878, social and political development of the Muslims, which is given here only in a few key words, seems to support both interpretations. In the late phase of the Ottoman empire, the Muslims were already losing their ruling class privileges, accorded to them on the basis of their religion, and when the Ottoman Empire collapsed in Bosnia, they definitely had to redefine their social position. Both the Austrian empire and the already well-developed Serbian and Croatian national movement confronted the Bosnian Muslims regarding their national identity. Religious interests and cultural traditions had to be defended against the new Christian rulers of Bosnia and against increasingly modernized and secularized surroundings. Here begins the attempt to mold the ties and loyalties of the "confessional nationality" into an ethnic and nationalistic consciousness. It addressed religious and educational autonomy—the first steps toward building a network of Muslim cultural and social organizations transcending purely religious goals—the administration of the *vakuf* (Arabic: *waqf*)[17] estates, newspapers, Muslim banks, and—since 1906—even political organizations.[18] It prepared at least part of the Muslim population of Bosnia to evolve from a pre- or protonational community of faith into an embryonic form of political community with an ethnic and national identity.

Compared to Serbian and Croatian nationalism, which was already established in the late nineteenth century, such stirrings of Muslim national ideology remained rudimentary at best. A national consciousness which transcended the feeling of religious community never took root among the mass of the Muslim population.[19] Until recent times— that is, until the Occupation—Bosnian "Muslims had no idea what nation they belonged to. The Begs, the respected Agas, and the intellectuals among them called themselves Bosnians and their language, Croatian, but the mass of the people do not understand it"—so writes the Croatian school teacher Anton Hangi, who taught in Bosnia at the beginning of this century.[20] But even among the potential leaders from the political and cultural elite an articulated national group consciousness was largely absent. Intellectuals, whom Hroch calls the engines of nation-building in "small nations," were not only few in number among the Muslims, but they wavered in their national loyalties until far into the new century. This changing of nationality mirrored the deep-seated insecurity typical of Muslims after the end of Ottoman rule in Bosnia.[21] Even beyond the time of World War I, the leading political elite did not tie its struggle for political, religious, and cultural rights of Muslims to the national cohesion of the Muslims, but sought to reconcile preservation of religious-cultural uniqueness with membership in the Serbian or Croatian nation. Even if cultural and religious difference from Serbs and Croatians developed and strengthened a separate consciousness, the Muslims ultimately lacked the popular consensus component of a nation.

The Attitude of the Communists toward the Muslims

If the Bosnian Muslims themselves lacked a well-developed national consciousness even beyond the turn of the century, certainly no one else took up the cause of their ethnic individuality. Serbs and Croatians, regardless of political persuasion, claimed the Muslims for their respective nations. In doing so, they answered the question "čija je Bosna?"—to whom does Bosnia belong?—each in their own way. This question surfaced not only in the territorial politics of the Serbian and Croatian bourgeois parties up to the time of World War II, but it created problems even for the Yugoslav communists, as will be seen later. For the politicians of Greater Serbia like Garašanin and Mustafa Pašić or for the patriarchs of Serbian Social Democracy like Svetozar Marković and Dimitrije Tucović the Serbian character of the Bosnian Muslims was uncontested.[22] Differences arose only in the consequences drawn from that certainty: would Bosnia simply be included in the envisioned Greater Serbia, or would the question "To whom does Bosnia belong?" be answered by incorporating it into the vision of a federation of autonomous Balkan republics.

On the Croatian side, the universal political consensus was shaped by the word of the founder of the Croatian "Rightist party," Ante Starčević, who called the Muslims the "purest Croatians."[23] It survived the times and political currents from the conservative camp via the Croatian Peasants' Party[24] to the Ustasha.[25]

The Yugoslav Social Democrats, and the Communists after them, were therefore rooted in a barely questioned tradition when their answer to the question of the national character of the Bosnian Muslims was at first no different from that of the bourgeois camp. The Social Democratic Party of Bosnia and Herzegovina, founded in 1908 and following the outline of Austrocommunism in its nationality policy, did not even pose the question of national affiliation. It simply asserted that "all citizens of Bosnia are part of a people that call themselves Serbs or Croatians." In the resolution concerning national identity from its Second Party Congress in 1910 it declared: "Our Muslims are without a national consciousness. This is a consequence of the economic conditions in which they live and from which their cultural backwardness originates. The solution of the agrarian question and the integration of large parts of the Muslim population into modern economic relationships is the premise for the national awakening of the Muslims."[26] Preservation of religious cultural traditions and separate consciousness were thus considered an expression of national indifference and a product of socio-economic backwardness; overcoming feudal survivals, industrialization, and modernization would stimulate the Muslims to confess themselves a part of the united nation of Serbs and Croatians. This concept bears a strong resemblance—as will be seen—to the attitude of the Yugoslav Communists in the first years after World War II.

The Bosnian Social Democrats also brought this attitude with them into the Communist Party of Yugoslavia (KPY), founded in 1919. To be sure, the individual Social Democracies who joined this union were of diverse ideological stripe. But all agreed, just like the bourgeois forces who took part in the unification process, that the population of the new Yugoslav state was a *troimenni narod:* a people consisting of the three tribes of Serbs, Croatians, and Slovenians, and speaking the same language, except for local dialects.[27] For the KPY, this answered the question of the national affiliation of the Muslims for the time being.

The conspectus of attitudes of the Yugoslav Communists regarding the problem of the national character of the Bosnian Muslims is divided into roughly four phases from the formation of the party to the present:

1. From the founding of the party in 1919 to about 1935. Regardless of certain changes in the party's concept of nationalism, the phase ignores the individual historical character of Bosnia and denies the special ethnic status of the Bosnian Muslims.

2. From the middle of the 1930s to the end of World War II. The existence of a special territorial and historical individuality of Bosnia is accepted and included in the federative plans of the KPY, but the attitude of the party toward the character of the Muslims is marked by two contradictory tendencies; namely, there are the beginnings of an acceptance of the special ethnic status of the Muslims on one side, and on the other this individuality continues to be denied.

3. The time from 1945 to the beginning of the 1960s. Regarding the national question, the attitude of the party during this period was shaped by a unionist concept of a solution, which openly denied any nationality-specific attributes of the Muslims and saw their future in their national identification as Serbs or Croatians.

4. From the early 1960s onward, there is a beginning recognition of the Muslims as a nation, which has become official since 1968.

The Unionist Phase

The first phase, from 1919 to the middle of the thirties, needs only a rough outline. Taken over from the prewar Social Democrats, the thesis of the ethnically unified character of the Yugoslav people reduced the concept of *Muslims,* a priori, to a religious category. In a "Proclamation of the KPY Leadership to the Working Populace of Bosnia" from the year 1921 (addressed to Muslims and people of other faiths) the demand for equal national rights for the Muslims was rejected as absurd, on the grounds that "it is unthinkable that a whole section of one and the same people would be disenfranchised simply because of religious faith."[28] The religiously and culturally motivated separate consciousness of the Bosnian Muslims was thus not understood as an element of an emerging "confessional nation." On the contrary: The leading party theoretician of the time, Sima Marković, stated that the Muslims are a prime example for how religion "can alienate a part of our people."[29] Even in 1923–24, when the party had to address the increasingly clear national antagonisms in the young Yugoslav state, the discussion showed no signs of a change regarding the Muslims. Although the party distanced itself more and more from the fiction of an ethnically unified Yugoslavia and regarded at least Serbs, Croatians, and Slovenes as self-contained nations,[30] the Muslims remained excluded from this political cleansing process. The same holds true for the proposed solution to the national question in which the party, prompted at least in part by pressure from the Comintern, from the end of the 1920s on, offered to dissolve the Yugoslav federation into individual states.[31] At that time, when in addition to Serbs, Croatians, and Slovenes, even Montenegrins and Macedonians were considered as individual nations, no mention is made of the Muslims at all.[32]

The KPY not only denied special ethnic status to the Muslims, it also almost completely ignored the role of Bosnia as a historically grown and individualistic region of Yugoslavia. There was no room for such thinking in the centralized state and party thinking of the years 1919 to 1924, and even in the late 1920s and early 1930s, Bosnia surfaces only sporadically in the vague plans of dissolving Yugoslavia into newly-to-be-formed individual states.[33] The lack of understanding for and lukewarm interest in Bosnia and the Bosnian Muslims exhibited by the KPY in the first decade of its existence was not only caused by the influence of Stalin's political theory, which simply could not conceive of a nation founded on religious confession and Islamic cultural tradition. A contributing factor was also the insignificant role played by the KPY in Bosnia-Herzegovina until the end of the 1930s. It was an isolated splinter group, far from the central party, and even in 1939 it had only about 170 members.[34]

In order to do justice to the attitude of the KPY toward the Muslims, scholars cannot simply put it aside as a "false start," as tends to be the case in contemporary Yugoslav historiography. In denying the ethnic and national character of the Bosnian Muslims, the party at that time knew itself to be in complete agreement with the political leadership of the Muslims. At no time did the "Yugoslav Muslim Organization" (YMO), which was the uncontested political force of the Muslims during the time between the wars, stake a claim for Muslim nationality. Rather, its national political creed was that of "Yugoslavism." In its platform of 1919, it declared itself in solidarity with the principle of "national unity" and "Yugoslovenstvo" and made it a point to refuse the "political nationalization" of the Muslims.[35] Mehmed Begović, a (Serb-leaning) Muslim, framed the question as whether the Muslims of Bosnia would evolve by means of an intermediate nationality as Serbs and Croatians or whether they would proceed directly to Yugoslavism.[36] The delegates of the YMO in the Belgrade parliament in 1923 and 1927 identified themselves overwhelmingly as Croatians (17 and 11 respectively), rarely as Serbs (0 and 1), and equally rarely as nationally undefined (1 and 6),[37] that is, the great majority gravitated toward Zagreb,[38] while only a few confessed themselves openly to the Muslim nation.[39]

Ultimately, however, the Muslim Yugoslavism of the YMO strengthened the Muslim feeling of separateness from the Serbs and Croatians, even if this did not happen under the banner of a special Muslim nation. It became a means for articulating specific Muslim concerns, continuing the modest prewar beginnings, widening the scope to transcend purely confessional interests, and expressing a common political will. After the founding of the state, which happened mostly without Muslim participation,[40] and which the Muslims eyed with neutrality and reserve, the Muslims withdrew into a kind of isolated autarky formed around mosque, cultural center, and YMO. From very early days the Muslims distanced themselves from the new state. For one thing, the Serbs took revenge against the anti-Serbian units of World War I, in which the Muslims had participated. Mehmed Spaho, leader of the YMO, claims that 2000 Muslims became victims of this vendetta between 1918 and 1920.[41] In addition, social conflicts following the agrarian reforms turned into nationalist altercations between Serbs and Muslims. Although the latter's social standing had long since declined to that of small farmers, the still partially indentured Serbian Kmetes saw in their status as free farmers a relic of Ottoman feudalism. Then there were political disadvantages and underrepresentation in the civil service and in political organizations.[42] These were not always only the result of deliberate harassment, but also of a falling behind in education and social skills compared to the non-Muslim strata. These were felt as deprivations and deliberately reinforced from the Serbian side.[43] In dealing with this conflict, the Muslim community began to understand itself more and more as a special population group with its own value system and infrastructure, even if it did not articulate this as objective national consciousness. As during the late phase of the Austrian domination, this collective self-isolation of the Muslims was not only an antidote against the national power of the Serbs, but also against the change in social structure which threatened to disintegrate the Muslim world.

Ambivalent Attitude

A gradual shift in the attitude of the KPY toward the Muslims is noticeable only in the second phase, beginning in the mid-1930s. Yugoslav historiography sometimes attempts to see this change as paralleling the rise of Marshal Tito to party prominence, but this places far too much importance on the stringency of the KPY's attitude toward the Bosnian Muslims. One can hardly say that the party had, at this time, reached unequivocal acceptance of a Muslim nation.[44] Its opinion remained ambivalent and contradictory.

However, in giving up the demand for the splintering of Yugoslavia in 1935 and in recognizing that the national question would have to be solved within the Yugoslav federation of states, the KPY was forced to come to grips with the national question in Bosnia. Starting in 1936, a prefederative concept based on seven administrative units was favored.[45] In this framework, the independent territorial-political unity of Bosnia was affirmed for the first time.[46] Demanding an autonomous Bosnia, however, was certainly not an original idea of the KPY. Long before the Communists and with much broader effect, the YMO, had sought to counter the Serbian and Croatian attempts at incorporation—which became more acute with the Croat-Serbian compromise (sporazum) of 1939—by drawing on the tradition of the Muslim independence movement dating from late Ottoman times.[47]

It was during this time that the special ethnic status of the Muslims was first openly discussed in the KPY. In December 1939 Bosnian students, fronting mostly for Communist intellectuals, published an "open letter" in which the demand for the autonomy of Bosnia was founded on the fact—among others—that Muslims as well as Serbs and Croatians lived in Bosnia and that they had always constituted "a special whole" (posebna cijelina).[48] At the same time, Edvard Kardelj was the first leading KPY functionary to take a similar position regarding the Bosnian Muslims. In his book on the "development of the Slovene national question" from the year 1938 he did not go as far as accepting the Muslims as a nation, but he did want them understood as a special "ethnic group."[49]

But even now the official Party documents remained contradictory, as evidenced by quotes from the Bosnian KP functionary Hasan Brkić. He called for "equal national rights" (!) for Serbs, Croatians, and Muslims in Bosnia[50] and shortly afterward called upon the "Muslims and their brothers of different faiths."[51]

Not even the last position paper of the Communist Party before the beginning of World War II—given at the Fifth National Congress in 1940—brought clarity into the attitude of the Party toward the Muslims. There was discussion of the character of the Muslims, between the Muslim delegate Mustafa (Mujo) Pašić and Milovan Djilas.[52] Djilas, assigned to speak on the national question at the Congress, attacked the thesis of his comrade defining the Muslims "not as a profiled nation, but definitely an ethnic group." Djilas wanted at best to accord them the character of a confessional entity. The documents of the Fifth Congress, which hinted already at the later federated concept of the Party, omitted the Muslims when enumerating the ethnic groups of Yugoslavia.[53] The divergence between Bosnian-Muslim party leaders, who favored upgrading the Muslims, and Serbian and Montenegrin functionaries, who wanted to preserve the confessional definition, emerged for the first time at the Fifth Congress—a dissent among the elite, which was to surface again and again until the definitive recognition of the Muslims in 1968.

Thus, the KPY had not yet reached a consensus regarding the special ethnic status of the Muslims when World War II began. There was a willingness to consider Bosnia as a yet-to-be-defined member in the future Yugoslav federation, but regarding the Muslims the attitude of the party remained nebulous and ambivalent.

The beginning of World War II in the Balkans created a wholly new situation for the party regarding its relationship to the Muslims. It now became imperative to woo this section of the populace for armed combat against the German occupation and against the Ustasha, or at the very least to secure its neutrality toward the partisans—an enterprise crowned with meagre success til far into the war.[54]

The great majority of Muslims accepted the division of Yugoslavia with passive resignation or, as in the case of the greater part of the leading strata, saw in the newly created Croatian puppet state of the Ustasha a chance for preserving and developing the religious and cultural rights the old Yugoslavia had offered them. One of the few Muslim partisans admitted at the end of the war that the "overwhelming majority of the Muslims was found in the occupiers' camp."[55] It is a fact that part of the leadership of the old Yugoslav Muslim Organization and of the clergy agreed early to support the Pavelić regime, and conversely the Ustasha sought to secure the loyalty of the Muslims by including Muslim representatives in parliament and government and by promising educational and religious autonomy. As early as 25 April 1941, Ante Pavelić, the leader of the Ustasha and of the "Independent State of Croatia" sent a message to the Reis-ul-ulema saying "that it is the wish of the Poglavnik to see Muslims free, equal, content, and at home in the free and Independent State of Croatia."[56] This assurance of full religious freedom was all the Muslim clergy needed to align itself verbally with the Ustasha state. The Reis-ul-ulema answered the message of the Poglavnik by calling it "a full guarantee that our eternal ideal of justice and equality will be completely realized."[57] The greater part of the secular leadership of the Muslims, whose leanings had been pro-Croatian all along, was equally ready to cooperate with the Ustasha regime. Eleven former YMO politicians were seated in the puppet parliament of the "Hrvatski Sabor,"[58] and the post of vice president was also filled by a Muslim.[59]

The initial hope for a prosperous lot for the Muslims in the Independent State of Croatia evaporated quickly. As the Muslims became involved in the bloody struggles between Ustasha, Serbian Četnici, and partisans, the legal rights they had hoped to gain with their pledge of loyalty were lost. In addition, since their political clout and their autonomous rights were never fully realized,[60] the disappointment with the Ustasha state grew. The alienation of part of the Muslim elite from the NDH began as early as 1941. In Sarajevo, Mostar, and Banja Luka, a group of clergy published several resolutions in which they distanced themselves from the atrocities committed against the Serbs which also made the position of the Muslims increasingly insecure.[61] Starting in November 1942, part of the Muslim leadership sought to extricate Bosnia from the Independent State of Bosnia, to gain autonomy for it as a German protectorate, and to create a separate Muslim legion.[62] Germany agreed to the latter by forming, at the end of 1943, an SS-Division (Handžar). But even this direct cooperation with Germany profited the Muslims very little. The division was deployed in Southern France instead of Bosnia, and autonomy for Bosnia was denied.[63] Their politics of accommodation and collaboration were less the result of an ideologically motivated tendency to collaborate than of an attempt to come closer, even under conditions of war and occupation, to the goal of an autonomous Bosnia. The Muslims strove to preserve the religious and cultural traditions of Islam, but they fell between all possible chairs.

In contrast, relatively few Muslim politicians, and these mostly of secondary rank, joined the bourgeois Serbian forces in and outside Yugoslavia. The massacre-like conflicts between the Muslims and the Serbian Četnici Draža Mihailović during the beginning phase of the war left little

maneuvering room for such cooperation.[64] The Muslims were not represented in the government-in-exile in London either. Since the Muslims
were discredited with the government-in-exile because of their cooperation with the Ustasha, they were offered very little to draw them to the
side of Germany's adversaries in the war. In spite of lip service to
the religious freedom of Muslims, the concessions never went beyond
the status in the old Yugoslavia. In its insistence on a tripartite, federated
Yugoslavia, in which Bosnia was not to be conceded a special position,
the bourgeois government-in-exile displayed little flexibility regarding
nationality politics.[65]

The efforts of the KPY to gain a foothold among the pro-Croatian and
pro-German Muslims proved equally difficult.[66] Only a very few politicians from the circles of the Muslims joined the Communist insurrection from the start. Nurija Pozderac, a former senator with the YMO,
was one of them. In many instances, it was only tactical considerations
that moved individual Muslim leaders to a provisional and superficial
rapprochement with the Communists.[67] In the first months, especially
in Herzegovina and eastern Bosnia, the insurrection was borne almost
exclusively by Serbs, on whom even the Communists had little influence. Therefore, the acts of vengeance perpetrated by Serbian nationals
on the Muslims prevented the latter from joining the Communist partisans. Many Muslims regarded the Communist partisans primarily as
Serbs. Svetozar Vukmanović-Tempo, who was at that time the political commissar of the partisans in Herzegovina, remembers that even
those units with Communist participation took part in anti-Muslim ex-
cesses which on occasion did not even make exceptions for Communist
Muslims.[68] Serbian Communist partisan leaders, too, were not free of
anti-Muslim resentments.[69] The strategy of the KPY, which sought to
bring the Muslims out of civil war, to get them to join the common
cause, and to separate the Muslim population from its pro-Ustasha and
pro-German leaders,[70] was slow in achieving success. A report of the partisans of August 1941 states that the Muslims had not yet recognized
who their enemies were.[71] Toward the end of 1941, purely Muslim bri-
gades of partisans began to be formed, but support from the Muslim side
was slow in coming. It picked up somewhat after Italy's capitulation in
1943, but even at the end of 1943 it had to be admitted that in spite of
increasing participation by Muslims, "the majority were still undecided
and under the influence of Begs, Hojas, and Čarsija,"[72] and half a year before the war was over, it was said that "many Muslims hold themselves
aloof." Those who joined the partisans were said not to have done it from

conviction, but to adjust to the emerging new situation.[73] According to Marshal Tito, the Yugoslav people's liberation army in the last months of the war included only 2.5 percent Muslims.[74]

The collaboration with the NDH-state and with Germany and the absence of communists among the Muslims kept the KPY at the end of the war from allowing a renaissance of the YMO in the pluralist fig leaf of the People's Front.[75] Instead, a "Muslim Executive Committee" was created inside the People's Front, in which Communist Muslims and Muslim clergy were to act as representatives of the Muslims. Little is known about its role other than that it was clearly a Communist-dominated control agency designed to prevent the resurgence of the old Muslim political forces.[76] It was dissolved as early as 1947, at the same time that suits were brought against Muslim clergy and former Muslim leaders. The postwar agrarian reforms and the confiscation of clerical property deprived the Islamic confessional community of its material base. Moreover, Muslim religious and educational institutions were abolished, and thus the activities of the old Muslim political forces were decisively curtailed.[77]

Even during the war, from 1941 to 1945, the efforts of the KPY on behalf of the Muslims did not imply unequivocal recognition of their ethnicity, much less of their nationality status. Contrary to the assertions of Muslim historians, an undoubted acceptance of the Muslims as a national unit cannot be documented during this time.[78] Unambiguous positions or resolutions bearing out such a claim are missing. The documents that do exist are ambiguous, and clear positions cannot be discerned.

What does exist is a plethora of war documents in which the Muslims are included in the canon of Yugoslav peoples and are thus given a quasi-national importance. Not least among these is Marshal Tito's program description of 1942, in which he writes, with regard to "the National Question in the Light of the People's War of Liberation," as follows: "The war of liberation would be a mere episode if besides the liberation of Yugoslavia it did not mean at the same time the liberation of Croatians, Slovenes, Serbs, Macedonians, Albanians, Muslims, and others."[79] The documents of the "Anti-fascist Council of Bosnia" (ZAVNOBiH), which was formed in 1943 as a provisional regional war parliament for Bosnia-Herzegovina, suggest a similar quasi-national ranking and equal status with the Serbs and Croatians for the Muslims. The "Proclamation of the Muslim Council Members of ZAVNOBiH" states that "representatives of the Serbian, Croatian, and Muslim peoples have created the ZAVNO-BiH" and that in Bosnia-Herzegovina "Serbs, Muslims, and Croatians shall have completely equal rights and freedoms."[80] The fact that during the war the KPY held meetings exclusively for Muslims in some areas also seems to indicate a growing awareness of the special Muslim consciousness.[81] The Muslim historian Atif Purivatra, historiography's guiding spirit in the Muslim national renaissance in the 1960s, has carefully compiled all the sources that suggest recognition of the special ethnic status of the Muslims by the KPY during the war.

If doubts about his thesis must be registered, it is because critical consideration of the sources permits a different interpretation. For one thing, there is any number of documents in which Muslims are not included in the enumeration of Yugoslav peoples and national minorities and are therefore obviously not understood in an ethno-national sense. In an article on the occasion of the Slavic Congress in Moscow in 1943, Muslims are excluded from the enumeration of Slavic peoples of Yugoslavia.[82] The Chiefs of Staff of the partisans decreed in 1941 that the Bosnian partisans should have one of two emblems on their uniforms, a Serbian or a Croatian one(!). The word *Muslim* is frequently used only as a regional or confessional designation.[83] Nowhere is there talk of a "Muslim people" (*muslimanski narod*). In contrast to *srpski* or *hrvatski narod*, they are only referred to as *muslimani* or *braćo muslimani*. But even when *muslimani* is used, it is not always clear whether it is understood in an ethnic sense, for the word is almost always spelled with a lower-case *m*, which should signify membership in a confessional group.[84]

Last, but not least, there were voices that openly opposed recognition of the Muslims as a national unit, the most outspoken among them being Veselin Masleša, a Bosnian Communist of Serbian descent. In a brochure that appeared during the war, he not only denied the Muslims the character of a nation, but—in the tradition of the Stalinist definition of a nation—did not even want them understood as an ethnic community, since they neither subjectively considered themselves a nation nor objectively fulfilled the criteria for a national community.[85]

This skeptical attitude toward a Muslim nationality also predominated in the documents that determined the politics and state laws of postwar Yugoslavia. In its constitutional draft for the federative model of Yugoslavia, the second session of the Anti-fascist Council for the Popular Liberation of Yugoslavia (AVNOY) of November 1943 does not name the Muslims as one of Yugoslavia's constituent groups. Also, during the deliberations about the future structure of Yugoslavia, attempts were made—mostly by a number of leading Serbian party functionaries—to prevent the incorporation of Bosnia into the federal republic on an equal footing with the others.[86] Moša Pijade and Milovan Djilas, true to the principles of Soviet federalism, envisioned Yugoslavia as consisting of the five republics of the five nations (Serbs, Croatians, Slovenes, Montenegrins, and Macedonians), whereas Bosnia, a territory lacking its own nation, was to be accorded the status of an autonomous province only.[87] But to which republic should the autonomous province of Bosnia belong? That was the old question "To whom does Bosnia belong?" and one answer considered was to put Bosnia directly under the jurisdiction of the federation. The Bosnian representatives resisted this plan and insisted on equal status for Bosnia as a federal republic. The plan was abandoned. Bosnia was incorporated into the Yugoslav federation of states.[88] In spite of this recognition of Bosnia as an autonomous republic, some reservations remained, as shown by the differing reason given for Bosnia's status as a republic: It is not, like the five other republics, a republic of one nation, but a republic of "parts of the Serbian and Croatian nation as well as the Bosnian Muslims."[89]

Return to Unity

Thus, although there were signs throughout the war which seemed to point to acceptance of the Muslims as a national unit, at the end of the war the Muslims were recognized only as a population with special cultural and religious characteristics, but not as a nation. Immediately after the end of the war, the third session of the ZAVNOBiH, in preparing the transition to peace, stated that "Bosnia-Herzegovina must not be divided between Serbia and Croatia, because for one thing Serbs and Croatians live intermingled throughout the whole territory and for another the Muslims who live there have not yet decided on a national affiliation."[90] The first prime minister of the member republic of Bosnia, Rodoljub Čolacovićs, said in the constitutional debate of 1946 that "the Bosnian Muslims are a Slavic ethnic group, the majority of which has not yet decided upon a nationality and which is allowed to develop on the same basis as Serbs and Croatians and to define itself nationally."[91] Thus the KPY came around full circle to the attitude of the Bosnian Social Democrats, who, a quarter of a century earlier, had been hoping for an eventual voluntary plebiscite of the Muslims for Serbia or Croatia. For this reason, the constitution of 1946—as well as the later party program of 1958—omitted the Muslims as one of the Yugoslav nations.

In so doing, the party leadership asserted itself against the openly voiced opinions of Bosnian Communists, who thought that the ambivalent attitude of the party during the war should be upgraded to official recognition of the Muslims as a nation. They proposed adding a sixth flame to the five representing the five peoples of Yugoslavia in the State Seal of 1946. It was to symbolize the Muslims.[92] An unverifiable source identifies Milovan Djilas as the one who turned down this proposal, basing his judgment that the term *Muslim* was of a purely confessional nature.

The attitude of the KPY for the first decade and a half after the war was determined by the thesis that the Muslims were not yet nationally defined. This did not mean, however, that the Muslims were allowed to develop toward nationhood on their own without outside influence. Until the beginning of the 1960s, there was considerable pressure on them to declare themselves as Serbs or Croatians. In fact, those who were members of the Communist party were forced to align themselves with one or the other of the two nationalities.[93] One of the delegates to the First Congress of the KP Serbia in the spring of 1945 reports that in the Serbian region of Sandžak, where—as in Bosnia—there are many Muslims, some of the leading functionaries had simply added the Muslims to the Serbs when listing the national affiliations of the delegates. "I think Muslims should remain Muslims," the delegate said, "and not be counted with the Serbs."[94] He was ahead of the times in terms of his party's nationality policy. The same pressure to assimilate was also exerted by the first two censuses, which denied the Muslims the possibility to declare themselves as belonging to an ethnic group of their own. In 1948, they could choose between "Muslim/nationality undefined," "Muslim/Croatian," "Muslim/Serbian," or "Muslim/Macedonian," where "Muslim" was clearly a confessional epithet.[95] In 1953, when the unitarian concept of *Yugoslovenstvo* had banned the concept *Muslim* completely from the census, they could only call themselves "Yugoslavs/nationality undefined."[96] Moša Pijade declared that it was obvious and beyond discussion "that the word *Muslim* signifies belonging to the Muslim faith and that it has no relation to the question of nationality."[97] Neither the federal nor the regional party congresses defined their attitude toward the Muslim problem before the 1950s came to a close.

In 1959, the Belgrade ethnologist Milenko Filipović stated that the national orientation of the Muslims toward Serbia or Croatia "is proceeding apace and will lead the Serbo-Croatian Muslims to see themselves as nationally conscious Serbs and Croatians rather than a segregated group. . . ."[98] This diagnosis was too hasty, however. In 1948, by far the greatest number of Muslims availed themselves of the possibility to declare themselves nationally indifferent: Only 170,000 declared themselves "Muslim/Serbian" or "Muslim/Croatian" as opposed to 778,000 who declared themselves "Muslim/nationally indifferent."[99]

The pressure to assimilate seems to have been strongest in the area of Sandžak, for in all of Serbia and Montenegro only 7,000 persons dared to declare themselves Muslims. In 1953 also, the overwhelming majority of Bosnian Muslims preferred the available category of "nationally un-defined Yugoslav" to identification with either Serbs or Croatians. At least this seems to be indicated by the fact that 891,800 "Yugoslavs" in Bosnia represented practically the same number which had voted themselves "Muslim/nationally indifferent" five years earlier. Also, the nationally undefined Yugoslavs were found almost exclusively (89 per-cent) in Bosnia-Herzegovina (cf. tables and figures in the appendix to this volume). Obviously, only those who thought it politically expedient to toe the official party line made use of the possibility to decide in favor of one of the two recognized nations of Serbs or Croatians. David Dyker examined the names of leading functionaries with definitely Muslim names in the Yugoslav "Who is who" for the year 1956 and found only 8.6 percent who listed themselves as "Yugoslavs"; 16.6 percent had de-cided on "Croatian," 61.5 on "Serbian," and 12.6 percent had given no nationality at all.[100] This shows not only the political identification pres-sure, but also the strong Serbian position in Bosnia during these years. The great majority of Muslims, however, were not to be persuaded to give up their collective identification as an integrated group separate from Serbs or Croatians, even though they were denied the possibility of autonomous national self-identification.

There are basically four reasons why the concept of Muslims as poten-tial Serbs or Croatians persisted in spite of efforts during the war to assign them equal national rights:

1. At that time, the KPY was oriented completely along Stalinist theo-retical lines and accepted the Stalinist definition of nations. The Mus-lims simply did not fit into this scheme.

2. Marxist-Leninist dogma held that national questions would lose their significance once socialism became victorious. Recognizing a "new" nation would therefore be an anachronism.

3. Because of the wartime experience, there was much skepticism regarding the loyalty of the Muslims toward the new state, for large sec-tions of the Muslims and their prewar elites had remained passive and openly distant.

4. Last but not least, there were the aspirations toward Greater Ser-bia—much as they had existed in Serbian bourgeois circles—which did not readily allow for an autonomous state.

Recognition as a Nation

The turning point came some fifteen years after the war, around 1960, when the federation of Yugoslav Communists realized that even in Socialist Yugoslavia the national question was an unsolved problem. They began to distance themselves from the heretofore dominant concept of *Yugoslovenstvo*.[101] The first sign of change came during the Third Congress of the League of Communists of Bosnia and Herzegovina (BiH) in 1959. The statements during the Congress still reflected the traditional understanding of the Yugoslav national question: the national question would slowly fade; in the long run, nations would "die off." Treatment of the Muslims remained especially conventional. The delegate Andrija Krešić, the only one to address the national question at length, stated: "neither is there any social-historical reason for the Muslims to feel as a nation, nor is now the time to form such a nation." However, the usual pressure brought to bear on the Muslims to declare themselves as Serbs or Croatians was called into question. "Such declarations," Krešić continues, "have so far had widely differing results in different regions. Only those who are more dependent on the political realities of the present have gone along with identification, and frequently only for pragmatic reasons, while the great mass of people remained undecided." In other words, only political opportunists had declared themselves as Serbs or Croatians. Whether a Muslim declared himself for one or the other nationality or whether he chose to remain nationally undefined should be left to each individual. The former is not to be considered more progressive than the latter.[102] This first tentative resistance to the pressure for identification evolved into a stronger trend in subsequent years. In 1963, and especially during the Fourth Congress of the League of Communists of Bosnia and Herzegovina in 1965, it was finally realized that insisting on a national identification with Serbs or Croatians had been a mistake.[103]

In practice, the first result of this recognition came in 1961, when during the census Muslims were offered the possibility to declare themselves "Muslims in the ethnic sense." The rules governing the administration of the census strive to separate the religious and ethnic components of this Muslim ethnicity. The difficulties involved in such an enterprise also become clear, for "only those persons of Yugoslav [that is, "south Slavic"] descent should list themselves as Muslims who feel thus ethnically. Members of other, non-Yugoslavian nationalities, such as Croatians, Macedonians, Montenegrins, Serbs, Šiptars, Turks, and the like, who understand themselves as members of the Islamic faith, need not register as Muslims. These persons are to designate their nationality as "Croatian," "Serbian," "Šiptar," "Turkish," "Montenigrins," "Macedonians," and so on, regardless of their religion."[104] The results of the census of 1961 show that this half-hearted step forward was not completely accepted by the Muslims: the number of those calling themselves Muslims turned out to be fewer than that of those who had declared themselves "nationally undefined Yugoslavs" five years earlier. At the same time, the number of "Yugoslavs" in Bosnia remained high. Eighty-seven percent of the 317,000 persons who still called themselves "Yugoslavs" in 1961 were living in Bosnia and were for the most part Muslims.[105] Thus, a large portion of the formerly "nationally undefined Yugoslavs" did not jump at the chance to declare themselves Muslims. Analysis of the census for the individual communities' regions shows, however, that the centers with a dominant Muslim population were the ones that made the change to Muslim identification in the census. In 20 out of 24 population centers with high Muslim concentrations, the percentage of "Yugoslavs" lay far below the average for the republic; the percentage was above average in communities where Muslims lived together with dominant Serbian majorities.[106] It may thus be concluded that it was, above all, local Muslim elites who activated the trend toward Muslim identification, whereas the political dominance of the Serbs was a retarding factor.

Two years later, the Muslims took a further step on their way to recognition as a nation. The constitution of 1963 anchored them with rights equal to those of Serbs and Croatians in the preamble to the constitution of Bosnia-Herzegovina.[107] The official label of "nation" was still avoided, but the Fourth Congress of the League of Communists of Bosnia and Herzegovina interpreted the constitution to say that "from a formal standpoint, the national affiliation of the Muslims has been decided and will be taken off the agenda, since we have made the Muslims a people—or an ethnic group—with the same rights as other peoples."[108] Although the recognition of the Muslims as a nation had thus been ordained in Bosnia, it was two more years before the Central Committee of the League of Communists of Bosnia and Herzegovina gave its formal blessing to their status as "a special nation."[109]

Clearly, the ground for the decision was thus prepared during the years 1961 to 1963, while the actual execution, especially in Yugoslavia as a whole, fell into the time from 1966 to 1968. This chronology has led scholars to associate the recognition of the Muslims as a nation with Aleksandar Ranković's fall from power in 1966.[110] Sources to support the view that Aleksandar Ranković was directly responsible for denying national status to the Muslims have so far not been offered in the literature, however. Theses of this nature are either accepted second-hand or are founded on post facto evidence taken from the same material that accused Ranković of nationalism and "état-ism" after he was deposed.[111] It is, of course, entirely within the realm of the possible that Ranković, like Djilas, Pijade, and other Serbian politicians before him, regarded a Muslim nation with skepticism, or he may have been against it. But the connection between Ranković's fall and the national upgrading of the Muslims should be seen as less direct. As has been shown here, first signs of an upgrading of the Muslim status had been present in Bosnia since the early sixties. Muslim historians and politicians had begun at this time, long before the fall of Ranković, to bring proof of the separate national identity of the Bosnian Muslims. Admittedly, they avoided expressly asking for national status, but claimed it indirectly by giving proof of the Muslims' traditional and historical independence and of their resistance to the two neighboring nations.[112] The historian Atif Purivatra, mentioned above, who was then chairman of the Commission for Nationality Questions in the mass organization of the Socialist Federation, was primarily instrumental in making these historical claims acceptable within the Bosnian party elite. Since this had already been achieved inside Bosnia through the Constitution of 1963, Ranković's fall might at best be considered a catalyst for the same acceptance throughout Yugoslavia. The sources admit only speculation: it does seem, though, as if the Ranković affair affected the interests of the Muslims favorably in several ways. For one thing, with Ranković's exit the concept of *Yugoslovenstvo* became obsolete once and for all, thereby discrediting the category the Muslims had been forced into in 1953— and which they had chosen for themselves to a large extent still in 1961. Now the Muslims had to be offered an identity, and in a time when Yugoslav unitarianism was being downplayed in favor of nationalism, the national claims of the Muslims had to be recognized. Above all, though, the Ranković affair brought a restructuring of relations between the federation and the republics. This process was mostly carried forward by Slovenia, Croatia, and Macedonia. Although Bosnia-Herzegovina kept a low profile in the discussion of federalization, its position improved after 1966, for the contemporary Zagreb historian Dušan Bilandžić reports that although the status of Bosnia as an autonomous emancipated republic was never openly questioned, there had been tendencies on the Croatian and especially on the Serbian side to regard the "statehood" of the republic as second-rank.

As long as the Muslims were not recognized as a nation, Bosnia was regarded as the hinterland of the republics of Serbia and Croatia. Since the Serbian element in Bosnia was dominant until the second half of the sixties, the political leadership of the time gravitated toward Belgrade. Bilandžić states that some of the older leaders had more or less "agreed" that Bosnian politics would be made in Belgrade.[113] The replacement of the Serbian elder Communist Party chief Djuro Pucar in 1965 might be interpreted as the first sign of a change in direction within the Bosnian elite which would give Bosnia more room to act on its own behalf.[114] It is possible that in the quest for liberation from Belgrade the interests of the Muslim component coincided with those of other political forces within the Bosnian leadership. Such a liberation would be easier to rationalize if Bosnia could point to the Muslims as belonging to a genuine "nationality" as did the Serbs and Croatians. It almost goes without saying that the Muslim component was interested in being upgraded to a nation, for the elite had already made several unsuccessful attempts to accomplish this since the war. Because federalization brought with it the proportional allocation of national offices and positions, the recognition of the Muslims as a nation considerably improved their access to political resources.

Ultimately, Bosnian-Muslim interest in upgrading the status of the Muslims also came at an opportune time for the federal party leadership around Marshal Tito, whose intention was to use Bosnia and the Muslims as internal and external buffers against the ever-increasing national antagonisms and controversies brought on by the federalizing process. Inside Bosnia, the discussions about the national identity of the Muslims which were still surfacing could be rendered moot. The alleged demands for "dividing Bosnia" at the Sixth Party Congress in 1974, reported by the Bosnian party chief Branco Mikulić,[115] were probably only an extremist fringe phenomenon and politically irrelevant. There can be no doubt, however, that the restructuring of the republics and the revitalization of national goals and emotions at the beginning of the 1970s had motivated the actions of some national Serbian and Croatian organizations, especially with respect to Bosnia and the status of its Muslims.[116] For Yugoslavia as a whole, the central party obviously speculated that a largely Muslim-defined Bosnia, with its quasi-natural antagonism against potential Serbian or Croatian aspirations, could function politically as a stabilizing supporter of the central powers.[117] In fact, Bosnia fulfilled that function a short time later, when it gave Marshal Tito unqualified support in his initiatives against the Croatian and Serbian party leadership.

During the post-Ranković era of the late 1960s, the efforts of the Bosnian Muslim elite to upgrade the status of the Muslims, begun in the early sixties, thus found a political climate favorable to extending their plans to all of Yugoslavia. But the "struggle for the capital *M*," as Bosnia's party chairman Mikulić called it, did not end without resistance.[118] It came first of all from the two republics of Croatia and Serbia. In Croatia, radically nationalistic circles outside the party, grouped around the cultural organization Matica Hrvatska found the Muslim nation unacceptable. In Serbia, there was resistance against the decision of the Bosnian party of May 1968 even from inside the leading party organs. During the fourteenth session of the Serbian Party's Central Committee, just a few days after the official recognition of the Muslims, the author Dobrica Ćosić and the historian Jovan Marjanović seized the opportunity to denounce the policy of nationalistic emphasis, declaring that it detracted too much from a reasonable "Yugoslavism" (not to be confused with the chauvinism and centralism of the Ranković era). According to Marjanović, "the senseless announcement of a new Muslim nation in Yugoslavia" is one expression of this policy.[119]

In view of the fact that, after Ranković's fall, the Serbian party organization had been especially discredited because of its chauvinistic suppression of the Albanians in the Kosovo, objections of this nature were ill-founded, particularly because the decision of Sarajevo was fully supported by the Muslims of the Sandžak, which belongs partially to Serbia.[120] But official resistance also came from Macedonia, not so much against the existence of a Muslim nation as such, but against the expansion of the category "Muslim" beyond the area of Bosnia and the Sandžak. The young Macedonian nation was struggling against Bulgarian claims and for national recognition, and the party leadership as its advocate had made it very clear that Macedonian-speaking citizens of Slavic descent would be considered Macedonians even if they were of the Islamic faith. Out of "considerations of principle" regarding the freedom of national identification, the Bosnian party disagreed.[121] Officially, the Bosnian position was accepted, but, de facto, the Macedonian position won the upper hand, at least for a while, as will be seen below.

The first tangible result of the recognition of the Muslims as a nation came in the census of 1971, when the Muslims could define themselves "in a national sense." The result of this officially encouraged option was a quantum leap in the number of Muslims to 1.7 million, giving them a plurality in the population. Parallel to this there was considerable shift in the population statistics in the individual communalities. In 13 of the 100 Bosnian communalities, the nation with majority status changed. In 1961, the Serbs had held the absolute or relative majority in 45 communalities, in 1971 in only 39; they had fallen to second place behind the Muslims in 5 communalities. Croatians had been the strongest in 27 communalities in 1961. After the census of 1971 they remained so in only 19, having to "cede" 9 to the Muslims. The latter had become the strongest national group in 42 communalities as compared to only 25 in 1961 (see Figure 2 in the appendix).

Recognition of the Muslims as a nation not only changed the nationality structure of the republic. It also reshaped the profile of nearly every political institution and every social elite in which the Muslims had been underrepresented until then.[122] Inside the party, where—because of pressure to assimilate—the Muslims had represented only 20 percent in the late 1940s, compared to more than 60 percent Serbs,[123] the Serbs remained overrepresented even after the national upgrading of the Muslims. This overrepresentation of the Serbs plays a role mostly in relations with the Croatians, whereas the Muslims are well on their way (35.3 percent in 1981) to representation commensurate with their share of the population (see Table 5 in the appendix). More significant were the positions won in the party leadership. In 1959 and 1965, only about 19 and 25 percent, respectively, of the party leadership was Muslim. By 1974 their number had risen to almost one-third in the Central Committee and to almost 40 percent in the Executive Committee. Similar gains were made in parliamentary committees on the federal and local level. The principle of nationally proportioned candidate lists dislodged above all the formerly dominant Serbian element and gave the Muslims considerable political influence.

Since the census of 1971, the quantitative development of the Muslims has run a smooth course, at least in the Republic of Bosnia. The results of the 1981 census, which for the first time since the war put the Muslims in the same statistical category [as in the previous census—translator's note], show an increase from 1.7 million to about 2 million persons. It is interesting to note, though, that growth in this time was much slower inside Bosnia than outside the republic. Only 54 percent of the increase in the Muslim population between the last two censuses occurred in Bosnia, whereas the percentage of citizens declaring themselves "Yugoslavs" grew disproportionally in this republic in 1981. A number of these "Yugoslavs" must have come from formerly Muslim circles. The facts do not bear out the conclusion that Bosnian Muslims once again have an identity problem or that their national consciousness is weak.[124] The phenomenon rather seems one of social change, for the new identification as "Yugoslav" is noticed mostly in the cities. Presumably, a higher percentage of mixed marriages is responsible. Also, it cannot be overlooked that in the city social values change and religiously connotated national definitions lose ground faster than in rural areas. The principal cause of the relatively slow growth of the Bosnian Muslim population is the strong rise in the Muslim population outside of Bosnia during the interval between the two censuses. In 1971, 86 percent of all Muslims lived in Bosnia; ten years later, that figure dropped to 81 percent. The dramatic increase of the Muslim population in the Republic of Slovenia, for example, can be understood as a consequence of the domestic "guest-worker migration" from Bosnia to the northern republics, which became very strong during the 1970s. In Serbia and Montenegro, growth can be explained as natural population growth among the Muslims of the Sandžak.

The strong growth among the Muslims of Macedonia and Kosovo requires a different explanation, however. In 1971, these two regions included only 1.6 percent of all Muslims, and yet they accounted for 26 percent of the population growth by 1981. As noted above, during the census of 1971 Macedonia had vehemently objected to extension of the Muslim category beyond Bosnia. Although its position did not officially win the day, the small number of 1,248 Muslims in this republic in 1971 shows that here was a de facto moratorium on declaring oneself Muslim. Ten years later, when this had obviously eroded or could no longer be rigidly enforced, the number of Muslims in Macedonia grew to almost 40,000. An exact identification of this population group is difficult, however. In the first years after the war, several thousand Muslim settlers from Bosnia migrated to Macedonia and took over land deserted by the Turks.[125] But these can only account for a small portion of the Macedonian Muslims. By far the larger portion must be descendants of the so-called Torbeši and of other Macedonian-speaking Slavs who converted to Islam during Ottoman rule. Since the dramatic increase in the number of Muslims, the Macedonian leadership had been trying hard to raise this group's consciousness of its membership in the "Macedonian mother-nation" and to discourage it from declaring itself Muslim in a national sense.[126]

It is also possible that, during the last census, part of the non-Slavic population, notably Turks, followed the principle of religious primacy and declared themselves Muslims. In any case, it is worth noting that the percentage of Muslims rose especially in communalities with strong Turkish components (Debar, Gostivar, Kičevo, Kruševo, Prilep, Tetovo). Also, comparing the dynamics of growth of the two groups reveals a certain correlation: while emigration caused the number of Turks to decline by 21 percent overall between the censuses, that figure declined even more dramatically in those communalities where the percentage of Muslims increased strongly. Wherever these "new" Macedonian Muslims may have come from, this development leads the Bosnian Muslims to a logical dilemma. On the one side, they define themselves as a nation separate from the Serbs and Croatians, with whom they share a common language. On the other, they consider themselves as one nation with the Macedonian Muslims, who speak a different language. The party's official definition, which says that the confessional aspect may be an historical component but never the determining element of a Muslim nation, seems to be eroding. In the case of the Muslims, historical consciousness, mores, and culture as "media of national identification"[127] are so closely linked to Islam, that it becomes next to impossible to legitimize a Muslim nation in purely secular terms. Thus it was that "Muslim nationalism," understood as the religious foundation of the Muslim nation, followed hard on the heels of the official recognition of the Muslims as a nation.[128]

Conclusion

This last consideration emphasizes the fact that a theoretical or historical derivation of a Muslim nation is not without its contradictions. But it would be shortsighted to regard it, in consequence, merely as an artificial construction. It needs to be remembered that other nations, too, are to a great extent products of a shaping process impelled by elites.[129] This fundamental aspect aside, the coming of age of the Muslim nation could be understood merely as the result of Communist political calculations. But as much as the upgrading of the Muslims may seem to the outsider to have come about "by the order of the mufti," it is ultimately also the result of multivariate processes in which the will of the people and the national ambitions of a political elite played equal parts. *Grown* and *created* nations are not mutually exclusive terms. The recognition of the Muslims as a nation at the end of the 1960s happened by decree, it is true, but it was also a response to a long-felt separate consciousness on the part of the Bosnian Muslims, who had more or less consistently resisted alternate offers of identification. It was also the result of the political interests of the Bosnian-Muslim party elite, who had worked long and hard and failed often before they could realize their national goals, in spite of Marxist-Leninist dogma and Serbian nationalist traditions in their party. Finally, it was the result of a new understanding of nationality in the post-Ranković era. All of this did not lead to an unambiguous definition of a Muslim nation, much less to a conflict-free practical application. That is the other side of the coin. But it must be affirmed that in their decision to recognize the Muslims as a nation the Yugoslavian Communists have shown more ability to learn than all other political forces before them, be they in the old Yugoslavia or in the camp of the bourgeois exiles.

Notes

1. See *Statistički Godišnjak SFRJ 1984* (Belgrade, 1985), p. 114.

2. In addition to the groups (*narodi*), such as the Croatians, Macedonians, Montenegrins, Serbians, Slovenians, and Muslims, who are considered to be the "state people" in their respective republics, the Yugoslavian constitution and theory of nationalities recognizes "peoples" (*narodnosti*), who have their national states outside Yugoslavia's boundaries; for example, Albanians and Hungarians.

3. Atif Purivatra, "O nacionalnom fenomenu bosanskohercegovačkih Muslimana," *Pregled LXVI* 10 (1974): 1019.

4. On the Muslims as a religious community, see the chapter by Alexandre Popović in this volume.

5. See, for example, Esad Ćimić, a sociologist of religion, whose reservations with regard to the recognition of the Muslims as a nation led to his exclusion from the party: *Politika kao sudbina* (Belgrade, [1984?]), pp. 70ff.

6. See the work of Serbian sociologist Vojislav Šešelj, *Šta da se radi* (London, 1985), pp. 31ff.; from a Croatian perspective, Franjo Tudjman, *Nationalism in Contemporary Europe* (Boulder, Colo., and New York, 1981), pp. 115, 122.

7. Jutta de Jong, "Die makedonische Nationswerdung: eigenständige Integration oder künstliche Synthese," in *Jugoslawien, Integrationsprobleme in Geschichte und Gegenwart,* ed. K.-D. Grothusen (Göttingen, 1984), p. 165.

8. Among those works of history—in the narrower sense—that are of non-Yugoslavian proveniance, the following are to be especially noted: Robert J. Donia, *Islam under the Double Eagle: The Muslims of Bosnia and Hercegovina 1989–1914* (New York/Boulder Colo., 1981); Ferdinand Hauptmann, "Die Mohammedaner in Bosnien-Herzegovina," in *Die Habsburger Monarchie,* vol. 4: *The Confessions,* ed. A. Wandruszka (Vienna, 1985). On the subject of the Muslims in socialist Yugoslavia, see especially Victor Meier, "Bosnien und seine Muslime als Problem des Vielvölkerstaates," in *Nationalitätenprobleme in Südosteuropa,* ed. R. Schönfeld (Munich, 1987), pp. 125–32; Alexandre Popović, *L'Islam balkanique* (Berlin, 1986), pp. 254–366; Bertold Spuler, "Die Lage der Muslime in Jugoslawien," *Welt des Islam* 26 (1986) (also, more briefly, in *Glaube in der 2. Welt* 14/1 [1986]: 25ff.); Pedro Ramet, "Primordial Ethnicity or Modern Nationalism: The Case of Yugoslavia's Muslims," *Nationalities Papers* 13/2 (1985): 165–87; Alexander Lopasić, "Bosnian Muslims: A Search for Identity," *British Society for Middle Eastern Studies: Bulletin* 8/2 (1981): 115–25; Mark Baskin, "The Secular State as Ethnic Entrepreneur: Macedonians and Bosnian Muslims in Socialist Yugoslavia," in *Beyond Ethnic Boundaries: New Approaches in the Anthropology of Ethnicity,* ed. William C. Lockwood (Ann Arbor, 1984); Zachary T. Erwin, "The Islamic Revival and the Muslims of Bosnia-Hercegovina," *East European Quarterly* 17/4 (1983): 437–58; Steven Burg, *The Political Integration of Yugoslavia's Muslims,* Carl Beck Papers in Russian and East European Studies, no. 203; Vladimir

Claude Fisera, "Ethnies ou groupes importants d'origine religieuse?" *Revue d'études comparative est-ouest* 11/9 (1980): 101–20; Smail Balic, "Die Moslems in Bosnien," in *Renaissance des Islam* (Graz, 1980), pp. 97–126; Robert J. Donia and William G. Lockwood, "The Bosnian Moslems: Class, Ethnicity, and Political Behavior in a European State," in *Muslim-Christian Conflicts* (Boulder, Colo., 1978), pp. 185–207; William G. Lockwood, *European Moslems: Economy and Ethnicity in Western Bosnia* (New York, 1975).

9. See, for example, Muhamed Hadžijahić, "Die Anfänge der nationalien Entwicklung in Bosnien-Herzegowina," *Sudostforschungen* 21 (1962): 168–193; "Nastanak i razvoj nacionalnih pokreta u Bosni i Hercegovini," in *Nacionalni odnosi danas* (Sarajevo, 1971), pp. 97–121; *Od tradicije do identiteta, Geneza nacionalnog pitanja bosanskih Muslimana* (Sarajevo, 1974). See also Enver Redžić, "O posebnosti Muslimana," *Pregled* 60/4 (1970): 457–88; Avdo Humo, "Istorijski i aktuelni aspekti nacionalnog položaja Muslimana," *Pregled* 60/4 (1970): 429–55; Avdo Sućeska, "Istorijske osnove nacionalne psebnosti bosansko-hercegovačkih Muslimana," *Jugoslovenski istorijski časopis* 4 (1969): 47ff.; Atif Purivatra, "On the National Phenomenon of the Muslims of Bosnia-Hercegovina," in *Nations and Nationalities in Yugoslavia* (Belgrade, 1974); Nedim Filipović, "Forming of Moslem Ethnicon in Bosnia and Hercegovina," in *Moslems in Yugoslavia* (Belgrade, 1985), pp. 1–20.

10. See especially Srećko Džaja, *Konfessionalität und Nationalität Bosniens und der Herzegowina. Voremanzipatorische Phase, 1463–1804* (Munich, 1984) (also published in *Südosteuropäische Arbeiten*, no. 80); a summary of the above, by the same author, can be found "Der bosnische Konfessionalismus: ein Phänomen der weltgeschichtlichen Peripherie," *Saeculum* 35/3–4 (1984): 267ff.

11. For an example of this approach, see the Soviet historian V.I. Freijdson, who— as in the case in Soviet scholarship generally—recognizes the existence of a Muslim nationality when considering socialist Yugoslavia, yet in the context of the Ottoman and Austro-Hungarian empires only speaks of a Muslim "ethnicity." In his view, it was only with slow and laborious steps that this Muslim ethnicity found its way to the path of becoming a modern nation, so that in its case the process could not develop the same intensity or take on clear form as it did with other southern and western Slavic peoples: V. I. Freijdson, "K istorii bosnii sko-musul'manskogo etnosa," in *Formirovanie natsii v tsentral'noi i iugo-vostochnoi Evrope* (Moscow, 1981), pp. 329ff.

12. Cf. Ferdinand Hauptmann, "Die Mohammedaner in Bosnien-Herzegowina," in *Die Habsburger Monarchie, 1848–1918*, vol. 4: *Die Konfessionen*, ed. A. Wandruszka (Vienna, 1986), pp. 670ff.

13. See, most recently, *Nationalismus in vorindustrieller Zeit*, ed. Otto Dann (Munich, 1986).

14. Rudolf Jaworski, "Zur Frage vormoderner Nationalismen in Ostmitteleuropa," *Geschichte und Gesellschaft* 5/3 (1979): 412.

15. Emanuel Turczynski, *Konfession und Nation: Zur Frühgeschichte der serbischen und rumänischen Nationsbildung* (Düsseldorf, 1976).

16. Turczynski, *Konfession*, p. 13.

17. See Robert J. Donia, *Islam under the Double Eagle: The Muslims of Bosnia and Hercegovina, 1878–1914* (Boulder, Colo., 1981) (also published in *East European Monographs*, no. 78).

18. On the Muslimanska narodna Organizacija, founded in 1906, and subsequent

organizations like it, see Atif Purivatra, *Jugoslavenska Muslimanska Organizacija u političkom životu Kraljevine Srba, Hrvat i Slovenaca* (Sarajevo, 1974), pp. 17ff. Hamdija Ćemerlić, "Alibeg Firdus—Borba muslimana za vjersko-prosvetnu autonomiju," in *Jugoslovenski narodi pred prvi svetski rat,* ed. V. Čubrilovič (Beograd, 1967), pp. 877ff. For an overview, see Holm Sundhaussen: "Jugoslavien," in *Lexicon zur Geschichte der Parteien in Europa,* ed. F. Wende (Stuttgart, 1981), pp. 320–21. On the Muslim cultural organization "Gajret," see Ibrahim Kemura, *Uloga "Gajreta" u društevenom životu Muslimana Bosne i Hercegovine (1903–1941)* (Sarajevo, 1986). On Muslim educational systems, see Hajrudin Ćurić, *Muslimansko školstvo u Bosni i Hercegovini do 1918* (Sarajevo, 1983).

19. Some Bosnian-Muslim historians concur on this point; see, for example, B. Dževad Jubašić, "Neke napomene o problematici etničkog i društvenog razvitka u Bosni i Hercegovini u periodu autrougarske uprave," *Prilozi* 11–12 (1975–76): 306.

20. Anton Hangi, *Die Moslims,* 2d ed. (Sarajevo, 1907), p. 1.

21. Two Muslim writers may be consulted for evidence of this uncertainty. One, Muza Ćazim Ćatić, identified himself in his poetry variously as a Serb, Bosnian, and Croat, during his brief creative period—less than 15 years—prior to World War I: see his *Sabrana Djela* (Tesanj, 1968), 1: 3, 15, 93–94. The other, Osman Nuri Hadžić, despite his ideas about linking Islamic heritage and secular modernization, nevertheless, prior to 1918, identified himself as a Croat prior to 1918, but as a Serb after the founding of the Yugoslav state: *Muslimansko pitanje u Bosni i Hercegovini* (Zagreb, 1902). On the subject of Osman Nuri, see also Ivan Pederin, "Islamischer Progressismus im Werk von Osman Nuri Hadžić und Ivan Miličević," *Südostforschungen* 44 (1985): 185–204.

22. See the following works, which include relevant documentation: Kasim Suljević, *Nacionalnost Muslimana* (Rijeka, 1981), pp. 123ff.; Enver Redžić, "Društveno-istorijski aspekti nacionalnog 'opredjeljivanja'muslimana Bosne i Hercegovine," in his *Prilozi o nacionalnom pitanje* (Sarajevo, 1963), pp. 104ff.; Muhamed Hadžijahić, *Od tradicije do identiteta: Geneza nacionalnog pitanja bosanskih Muslimana* (Sarajevo, 1974), pp. 46ff.; Nikola Babić, "Bosna i Hercegovina u koncepcijama gradjanskih političkih snaga i Kommunističke Partije Jugoslavije," *Prilozi* 4/3 (1967): 11ff.

23. Ante Starčević, *Izabrani spisi* (Zagreb, 1908), p. 34.

24. On the stance of the Croatian Peasants' Party during the Radić era, see Stjepan Radić, *Živo pravo Hrvatske na Bosnu i Hercegovinu* (Zagreb, 1908), p. 34.

25. On the stance of the Ustasha: Fikret Jelić-Butić, *Ustaše i NDH* (Zagreb, 1978), pp. 196ff.

26. *Arhiv Komunističke partije Bosne i Hercegovine,* vol. 2: *Socijalistički pokret u Bosni i Hercegovini, 1905–1919* (Sarajevo, 1951), p. 114.

27. On the stance of the KPY on the Nationality Question during the first years of the Yugoslavian state, see Desanka Pešić, *Jugosloenski komunisti i nacionalno pitanje, 1919–1935* (Beograd, 1983), pp. 26ff; Latinka Perović, *Od centralizma do federalizma: KPJ u nacionalnom pitanju* (Zagreb, 1984), pp. 97ff.; Dušan Lukać, *Radnićki pokret u Jugoslaviji i nacionalno pitanje, 1918–1941* (Belgrade, 1972), particularly pp. 26ff.

28. *Gradja o djelatnosti KPJ u Bosni i Hercegovini, 1921–1941* (Sarajevo, 1971), p. 397.

29. Sima Marković, *Nacionalno pitanje i Jugoslaviji u svetlosti marksizma* (Belgrade, 1923), p. 123.

30. See the resolution on the "nationality question" at the III. National Party Con-

ference in January, 1924: *Istorijski Arhiv Komunističke partije Jugoslavije*, vol. 2: *Kongresi i zemaljske konferencije KPJ, 1919–1937* (Belgrade, 1950), pp. 67–71.

31. *Istorijski Arhiv*, 2:162–63.

32. See, for example, in *Proleter* (repr., Belgrade, 1968): no. 22 (December 1931): 115; no. 7 (15 December 1929): 43; no. 26 (September 1932): 141. In the context of participation that would be territorial rather than national, in August 1935 the Communist *Narodna prava* listed both "Bosniaks" and "Voivodins" in addition to Croatians, Macedonians, Montenegrins, Serbs, and Slovenes: "Gradja o djelatnosti KPJ u Bosni i Hercegovini," p. 254.

33. See Nedim Šarac, "Osvrt na politiku Komunističke partije u Bosni i Hercegovini," *Prilozi* 6 (1970): 117ff.; Enver Redžić, "KPJ i Pitanje Basne i Hercegovine," *Prilozi* 5 (1969): 19ff.; Atif Purivatra, "Komunistička partija Jugoslavije i nacionalno pitanje u Bosni i Hercegovini," in his *Nacionalni i politički razvitak muslimana* (Sarajevo, 1969), pp. 43ff.

34. See the relevant documentation in the memoirs of Ugljesa Danilović, "Iz rada partiske organizacije u Bosni i Hercegovini od 1938 do 1940 god.," in *Četrdeset godina. Zbornik sećanja* (Belgrade, 1961), 3:51; also Marshal Tito [Josip Broz], *Sabrana Djela* (Belgrade, 1978), 5:15, 23, as well as his work included in the same work, 6:15, 23, 98. See also Ubavka Vujošević, "O organizacionom razvoju KPJ u Bosni i Hercegovini, 1919–1941," in *Četvrta i Peta Pokrajinska konferencija KPJ za Bosnu i Hercegovinu u istoijskom razvitku revolucionalnog pokreta, 1938–1941*, ed. Institut za istoriju Sarajevo (Sarajevo, 1980), pp. 51–65.

35. Printed in *Jugoslavia 1918/1984: Zbirka dokumenata*, ed. B. Petranović and M. Žecević (Belgrade, 1985), pp. 189–90.

36. Mehmed Begović, *Muslimani u BiH* (Belgrade, 1938), p. 37.

37. Branislav Gligorijević, "Jugoslovenstvo izmedju dva rata," *Jugoslovenski istorijski časopis* 1–4 (1986): 80–81.

38. See, among others, Abdullatif Dizdarević, *Bosansko-hercegovački muslimani hrvati* (Zagreb, 1936).

39. See, for example, Suljaga Salihagić, *Mi bosansko-hercegóački muslimani u krilu jugoslovenske zajednice* (Banja Luka, 1940), cited by M. Hadžijahić, *Od tradicije do identiteta*, pp. 38–39.

40. Vladimir Čorović, *Političke prilike u Bosni-Hercegovini* (Belgrade, 1939), pp. 55ff.

41. Purivatra, *Jugoslovenska*, pp. 47–48; S. Ćerić, *Muslimani srpskohravtskog jezika* (Sarajevo, 1969), p. 186.

42. Only 1.2 percent of Yugoslavia's civil servants during the interwar period were Muslims; see Salihagić, *Mi bosansko-hercegovački*, p. 59.

43. Begović, *Muslimani*, pp. 22–23; Purivatra, *Jugoslovenska*, pp. 62–63.

44. Such is the thesis of Muslim historians; for example, see Atif Purivatra, "On the National Phenomenon," p. 307, and Avdo Humo, "Radnički pokret i zahtjev za autonomiju Bosne i Hercegovine izmedju dva svjetska rata," *Pregled* 65/1 (1972): 22; Nijaz Duraković, "National Question of Moslems in Yugoslavia," in *Moslems in Yugoslavia*, pp. 21ff.

45. Tito, *Sabrana Djela*, 3:36ff.; *Proleter* 12/4–5 (1936), repr., p. 433.

46. *Gradja o djelatnosti KPJ u Bosni i Hercegovini*, pp. 452ff.

47. See Dana Begić, "Pokret za autonomiju Bosne i Hercegovine u uslovima sporazum Cvetković-Maček," *Prilozi* 2 (1966): 177–91.

48. *Gradja o djelatnosti KPJ u Bosni i Hercegovini*, p. 467.

49. Sperans (Edvard Kardelj), *Razvoj slovenskega narodnega vprašanja* (Liubliana, 1938), p. 347. In this regard, see also the resolution of the Fifth Conference of the Provincial Committee of the KPY for Bosnia of July 1940, where another issue was that the Muslims only followed the YMO because they felt threatened as an "ethnic group" by the Serbian bourgeoisie. This resolution is printed in *Godišnjak Društva istoričara NR Bosne i Hercegovine* 10 (1959), pp. 48ff.

50. *Gradja o djelatnosti KPJ u Bosni i Hercegovini*, pp. 319–20.

51. *Gradja o djelatnosti KPJ u Bosni i Hercegovini*, p. 323; similarly, Tito, *Sabrana Djela*, 6:43.

52. Pero Damjanović, *Tito pred temama istorije* (Belgrade, 1978), p. 187. Milovan Djilas does not mention this debate at all in his memoirs, restricting himself to a discussion—doubtless of greater political consequence—of his disagreement with the Bulgarian-Macedonian delegate Metodije Šarlo regarding the character of the Macedonians. See Milovan Djilas, *Der junge Revolutionär: Memoiren, 1929–1941* (Vienna and Munich, 1979), p. 338.

53. Tito, *Sabrana Djela*, 6:43, 63ff.

54. Yugoslavian historical investigations have thus far scarcely considered the question of the Muslims' role in World War II. The question was surrounded with further taboo at the end of the 1960s, following the recognition of the Muslims as a nation, since the fact of the Muslims' having been compromised—at least to a certain degree—by cooperation with the Ustasha and with the Germans was not in line with the trend toward the Muslims' political revaluation. The Bosnian historian Enver Redzić, in his *Muslimansko autonomaštvo i 13. SS-divizija* (Sarajevo, 1987), has made an initial investigation of one aspect of the problem.

55. *ZAVNOBiH: Dokumenti, 1945* (Sarajevo, 1968), 2:430. See also, *Osnivački kongres KP Srbije (8–12 May 1945)* (Belgrade, 1972), p. 100.

56. *Glasnik Islamske vjerske zajednice* 9/4–5 (1941): 147.

57. Alija Nametak, "Muslimani u Nezvisnoj Državi Hravtske," *Glasnik Islamske vjerske zajednice* 9/8 (1941), p. 215.

58. Branko Petranović, *Revolucija i kontrarevolucija u Jugoslaviji, 1941–45* 1 (Belgrade, 1983): 1:56.

59. Jelić-Butić, *Ustaše i NDH*, pp. 198ff.

60. Jelić-Butić, *Ustaše i NDH*, pp. 200ff.

61. See, among others, "Stav Sarajevskih muslimana," *Glasnik Vrhovnog Islamskog starješinstva* 2/1–3 (1951): 23ff; "Muslimanske rezolucije," in *Jugoslovesnki federalizam: Tematska zbirka dokumenata*, vol. 1, ed. B. Petranović and M. Zečević (Beograd, 1987), pp. 697–713; Milica Bodrozić, "Prilog razmatranju drzanja gradjanskih stranaka u Bosni i Hercegovini, 1942–43)," *AVNOJ i Narodnooslobodilacka Borba u Bosni i Hercegovini* (Belgrade, 1974), pp. 122ff.

62. See Rasim Hurem, "Koncepcija nekih muslimanskih gradjanskih politicara u vremenu od sredine 1943 do kraja 1944 godine," *Prilozi* 4 (1968): 533ff.

63. On the SS-Division (Handžar), see Martin Brosszat and L. Hory, *Der kroatische Ustascha-Staat, 1941–1945* (Stuttgart, 1964), pp. 154–61; Holm Sundhaussen, "Zur Ge-

schichte der Waffen-SS in Kroatien 1941–1945," *Südostforschungen* 30 (1971): 176ff.; Enver Redžić, *Muslimansko autonomaštvo i 13. SS-divizija* (Sarajevo, 1987) (a concise summary can be found in *NIN*, nos. 1920 and 1921 [18–25 October 1987]), pp. 45–46 and 52ff.

64. See Radoje Pajović, "Pokolj Muslimana u Sandžaku i dijelu Istočne Bosne u Januaru i Februaru 1943," in *Neretva Sutjeska 1943: Zbornik radova* (Belgrade, 1969), pp. 510ff.

65. Bosdrović, *Prilog razmatranju*, pp. 117ff.

66. Enver Redžić, "Političko jedinstvo naroda Bosne i Hercegovine u svjetlu ustanka 1941 god," *Pregled* 62/7–8 (1972): 947–48; Rasim Huren, "Neke karakteristike ustanka u Bosni i Hercegovini 1941," *Godišnjak društva istoričara Bosne i Hercegovine* 18 (1970): 218ff.

67. For pertinent examples, see the memoirs of Meša Selimović, *Sjećanja* (Belgrade, 1983), p. 234.

68. See Svetozar Vukmanović-Tempo, *Revolucija koja teče: Memoari* (Belgrade, 1971), 1:224 and 243–44; by the same author, *Četrdeset godina: Zbornik sećanja* (Belgrade, 1961), 5:250ff; Milovan Djilas, *Der Krieg der Partisanen: Memoiren, 1941–1945* (Vienna and Munich, 1978), pp. 19, 55–56, 187–88; "Izvještaj Uglješe Danilovića Svetozaru Vukmanoviću-Tempu, 17.9.1941," *AVNOJ i Revolucija*, pp. 550–51.

69. Cf. the recollections of the former muslim partisan Adil Zulfikarpašić, "Put u Foču," in *Godisnjak, 1957* (Vienna, 1957), pp. 44–54.

70. On this point, see also Tito, *Sabrana Djela,* 7:137; *Oblasna konferencija KPJ z Bosansku Krajinu* (Banja Luka, 1982), p. 60.

71. *Arhiv Saveza komunista Bosne i Hercegovine* 3:1 (Sarajevo, 1952), p. 32.

72. *Zemaljsko Antifašističko Vijeće Narodnog Oslobodjenja Bosne i Hercegovine: Dokumenti 1943–1944,* book 1 (Sarajevo, 1968), pp. 86–87, as well as *Oblasna konferencija KPJ za BiH,* p. 60.

73. *ZAVNOBiH: Dokumenti, 1943–1944,* book 1, p. 187.

74. *V. kongres Komunističke partije Jugoslavije: Stenografske beleške* (Belgrade, 1949). An analysis of veterans in 1977 underscores the Muslims' small rate of participation: the data suggest that, for the total Yugoslav population, of which Muslims constituted 8.5 percent, they comprised only 3.5 percent of war veterans; the ratio in Bosnia was 39.6 versus 23.0 percent. See Lenard Cohen and Paul Warwick, *Political Cohesion in a Fragile Mosaic: The Yugoslav Experience* (Boulder, Colo., 1983), p. 64.

75. Cf. the discussion by Hamdija Ćemerlić during the III. Session of ZAVNOBiH, described in *ZAVNOBiH: Dokumenti, 1945,* book 2, p. 420; also *Arhiv KP BiH,* vol. 1, book 1 (Sarajevo, 1950), pp. 280–81.

76. Budimir Miličić, "Organizaciono-politicka struktura izgradnja Socijalističkog Saveza Radnog naroda Bosne i Hercegovine, 1945–1963," *Prilozi* 14/14–15 (1978): 311ff.; Branko Petranović, "Gradjanske stranke u Jugoslaviji, 1944–1948," *Istorijski glasnik* 1 (1969): 82.

77. The resistance of the clergy to this social reorganization was finally broken in 1947, by the imposed replacement of the leadership of the "Islamic community" by figures who were cooperative and loyal to the state and party: Branko Petranović, *Politička i ekonomska osnova narodne vlasti u Jugoslaviji za vreme obnove* (Belgrade, 1969), pp. 157–58.

78. See, for example, Arif Purivatra, "Stav Komunističke partije Jugoslavije prema nacionalnom pitanju Muslimana u toku narodnooslobodilačkog rata," *Prilozi* 4 (1968): 491ff.

79. Tito, *Sabrana Djela* 13:99; also, from the same collection, no. 10, p. 123; no. 11, p. 188, and elsewhere. The first AVNOY session, in 1942, made a statement to the effect that, "This historic meeting is a testimony to the unity of our peoples: Croatians, Montenegrins, Muslims, Serbs, Slovenes, and others, without regard to belief or nationality. . . .": *Prvo i Drugo zadeanje Antifašističkog Veća Narodnog Oslobodjenja Jugoslavije* (Belgrade, 1953), p. 17.

80. *ZAVNOBiH: Dokumenti, 1943–1944,* book 1, p. 231; also pp. 163 and 185.

81. *Arhiv KP BiH,* vol. 1, book 2 (Sarajevo, 1950), p. 287.

82. *Istorijski Arhiv KPH,* vol. 1, book 2 (Belgrade, 1949), p. 256. See also Tito, *Sabrana Djela* 7:27, 45, and 60; *Proleter,* repr., p. 784.

83. Tito, *Sabrana Djela,* 13:149; no. 8, p. 123; no. 9, where he speaks of the "brotherhood and unity of all Bosnians, regardless of belief."

84. Regrettably, appropriate use of the term *Muslim* in the sources has been hindered by Yugoslav historians' more than problematic editorial practice of altering the term in lower case, as it was originally written, to the capitalized form, in the source publications that came out after the national-political reevaluation of the Muslims in the 1960s. This practice has given, even for the period of war, the impression of a uniformly ethno-national use of *Muslim;* see, for example, Marshal Tito's original article about "The Nationality Question in Light of the War of Liberation" in the reprint of *Proleter,* pp. 807ff., and in vol. 13 of his *Sabrana Djela.*

85. Veselin Masleša, *Dela,* book 2 (Sarajevo, 1956), pp. 152–53.

86. On this point, see Nikola Babić, "KPJ i pitanje BiH," pp. 236ff.; Hamdija Ćemerlić, "Položaj Bosne i Hercegovine u jugoslovenskoj zajednici od ZAVNOBiH-a do Ustava SR BiH," *Prilozi* 4 (1968):338ff.; Drago Borovčanin, "O izgradnji bosansko-hercegovačke državnosti poslije II. zasedanja AVNOJ-a," *Prilozi* 13 (1977): 267ff.

87. Rodoljub Čolaković, *Tako je rodjena nova Jugoslavija* (Beograd, 1963), pp. 118–19; Čolaković, "Pravi odgovor na pitanje: čija je Bosna," in *AVNOJ i Narodnooslobodilačka borba u Bosni i Hercegovini,* ed. Institut za istoiju Sarajevo (Belgrade, 1974), pp. 15ff. A divergent opinion is expressed by Milan Djilas, in *Krieg der Partisanen,* pp. 463–64, where he states that the reduction of Bosnia to an autonomous region was supported by a majority Party opinion, which the Bosnian leaders sought to counter by demanding republic status.

88. *ZAVNOBiH: Dokumenti, 1943–1944,* book 1, p. 231.

89. Moša Pijade, "Ravnopravnost SRBA i Hrvata u Hrvatskoj," in *Izabrani spisi,* vol. 1, book 3 (Belgrade, 1965), p. 136; see also R. Čolaković, *Izabrani govori i članci,* 1:288.

90. *ZAVNOBiH,* book 2, pp. 410–11.

91. Rodoljub Čolaković, *Izabrani govori i članci,* 1:128, 288ff.; *ZAVNOBiH,* book 2, pp. 410–411.

92. Kasim Suljević, *Nacionalnost Muslimana,* pp. 226ff.

93. Enver Redžić, *Tokovi i otpori* (Sarajevo, 1970), p. 109.

94. *Osnivački kongres KP Srbije,* pp. 100–101.

95. *Savezni zavod za statistiku: Popis stanovništva 1948 god.,* book 9 (Belgrade, 1954), pp. xiv ff.

96. *Savezni zavod za statistiku: Popis stanovništa 1953 god.*, book 1 (Beograd, 1959), p. xxxviii.

97. Moša Pijade, "O popisu stanovništva," in his *Izabrani spisi*, vol. 1, book 5 (Belgrade, 1966), pp. 947–48.

98. Milenko Filipović, "Die serbokroatischer Mohammedaner," *Tribus* 9 (1959): 58.

99. Savezni zavod za statistiku, *Popis stanovništva 1948 god.*, pp. xiv ff. Some information on the dates of censuses since 1948 can be found in Jure Petričević, *Nacionalnost stanovništva Jugoslavije* (Brugg, 1983).

100. David A. Dyker, "The Ethnic Muslims of Bosnia-Hercegovina: Some Basic Socio-Economic Data," *The Slavonic and East European Review* 50 (1972): 245.

101. For more detail, see Paul S. Shoup, *Communism and the Yugoslav National Question* (New York and London, 1968); also Othmar N. Haberl, *Parteiorganisation und nationale Frage in Jugoslawien* (Berlin, 1975).

102. *Treći kongres Saveza komunista Bosne i Hercegovine* (Sarajevo, 1959), pp. 290–91.

103. See, for example, *Četvrti kongres Saveza komunista Jugoslavije: Stenografske beleške* (Sarajevo, 1965), pp. 36, 55.

104. *Demografska kretanja i karakteristike stanovništva Jugoslavije prema nacionalnoj pripadnosti* (Belgrade, 1978), p. 15.

105. Atif Purivatra and K. Suljević, *Nacionalni aspekti popisa stanovništvau 1971 g.* (Sarajevo, 1971), pp. 26–27.

106. A disproportionate number of the twenty-eight members were "Yugoslav"; twelve of them were concurrently in the Center Party of the Bosnian population.

107. "Bound by their past communal life and by the struggle for freedom and progress . . . the Serbs, Muslims and Croatians are now free for the first time, enjoying brotherly equality in their republic . . . ," *Ustav Socijalističke Republike Bosne i Hercegovine sa ustavnim amandmanima i ustavnim zakonima* (Sarajevo, 1969), osnova nacela 1, pp. 7–8.

108. *IV Kongres SK BiH*, p. 55.

109. Printed in *Nacionalni odnosi danas: Prilog sagledavanju nacionalnih odnosa u Bosni i Hercegovini* (Sarajevo, 1971), pp. 207–08.

110. See, for example, P. Ramet, *Nationalism and Federalism in Yugoslavia, 1963–1983* (Bloomington, Ind., 1984), pp. 144ff., and the same author's *Primordial Ethnicity*, p. 171; Zacharin T. Irwin, *The Islamic Revival*, p. 443.

111. See Dušan Bilandžić, who asserts that "the promoters of reactionary ideology" had taken hold of the national individuality of the Muslims: *Historija SFRJ: Glavni procesi* (Zagreb, 1978), p. 439. Yet he, too, does not attribute to Ranković unmitigated responsibility for the attitude toward the Muslims.

112. See, for example, Atif Purivatra, "Prilog proučavanju koncepcije o nacionalnom opredeljivanju muslimana," *Pregled* XVI/10 (1964): 331ff.; also, as early as 1961, Enver Redžić, "Društveno-istorijski aspekt 'nacionalnog opredeljivanja' muslimana Bosne i Hercegovine," *Socijalizam* 4/3 (1961): 31–89.

113. Dušan Bilandžić, *Historija SFRJ* (Zagreb, 1978); on Bosnia's weak economic autonomy, see also Avdo Humo, "Daljni razvoj nacionalnog pitanja u Bosni i Hercegovini i reforma Saveza komunista (2)," in *Vjesnik*, 7 June 1971, p. 6.

114. See April Carter, *Democratic Reform in Yugoslavia: The Changing Role of the Party* (London, 1982), p. 19.

115. *Šesti kongres Saveza komunista Bosne i Hercegovine* (Sarajevo, 1974), p. 21.

116. See Steven Burg, *Conflict and Cohesion in Socialist Yugoslavia* (Princeton, 1983), pp. 55ff.; P. Ramet, *Nationalism and Federalism*, pp. 151ff.

117. See the indirect reference by Džemal Bijedić, "Savez komunista Bosne i Hercegovine i bosansko-hercegovački medjunacionalni odnosi," in *Reforma Saveza komunista Bosne i Hercegovine* (Sarajevo, 1971), p. 34, when he speaks of Bosnia as a factor of harmony in relations between Serbia and Croatia. In this regard, see also Avdo Humo, "Muslimani u Jugoslaviji (5)," *Komunist*, no. 590 (8 August 1968), p. 12.

118. *XXI sjednica Centralnog komiteta Saveza komunista Bosne i Hercegovine* (Sarajevo, 1970), p. 322.

119. *Proceedings of 31 May 1968*, p. 7. The input of Dobrica Ćosić can be found in the more recent publication *Stvarno i moguce* (Rijeka, 1986).

120. Cf. the delegate Ramiz Crnimani, who spoke in the name of the 130,000 Muslims of Sandžak at the Fourteenth Session: *Proceedings of 30 May 1968*, p. 5.

121. For the Macedonian criticism, see *Vjesnik* of 21 January 1971 (a reprint of an article from *Nova Makedonija*); *NIN*, no. 1648 (8 February 1971), pp. 29ff.; *Proceedings of 12 September 1970*, p. 6. For the Bosnian opposition view put forth by Mustafa Imamović, see "Nesporazumi oko Muslimana," *Gledišta* 12/2 (1971): 247–50.

122. See Lenard Cohen, "Balkan Consociationalism: Ethnic Representation and Ethnic Distance in the Yugoslav Elite," in *At the Brink of War and Peace: The Tito-Stalin Split in a Historic Perspective*, ed. Wayne S. Vucinich (New York, 1982), p. 34 (also found in *War and Society in East Central Europe* 10).

123. See Vera Kac's contribution to discussion in "Problemi istraživanja historije SFRJ," *Časopis za suvremenu povijest* 17/1 (1985): 79.

124. Viktor Meier, *Bosnien und seine Muslime*, pp. 130–31.

125. M. Imamović, *Nesporazumi oko Muslimana*, pp. 248ff.

126. Cf. the collection *Makedonci Muslimani* (Skopje, 1984), particularly pp. 51, 83, 88.

127. Peter Alter, *Nationalismus* (Frankfurt am Main, 1985), p. 17.

128. See Dennison Rusinow, "Nationalities Policy and the National Question," in *Yugoslavia in the 1980s*, ed. P. Ramet (Boulder, Colo., and London, 1985), pp. 148ff.

129. Heinrich August Winkler, "Der Nationalismus und seine Funktionen," in his *Nationalismus* (Hanstein, 1978), pp. 7–8.

Part III *Muslim Opposition*

11. "Holy War" against Czarism: The Links between Sufism and Jihad in the Nineteenth-Century Anticolonial Resistance against Russia

Uwe Halbach

In recent times, Soviet media have provided numerous accounts of the growing vitality of Islam in Central Asia. Among them, there is one especially worth noting. In early 1987, the Tajikistan Communist Party journal, *Kommunist Tadzhikistana*, reported that, in the summer of 1986, unrest broke out among the population when an unregistered mullah was arrested. The occasion of his arrest "impelled his co-religionists—those believers who had sworn him loyalty and fidelity—to take action on the very same day" and to disrupt public order.[1]

In addition to the fact that it took place not far from the border with Afghanistan, one circumstance of this event must have caused Soviet authorities to take particular notice: the words of the believers who had sworn "loyalty and fidelity" to a leader is indicative of a phenomenon that both czarist and Soviet authorities had experienced in a very negative light in the Muslim regions of Russia and the Soviet Union. That phenomenon, called Muridism, is a singular system of religious communication, in which a circle of students (*murids*) oriented toward mystical Islam swears to follow a certain teacher and master (*murshid*), who treats them in an almost totalitarian manner.

The most significant cases of Islamic resistance against Russian central authority were grounded in this type of relationship. One outstanding example is that of the struggle of the North Caucasian mountain people against Russian colonial forces in the Caucasus in the nineteenth century, along with ensuing resistance in the same region during the period of Sovietization. Other more local incidents in Turkistan and among the Volga Tatars, during the late nineteenth century, follow a similar pattern. During the past few years, Soviet sources have confirmed the fact that Muridism has remained active until this day and that it is a kind of "underground Islam" that is not linked to mufti or mosque. One Soviet commentator admits, in brief, that Murid groups— under the influence of foreign propaganda, of course—have the potential "to form a political opposition within our country."[2]

The present essay will describe three cases of "Holy War" against czarist rule in the nineteenth century, all of which were organizationally and ideologically based in Muridism. Furthermore, all of them have importance in the context of the anticolonial jihad that was taking place throughout the Islamic world during this period.

The Relationship between Islamic Anticolonial Resistance and Sufism

In 1846, in the colonial newspaper *Kavkaz* that had recently been established in Tbilisi, a Russian wrote with regard to the "Muslim Holy War":

> But, thank God, Muslim fanaticism is dying out now. From north to south, the Muslim world stands under the flags of England, Russia and France; more and more its force is tempered, so that Algeria and the Caucasus are now the only places on earth where blood is spilled in the name and for the glory of the Prophet of Medina.[3]

This statement epitomizes the European perception of Islam at the time: it obviously follows the coarse stereotype of "Muslim fanaticism" —and it turned out to be utterly wrong in its pronouncements about the death of Islamic resistance. The Caucasus and Algeria were not to be the only regions where Occidental expansion into the Dar al-Islam met vigorous resistance.

On one point, at least, the author reported accurately, in describing two events of exemplary significance for anticolonial Islamic resistance throughout the world. The first is the struggle of Berber and Arab tribes, under the leadership of the amir Abd al-Qadr, against French expansion into Algeria, lasting from 1830 to 1845. The second is the much longer struggle of the North Caucasian mountain people against czarist colonial policies in the Caucasus during the first half of the nineteenth century. Confronting this resistance was a matter of considerable military exertion for the Russian Empire; the conflict damaged its prestige and threatened its self-assurance even before the Crimean War.

These two events are typical of a form of Islamic resistance that presented a strong and persistent challenge to Europe's colonialist enterprises. This resistance drew its force from pre-national and tribal sentiments and, even more significantly, "mysticism" guided it.[4] There were other types of Islamic resistance, including the later and more enlightened forms of Islamic self-assertion such as Jadidism and Pan-Islamism, but this earlier type became sensational news in Europe and thus had a special role in shaping the image of the "Orient." In this image, the dervish is linked with the "holy warrior" in the cliché of the Muslim fanatic, who, with ignorant refractoriness, seeks to thwart the West's "civilizing mission."

Against the background of experience of the French, Russians, British, and Dutch with mystically inspired Muslim guerrillas, the nineteenth-century European picture of Islam outlined an exciting connection between jihad and *tariqa;* holy war and Sufi brotherhood. The Atyeh War against the Dutch in Sumatra (1821–39), the Sepoy uprising in India, the Mahdi in the Sudan and, in the twentieth century, the resistance of the Libyan Sanussi against Italy, all provided support for this view.

More than any others, however, it was two protagonists of early Islamic resistance who brought the links between jihad and Sufism to European attention. One was Abd al-Qadr, the leader of the Qadiriyya Order in Algeria and the leader of the Algeria war of liberation against the French between 1832 and 1847. The second was an Avar named Shamil, the third and most notable imam of the Northeast Caucasian Murids. From 1834 until his capitulation in 1859, he led the struggle of the mountain people (Russian: *gortsy*), building on the ideological, psychological, and organizational foundations laid by the Sufi Naqshbandi Order in the Eastern Caucasus several decades before.

A contemporary expert on the Caucasian War, the Russian Fadeyev, described the Algerians and the Caucasians as the first non-European groups to raise serious resistance against the expansion of European dominance. Struck by the fact that these fighters persisted even in the face of the opposition's vastly greater material means, Fadeyev pointed to their "uncivilized, pugnacious, and noncentralized condition" ("one can destroy a center")—a situation that Soviet troops were to encounter once again in Afghanistan.[5]

For those writing about the Orient in the nineteenth century, it was customary to mention Abd al-Qadr and Shamil in the same breath. These two guerrilla leaders, who carried on a brief correspondence in 1860, naturally invited comparison because of their roles as prominent members of the *ulema* in their homelands, as *murshids* (spiritual leaders) and as founders of states. So, too, did the social conditions of Algeria and the Caucasus that gave rise to Islamic resistance. It is thus surprising that modern historical discussions of anticolonial Islamic resistance often neglect this connection—or treat it only superficially.[6] In particular, the activities of Shamil and of Caucasian Muridism generally, with which all of Europe was intensely preoccupied during the 1840s and 1850s, seem now to be consigned to oblivion.[7] Alexandre Bennigsen's term, *musul-mans oubliés*, referring to contemporary Islamic scholarship's lack of interest in Soviet Muslims, also applies to earlier studies of Islamic history in the West. But in Muslim countries, with the exception of Turkey,[8] interest in Shamil seems to have awakened only recently, inspired by the Afghan jihad.[9]

It is thus clear that there are possibilities for comparative study of Caucasian Muridism. These are evident in the framework of the universal history of Islam in the 1800s, but even more in the narrower context of the history of the eastward expansion of Russian and czarist domination of Muslims. Sufi-inspired Islamic resistance that declared itself as jihad, or *ghazawat* ("war for the faith"; this was the term used particularly in the Caucasus and Central Asia; plural of the Arabic *ghazwa*, "military expedition") in the nineteenth century was not restricted to the Caucasus: it also existed in other regions of the Russian Empire that had Muslim populations, although to a far lesser extent than in the Caucasus. A particularly promising study could be made comparing the struggles of the Northeast Caucasian Murids with those of the Northwest Caucasian Cherkess, who did not associate themselves with Shamil and whose motivation was not primary religious. These two movements were largely contemporaneous, yet they were not coordinated in any way and took place under different ethnic and cultural conditions.[10]

"Holy War"

No concept in Islam has engendered such a one-sided and distorted response in the West's perception of Islam as that of jihad. It is usually interpreted as meaning "holy war," which is a mistake from the beginning. The word does mean—among other things—"armed struggle against heathens," and it ranks as a "sacred duty" in the doctrines of a Muslim's responsibilities (*fiqh*), but there has never been an exclusively religious war in Islam. Because the Muslim community has always been a political body, its conflicts with groups outside the 'Umma have always had motivations other than religious ones. The Caucasian Murid War is a good example: it was not only a struggle in the name of religious belief, but also—and above all—for ethnic self-defense. In the image of Islam created by European Romanticism, Islamic "Holy War" was the key to understanding the Orient. François-Auguste-René, Vicomte de

Chateaubriand, in his *Itinéraire de Paris à Jérusalem* of 1811, influenced by the "holy war" line of thought, proposes that Islam is the "enemy *par excellence.*"[11]

This picture of an extremely militant and intolerant religion also pervaded Russian writings during the Caucasian war. In Caucasian journalism of the time, views of the mountain people tended to fluctuate between an image of them as noble savages, toward whom there was a certain sympathy despite their being enemies, and an image of them as "Muslim fanatics." This ambivalence is often apparent in Russian descriptions, as well. Thus, the Soviet author of a general history of religion remarks with regard to jihad:

> In this regard, the Qur'ân states clearly and unmistakably that war should be waged against polytheists and unbelievers for eight months of the year; these people should be destroyed; their property should be confiscated. This is a blatant expression of Islam's fanaticism and intolerance toward members of other faiths, the degree of which is matched by no other world religion. . . . Under the banner of Jihad, the Mohammedan clergy has incited believers to undertake wars of total destruction against all unbelievers, time and time again, as, for example, against the Russians and the Red Army.[12]

Several factors distorted the common European conception of jihad, during both the nineteenth and twentieth centuries.[13] Foremost was the one-sided view of jihad that resulted from its incorrect translation as "holy war," which was based in turn on the meaning that term had had during the Crusades. Etymologically, however, *jihad* does not mean "war," but rather, "effort." This "effort" is not limited to its external application in terms of armed struggle for the faith. War for the sake of Islam, especially when it was understood in terms of fighting against the "world of unbelief," always had an inward dimension as well. In this sense, it was also the struggle against lapse of faith within the community of believers; the struggle for unity and solidarity and against neglect within the faith's own house—the Dar al-Islam. Particularly during the nineteenth century, during the period of anticolonial resistance, the idea of jihad was linked with "re-Islamicization" and the adoption of religious law within the regions to be protected. Fitting examples for the dual nature of jihad can be found in Shamil's imamate, in the regime of Abd al-Qadr and in other Islamic resistance movements.

In Western writings, jihad is generally described as being offensive. Then it is treated as the ideological foundation of Arabic or Ottoman expansion. The fact that jihad reveals a defensive side, both during the time of the Prophet and during the nineteenth-century confrontations of Orient and Occident, is often ignored.

The status of the duty of jihad, in the sense of battle, within the doctrine of Muslim responsibilities, is often grossly overestimated. Sometimes "holy war" is even ranked among the basic duties of Muslims—the so-called Five Pillars of Islam.

In the European view of Islam, jihad is often considered to be a single concept that is based on unambiguous statements in the Qur'ân. Evidence is then cited from the most militant Qur'ânic passages: those that speak of the destruction of opponents. But even the Qur'ân does not express a uniform and uniformly militant understanding of jihad. Rather, it makes various statements regarding situations faced by the early Muslim community.

The earliest references to jihad occur in the period of the Hijra: they speak of the need to avert *fitna* (apostasy), putting internal, defensive motivations ahead of all others. Subsequently, the concept of jihad shifted toward a more offensive, outwardly directed stance, in the context of active struggle against unbelievers. It was not until after the life of the Prophet that universalist objectives for jihad were formulated, by traditionalists. In this view, jihad became the basic principle of relations between Islam and the world of unbelief. During the nineteenth century, particularly during the Sepoy Uprising of 1857, classical teachings about jihad were adapted to fit the circumstances and needs of anticolonial resistance.[14] This revision emphasized the internal dimensions of the concept: unity, the overcoming of tribal factionalism, intensification of faith, and application of the Shari'a. This mobilizing effect of jihad meant that Islam began "increasingly to play the role of pronationalist ideology against foreign domination, as a force that could override local or regional loyalties."[15]

The "Mystical" Dimension of Islamic Resistance

History has used the terms *Muridism* and *Murid War* to characterize the struggle for liberation waged by the Chechen and mountain people of Daghistan: the most important Islamic anticolonialist guerrilla movement of the nineteenth century. The use of these terms points to the "mystical dimension of Islam," that is, to Sufism.[16] The word *murid* (from the Arabic *murīdun*, "one who desires") refers to a student of a Sufi master and teacher. The Arabic term for the teacher is *shaykh* (meaning "elder") or *murshid* (meaning "one who gives guidance"); the Persian term is *pir* ("elder") or *ishan* (the third person plural pronoun, used in formal speech for the third person singular). Muridism can also be described from the perspective of the teacher; hence, in Russian sources, it is sometimes referred to as Ishanism, Pirism, or Shaykhism. This range of terms is a good indication of the centrality of the student-teacher relationship for organized and politicized Sufism.

One of the most striking features of early anticolonial resistance in the Islamic world is the fact that its best-known manifestations have been linked, both organizationally and psychologically, with Sufism. Yet the tenets of Sufism, in themselves, would appear to have very little to do with war or struggle. If Sufism is identified with "Islamic mysticism," it is possible to speak of "mystic tendencies" of resistance movements. The concept of mysticism, however, is not essentially applicable to this specific historical context without further elaboration. In its original form, Sufism is more oriented toward asceticism (*zuhd*) than toward struggle and political activism.

It would be presumptuous to attempt to give a serviceable, concise definition for Sufism here. In the oldest textual sources that discuss Sufism there are seventy-eight different definitions for it.[17] Throughout all of the diverse Sufi currents, schools and teachings, however, one feature remains the same: the adherent's search for union of the soul with God; for transcendence of the self and self-annihilation (*fana*) in God. As a "religion of the heart," Sufism goes beyond the normative and formal elements of Islamic orthodoxy, but it does not do away with all formal religiousness. The Shari'a, for example, is revealed law and, as such, is binding for all Muslims; for the esoteric *tariqa* (Arabic, meaning "means; way; system; creed; faith") it provides the *itinerarium mentis ad Deum*: the path toward direct experience of God, moving through various stages of spiritual development that can only be reached by certain believers.[18]

The historical reality of Sufism, however, stands in apparent contrast to its esoteric nature. In fact, it has played a very active role in the social and political life of Islam that cannot be founded on principles of renunciation of the world and self. Western researchers' investigation of this historical-political dimension of Sufism has lagged far behind interest in its philosophical and religious value, with the exception of a few general descriptions[19] and individual studies of regions, such as the works of Alexandre Bennigsen and his students on Sufism in the Soviet Union.[20]

In its earliest phase, during the eighth and ninth centuries, Sufism was exclusively oriented toward renunciation of social activity, seeing ascetic life as requisite for the possibility of mystical contact with the Divine. In its subsequent centuries of development, however, as it spread throughout the Islamic world and elaborated both its concepts and organizational forms, it came to embrace social and political activities of various kinds. In the course of this development, Sufi groups sometimes upheld and even formed the state; sometimes they acted as social revolutionaries; at other times they were linked with military bodies.

More than any other Islamic group, Sufis acted as powerful agents for missionary activity, playing an especially conspicuous role in the Islamicization of African, Balkan, Turkic, and Caucasian people. Sufism not only became an effective force in stimulating and organizing resistance to external pressure from non-Muslim societies, but also against internal oppression by unjust Muslim administrations. Sufi brotherhoods took up the cause of "national" liberation movements particularly in border areas with strong tribal influence: in the Maghreb (Abd al-Qadir), Indonesia (the Atyeh War), Black Africa (the struggle against the French in Senegal, led by the Tidyaniyya Order, 1852–64), and in the Caucasus.

In the eastern part of the Islamic cultural area, in Turkistan, Sufism showed its militant face. Even before the Russian conquest, Central Asians had waged jihads that were initiated by Sufi orders. In the seventeenth and eighteenth centuries, for example, Naqshbandi preachers mobilized Kazakh clans to resist the Buddhist Oirats,[21] and the Turkmens were unified by *murid*s in battle against Persian troops.[22]

Contemporary observers of Sufism have expressed their bewilderment at the "Sufi Paradox": the fact that leaders on the mystic path to God become leaders in war; that thirst for war and fierce capacity for hate can emerge from a doctrine centered on love and self-renunciation. Baron Haxthausen, writing in *Transcaucasia*, about the first leader of politicized muridism in Daghistan, Mullah Muhammad, states, "He lived only in his religious observances and in the reflections and teachings on the holy books he gave his students. And this old man, with his peaceable and unpresuming demeanor . . . preached the uprising of the people as one body, as well as bloody struggle; ceaseless war and raging, unquenchable hatred."[23]

Many similar statements of perplexity can be found among contemporary French, English, German, and, of course, Russian writers on the Caucasus War. Even today, Soviet authors are inclined to distinguish politicized and militant muridism from the principles of Sufism, citing the monastic and apolitical nature of *tariqa*.[24] In contrast to this view, the following four points should be considered:

First, such a separation is based on a conception of a pristine form of Sufism that invoked quietism, which was characteristic only of the early phase of Islamic mysticism. In later stages, however, it was hardly the case that Sufi "renunciation of the world" always entailed isolation from the larger community and abstention from social activities. Beginning in the eleventh century, movements toward collectivization and organization came more and more into the foreground of Sufi life. The *tariqa*, the mystic path to God followed by the Sufi, began to be embodied in organizational forms. It came to be described in terms of a specific method for spiritual progress in connection with a community—the order—that followed this method under the guidance of a master. Hence, Sufism became, in essence, an alternative religious organization.[25] The more institutionalized Sufism became, the greater was its social and political potential.

Second, struggle is not a major concern of mystic teachings, but it is part of Sufi socialization. The pursuit of a *tariqa* was a singular type of struggle: that against the self, but it could only be undertaken under the guidance of an experienced master/teacher. Sufi literature issued stern warnings against false paths: these admonitions were directed especially toward anyone who sought unmediated contact with God without the help of a guide. As a consequence, the group, the brotherhood, and the order evolved as the organizational framework of Sufism. The remarkably strong coherence of the Sufi community would thus appear to be a favorable condition for the growth of socio-political activities.

Third, the master-student relationship, in which the *murid* stood in total submission to the teacher, provided the basic framework for this cohesive system. Russian sources from the nineteenth century emphasize this dynamic in manifestations of Muridism in the Muslim regions of the Russian Empire. From among the countless sayings used by Sufis to describe this relationship, these sources tend to cite one in particular; namely, that the *murid* in the hands of a *shaykh* should be "like a corpse in the hands of the corpse-washer." Sufi literature in Russia-dominated regions speaks repeatedly of this principle. Tazeddin Yaltshigul, a Sufi *shaykh* from Central Asia, states: "The rays of God's love cannot shine if there is no *murshid* with holy wisdom among the *murid*s. The community of *murid*s cannot be victorious over the Devil's forces if they have no leader at the helm."[26] Aleksandr Kazembek, Russia's leading orientalist at the time of the Caucasus War and the writer of one of the earliest serious studies of Muridism (1859), gives an appropriate definition of this principle in calling it *predannost' dukhovnomu vospitatelyu* (submission to a spiritual instructor).[27] Unconditional subordination to the will of a master was the first step toward transcendence of the self, on which the whole mystic endeavor depended, but it was also the basis for a totalitarian principle of leadership that could easily carry over into the political realm.

Fourth, the concept of jihad is, to be sure, not originally a Sufi teaching; rather, it is one of the duties commanded by orthodox Islam. Contrary to what might be expected, however, Sufism does not take a renunciatory, quasi-pacifistic stance toward this principle.[28] Sufis have always endorsed jihad when it was seen as a means of defense against foreign domination, on the grounds that, for the soul to belong exclusively to God, the believer must be externally free and independent. Submission to foreign domination is a religious crime, even for Sufism. Consequently, when there was a need to avert danger from outside the Dar al-Islam, Sufism could draw on the idea of jihad, which already served as a mobilizing force in orthodox Islam. It could rouse the public to action by investing the concept with mystic value that satisfied the need for "meaningful" faith, awakening inspiration and religious passion.

The Naqshbandi Order

The above points are especially applicable to the Sufi orders that played the greatest historical role among Muslims, especially in Asia: the Naqshbandis, who exerted influence over a broader area than any other universalist Sufi order. In the fourteenth century, from its historical center in Bukhara, the Naqshbandi Order began to spread to other settled regions of Central Asia, where it shaped the political history of the Timurid, Shaybanid, and other dynasties, and then to the rest of Muslim Asia. In its Central Asian homeland, it gained immense prestige through organizing a jihad against non-Islamic expansionist powers such as the Buddhist Oirats. The influence of the Naqshbandi Order can still be observed in the North Caucasus, Azerbaijan, Turkmenia, Uzbekistan, and Karakalpakia.[29] The Naqshbandis have played a part in raising Islamic and national resistance against foreign domination throughout Asia: against the Dutch in Indonesia; against the Thai in the northern Malay Peninsula; in Muslim uprisings against Chinese rule in Shanxi, Kansu and Xinjiang; in the southern Philippines, India, Afghanistan; and, last but not least, in the Caucasus.[30]

Several features characterize the Naqshbandi Order and have made possible its unique historical role:

The Naqshbandis are a distinctively level-headed and pragmatic order. Annemarie Schimmel has proposed a contrast between the "Naqshbandi reaction" and more emotional forms of mysticism.[31] The "nonecstatic" is the focus of the Naqshbandi *tariqa*, as, for example, the silent *dhikr*: the voiceless invocation of God's presence in the believer's heart through inward repetition of a formula. The Naqshbandis thus stand conspicuously apart from the practices of the "wailing" or "dancing dervishes."

All Sufi orders maintain some kind of balance between the exoteric and esoteric sides of Islam—between Shariʿa and *tariqa*. The Naqsh-bandis emphasize the exoteric more than any other group.[32] External observers therefore have difficulty distinguishing Sufism and orthodoxy in this order.

The relationship between master and student—the acquiescence of *murid* to the *murshid* or *shaykh*—is especially cultivated in this order, as in *tawajjuh*, the pair's focused concentration on one another.[33]

More than any other order, the Naqshbandis place great value on the prophets of Islam and the early period of the Islamic community.

Naqshbandi teachers and leaders have clearly expressed their willing-ness to participate in political power structures and social life. The order advocates *khalwat dar anjuman:* solitude within society. According to this principle, one does not need to turn away from society to be a Sufi. Khwajah Ubaydullah Ahrar (1404–90), one of the most important Naqsh-bandi leaders during the period when the order virtually ruled parts of Central Asia, taught that:

> To serve the world, one must exercise political power appropriately. In this age, if we were to act only as shaykhs, no shaykh would ever find another student. We have another task before us: to protect Muslims from the evil of oppression, and, with this end in view, we must consort with kings and conquer their souls.[34]

The *Murids'* "Holy War" in the North Caucasus

The "Caucasus War" and the Russian conquest of the Caucasus date from the beginning of the nineteenth century to the final subjugation of the Circassians in 1864. One part of this event, the murid War, was to be the Muslims' most significant defensive struggle during the nine-teenth century, in terms of its duration and scale. The term *Caucasus* here is used in the usual nineteenth-century Russian sense of *Kavkaz*, designating the Caucasian mountain region extending from the Black Sea to the Caspian (now, Severnyi Kavkaz, "North Caucasus"), that lay between the Russian Empire's newly gained Transcaucasus lands and the steppe region north of the Caucasus that had long been settled by the Cossacks. To the east, this region bordered on the Caspian coastal region, with its minor Muslim sovereignties (Shirwan, Kura, and others), which had been under indirect Russian rule since the beginning of the nine-teenth century. This geographic situation, which made the Transcau-casian holdings into something resembling "overseas" colonies, meant that St. Petersburg could represent the conquest of mountainous Caucasus as an unavoidable strategic necessity.

In the 1820s, Russian colonial forces in the Caucasus stepped up maneuvers against the mountain people who had still not been conquered and who had been causing unrest with raids on regions under Russian dominion. At this time, a local branch of the Naqshbandi *tariqa* in the coastal region of Daghistan began to agitate against the "unbelieving" enemy. The Naqshbandis had come rather late to the Islamic areas of the Caucasus. The first Naqshbandi preacher to call for jihad against the Russians was the Chechen shaykh Ushurma. At the end of the eighteenth century, he united the inhabitants in the western part of the region in battle against Russian expansion.[35]

The second chapter of Naqshbandi agitation against czarist colonialist policies began in the early 1820s in Shirwan, with the sermons of a shaykh from Kurdamir, named Ismail. In 1825, one of this shaykh's students, Mullah Muhammad, from Jaraglar in the Khanate of Kura (in south Daghistan), called for the first jihad against the Russians in Daghistan. With Mullah Muhammad there began a chain of initiation (*silsila*) to the leadership of a politicized Muridism, leading to Ghazi Muhammad, the first imam of Daghistan (1828–32), then to his follower Hamzad Beg (1832–34), and to Shamil (1834–59; d. 1872).

The emergence of politicized Muridism in Daghistan took place alongside the escalation of Russia's violent incursions into the region. The *murid* struggle, despite its frequently aggressive arguments, was a case of defensive jihad, or *ghazawat*. After the historiographic reinterpretation of this event during the late Stalinist period, beginning in 1956, Soviet scholars returned to an interpretation that considers Muridism a defensive movement. They insist, however, on the "objective fact" that the forcible annexation of the North Caucasus to the Russian Empire brought progress to the people of the region.[36]

The Muridist program, harkening to the Shari'a and to *ghazawat*, brought about the integration of an ethnically fragmented population and moved toward the goal of defense against colonial domination. More than once in the speeches of the czarist governors of the Caucasus, particularly in that of General Aleksandr P. Yermolov's, the will to dominate had been expressed in terms of punitive expeditions and threats to exterminate the insubordinate mountain people (*gortsy*).

The harshness of Russian military feudalism in the Caucasus was noted with shame by critical Russian contemporaries. N. N. Raievski compared the Russians' actions to "the atrocities of the first conquest of America" and, thus, to the European colonialist undertakings that had brought about genocidal atrocities on a massive scale.[37] For their economic survival, at the very least, the *gortsy* would have to struggle, for they were being cut off from the lowlands of Daghistan—already largely under Russian domination—and were being robbed of their vital trade connections and forced ever deeper into the mountains.

Russian colonial dominion in the Muslim areas of the Caucasus was based on a form of "indirect rule," and, particularly on account of its policy of rank, it provoked the resistance of the local population and the politicization of Muridism. It actually put in place what were presumed to be trustworthy local rulers, strengthened the social and economic powers of the secular aristocracy of khans and begs, thus intensifying the exploitation of a peasantry that already lived in a state of feudal dependency. Russian-supported local despotism was strongest in the khanates of the lowlands of south Daghistan, as in Kura under Aslan Khan. It was from this region that Muridism began to branch out, before it had created the basis for jihad against the czars in the mountains of central Daghistan and in the Chechen region.

In this way, czarist policies secured a broad social base for the Muridist movement, with an Islamic egalitarianism as its focal point. The Russians were much too late in recognizing Muridism as mass movement; when they did, they reacted with an intensification of the very policies to which Muridism was a response. "Only the principle of aristocracy can overcome the democratic movement that has arisen and become deeply rooted in Daghistan, a movement which, thus far, nothing but armed force has been able to confront."[38]

The *murids'* struggle against czarist forces in the Caucasus was long and bloody, tying up large contingents of the Russian army, a total of 350,000 men, for some three decades. In the 1840s, Shamil was able to set up a real state, with a centralized structure, in his domain: a large part of Daghistan and the whole Chechen region. Internal deterioration, along with an increase in feudalization and intensified pressure from without led to a weakening of resistance in the 1850s. When Shamil, along with his few remaining followers, capitulated to Field Marshall Bariatinskii in 1859, Russia breathed a sigh of relief. The Imam of Daghistan, now famous throughout the world, was imprisoned at Kaluga as a most respected enemy.

Basic Ideological Elements of North Caucasus Muridism

Origins in Sufism

Discussion above has indicated the difficulties involved in characterizing militant Muridism as "Sufism." These difficulties are diminished, however, if Sufism is considered as a multifaceted phenomenon, rather than simply as a form of quietism. An understanding of the features of the Naqshbandi Order can further clarify the transformation of the "mystical" into political activity.

The association of Caucasian Muridism with this most important of the brotherhoods in the East cannot be denied. The *silsile*, or chain of initiation into leadership of the order, of the Caucasus Naqshbandi branch provided the three imams of Daghistan who waged war against Russian expansion: Ghazi Mullah, Hamzad Beg, and Shamil. The organization of resistance in the Caucasus, and in Shamil's resistance state (his imamate), was grounded in the basic principles of the *tariqa* of late Sufism: on the hierarchical structure and the cohesiveness of brotherhoods; on the cult of the leader and the unconditional obedience of *murid*s. Nineteenth-century Russian sources often call *murid*s "*tarikatisty.*" Shamil himself spoke of a split between *tariqa murid*s and the *na'ib murid*s (*na'ib*—Arabic for "allotment"—was a term designating Shamil's agents in the local civil and military administration), and he never referred to himself as a shaykh in the mystic sense, but this does not suggest any separation of Muridism from its Sufi origins.[39] In other parts of the Islamic world, there was a similar "division of labor" within Sufi orders between those who devoted themselves to mystic contemplation and those who went to war. Accordingly, Mahi al-Din, the head of the Qadiriyya in Algeria and father of Abd al-Qadir, handed on the leadership of the resistance movement to his son saying, "I am a man of peace who has given himself to the service of Allah."[40]

Islamic Orthodoxy

In this case, Sufism does not mean heterodoxy and sectarianism. Nineteenth-century Russian authors who treat Muridism always discuss the teachings of the *tarikatisty* and *murid*s under the heading of "sectarianism." But Baron Haxthausen, writing in 1856, put forth an opposing view:

> In fact, it is wrong to call Muridism a Mohammedan sect. It would be more correct to call it a political and religious schism. There is no doctrine of Muridism that distinguishes it in any essential way from Mohammedanism; on the contrary, it openly teaches the harmony and unity of Shiʿa and Sunni.[41]

During more recent periods of Sufism's development, the boundaries between mysticism and orthodoxy become blurred, particularly in the phase of anticolonial resistance. In Algeria in the nineteenth century, the Qadiriyya were scarcely distinguishable from orthodoxy.[42] In the case of the Naqshbandi order, the essentials of doctrine have long been orthodoxy on a foundation of mysticism. Sufis have carried out their most intensive activities in regions where the process of Islamicization was not yet complete. In such regions, Orthodox Islam has been imposed through Sufism, because these have tended to be areas with strong tribal influence, where Islamic law has had to compete with other norms, such as clan practices. But, in these areas, Sufi teachings have often been much more orthodox than mystical, so that an outside observer may not recognize them as part of Sufism. Alexandre Dumas, for example, like other travelers in the Caucasus during the nineteenth century, often confuses Muridism with Wahhabism, a form of Arabic puritanism that is actually strongly opposed to Sufism.

Strengthening the Faith

Prior to the call to jihad against the Russians, the primary objective of Muridism in the North Caucasus was to create a deeper faith—an intensified Islamicization. At a gathering of mountain people in 1824, Mullah Muhammad explained, "The way we live now, we are neither Muslim nor Christian nor idol worshippers. But one must hold fast to what one knows to be good in the world. And this one good for us is the belief of our fathers."[43] Deepened faith came to be seen as the condition for the possibility of Muslim self-defense. In the case of Caucasus Muridism, as in similar resistance ideologies, the interdependence of "greater" and "lesser" jihad—the internal and external faces of "holy war"—is particularly clear.

Orientation toward Early Islam

Shamil stated repeatedly that a number of Muridism's ideas were borrowed from early Islam. Other Islamic movements of the nineteenth century that were guided by Sufi brotherhoods—as in Algeria—had a similar orientation toward the early Islamic community, toward the time of the Prophet and the rightly guided caliphs, considered to be the period of fullest unity and purity of Islam.[44] In some respects, Sufism developed a particular attitude of submission to the Prophet as a model, becoming a sort of tariqa al-Muhammadiyya. The Naqshbandis were prominent among those who stressed the Prophet's example. As a contemporary member of the order has said, "True Sufism means submitting oneself to the Book of God and following the Sunna of His Messenger. It means re-experiencing the time of the Messenger and the companions in one's inner being and outward actions."[45]

Shamil himself also strove to imitate the Prophet. He called his flight from Himry to Ashilta the "Hegira" and those who accompanied him there, *muhajirun* (the term for those who fled with Muhammad to Medina) and *al-ansar* (the term for the Medinan followers of the Prophet who granted him refuge after the Hegira). Kazembek goes so far as to propose that his fragmentary written testimony—Shamil wrote on scraps of leather and tree bark—was done in conscious imitation of the Prophet.[46] Even Shamil's opposition recognized the similarity with the early history of Islam, and with its fierce character. The first Russian historian of the Caucasus War, Golovin, wrote in 1841, "We have never known such a wild and dangerous opponent as Shamil . . . his power has religious and militant roots, just as did Mohammed's in early Islam, when he threw three-quarters of the world into disorder."

Puritanism

Public life in Shamil's domain was governed by an extreme form of puritanism, essentially alien to the people of the Caucasus. This code resulted from the principles enumerated above, but also from the requirements of the guerrillas, for it was a system that could concentrate all forces in defense and bring about the discipline of the people that was required for war. This puritanism also characterizes other Islamic resistance movements of the nineteenth century. A Soviet author says of the Atyeh War, "Spiritual leaders regarded the smallest diversion from moral/ethical and legal standards as a religious crime, and one that could lead to failure in battle against the unbelievers."[47]

The Shariʿa versus ʿAdat (Customary Law)

Early Islamic history was repeated in Daghistan with the effort to replace tribal organization by a community of believers. This attempt at integration was quite remarkable, in view of the ethnic fragmentation of this region. It gave impetus to the acceptance of the Shariʿa, Islamic canon law, in place of local customary laws, ʿadat, which had helped preserve tribalism and fragmentation. Like the Prophet, Shamil rejected every form of solidarity that was not Islamically based, such as the solidarity of clans, identifying ʿadat with jahiliyya; that is, with pre-Islamic ignorance.

This emphasis on Shariʿa does not contradict the principles of Sufism. Shariʿa and *tariqa* do not form a dichotomy. Sufism does not reject the Shariʿa at all; rather it uses *tariqa* as a path to reach the Shariʿa and then to go beyond it. In places where Shariʿa had not yet been accepted, Sufi organizations often made strong progress toward that goal. Shamil, however, could not enforce the Shariʿa in his imamate without some compromise: the Islamic legal system would have to fit the socio-cultural realities of life among the mountain people. In the northwestern Caucasus, with its religious syncretism and very superficial acceptance of Islam, Shariʿa had no chance of winning over ʿadat, just as Muridist propaganda faded in influence among the Abaza, Circassians, and Kabardines.

The significance of "Shariʿa versus ʿadat" became particularly clear in the suppression and regulation of blood feuds (*qanli*), the most egregious customary institution of the Caucasus. It was clear that blood feud in the region could take on dimensions that would substantially reduce the capacity for battle against a much larger external opponent.

Russian counter-ideology focused on this aspect of Muridism's program and set out to reinforce ʿadat/customary law. Codification of local customary laws was carried out under Russian guidance, and research was done on ʿadat. The Russian administration of the mountain region (Kavkazskoe Gorskoe Upravlenie) was initiated in the 1840s with the collection of information on the ʿadats of the mountain clans.[48] Czarism also made use of coopted Muslim spiritual leaders from other Islamic regions of the Empire to denounce the Murids as "false servants of Allah, who deviate from the Shariʿa and spread erroneous teachings."[49]

Ghazawat: "Holy War"

The exhortations of Muridist leaders linked Shariʿa with *ghazawat/ jihad*, praising both of these principles for their integrative and mobilizing potential. In Mullah Muhammad's exhortation in 1824, he says,

> And the highest law of the faith is freedom in all relations. The Muslim is not to be a subject; much less is he to live enslaved to a foreign people. . . . The second law is similar to the first: the one does not stand without the other. This law commands war against the unbelievers and the following of the Shariʿa. Whoever does not uphold the Shariʿa and does not take up the sword against the unbelievers— for him there is no salvation.[50]

Ghazawat was scarcely a new word or concept in Daghistan: the people of that region had rallied around it in the eighteenth century to resist the Persian troops under Nadir Shah. "Holy war" could be waged against Muslim oppressors as well. "Unbeliever" must not be understood in a purely confessional sense, for it pertains to all who oppress faith and the faithful. The "confessional intolerance" that Russian sources ascribe to Muridism is contradicted by the fact that Russian, Ukrainian, and Polish deserters played a significant role in Shamil's forces. Maintaining their Christian faith, they were integrated into the society of the mountain people.

Egalitarianism

One of the reasons Muridism appealed so broadly to people was that it preached the need not only for deepened faith, the Shari'a and *ghazawat*, but for social justice as well, citing the principle that "in Islam all men are brothers." In his domain, Shamil introduced reforms such as the abolition of slavery as well as the limitation of rights of secular feudal landholders and, to some extent, the divestment of their power. Russian contemporaries like Apollon Runovskii acknowledged this aspect of Muridist policy.[51] Soviet historiography, too, has described features of the social reformism in Muridism, although not in the sense of any real progressiveness.[52]

Imamate

In the territory where Muridism predominated. Shamil established a theocratic state that was called the "imamate." This was a truly Islamic form of government, whose head, the *imam*, possessed both spiritual and worldly power. The system of Sufi orders, already structured around loyalty to leaders, served as the primary organizational basis of this state. The theoretical basis was Islamic theology, one of the most important of *'ilm al-qalam* (the science of the pen).

Muridism/Ishanism in Turkistan and the Revolt of Andijan

From the sixteenth century onward, Turkistan was a bastion of Sunni orthodoxy, with Bukhara as a world center for orthodox Islamic scholarship. During the sixteenth century, too, this region began to figure prominently in the history of Sufism, especially in its organizational development. Mystical orders like the Naqshbandis had sprung up in Bukhara. According to Russian writers, the influence of the *ishans*—as Sufi *shaykh*s were called—in this region in the nineteenth century was greater than the "normal Islam" of the *imam*s and *asanchi* (muezzins), an approach that had frozen into scholasticism. "All control over the views and convictions of the people rests in the hands of the *ishans*." The dervishes, the majority of whom belonged to the Naqshbandi Order, "form brotherhoods that are usually closed, concealing within their societies great strength that sometimes lashes out, unexpectedly and violently, as it did in the Caucasus," wrote a Russian author at the end of the nineteenth century.[53]

Contrary to the situation in the Caucasus, Muridism in Turkistan failed to take hold. In the second half of the nineteenth century, the *ishans* of Turkistan could not agree on a coordinated revival and resistance movement against the spread of Russian rule. The single initiative toward concerted regional resistance, the revolt of Andijan in 1898, ran aground in its early stages. In this region, movements headed by *ishans* were entirely lacking in the powerful dynamism possessed by Muridism in the Caucasus. Compared with the long, hard struggle in the Caucasus, Russian expansion into Central Asia was a casual promenade.

Russian rule in Turkistan favored the principle—introduced by its first governor-general, K. P. von Kaufmann—of "conscious neglect": nonintervention in local customs, the promotion of Islamic conservatism and the exploitation of the drive led by *ishans*. The *ishans* could manipulate foreign rule toward their own ends of mobilization, without becoming subject to its intimidation or control.

Russian sources emphasize the fact that the revolt of Andijan, in the administrative district of Farghana, was completely unexpected and unprovoked. In fact, however, the seeds of revolt had been sown years before its occurrence, when Ishan Madali formed a Muridist group near the garrison city of Andijan and the administrative center of Marghelan, in the Farghana Valley. He mobilized the population and eventually preached in public of the need for "holy war."

The Farghana region encompassed the Khanate of Kokand, which the Empire had annexed by 1876. The goal of the *ishans'* drive in this part of Turkistan was the restoration of this khanate as an independent Islamic state. At the end of the nineteenth century, memory of the time prior to the Russian conquest was still very much alive, partly as a result of the *ishan's* efforts. Some former khanate officials, both temporal and spiritual, were among Ishan Madali's followers. The objective of restoration in Turkistan constitutes a significant difference with Muridism in the North Caucasus, which could not link itself to the recollection of any history of an autochthonous Islamic state. Rather, it sought to create such a state for the first time by struggling against the minor fiefdoms of Daghistan that had been coopted by the Russians.

Madali himself, born in 1856, was the son of a Sart craftsman. At the age of ten, he went to study with an *ishan*, with whom he remained for nine years. In 1883, after the death of his teacher, he took on his own students, led an ascetic life, and gained a reputation as a holy man. He made the pilgrimage (*hajj*) at the age of thirty and, on his return from Mecca, began to be regarded explicitly as an *ishan*.

Russian sources describe him in terms of the dervish stereotype that was widespread in Europe: fiery eyes, grimness, unlaughing, obstinately "fanatic." The picture of *ishan* movements always alleges the exploitative and parasitic nature of *ishans'* activities. Ishan Madali is not only said to have taken money out of people's pockets, but also to have raped women who came to him for medical consultations.[54] Such calumny still appears in Soviet writings about present-day "parallel Islam," where the word "parasite" is a synonym for unregistered mullahs and "religious fanatics."

In 1898 a delegate from Constantinople is supposed to have come to Ishan Madali with a document, said to be from Sultan Abdülhamit II, urging that the Shariʿa be strengthened and that jihad be waged against the unbelievers in Turkistan. The document is thought to have been a fake. Presumably, Madali's deputy, a Kirghiz named Ziyauddin, created this forgery in order to initiate action. A plan of action drawn up in 1898 proposed attacks on Russian barracks in Andijan, Marghelan, and Osh. The next steps were to be the conquest of Namangan, the restoration of the Kokand Khanate, and the instigation of revolt throughout Turkistan. But the planned revolt was limited to a feeble action against the garrison of Andijan that lasted scarcely a quarter of an hour and cost twenty-two Russian soldiers their lives.[55]

Despite the pitifully small scale of the ishan's actions in Turkistan, they did shake up local Russian authorities, and they provoked changes in policies toward the local population. It was evident that the time for "conscious neglect" was over. The Russian colonial administration began to show its true colors.

Ishan Madali and seventeen of his followers were hanged on a Friday— the Muslim Sabbath. During the preceding trial, these reasons were given for the uprising: corruption of traditions after Russia's conquest, neglect of the Shariʿa, restrictions on Muslim pilgrimage imposed by Russian authorities, elimination of *zakat* (the alms required by Islamic law, which had consisted of one-fortieth of a person's income in this region), and restrictions of *waqf* (religious endowment) rights.[56]

Other factors in addition to these religious ones served to increase popular support for the ishan. Among these were the ruination of farmers as a consequence of the compulsory cotton cultivation, the corruption of local officials, and the census of 1897 that had especially incensed the local Kirghiz population, who had played a notably active role in the uprising.[57]

Sufism among the Tatars and the Vaisov Movement

The Tatar region centered on the Middle Volga was the Muslim area longest under Russian rule. There, Sufi influence was channeled primarily through trade relationships with the centers of the Islamic world. According to descriptions by Tatar historians, the beginnings of Sufism in this region go back to the eleventh and twelfth centuries: the age of the medieval Bulgarian Khanate. In the centuries after Russian rule began, after the 1500s, the *ishan*s began to gain influence over the population, increasing in strength especially at the end of the nineteenth century. Tatar Sufism extended well beyond the mid-Volga region, as far away as Siberia.[58]

To a greater extent than in other Muslim regions, the drive led by the *ishan*s became a strong vehicle for the communication of nationalist ideas. The expression "tribal resistance" does not apply here. The association of Sufism with nationalism in the nineteenth-century Vais movement brought about one of the most peculiar cases of Sufi-inspired "holy war." In this region, as in Turkistan, Russian authorities did not regard Sufism as a threat. To an extent, in fact, the Orenburg Muslim Directorate even supported the *ishan*'s authority.

In the 1860s in Kazan, a sectarian leader named Bahaeddin Vais (in Russian, "Vaisov"), who was influenced by the Naqshbandi Order, established an alternative Islamic organization that was explicitly opposed to the official Tatar clergy. Its first embodiment was a house of worship "for the advancement of the true faith"; the next was a "Muslim academy," set up in opposition to the Orenburg Spiritual Directorate. Vaisov defined his organization as "Islam outside the mosque" and separated it *ot mechetskikh Tatar* (from the Mosque Tatars). He named it *Vaisov Bozhii polk musulman Staroverov* (God's Host of Old-Believer Muslims [led by] Vaisov) and defined its mission as that of jihad. His sermons proclaimed that it was wrong for any temporal body to claim authority over these warriors of God: the Qurʾân and Shariʿa were their sole authority. Vais's followers regarded themselves as subjects of God and the czars, but they did not acknowledge the authority of the czarist state and its bureaucracy nor that of the orthodox Muslim clergy: "Our sole responsibility is to follow the precepts of the Qurʾân, and to carry out this duty we must be free: a horse cannot wear two bits at once. We honor the sovereign; we pray for the sovereign, but we have no use for the state."[59]

Jihad against clergy and bureaucracy was waged without violence.

Vais's warriors of God refused to accept Russian passports and did not pay their taxes. In 1884, Russian authorities destroyed the organization and sent its leader to a psychiatric institution, where he died in 1893. In 1897, the sect once again showed signs of life when it refused to participate in the census. In 1905, Vais's son, Iman ad-Din, set out to further his father's work, establishing a new community house and an "academy" in Kazan.

Vais's ideas bear certain marks that place it somewhat outside the framework of the Islamic resistance movements based on Sufi principles that have been discussed here, notably three:

First, the passive nature of its jihad. Vais's followers refused to recognize the czarist power structure, while nevertheless maintaining loyalty to the person of the czar. This is reminiscent of the anarchism of certain Christian heterodox Russian sects.

Second, the emphasis on "old belief." The recognition of pure and uncorrupted teachings accords with the Islamic fundamentalism evident in other Sufi-inspired Muridist movements of the nineteenth century. The term *starovery* (old believers), however, suggests influence from "old-rite" Russian sects, who were strongly represented in the Volga region. This emphasis on "old belief" distinguishes Vais's ideology from the Jadidist revival movements that were gaining impetus among the Tatars at this time.

Third, nationalism. The most striking feature of Vais's movement is its bizarre form of nationalism, both anti-Russian and anti-Tatar. Vaisov's followers associated themselves with the ancient Khanate of the Volga Bulgars, which they sought to regain for their community through grotesque petitions sent to the czar. They called themselves, in Russian, *Bolgary* and were concerned that they not be regarded as Tatars: "We are not Tatars. Between ourselves and them there is as great a difference as between Heaven and Earth; fire and water."[60]

At the same time, however, Vais's sect had certain features in common with the Muridism and *ishan* drives of the Caucasus and Turkistan. Vais's tenets reveal a distinct puritanism, stressing Islamic criminal law, the status of women, the sharp divergence from Islamic conformism and from spirituality as coopted by czarism, as well as in its emphasis on the authority of the sect leader, the *murshid*, who held the powerful Persian title of *sardar* (governor). Chantal Lemercier-Quelquejay has proposed that the emergence of this unique movement should be seen in the context of a three-fold crisis in Tatar society. Scarcity of land and Tatar farmers' discontent with the regional consequences of agarian reform, aggravated by the introduction of a new system of local taxation in 1878, created an economic and *social* crisis, resulting in unrest among farmers and emigration to Turkey. The intensification of czarist assimilation policy among the Tatars (Il'minskii reforms) precipitated a *national* crisis. And, finally, a *spiritual* crisis was precipitated by the collaboration of the Orenburg Muftiate and Tatar clergy with the Russian authorities, as well as by certain manifestations of decadence among the local clergy.[61]

Conclusions

The cases of Sufi-inspired jihad against czarism that have been outlined here occurred independently of one another in the three principal Muslim regions of the Russian Empire, under very different regional conditions. Their proportions differ, for example, with regard to popular participation. Jihad/*ghazawat* in the North Caucasus, was able to mobilize entire ethnic groups; Vais's sect drew about 15,000 followers in 1908, while only some 1,500 to 2,000 Muslims participated actively in the uprising in Andijan. In the North Caucasus and among the Tatars the social basis of these movements lay primarily among the peasantry (for Vaisitism, among artisans as well), and both were led by ʿulama organized by Naqshbandi affiliates. In the Andijan uprising, in contrast, there was a conservative, secular element, with the participation of certain officials of the Khanate of Kokand. Yet, despite these differences, all three cases are alike in their Sufi instigation, their *tariqa* organizational structures, and in their Islamic ideological characteristics, such as puritanism and adherence to the Shariʿa.

Muridism is obviously not a dead historical phenomenon. It is still active today—particularly through the Naqshbandi *tariqa*—in jihad in Afghanistan; in the Islamic "renaissance" in the Soviet Union; in anti-secular opposition in Turkey, where Ataturk's first measure against Islam was the banning of mystic brotherhoods. The nineteenth century's much-popularized figure of the "fighting dervish" lives on in the twentieth century.

Notes

1. *Kommunist Tadzhikistana,* 31 January and 12 February 1987.

2. I. Makatov, "V ushcherb interesam obshchestva i lichnosti," *Sovetskii Dagestan* no. 6 (1987): 37–44; here, p. 42.

3. *Kavkaz,* no. 20 (1846).

4. Regarding this description, see Baber Johansen, *Islam und Staat*, Argumente Studienhefte, no. 54 (Berlin, 1982), pp. 25–26.

5. R. A. Fadeev, *Sobranie Sochinenii, Vvedenie: 60 let kavkazskoi voiny. Pisma c Kavkaza* (1889). See especially "Pis'mo tret'e, pp. 118–19).

6. An exception can be found in the work, otherwise not especially useful, of M. Canard, "Chamil et Abdelkader," *Annales d'Etudes Orientales* 44 (Algiers, 1956), pp. 231–56.

7. For example, the general study by Rudolph Peters, *Islam and Colonialism: The Doctrine of Jihad in Modern History* (The Hague, 1979) makes no reference whatsoever to Muridism in the Caucasus.

8. Several publications on Caucasian history that discuss Shamil in some detail have appeared in Turkey; for example, Ismail Berkok, *Tarihte Kafkasya* (Istanbul, 1958); Serafeddin Erel, *Dagistan ve Dagistanlilar* (Istanbul, 1959).

9. In 1986 in Lahore, Pakistan, a book about Shamil appeared that represented him —to a public evidently unacquainted with him—as "the first Muslim guerilla leader": Muhammad Hamid, *Imam Shamil: The First Muslim Guerilla Leader* (Lahore, 1986).

10. See Paul B. Henze, "Circassia in the Nineteenth Century: the Futile Fight for Freedom," in Chantal Lemercier-Quelquejay, ed., *Passé turco-tatar, présent soviétique. Etudes offerts à Alexandre Bennigsen* (Paris, 1986); pp. 243–75.

11. Claudine Grossir, *L'Islam des Romantiques*, vol. 1: *1811–1840, Du réfus à la tentation* (Paris, 1984), p. 24.

12. S. A. Tokarew, *Die Religion in der Geschichte der Völker* (East Berlin, 1976), p. 686.

13. On the persistence of distorted views of jihad, see Monika Tworuschka, *Analyse der Geschichtsbücher zum Thema Islam* (Braunschweig, 1986), Studien zur internationalen Schulbuch Forschung (vol. 46), part 1 of *Der Islam in den Schulbüchern der Bundesrepublik Deutschland*, ed. Abdoldjavad Falaturi, pp. 113–22.

14. Peters, *The Doctrine of Jihad*, pp. 39–44; 105–51.

15. W. F. Wertheim, "Nationalismus und Führungselemente in Asien," in *Nationalismus*, ed. H. A. Winkler (Konigstein, 1978), pp. 189–201; here, p. 191.

16. Annemarie Schimmel, *Mystische Dimensionen des Islam: Die Geschichte des Sufismus* (Cologne, 1985).

17. See I. P. Petrushevskii, *Islam v Irane v VII–XV v.* (Leningrad, 1955), p. 319.

18. On the teachings of Sufism see, in addition to Schimmel, Richard Gramlich, *Die schiitischen Derwischorden Persiens*, part 2: *Glaube und Lehre* (Wiesbaden, 1976). On *tariqa*, see the same work, in the section, "Der mystische Weg," pp. 253–455. See also J. Spencer Trimingham, *The Sufi Orders in Islam* (Oxford, 1971), pp. 4–5 ("A *tariqa* is a practical method to guide a seeker by tracing a way of thought, feeling, and action, leading through a succession of 'stages' "), as well as E. E. Bertel's, *Sufizm i sufiiskaia literatura* (Moscow, 1965), p. 37.

19. One fundamental work on this subject is Trimingham, *The Sufi Orders in Islam*.

20. Alexandre Bennigsen and Chantal Lemercier-Quelquejay, *Le soufi et le commissaire: Les confrèries musulmanes en URSS* (Paris, 1986); Lemercier-Quelquejay, "Sufi Brotherhoods in the USSR: A Historical Survey," *Central Asian Survey* 2/2 (1983): 3–35.

21. Alexandre Bennigsen and Chantal Lemercier-Quelquejay, *Les musulmans oubliés: l'Islam en Union soviétique* (Paris, 1981), p. 120.

22. Emanuel Sarkisyanz, *Geschichte der orientalischen Völker Russlands bis 1917* (Munich, 1961), pp. 221–22.

23. August Freiherr von Haxthausen, *Transkaukasia: Andeutungen über das Familien- und Gemeindeleben und die socialen Verhältnisse einiger Völker zwischen dem Schwarzen und Kaspischen Meere*, part 2 (Leipzig, 1856), p. 132.

24. See, for example, G.-A. D. Daniialov, "K voprosu o Sotsial'noi baze i kharaktere dvizheniia gortsev pod rukovodstvom Shamila," in *O dvizhenii gortsev pod rukovodstvom Shamilia: Materialy sessii Dagestanskogo Filiala Akademii Nauk SSSR 4–7 oktiabria 1956 goda* (Makhachkala, 1957), pp. 7–66; here, p. 52.

25. For the periodization of the historical development of Sufism, see Trimingham, *The Sufi Orders in Islam*, pp. 163–64, who distinguishes three stages of development. The first is the period between the seventh and tenth centuries, the "Golden Age of Mysticism," characterized by a minimum of regulation and institutionalization. The second, from 1100 to 1400, the "*Tariqa* Stage," is characterized by "devotion to method," doctrine, rule, tradition, and legalism, as well as to "continuative teaching schools." During the third stage, Sufism becomes a "popular movement," with cults of saints and veneration of *shaykh*s.

26. Quoted by Izmukhamedov, *Islam v Tatarii* (Kazan, 1979), p. 47.

27. Aleksandr Kazembek, "Miuridizm i Shamil'," *Russkoe Slovo* 12 (1859): 182–242.

28. Concerning the relationship between classical Sufism and jihad, see Albrecht Noth, *Heiliger Krieg und Heiliger Kampf in Islam und Christentum* (Bonn, 1966), pp. 59–60.

29. Bennigsen and Quelquejay, *Le soufi*, pp. 64–67; for the Naqshbandi Order in the Caucasus, Quelquejay, *Sufi Brotherhoods*, pp. 5–8.

30. Hamid Algar, "The Naqshbandi Order: A Preliminary Survey of its History and Significance," *Studia Islamica* 44 (1977): 123–52.

31. Schimmel, *Mystische Dimensionen*, pp. 514–26.

32. Hamid Algar, *The Naqshbandi Order in Republican Turkey* (Berlin, 1984), p. 1.

33. Schimmel, *Mystische Dimensionen*, p. 517.

34. Algar, *Naqshbandi Order*, p. 123.

35. Alexandre Bennigsen, "Un mouvement populaire au Caucase au XVIII. siècle. La guerre sainte du sheikh Mansur (1785–1791)," *Cahiers du Monde Russe et Soviétique* 5/2 (1964): 159–205.

36. Regarding the repressive nature of this annexation, see Kh. M. Khashaev, *Obshchestvennyi stroi Dagestana v XIX veke* (Moscow, 1961), p. 45; Kh. Kh. Maramzanov, "Kolonial'naia politika tsarizma v Dagestane v pervoi polovine XIX veka," *Materialy sessii Dagestanskogo Filiala Akademii Nauk SSSR 4–7 oktiabria 1956 goda* (Makhachkala, 1957), pp. 134–55.

37. *Archiv Raevskikh*, vol. 3 (n.p., 1916), p. 342.

38. Statement by the Caucasus governor Vorontsov, cited by A. D. Iandarov, *Sufizm i ideologiia natsional'no-osvoboditel'nogo dvizheniia* (Alma-Ata, 1980), p. 125.

39. A minority of *tariqa* followers was excused from *ghazawat*. Shamil's domain and his war efforts rested on the Naib *murid*s, who represented the "heroic side" of

Muridism. For Shamil's remarks in this regard, see Apollon Runovskii, "Miuridism i gazavat v Dagestane po ob'iasneniiu Shamilia," *Russkii viestnik* 12 (1862). See also Mohyieddin I. Quandour, *Muridism: A Study of the Caucasian Wars of Independence 1819–1859* (Ann Arbor, Mich.: University Microfilms, 1969), pp. 218–19.

40. Ahmed Nadir, "Les ordres religieux et la conquête française," *Revue algérienne des sciences juridiques, économiques et politiques* 9/1 (1972): 819–68; here, p. 837.

41. Haxthausen, *Transkaukasia,* p. 130.

42. A. Nadir, "Les ordres religieux," pp. 839–40.

43. Quotation from Khashaev, "Dvizhushchie sily miuridizma v Dagestane," pp. 67–101; here, p. 82.

44. Nadir, "Les ordres religieux," p. 844.

45. Quoted by Algar, *Naqshbandi Order,* p. 1.

46. A. Kazembek, "Miuridizm i Shamil," *Russkoe Slovo* 12 (1859).

47. V. A. Tiurin, *Achekhskaia voina* (Moscow, 1970), pp. 160–61.

48. R. I. Leontovich, *Adaty kavkazskikh gortsev. Materialy po obychnomu pravu severnago i vostochnago Kavkaza* (Odessa, 1882); see introduction.

49. A. V. Avksent'ev, *Islam na severnom Kavkaze* (Stavropol', 1973), p. 39.

50. Quoted by Khashaev, "Dvizhushchie sily miuridizma," p. 82.

51. A. Runovskii, "Vzgliad na soslovnyia prava i na vzaimnyia otnosheniia soslovii v Dagestane," in *Voennyi Sbornik* 26, no. 2 (1862).

52. See the essays by G. A. Daniialov, Kh. M. Khashaev, and V. G. Gadzhie in *Materialy sessii Dagestanskogo Filiala Akademii Nauk SSSR 4–7 oktiabria 1956 goda* (Makhachkala, 1957). See also A. M. Pikman, "O bor'be kavkazskikh gortsev c tsarskimi kolonizatorami," *Voprosy Istorii* 3 (1956): 75–84.

53. E. T. Smirnov, *Dervishizm v Turkestane* (Tashkent, 1898), p. 3.

54. V. P. Sal'kov, *Andizhanskoe vosstanie v 1898 g.* (Kazan, 1901), pp. 29–33.

55. Concerning the events of the Andijan Uprising, see Ann Sheehy, "The Andizhan Uprising of 1898 and Soviet Historiography," *Central Asian Review* 14/2 (1966): 139–50; G. Gafurov, "Ob Andizhanskom 'vosstanii' 1898 goda," *Voprosy Istorii* 2 (1953): 50–61.

56. Sal'kov, *Andizhanskoe vosstanie,* pp. 79–81.

57. Sheehy, "Andizhan Uprising," p. 142.

58. Izmukhamedov, *Islam,* pp. 43–58.

59. Quoted by E. V. Molostvova, "Vaisov Bozhii polk," *Mir Islama* 1/2 (1912): 143–52; here, p. 147.

60. Molostvova, "Vaisov Bozhii polk," p. 148.

61. Chantal Lemercier-Quelquejay, "Le 'Vaisisme' à Kazan. Contribution à l'étude des confréries musulmanes chez les Tatars de la Volga," *Die Welt des Islams* 6/1–2 (Leiden, 1959): 91–113; here, pp. 92–94.

12. Economic Bases of the Basmachi Movement in the Farghana Valley

Richard Lorenz

The movement called "Basmachi,"[1] centered in Russian Turkistan as well as in the former amirate of Bukhara and khanate of Khiva,[2] struggled against the Soviet regime after the October 1917 Revolution. In the increasing amount of research in recent years about the history of this movement, considerable difference of opinion is apparent.[3] Soviet scholars speak of a counterrevolution supported by British imperialism and denounce the Basmachis as robbers and brigands. Western scholars, in contrast, tend to emphasize the nationalist and religious underpinnings of the movement: the term *freedom fighters* is often used in this context.[4] The present chapter will attempt to discuss the origins of the Basmachi movement in the colonial history of the region, and to investigate its national and religious objectives, in connection with the region's socio-economic development. The Farghana region will be the focus of the discussion, for it was the most important territory of the former Governor-generalship of Turkistan.

The Economic and Social Development of Farghana prior to 1917

The Farghana valley is the oldest of the Central Asian agricultural oases. Surrounded by high mountain ranges, it is linked to other Central Asian cultural areas by only one narrow pass on its western edge.[5] An ancient trade route cuts through it to the southeast and into Chinese Turkistan. From very early times, intensive agriculture was made possible by two tributaries of the Sir Darya, the Kara Darya and the Naryn, as well as a number of smaller mountain streams. Fertile soil, a mild climate, and an abundance of water, in addition to a favorable geographic situation, all helped to promote a very early agricultural civilization, as well as the development of an independent culture. There were continuous settlements in the valleys from earliest times, but the uplands were settled considerably later: even as late as the early nineteenth century they were used principally as pasture lands.

The population of the Farghana valley comprised numerous ethnic groups, with a predominance of Tajiks, Sarts, and Uzbeks.[6] The Kirghiz arrived between the sixteenth and eighteenth centuries, working the pasturelands of the eastern and northeastern edges of the region. In the first half of the seventeenth century tribes of Kipchaks, nomadic herders, appeared in Farghana. Ethnographic researchers have tended to group the Kipchaks with the Uzbeks, but their economy and way of life was distinctly different. In the eighteenth century extensive migrations caused by the political shocks suffered by the Central Asian area considerably increased both the population and the ethnic diversity of Farghana. The population of this agricultural oasis thus came to be distinguished by its great density and its exceptionally diverse ethnic composition.

There were certain processes of assimilation and acculturation that helped to integrate the region's tribal people, who were primarily Uzbek, with the people who had long been settled. Even by the nineteenth century, however, integration of the various ethnic groups was by no means complete. At that time, as previously, large areas were inhabited by a homogeneous Tajik population, while the mountains of Khojand were populated by the descendants of the indigenous Iranian-speaking people: the so-called Mountain Tajiks.

The complex relationships among the inhabitants of Farghana restricted economic development and often led to conflicts.[7] As in other parts of Central Asia, there was a division of labor between the agricultural oasis itself and the surrounding areas that were inhabited by nomadic people. The agriculturalists of the oasis often lived in close proximity with nomadic people, and conflicts flared up frequently over the increasing scarcity of land and water, especially in the uplands where those resources were in demand both for agriculture and for husbandry. By the nineteenth century the shortage of water and land became so severe that the state organized a large irrigation system, including the first large canals to be built in the region.

These irrigation works opened up the possibility of cultivating regions that had hitherto served only as pasturelands, so that many former pastoralists turned to agriculture. This transition led to bitter conflicts between the newly settled nomads and their agriculturalist neighbors, but it did accelerate economic development in the region. Travelers who visited Farghana during the first half of the nineteenth century spoke of dense settlements and of the industriousness of their inhabitants. In addition to widespread cultivation of fruit, vegetables, and grain, cotton and silk were produced, with some being exported. Neighboring nomadic people were the primary trading partners, and small-scale industry played a significant role.

Urban life in Farghana was more developed than in other Central Asian regions. In Khokand, the economic and political center, there were 8,000 houses, 360 mosques and 12 madrasahs.[8] A. F. von Middendorf, a Russian researcher who traveled in the Farghana valley in the 1870s, emphasized the extraordinary fruitfulness of the land and the diligence of its inhabitants. He admired the high quality of agriculture, the intensive methods of soil utilization and the simple yet effective irrigation works.[9] Farghana had achieved an economic significance of which the Russians, despite their recent conquest of Central Asia, were scarcely aware.

The khanate of Khokand, like the khanate of Khiva and the amirate of Bukhara, was structured on Islamic principles.[10] It arose during the eighteenth and nineteenth centuries in the Farghana region and its surrounding areas. By the early nineteenth century it had reached its fullest extent of territory and of political power, embracing the vast region between the Pamirs in the south to the Ili River in the northwest. Russia and China, as well as the neighboring Central Asian khanates, had to take this important state into account in their affairs. The khans of Khokand subjugated Tashkent, the largest city of Central Asia.

Such early prominence notwithstanding, wars with the amirate of Bukhara and intense internal discord set back the khanate's subsequent economic and political development considerably. Eventually it came to a fatal conflict with Russia, arising from both sides' competing claims to sovereignty over the Kazakh and Kirghiz plains. The armies of Khokand put up strong resistance, but they lacked the Russian troops' discipline and weaponry. By the mid-1860s, the khanate of Khokand had been subjugated; in 1868, a peace treaty was concluded by General K. P. von Kaufman, who was in charge of the administration of the Governor-generalship of Turkistan that had been created the previous year.

The khan was compelled to surrender many occupied cities and regions and to grant the Russians the right of free trade. Initially, he retained the Farghana valley, the core of the khanate, but in 1875 the khanate was completely brought down by disturbances that led to anti-Russian resistance. The Russian troops brought bitter defeat upon the resisters and occupied the cities. In 1876 the Farghana region was incorporated into the Governor-generalship of Turkistan, thus coming directly under Russian rule.

This development initiated a new period in the history of the Farghana valley; one that was characterized by far-reaching administrative and economic changes.[11] As was the case in the four other regions of the governor-generalship, a military regime was established, in which local inhabitants only occupied lower-level positions. The right to elect the heads of the district, *aul*, and *qishlaq* (village) meant substantial weakening of the aristocracy, and the Muslim clergy lost a large part of its former power because of cutbacks in its land holdings.

Russian agricultural policy further limited the amount of property held by the aristocracy, favoring ownership of land by farmers. A decree in 1886 that detailed the future development of agricultural relations specified that the lands cultivated by farmers were to become hereditary property, declared the lands hitherto used by nomadic people to be the property of the state. At the same time, the old land tax was replaced by a state tax on all real property that amounted to about one-tenth of its average gross yield.

A series of subsequent measures undertaken by the state—particularly the construction of a railroad beginning in 1880—laid the groundwork for more rapid economic development throughout Turkistan. Conditions for such development were also improved by cessation of frequent wars and disputes in the region, as a result of the introduction of the centralized Russian administration.

Turkistan, and the Farghana valley especially, took on great importance as a source of cotton for the Russian textile industry.[12] Prior to the initiation of extensive cotton cultivation, the primary crop had been cereals, primarily wheat. Cotton had already been cultivated in the region for centuries, but the local variety, which had a short fiber and was relatively easy to grow, had not been very profitable. In consequence, General von Kaufman ordered that long-fiber American varieties be put under cultivation as soon as possible. The conditions needed to grow these varieties—rich soil with plenty of moisture for the roots, as well as a great deal of sunlight for the leaves—were more than adequately supplied for the Central Asian agricultural oases, with their well-watered loess soils and abundance of sunlight.

In addition to textile material produced by the new long-fiber cotton types, oil could be pressed from the seed, and the stalks and seed capsules could be used as fuel. These American cotton types, which were used exclusively for export production, were quickly adapted to

Turkistan. Beginning in the 1880s, exports increased dramatically, so that Turkistan took on a strong role in the Russian economy and in the international market as well. By the end of the 1890s, there was talk within the Russian administration of independence from imports of American cotton, which had been indispensable until that time. Czar Nicholas II commented in 1894 that: "It is very desirable that this goal be accomplished."

The expansion of cotton cultivation led to a complete transformation of the local economy. No one could afford to ignore cotton, since it brought greater profits than grain. Great numbers of farmers who had been growing grain for their own use now turned to cotton, thus enmeshing themselves in the market economy, in pursuit of greater profits. Farmers with small holdings were initially able to resist efforts to organize the system of cotton cultivation into large plantations. It was these independent farmers who were best able to cater to the requirements of the cotton plant for exactingly careful cultivation.

There was also considerable resistance, however, manifested in different forms, to the abrupt shift in economic patterns. Stories circulated in the Farghana region about how "the white cotton-wool" would bring "black disaster." Many believed that Allah would only permit a family to cultivate the amount of cotton necessary in a year to make three *khäläts* (a local type of robe). The Muslim clergy was particularly insistent in its opposition to mandatory cotton cultivation, believing that it could only lead to trouble.

In the end, however, economic motivations proved stronger than these kinds of fears. It became more and more difficult to stay away from the raging "cotton fever." Russian industrial and bank capital, aided by extensive loans and local intermediaries, succeeded in transforming the heart of Turkistan—the Farghana valley—into cotton land.[14] Various firms and offices usually made loans on the basis of future production. In this aspect of the development, the system of contracts between cotton companies and the local administration was particularly effective. Offices of Moscow merchants sprouted up like mushrooms in the Farghana region. The community of buyers and commissioned agents, who profited most from the new system, soon became a privileged social class.

The dramatic increase in capital flowing into the region with the expansion of cotton cultivation was accompanied by unforeseen consequences, however. Price increases began to cripple the smaller cotton industries, resulting in an economic crisis for the whole community. By the turn of the century, it was clear that the expansion of cotton production had not improved the standard of living for the population as a whole. Rather, it had allowed certain social groups to prosper, particularly the *bays* (well-to-do men), who acted as agents and middlemen.

Official records also note the result of the widespread practice of taking loans: the widespread indebtedness.[15] This indebtedness followed from the conditions of cotton cultivation, an extremely labor-intensive form of agriculture. Because of the low level of agricultural technology in that society, cotton cultivation demanded all of the farming family's time and energy. This was not the only requirement, however: working capital was also required to hire the outside labor that was needed during certain critical stages of the crop's production.

Financial resources were also needed for the purchase of seed and, above all, to feed the family, who no longer grew enough grain for their own needs. To meet these financial demands, it was necessary to rely on loans, which the farmers sometimes obtained from Moscow firms and banks, but more often from wealthy Sarts and from the bays, who often extorted usurious rates of interest. The farmers, thus forced deeper and deeper into debt and chronically unable to make payments, had to take on larger loans with even steeper interest rates.

Even during good years, when abundant harvests brought in relatively high profits, the farmer had to advance a large sum early in the season toward the next cotton harvest. In poor years, the farmer was reduced to the state of an impoverished debtor. Whenever there were successive crop failures, the farmer had to relinquish all his property rights, and remained on the farm only as a laborer or tenant of the bays. The administration was well aware of the plight of the cotton farmers, but did little to change the system of credit, which could have helped to check the exploitation of the farmers.

The consequences of this exploitation and neglect were the massive collapse of the smaller cotton farms, which constituted nearly a third of all the farms in the Farghana region, and thus the emergence of a landless—and often unemployed—rural proletariat.[16] In the worst cases, the impoverished farmers would seek irregular and temporary work. At the same time, however, the size of the rural proletariat was increasing, because of the decline of local workshops and cottage industries, which had been unable to compete with Russian manufactured goods. Large numbers of artisans lost their livelihoods and were thrown onto the job market.

In view of this agricultural crisis in Turkistan, which threatened to destroy the most important source of cotton in the empire, the administration finally organized a series of investigations and audits.[17] It was believed that conditions for production could be improved by means of new technology and less costly small loans, and that extensive irrigation works would help create a second Turkistan that would produce even more cotton: cotton sufficient to meet the needs of the Russian textile industry. "All imported cotton must be replaced by Russian domestic production; the goal set by the Czar must be achieved," stated an official memorandum from 1912.[18]

The anticipated improvements failed to materialize, however. Cotton cultivation continued to spread, replacing cereal crops, but there was no increase in the area of lands under irrigation. Because there was no concomitant advance in agricultural technology, cotton cultivation also proceeded at the expense of the health of the soil, leaching out nutrients and causing soil exhaustion. In addition, the state organization for small loans that had been established to help the farmers failed to go beyond preliminary measures toward that goal, so that there was no curb on indebtedness and destitution. In the end, the Farghana valley became a cotton plantation run by Russian capitalists. Before the advent of the war, there were large areas where cotton cultivation had led to a one-crop economy, meaning that the Farghana valley, more than any other region, was dependent on grain imports and, consequently, on a functioning transportation system.

Russian domination brought about substantial changes in nonagricultural sectors of the economy as well. The expansion of cotton cultivation had led to the establishment of a large number of small factories for the initial processing of raw cotton.[19] Most of their operations were seasonal: between September and February, the factories operated at full capacity, but they employed only a small body of workers at other times. In contrast to other types of industry, these factories applied mechanized processes. By the early twentieth century, the cotton-cleaning industry employed the largest number of workers of any in the region. In the Farghana region at that time there were about one hundred cleaning mills, a number that increased over the years.

No textile mills were established in the region: the cleaning mills sent their cotton to factories in the large Russian cities. Nevertheless, the Farghana region was far ahead of the rest of Turkistan in terms of industrial development. The average sector of the population employed in industry elsewhere in Turkistan was 35 percent, but in the Farghana valley it reached 57 percent.[20] Besides the cleaning mills, industries in the region processing cotton products included a large number of oil mills and soap factories, as well as several other types. In 1911, there were said to be 3,892 small factories, employing a total of 29,563 workers, and

250 larger concerns, with a total of 18,309 employees; there were also 14 businesses associated with coal-mining and 8 with petroleum; the employees of these two industries totalled 1,392.[21] In addition, there were numerous businesses concerned with trade, most of them quite small. The economic structure of the Farghana valley was completely transformed within a very short time, and rapid industrial development was a crucial component of this change.

With the growth of industry, a local labor force emerged, comprising large numbers of women and children.[22] Most of these workers were unskilled laborers who found seasonal employment in cotton cleaning mills, oil mills, and similar industries. Their wages were far below the average in European Russia, meaning that employers' profits were potentially very high. Positions requiring skilled labor were generally filled by Russian workers; their jobs were most often permanent ones, and they earned more than the local workers. Considerably more Russians than local workers worked in the mines, which also provided year-round employment. The railroad employed Russians almost exclusively, drawing on the local labor force only when Russian workers were in short supply. These differences in employment patterns between Russian and local workers led to the development of two separate classes of workers, which would later have far-reaching political consequences.

The economic and social transformation of the Farghana region brought with it a great influx of wealth, but also great increase of poverty, and it effected profound changes in religious and moral values, as well as in traditional social life. Whereas von Middendorf could still praise the peaceful and secure life of the Farghana valley in the early 1870s, only a few decades later, all sorts of vices and crimes became widespread, particularly among the local youth. Theft became much more common, and there were numerous raids on management premises.[23] The number of crimes, which were committed primarily by local residents, increased even more rapidly after the Revolution of 1905, to a level far above the average for the Russian empire as a whole.

Increased consumption of alcohol, with associated problems, had also become more prevalent since the beginning of Russian domination in the region, and it grew along with crime. "The Sart has quickly adopted the habit of drinking beer (the Qur'ân is no hindrance), and now takes it in the same quantities that he once did tea; that is, in great and endless amounts," reported Otto Hoetzsch, who spent time studying in Turkistan in 1912.[24] Many taverns sprang up, both in cities and in rural areas, and vodka was even served in the old tea houses. Gambling and other types of intemperate activities became especially popular. The Muslim

clergy and the older generation, who continued to uphold orthodox beliefs, sought in vain to counteract the decline of religious values. The
reign of cotton had completely upset the balance of life in the Farghana
region.

World War I provoked an intensification of the crisis in the cotton
economy, thus accelerating the degeneration of the old way of life that
had been grounded in Islamic values.[25] At first, it seemed as though the
increased demand for cotton that accompanied the war might improve
the material conditions of life and ameliorate the destitution of the prewar years. But although prices for cereals and industrial goods rose, cotton prices were fixed at low rates, and poverty spread. Reports from the
Farghana region indicate that the situation in the cotton centers grew
worse from day to day.[26]

Further burdens came from demands for requisitions, as well as from
the wartime taxes and levies that fell most heavily on the local population. When the authorities finally called for the mobilization of the
local male population for duty behind the front lines, in 1916, there were
abuses in the recruitment process. In response, a mass uprising took
place throughout Central Asia, including most of the Farghana region.
The unrest lasted from 8 to 18 July 1916 and was countered by extensive
and severe punitive measures, which served to deepen the rift between
Central Asians and Russians.

The October Revolution of 1917 found the Farghana region, like the
rest of Turkistan, in a state of economic, social, and political crisis.
Russian colonial domination, which had lasted some 50 years, had left
a legacy of mass poverty, which had its source in—and further aggravated—the collapse of cotton production. The incidence of theft was
growing in 1917, and crime was becoming more organized, with the
formation of robber bands that looted throughout the Farghana valley.
When political motivations compounded these social conditions with
the fate of Khokand Autonomy, the Basmachi movement was born.[27]

Khokand Autonomy

Since the end of the nineteenth century, there had been efforts to bring
the medieval form of Islam prevalent in Turkistan into harmony with
movements toward modernization. Jadidism sought to meet these goals
by means of innovations in education, and it gained strength in Central
Asia in the early twentieth century.[28] The first "New Method" schools
were established in the cotton and commercial centers in the Farghana
valley, which had long been a cradle of critical literary activities as well.

Religious and cultural reform movements became even more politicized under the influences of the Revolution of 1905 and the ideas of the Young Turk organizations of the Ottoman Empire, and they were attacked equally by the traditional Muslim clergy and by the Russian colonial authorities. During World War I, the reform movements were forced into illegitimate status, but they regained strength with the support of the czarist autocracy. Working in close cooperation with political activists in other Muslim regions of Russia, a national movement took shape in Turkistan. Its goals were cultural and religious autonomy and a high degree of political independence.[29]

The most important supporters of this movement were the Shura-i Islam (Islamic Council) and the Shura-i 'Ulema (Council of Religious Scholars). The Shura-i Islam had been set up in Tashkent in March 1917 and branched out so quickly to other cities that the first conference of Central Asian Muslims was held in April of that year. This conference, which also elected a Regional Council of Turkistanian Muslims, consolidated the progressive and enlightened forces of Turkistan who sought to reform traditional Islamic structures but also wanted close ties with the new democratic Russia. This relationship was sought in the belief that the new federative policies of the former czardom would guarantee national self-determination.

The conservative clergy took issue with these objectives, however, as they did with every form of social change, bound as they were to the idea of the "Golden Age of Islam." Their inclination was to work in line with reactionary forces in the Russian colonial administration. In June 1917 the conservatives left the Shura-i Islam to form their own group, the Shura-i 'Ulema, and proceeded to set up other organizations throughout Central Asia to provide education.

Among the other organizations that appeared in 1917 were smaller Muslim groups that made demands for nationhood according to Islamic principles. One of them was the Association of Working Muslims, in Farghana, which proposed that a federative democratic republic be established to secure freedom of national development, the use of indigenous languages and democratic rights. During its first congress in Khokand, this association passed a resolution calling for national self-determination for Turkistan that would involve close ties with democratic Russia, a prospect backed by most of the press.[30] The prevailing view was that Turkistan—the land of the Turks—should become a federative republic based on Islamic principles. Toward this end, the Society of Turkistanian Federalists, in cooperation with the Society of Turkic Federalists, planned to unite all Muslim organizations in the struggle for a federative Turkic state that would be oriented toward a revitalized Ottoman empire. The idea of an autonomous Turkistan was the most important nationalist vision of the Muslim popular circles that were organized in 1917.

The second conference of Central Asian Muslims, which took place in September 1917, passed a series of concrete resolutions.[31] The regions of the former governor-generalship—most probably with the incorporation of Jeti Su (in Russian, Semirechie) and certain other Kazakh territories—should be joined in a Federative Republic of Turkistan, in which separate ethnic groups could organize themselves autonomously. This Turkistani federation would be governed by its own parliament, to be elected every five years in a secret ballot—on the basis of one vote per person—and in which all the ethnic groups in the region would be represented in proportion to the size of their populations. The foundations of its legislative functions would be drawn both from the principles of the Russian Republic's constitutional law and from the Islamic Shari'a. There would be a senate that would interpret parliamentary law and the Shari'a, in addition to supervising the executive branch of the government and the court authorities. The Shaykh-ul Islam would preside over the senate, making sure that all proceedings were in accordance with Islamic law. This point of the resolution marked the endorsement of continuing control by the conservative clergy over a democratically elected parliament.

The Muslim conference also considered the current political interests of Turkistan with regard to central Russia and the provisional government in Petrograd. At least 50 percent of the members of the Turkistan Committee (appointed by the provisional government), which had replaced the old colonial administration and represented the central governing body, were to be representatives from the local population, to whom the position of commissar, at various administrative levels, must also be open. The Regional Council of Turkistanian Muslims would be an advisory body for both the Turkistan Committee and for the parliament.

The First Special Muslim Regional Congress advocated the consolidation of all of the Muslim organizations of Turkistan into a single party, the League of Muslims, which would devote itself to the program set forth by the Congress and help to set up an autonomous Turkistan on an Islamic basis. Another topic under consideration at the Congress was that of Turkistan's economic interests. It resolved that fixed prices for cotton, as well as requisitions and monopolies, should be abolished: Turkistan should no longer serve as Russia's cotton plantation. The cultivation of American cotton varieties—which had already decreased considerably—should be further restricted, being replaced by the cereal crops that were so desperately needed by a population on the verge of starvation. Finally, the Congress declared itself against Russian interference in the local affairs of the Kazakhs of Jeti Su, advocating autonomous rule for this community.

Meanwhile, considerable changes were taking place among the Russian population, now a dwindling minority, which paved the way for new political developments.[32] The Petrograd provisional government, along with its Turkistan Committee, had only limited influence, and had to rely on the support of the Committees for Security, which had grown up in other cities. Workers and soldiers generally aligned themselves with the soviets, which were organized after the February Revolution.

The Tashkent Soviet drew most of its support from railroad workers, garrison soldiers, as well as a number of communications specialists who were returning from the battlefront and from central Russia. Most of the members of this soviet espoused leftist Socialist Revolutionary ideology, and it adopted notably radical lines of action. In September 1917, the Tashkent Soviet attempted to seize power. It removed the commander of the Turkistan military—who had charge of some fifteen thousand men—replacing him with a Socialist Revolutionary. In response, Aleksandr Kerensky, the provisional premier, sent an enforcement expedition, led by General P. A. Korovnichenko, to Tashkent. General Korovnichenko took over the position of Commander of the Turkistan military, as well as that of General Commissar of the Provisional Government, but he was able to wield power only for a brief period.

On 28 October 1917, under Bolshevik leadership, an armed uprising took place among railroad workers. They not only had weapons of all kinds, including machine guns, at their disposal, but could also get reinforcements from other areas. Somewhat later, the Third Congress of Soviets convened, claiming to represent the power of revolutionary democracy throughout Turkistan. This congress set up the Council of the People's Commissar: a regional government initially comprising eight Socialist Revolutionaries and seven Bolsheviks, under a Bolshevik chairman, F. I. Kolesov.

Other efforts were made, however, to establish a government with a broader political base.[33] The regional soviet, in particular, which was dominated by Mensheviks and Socialist Revolutionaries, proposed the organization of a Provisional Executive Committee of Turkistan and an advisory body, composed of representatives from all democratic organizations. Some Muslim organizations, notably the Shura-i 'Ulema, voiced similar opinions. But the Third Congress of Soviets rejected the idea of a government shared with any organizations that had cooperated with the Provisional Government, as it did the participation of the Muslims. It stated that the Muslims' relationship to the Russian inhabitants was unreliable, and that they did not have any organizations for the proletariat.

Consequently, the Council of the People's Commissar, which had wielded full power when Turkistan was a colony, was left with a political base that was restricted to the Russian sections of the city, the railroad stations, and the garrisons of the Turkistan military. When the new administration became embroiled in conflicts with the Cossacks, it could only turn to a few small groups of railroad workers and soldiers for support: the local population was indifferent to the disputes of Russians. In the cities, the way was being paved for the establishment of a government rooted in indigenous national tradition.

The attempt to form a democratic state, based on local political forces, took place in Khokand, the economic and political center of the Farghana region and the site of the Fourth (Extraordinary) Conference of Central Asian Muslims, from 26–29 November 1917.[34] Groups participating in this meeting included the Shura-i Islam, the Shura-i 'Ulema, and the Alash Party, which represented the Kazakh national movement. The conference declared Turkistan to be autonomous, invoking the principles of the Russian Revolution in its demands for self-determination, as well as for the unification of an autonomous Turkistan with a federative and democratic Russian Republic. A constituent assembly, to be convened as soon as possible, was to set forth in detail the form of autonomy to be adopted, with careful attention to the rights of all national minorities living in Turkistan.

The conference also organized a provisional government, with Muhammedjan Tanyshbaev as prime minister and Mustafa Chokaev as foreign minister. A provisional council, including representatives from the different regions, from the autonomous metropolitan administrations and from the Russian democratic organizations, was to govern, in conjunction with a people's administration, until the constituent assembly could be held.

A further goal, conceived particularly in the hope of obtaining grain, was that of joining together with the Southeastern League of the Cossack Army, the Mountain Peoples of the Caucasus, and the Free Steppe Peoples, which had been formed in the Northern Caucasus in the fall of 1917. Cooperation was also sought with the Alash party which, about a month after the Congress took place, organized the Alash Orda as an autonomous Kazakh government in Orenburg.[35] Through cooperation with such groups, it was hoped that the common ties of Islam and ethnic kinship might finally end the old conflicts between nomadic pastoralists and settled agriculturalists, allowing consolidated resistance to Russian domination. Turkistan's autonomy was to be proclaimed in Tashkent on 13 December 1917.

Initially, the Tashkent administration hailed the Khokand Autonomy as "an achievement of the revolution," but it immediately imposed several significant limitations. First, as long as the revolution—and, with it, the autonomy of Turkistan—was endangered, Tashkent itself would govern the region. Second, the congress's declarations would be supported, but they must apply only to the old section of Tashkent.[36] On 13 December, the entire male population of Muslim Tashkent, as well as some Russian anti-Bolshevik groups, took part in a demonstration. Violence ensued in conflicts with Russian soldiers and members of the Red Guard, and a number of demonstrators were killed.[37] After this incident conflicts intensified between the Khokand Autonomy and the Tashkent administration.

The Khokand Autonomy found itself in a very difficult position. Its support came from both Muslim and European—in some cases Russian—organizations. But it had no armed forces with which to oppose the Tashkent administration, which could turn for support to the Russian military and Red Guard, as well as to the armed members of the Armenian anti-Turkish Dashnak Party. The Muslim population, in contrast, had neither soldiers nor qualified officers. The only hope for a military force lay with the armed robber bands, who were perpetrating their misdeeds in Farghana under the leadership of Irgash, a former convict. It was under these precarious political circumstances that the Khokand administration proclaimed an amnesty and invited the brigands to join a Muslim military unit. The robber bands accepted the offer, and the administration—which had undergone a change of leadership in the meantime—designated Irgash as *qorbashi:* military commander.

At the same time, in Russian Khokand armed divisions were being marshaled and prepared to fight. Tensions in the city grew noticeably; the incidence of assaults and vandalism increased; conditions approached a state of civil war. There was a new regional soviet, made up of workers, soldiers and deputations of farmers, that sought to take over the power of the Khokand Autonomy, but it failed to produce any moderating influence. There were outbreaks of violence, followed by negotiations; finally, after the arrival of reinforcements from Tashkent and Samarkand, there was a full-scale assault on Muslim Khokand.

According to testimonies of numerous eyewitnesses, as well as the reports of the Soviet press, the victory of the Russian and Armenian units was accompanied by a horrible pogrom, in which Armenians were especially active.[38] Slaughter was heaped on slaughter; the old city was completely plundered and then went up in flames. "All of the shops were destroyed; whatever could be taken away was stored; the rest was burned"—such was the description given by an early Soviet account.[39]

The Khokand pogrom marked the beginning of a policy of terrorism against the Muslim population of Turkistan. Its scope increased over time, being carried out mainly by the armed forces. Kolesov's campaign of March 1918 against Bukhara, where many of the representatives of the Khokand Autonomy had fled, was part of this phase of the region's history.[40] The Tashkent authorities had made several demands on the amir of Bukhara: his relinquishing of control over the Russian settlements there and reform of the system of administration, including the acceptance into it of members of the Young Bukharan movement.

While negotiations over these demands were in process, new armed conflicts broke out. The amir called for battle against the unbelievers; Russian inhabitants were hunted down; enraged crowds destroyed a large section of the railway, and soon a sizeable Muslim army was ready to fight. After Kolesov had received reinforcements from Tashkent, bitter battles were fought, carried out with utmost savagery on both sides.

Although this military campaign had originally sought political goals, it, too, quickly turned into a raid for plunder and booty, accompanied by terrorization and slayings. "Beautiful carpets and entire silk warehouses were our bounty. We repaid them for the atrocities they committed by carrying off whatever we could," reported R. Köstenberger, who took part in the campaign as an Austrian prisoner of war.[41] The news of these events in Bukhara, the religious center of Central Asia, must have further agitated the Muslim population, especially since their economic circumstances had worsened considerably under the new administration.

The Muslim Uprising

The Russian Revolution, particularly the overthrow of October 1917, had further increased the misery of the Muslim population. Not only were they shut off from access to political power; they also suffered from a critical shortage of supplies that was caused by the collapse of the transportation system and military conflicts, compounded by a severe drought in 1917.[42] The grain imports on which they depended were cut off. Whatever grain could be procured from neighboring regions during the harsh winter of 1917–18 was distributed exclusively to the Russian inhabitants. "The inhabitant of the *qishlaq* was a pariah: the only thing he could do was die," wrote Georgi Safarov, a leading Bolshevik functionary.[43] The winter of 1917–18 devastated much of the fodder crop of the nomadic pastoralists, so that there was no meat on the market.

Rather than trying to ameliorate these conditions, as the food crisis grew more and more severe, the Tashkent administration further drained available resources through frequent confiscations and requisitions that fell most heavily on local farmers. The small population of Russians tried to live at the Muslims' expense. Numerous Soviet reports and descriptions bear witness to the transition under the new administration in Turkistan: from the old colonialist policy to one of "overt armed robbery" that caused untold suffering in the region.[44]

The Cotton Decree of 28 February 1918, which was made in an attempt to satisfy the Russian textile industry, had a particularly disastrous effect on economic and political development. The Council of Peoples' Commissars sent out special authorized agents to bring all available cotton to the Tashkent railway station for confiscation. Any resistance was to be countered with severe retaliation, not excluding execution on the spot.[45] This decree opened the way for arbitrary use of force and completely destroyed Turkistan's cotton production.

The inhabitants of Farghana whose lives had depended on cotton production were now unable to find any employment whatsoever. The rapid spread of unemployment was furthered by the economic policy of which the decree had been a part. Some industrial committees were formed, according to Russian models, but they were mainly concerned with product distribution. Nationalization and state control, which affected the large number of small industries involved in crafts and trade, also accelerated the trend toward economic chaos. Even gardens were nationalized: "When the time for harvest came, the fruits rotted."[46] The collapse of the economy destroyed the means of subsistence for the entire population. Rich and poor were affected, although not to the same degree: the upper classes became less affluent, but tenant farmers, agricultural laborers and seasonal workers lost their entire base of existence. The destitute and unemployed masses, threatened by starvation, formed the social force for a popular movement, whose political goals were to take shape in the struggle against brutal foreign domination.

The forcible destruction of the Khokand Autonomy, as well as similar incidents, played a decisive role in these developments.[47] Those who had fled from Khokand brought reports of their experiences to the new areas they settled. The Basmachis, who had been driven from the city, did not consider themselves to be defeated: they called for holy war against the unbelievers and tried to wage their struggles in other regions. Irgash, the commander of the Muslim troops, had fled to a *qishlaq* near Khokand and turned it into a fortress. He saw himself as a "warrior for Islam" and "defender of the righteous"; adopting the title of "Supreme Leader of the Islamic Army," he proclaimed holy war against the Russian administration. He was recognized by the Muslim clergy, and his division, into which local people crowded enthusiastically, soon became a considerable military force.

A powerful movement was thus resurrected from the ashes of the Khokand Autonomy. The War between Russians and Muslims, as it was commonly called, took on increasingly greater dimensions. The Basmachis always operated in small guerrilla bands, relying on popular support; their frequent raids on Russian and Armenian garrisons provoked grim retaliatory measures.[48] In one case, the Basmachis' successful attack on Andijan provoked the Armenian garrison there to exact revenge from the entire Muslim quarter of the city. After a week of punitive measures, a large number of the residents joined the Basmachi movement.

The Basmachis' numbers were further increased by Muslims from Tashkent, where the administration issued more and more frequent accusations that the Muslim inhabitants of Farghana had been sympathizing with the Basmachis. When enforcement divisions were sent out, they destroyed entire villages and persecuted the residents, causing them to take recourse with the Basmachis. In addition, Tashkent's administration found that it could play on the Russian residents' fear of the Basmachis to gain support. A report on actions of vengeance taken by Russian farmers against a Muslim settlement reads, "At first they simply robbed; then they began their slayings, killing everyone indiscriminately. They fell on the men, believing that they supported the Basmachis; they fell on children, believing that they would become Basmachis in a few years."[49] Soviet military authorities were evidently not displeased by such atrocities, and soon began to consider the Russian settlers as allies and to supply them with weapons.

In addition to Irgash's bands, there were countless other Basmachi contingents in Farghana. One important figure was Madamin Bay, the former head of the Muslim militia of Margelan.[50] Having once been involved in fighting against the incipient Basmachi movement, he changed his views and left his job in protest against Soviet policies of violence and theft. Finding himself persecuted, he and several assistants formed a Muslim military contingent to take action against the offences perpetrated by the Soviet regime. The entire population backed him, and within a few months his small contingent had grown into a proper army of about one thousand men, controlling a broad area of Farghana.

Initially Madamin Bay and Irgash cooperated, but, after a series of clashes that had led to armed conflicts, Madamin Bay set up independent operations. His considerable organizational skills enabled him to unite the guerrilla groups, who had long worked independently; he instituted rigid discipline and set up his own centralized administration, intent on reinstating order in the Farghana valley. Toward that end, he curtailed much of the theft and violence in the region, by which he gained the trust of the local population. Eventually he also created an alliance with the leaders of an army of farmers that had originally been formed to protect Russian settlements.

The Tashkent administration, which was backed by Armenian fighting forces, was in no position to defend the Russian settlements alone, particularly since the outbreak of the Russian Civil War in 1918. Consequently, they made concessions to long-standing demands of the settlers in exchange for their agreement to form a military contingent headed by a staff of their choosing. In the summer of 1918, the soviet of the heavily populated valley of Jalalabad resolved to raise an army comprising farmers and other local people, on the basis of the territorial principle.[51] Individual settlements were also prepared to provide militia.

At the end of 1918, Soviet authorities granted legitimacy to this army —a status that also authorized financial credit and weapons—specifying that its objective should be to work together with other armed forces against the Basmachis. Technically, the new coalition army was responsible to the commanders on the Farghana front, but in actuality it operated independently. A commanding officer was appointed and, at the head of this popular army, there was an appointed war council, of which the war commissar of Jalalabad was a mandatory member. In late 1918 and early 1919, this military collaboration led to concerted maneuvers against Madamin Bay and other Basmachi leaders, often involving attacks on local settlements.

In the course of the year 1919, the Tashkent administration came to be more and more exclusively controlled by the Bolsheviks. As its policies, in consequence, became those of War Communism, oriented toward central Russia, conflicts began to break out in the Russian-sponsored military coalition. Soviet authorities tried in vain to disarm the farmers' army: its leadership soon became aligned with that of Madamin Bay. K. I. Monstrov, who took over the command of the coalition army in May 1919, made an agreement with Madamin Bay in the summer of that year. Madamin Bay pledged not to attack any more Russian settlements; Monstrov, for his part, promised not to initiate any military action against Muslim troops.

The introduction of mandatory delivery of grain further intensified conflict with Soviet authorities. The war council of the farmers' army took issue with the Boksheviks' dictates and set its own political and economic agenda. The council demanded the reorganization of the regional soviet so that half of the deputy seats would be filled by Muslims; it also demanded basic political, economic, and cultural rights, as well as the abolition of the numerous forms of systematic repression and of the grain monopoly. "If necessary, we will defend the rights and demands of the free farmers with arms," stated the war council's resolution of August 1919.[52] At the same time, it was proposed that Madamin Bay's Muslim troops become part of the coalition army. On 1 September 1919, after Madamin Bay had accepted this proposal, an official agreement was concluded that made provisions for collective action against the Tashkent administration's military forces.

The united Russian and Muslim troops constituted a formidable power, with Jalalabad, which they were able to take over quickly, as their most important base. After Jalalabad, they conquered Osh and besieged Andijan. At Andijan, however, they were beaten by the Red military units and were forced to surrender their previous conquests, which precipitated the disbanding of the farmers' army. Political activities were subsequently pursued with particular vigor, including those that had as their objective the formation of a separate state. With the mediation of the former Russian consul in Kashgar, a provisional government, headed by Madamin Bay and his deputy Monstrov, was established for Farghana.[53]

This government enacted a number of administrative reforms, yet it was not acknowledged by all of the *qorbashi*s: there were repeated demands that a Russian be its chief. An Afghan delegation tried to persuade the fragmented forces to join together around the principles of Islam, but met with no lasting success. Since achieving independence, Afghanistan had represented itself as a model Islamic state, so that the possibility of a religious orientation was very much on people's minds, but the leaders of the farmers' army found no reason to adopt that orientation. Consequently, the alliance between the Russian farmers and the Muslims of Turkistan soon fell apart.

In the meantime, the political and military situation in Turkistan had changed a great deal. Early in 1918, it had been designated as the "Autonomous Turkistan Socialist Republic." In the fall of 1919, relationships with central Russia were resumed, so that the central authorities could provide direct military assistance and support for the region's development. The central Bolshevik administration dispatched a special commission for Turkistanian affairs—the so-called Turk Commission—which succeeded in bringing the excessive power wielded by local agencies under control, and in creating a centralized system of administration, in which the local population was generally included.[54]

At this time, the Basmachi troops, well equipped and relatively well disciplined, were facing the Red Army. Conflicts within the Basmachi movement were intensifying, however: during the first months of 1920, several units had defected to the Soviet side, followed shortly thereafter by Monstrov and several of his cohorts. Madamin Bay, however, led his numerous bands in fighting until February 1920. But, after suffering military defeat, he entered into negotiations in which he was pressed to relinquish his units and recognize the Soviet administration. On 6 March 1919, after the Revolutionary War Council of the Farghana front had guaranteed Madamin Bay that his troops would be accepted into the Red Army as armed units, a peace treaty, based on the Shariʿa, was concluded.[55] In celebration, Muslim and Russian troops paraded together, and Madamin Bay was hailed by the crowds.

Not all the *qorbashi*s joined him, of course: one leader named Kurshirmat, especially, being a particularly ardent opponent of the Soviet administration, continued to try to muster Basmachi units and keep up the fight. By the middle of March 1920, however, most of the Basmachis had gone over to the Soviet side. They received weapons and were incorporated into the Red Army, so that there were now Soviet Basmachis and *qorbashi*s. It appeared that the bloody battles that had devastated the Farghana valley and brought so much suffering upon its people were coming to an end.

Matters were not destined to be so simple, however. During the summer of 1920, Soviet policy sought to replicate the entire central system of War Communism in Turkistan.[56] Actions taken toward this goal once again drove large numbers of Muslims to rebellion and to renewed collaboration with the Basmachis. As this Muslim movement rapidly gained momentum, people from all sectors of the society became involved. They prepared themselves to resist the forcible destruction of their traditional ways of life and their Islamic values.

All of these dimensions of the Muslims' lives were now imperiled by Soviet initiatives such as the abolition of the *madrasah*s (religious seminaries) and religious courts, the appropriation of *waqf* lands and other attempts to eliminate Muslim customs and traditions. A further form of intervention that provoked the population's resistance was the closing of the bazaars, which were not only centers of private enterprise, but centers of social life as well.

The final blow came when the Soviet administration called for Muslim men to enter the Red Army: a large number of them—who remembered all too well the abuses that had taken place during the mobilization of 1916—took their weapons and joined the Basmachis, under Kurshirmat. Kurshirmat proclaimed himself "Commander of the Warriors for Islam"; Islamic battle-cries were used, and the resistance movement saw as its goal the defense of the foundations of Islamic society. The movement now became one of extraordinarily great proportions, gaining importance well beyond Farghana's boundaries. As a military force, the Muslims were apparently invincible.

The course of events began to shift significantly when, in 1921, the Soviet administration put an end to its destructive policies, adopting instead the so-called New Economic Policy and concluded a series of compromises.[57] Businesses involved in trade and crafts, banks, and small industries all rushed to capitalize on the new opportunities that opened up with the reauthorization of the market economy. The clergy, too, became more satisfied with the situation, since the madrasahs and religious courts were allowed to operate once again; the *waqf* lands had been restored, and the authorities had ceased their continual assaults on the Islamic way of life. A number of influential people native to the Farghana valley were prepared to cooperate with the administration, and even the farmers, who had suffered the most in the violent conflicts, showed willingness to return peaceably to work.

Consequently, the Basmachis, who did not want to give up the struggle, found themselves more and more isolated. After most of the Islamic institutions were restored to their former functions and old customs were more or less back in place, the religious slogans that had roused the faithful to fight lost their mobilizing effect. As the Basmachis continued to demand contributions and levies for the maintenance of their Muslim troops, therefore, they began to encounter the population's refusal. There were conflicts with cotton farmers who were trying to reclaim their former livelihood.

Finally, in the autumn of 1921, Soviet authorities were able to use peace treaties to split the Basmachi movement.[58] Basmachi leaders were unable to forestall the further disintegration of the movement, which was not only facing stronger military forces but was also under attack by a newly formed Muslim militia. The Basmachis, lacking the support of the general Muslim population, found it increasingly difficult to subsist in the *qishlaq*s and lost their military superiority. Many of their number capitulated, while others returned to their former careers as brigands.

Despite the Basmachis' decline, when the farmers found themselves once again under economic and political pressure from administrative authorities later in the 1920s, there were occasional insurrections and even some clashes with the Red Army.[59] The renewed attempt to transform the region as rapidly and completely as possible into a "cotton bowl" for the Russian textile industry thus met with vigorous resistance from the local population, who remembered all too well the sufferings caused by such efforts in the past. It was only with forced collectivization that the Soviet administration was able to achieve the economy it sought for the Farghana region.

Although the resistance movements of the former amirate and khanate of Bukhara and Khiva had different social origins from those in Farghana, they were similar in invoking Islamic values, and they met with a similar fate. The Basmachi movement in Bukhara dissolved after the downfall of the amir, who subsequently fled to Afghanistan.[60] Its supporters, who came mainly from the mountain clans of eastern Bukhara, initially fought for their independence, but now they allied themselves with the toppled amir, receiving material support from him in compensation.

The Basmachi movement gained further impetus and became a threat to Soviet leadership with the arrival in Bukhara of Enver Pasha in November 1921. The most prominent member of the Young Turk movement, Enver Pasha was the former Minister of War of the Ottoman Empire and son-in-law of the Ottoman sultan. Calling himself "commander-in-chief of all warriors for Islam and representative of the amir of Bukhara," he set out to unite the scattered resistance fighters under his command and to give the whole movement a political agenda. Enver Pasha, who was also supported by Afghanistan, aspired toward the establishment of a Central Asian caliphate: an Islamic empire that would include Afghanistan, Bukhara, and Turkistan. He contracted an alliance with the most important leaders of the Basmachi movement, who were all the more willing to cooperate now that their decline in power and popularity in Farghana had become evident.

To some extent, Enver Pasha's defeat by the Red Army was inevitable when he decided to wage a conventional battle against them with his guerrilla bands in the summer of 1922.[61] After his death, on 4 August 1922, the Basmachi movement in Bukhara quickly became weakened and fragmented. During subsequent years, it was only in their strongholds in the impenetrable mountain regions of eastern Bukhara—the heart of Tajikistan—that the Basmachis were successful in resisting Soviet attempts to eradicate them. As collectivization swept the region, finally destroying the traditional Islamic ways of life, there were outbreaks of violence in many areas.

The Basmachi movement in the distant Khwarazmian basin—the former khanate of Khiva—had a very different character. In this region there lived numerous Turkmen clans who had suffered economic disadvantage and political oppression under Uzbek rule. Joining together under the leadership of Muhammad Qurban Junaid Khan, they carried out a successful attack on the Uzbek khan in 1918. The new khan acted as their willing agent and helped the Turkmens to establish their own despotic rule, bringing particularly harsh oppression to bear on the region's Uzbek majority. In 1920 the new ruler of the Turkmen-Uzbek coalition was overthrown by the Red Army's efforts. He shifted his base of operations to the Karakum desert, from whence he attempted to regain power.

The new administration of Khwarazm enacted broad social reforms that took no consideration of Islamic tradition. These actions brought Junaid Khan renewed support from all social and ethnic sectors of the former khanate. With his war-seasoned Turkmen fighters, he conquered numerous settlements and, in the beginning of 1924, besieged Khiva, the capital.[62] Forced back by superior Soviet forces, he withdrew to the Karakum desert, where he and his fighters continued their resistance for many years. He was finally exiled in 1928. Mass resistance flared up again in Turkmenistan during the years of collectivation, but there was no longer any possibility of serious challenge to Soviet rule.

Notes

1. The term *Basmachi* derives from the Turkic verb *basmaq:* "to attack." In Turkistan, the name *Basmachi* was originally applied to robbers who attacked caravans and settlements. After 1917, however, the name took on a whole new significance: it designated the members of the movement for national and religious independence that was directed against Soviet domination, as well as being synonymous with *mujaheddin:* "warrior for the faith." The term *Basmachi* with this sense appeared in the literature of the period, particularly in the works of Castagné and Chokaev (see below). Soviet literature, in contrast, retains the pejorative sense of the term.

2. In this article the term *Turkistan* (from the Persian for "land of the Turks") will be used to designate the Central Asian territories that were completely subjected to Russian domination; that is, Russian, or Western, Turkistan. Between 1918 and 1924, this region was called the "Turkistanian Autonomous Soviet Socialist Republic." A more comprehensive sense of the term *Turkistan* also includes the amirate of Bukhara

and the khanate of Khiva. In addition, there was also a Chinese, or Eastern, Turkistan, in the Xinjiang Province of China, as well as an Afghanistanian, or Southern, Turkistan located in northern Afghanistan. These regions were—and are—populated primarily by Turkic people.

Middle Asia is an imprecise term that came into use during the Russian expansion of the nineteenth century, primarily designating the territory between the Caspian Sea and the Chinese border that was dominated—directly or indirectly—by Russians, particularly the Governor-generalship of Turkistan as well as the amirate of Bukhara and the khanate of Khiva. In Soviet scholarship, especially, *Middle Asia*—traditionally defined in terms of history and geography—is distinguished from the concept of *Central Asia*, which cannot be clearly defined either on the basis of geography or cultural history. *Middle Asia* designates the Inner Asian regions of the Tarim Basin (in Eastern Turkistan), Dzungaria, Mongolia, and Tibet; that is, the territory from the Pamirs to the Great Khingan Range in Inner Mongolia; from Lake Baikal to the Himalayas. The terms *Inner Asia* and *Upper Asia* are occasionally used. The term *Central Asia* has recently come to refer to the entire historical and cultural region comprising eastern Iran, Afghanistan, Pakistan, Northern India, Nepal, western China, and Mongolia, as well as Soviet Kazakhstan and Middle Asia. See Gavin Hambly, ed., *Zentralasien*, Fischer Weltgeschichte 16 (Frankfurt am Main, 1966); V. N. Fedchina, *Kak sozdavalas' karta Srednii Azii* (Moscow, 1967); D. Sinor, *Inner Asia* (Bloomington, Ind., and The Hague, 1969); A. von Gabain, *Einführung in die Zentralasienkunde* (Darmstadt, 1979). On the historical and cultural unity of Turkistan see, especially, V. V. Bartol'd, "Sostoianie i zadachi izucheniia istorii Turkestana," *Sochineniia* 9 (Moscow, 1977); B. A. Litvinskii, ed., *Vostochnyi Turkestan i Sredniaia Aziia v sisteme kul'tury drevnego i srednevekovogo Vostoka* (Moscow, 1987).

3. Martha Olcott, "The Basmachi or Freemen Revolt in Turkestan, 1918–1924), *Soviet Studies* 33, no. 3 (1981); Glenda Fraser, "Basmachi I," *Central Asian Survey* (hereinafter *CAS*) 6, no. 1 (1987); G. Fraser, "Basmachi II," *CAS* 6, no. 2; H. A. de Lageard, "The Revolt of the Basmachi According to Red Army Journals (1920–1922), *CAS* 6, no. 2; M. Mobin Shorish, "Islam and nationalism in West Turkestan (Central Asia) on the Eve of the October Revolution," *Nationalities Papers* 1985; Marie Broxup, "The Basmachi," *CAS* (July 1983). For representative works in Soviet scholarship, see A. I. Zevelev et al., *Basmachestvo: vozniknovenie, sushchestvo, krakh* (Moscow, 1981). Among earlier studies, see especially J. Castagné, "Le Turkestan depuis la Revolution Russe," *Revue du Monde Musulman* 50 (1922): 28–73; Castagné, "Le Bolchevisme et l'Islam: les organisations soviétiques de la Russie musulmane," *Revue du Monde Musulman* 51 (1922); Castagné, *Les Basmachis* (Paris, 1925); Mustafa Chokaev, "The Basmaji Movement in Turkestan," *Asiatic Review* 24 (1928): 273–88; N. Paskutskii, *K istorii grazhdanskoi voiny v Turkestane* (Tashkent, 1922); N. Batmanov, "Basmachestvo i bor'ba s nim," *Krasnaia Armiia* 9 (1921); P. Alekseenkov, *Chto takoe basmachestvo?* (Tashkent, 1931); Faizulla Khodzhaev, *Basmachestvo* (Tashkent, 1927); T. Ryskulov, *Revoliutsiia i korennoe naselenie Turkestana* (Tashkent, 1922), pp. 87–120 (includes important contemporary documentation); A. Syrkin, *Vostok v ogne* (Leningrad, 1925); T. Dervish (N. Tiurakulov), "Sovremennoe basmachestvo, *Kommunist* 1 (1922); T. Dervish, "Ferganskaia problema," *Voennaia mysl'* 2 (1921); G. Skalov, "Sotsial'naia priroda basmachestva v Turkestane," *Zhizn'*

natsional'nostei 3–4 (1923); S. Ginzburg, "Basmachestvo v Fergane," *Ocherki revoliutsionnogo dvizheniia v Srednei Azii* (Moscow, 1926); D. D. Zuev, "Ferganskoe basmachestvo," in *Grazhdanskaia voina* (Moscow, 1924), vol. 3 (with useful documentation in appendix). The early Soviet studies are particularly informative.

4. The idea of "freedom fighters" receives particular emphasis in studies by Baymirza Hayit; for example, *Turkestan im XX. Jahrhundert* (Darmstadt, 1956), pp. 173–214; *Turkestan zwischen Russland und China* (Amsterdam, 1971), pp. 268–71.

5. Iu. A. Zadneprovskii, *Drevnezemledel'cheskaia kul'tura Fergany* (Moscow-Leningrad, 1962); A. F. Middendorf, *Ocherki Ferganskoi doliny* (Moscow, 1913), pp. 415–650.

6. On the distinctions between the terms "Tajik," "Sart" and "Uzbek," see the article by Bert Fragner in this volume, as well as V. Nalivkin, *Kratkaia istoriia* (n.p., n.d.), and P. P. Ivanov, *Ocherki po istorii Srednei Azii* (Moscow, 1958), pp. 178–212.

7. Ivanov, *Ocherki.*

8. *Istoriia Kokanda* (Tashkent, 1984), pp. 5–41.

9. Middendorf, *Ocherki.*

10. Nalivkin, *Kratkaia istoriia.*

11. V. I. Masal'skii, *Turkestanskii krai* (Moscow, 1913); A. P. Savitskii, *Pozemel'nyi vopros Turkestana* (Tashkent, 1963); L. Kostenko, *Sredniaia Aziia i vodvorenie v nei russkoi grazhdanstvennosti* (St. Petersburg, 1871); *Otchet revizuiushchego po vysochaishemu poveleniiu Turkestanskii krai tainogo sovetnika D. Girsa* (St. Petersburg, 1883); V. Voshchinin, *Ocherki novogo Turkestana* (St. Petersburg, 1914); R. A. Pierce, *Russian Central Asia 1867–1917: A Study in Colonial Rule* (Berkeley and Los Angeles, 1960).

12. S. A. Melik-Sarkisian, *Khlopkovoe delo v Ferganskoi oblasti i mery ego uporiadocheniia* (Moscow, 1904); S. Poniatovskii, *Opyt izucheniia khlopkovodstva v Turkestane i Zakaspiiskoi oblasti* (Moscow, 1913); V. Juferev, *Trud v khlopkovykh khoziaistvakh Turkestana* (Moscow, 1914); V. I. Juferev, *Khlopkovodstvo v Turkestane* (Leningrad, 1925).

13. *Denkschrift des Chefs der Hauptverwaltung für Landeinrichtung und Landwirtschaft über seine Reise nach Turkestan im Jahre 1912* (Berlin, 1913), p. 5; see also V. I. Masal'skii, *Amerikanskaia monopoliia russkogo khlopkovodstva* (Petrograd, 1914).

14. A. I. Shakhnazarov, *Sel'skoe khoziaistvo v Turkestanskom krae* (Moscow, 1908); P. G. Galuzo, *Turkestan—koloniia* (Moscow, 1929); V. Lavrent'ev, *Kapitalizm v Turkestane* (Moscow, 1930); A. K. Silanov, *K voprosu o roli rostovshchicheskogo kapitala v sel'skom khoziaistve Srednei Azii* (Tashkent, 1926).

15. *Denkschrift,* pp. 14–18; I. I. Geier, *Turkestan,* 2d edition (Tashkent, 1909); E. Zel'kina, *Ocherki po agrarnomu voprosu v Srednei Azii* (Moscow, 1930), pp. 24–66.

16. G. Safarov, *Kolonial'naia revoliutsiia: Opyt Turkestana* (Moscow, 1921), pp. 28–52; A. Ch. Valiev, *Polozhenie dekhkanstva Fergany v kontse XIX—nachale XX vv.* (Tashkent, 1958); R. Navlikin, "Tuzemnyi proletariat," *Russkii Turkestan* (10 August 1906).

17. K. K. Palen, *Materialy k kharakteristike narodnogo khoziaistva v Turkestane* 2 and 1/I (1910–11); Zel'kina, *Ocherki,* pp. 25–66.

18. *Denkschrift,* p. 5.

19. Galuzo, *Turkestan*, pp. 65–72; V. V. Zaorskaia and K. A. Aleksandr, *Promyshlennye zavedeniia Turkestanskogo kraia* (St. Petersburg, 1915); V. N. Oglobin, *Promyshlennost' i torgovlia Turkestana* (Moscow, 1914).

20. M. P. Viatkin, *Sotsial'no-ekonomicheskoe razvitie Srednei Azii* (Frunze, 1974), pp. 123–45.

21. Ibid.

22. R. Ismailova, "Aus der Geschichte der Arbeiterbewegung in Turkestan im Jahre 1905," in *Jahrbuch für Geschichte der UdSSR und der volksdemokratischen Länder Europas* (Berlin, 1959), 3:247–68.

23. Galuzo, *Turkestan*, pp. 133–160.

24. O. Hoetzsch, "Russisch-Turkestan und die Tendenzen der heutigen russischen Kolonialpolitik," *Schmollers Jahrbuch* 37 (1913): 403.

25. Zel'kina, *Ocherki*.

26. Galuzo, *Turkestan*.

27. The European studies of the Basmachi movement cited in note 3, above, have tended to overlook the collapse of the cotton economy as a primary cause of the crisis in Turkistan, yet this economic factor is of crucial significance in understanding the movement's dimensions.

28. M. G. Vakhabov, "O sotsial'noi prirode sredneaziatskogo dzhadidizma i ego evoliutsii v period Velikoi Oktiabr'skoi Revoliutsii," *Istoriia SSSR* 2 (1963); S. G. Batiev, "Tatarskii dzhadidizm i ego evoliutsiia," *Istoriia SSSR* 4 (1964).

29. Hayit, *Turkestan*, pp. 206–25; P. Alekseenkov, "Natsional'naia politika Vremennogo pravitel'stva v Turkestane v 1917 g.," *Proletarskaia Revoliutsiia*, no. 8 (79) (1928): 104–32; *Revoliutsiia i natsional'nyi vopros* (Moscow, 1930), 3:283–327, 345–68.

30. *Istoriia Kokanda*, pp. 45ff.

31. *Turkestanskii Kur'er*, 8 October, 11 November 1917.

32. Safarov, *Kolonial'naia revoliutsiia*; L. Reztsov, *Oktiabr' v Turkestane* (Tashkent, 1927), pp. 31–115.

33. *Nasha gazeta*, 8, 10, 23 November 1917; Safarov, *Kolonial'naia revoliutsiia*, pp. 66–69.

34. *Turkestanskii Viestnik*, 1 December 1917; Hayit, *Turkestan*, pp. 238–44, P. Alekseenkov, *Kokandskaia avtonomiia* (Tashkent, 1931); "Kokandskaia avtonomiia," in *Tri goda Sovetskoi vlasti* (Tashkent, 1921).

35. A. K. Bogachov, *Alash-orda* (Kzyl Orda, 1927); Martynenko, *Alash-orda* (Kzyl Orda, 1929); S. Brainin and Sh. Sha'firo, *Ocherki po istorii Alash-Ordy* (Alma-Ata, 1935).

36. *Turkestanskie Viedomosti*, 12 December 1917.

37. *Nasha gazeta*, 15 December 1917; Safarov, *Kolonial'naia revoliutsiia*, p. 74.

38. *Novyi Turkestan*, 2 March 1918, cited by Safarov, *Kolonial'naia revoliutsiia*, p. 80.

39. Safarov, *Kolonial'naia revoliutsiia*.

40. *Nasha gazeta*, 3 April 1918.

41. R. Köstenberger, *Mit der Roten Armee durch Russisch-Zentralasien* (Graz, 1925), p. 19.

42. Ryskulov, *Revoliutsiia*, pp. 35–48. On Soviet rule in Turkestan in general, see A. G. Park, *Bolshevism in Turkestan, 1917–27* (New York, 1957); Ch. W. Hostler,

Turkism and the Soviets: The Turks of the World and their Political Objectives (London, 1957).

43. Safarov, *Kolonial'naia revoliutsiia*, p. 81.

44. Ginzburg, *Basmachestvo*, p. 132.

45. *Nasha gazeta*, 28 February 1918; on 5 March 1918 this newspaper published corrections and additional information, but these were generally disregarded.

46. Safarov, *Kolonial'naia revoliutsiia*, p. 85.

47. Zuev, *Ferganskoe basmachestvo*; pp. 27–36.

48. Ibid.; Ryskulov, *Revoliutsiia*, pp. 87–120.

49. Ryskulov, *Revoliutsiia*, p. 108.

50. Zuev, *Ferganskoe basmachestvo*, pp. 73–74, figure 2.

51. Ibid., pp. 37–44 and 75–76, figures 4–7.

52. Ibid., p. 40.

53. Ibid., pp. 41–44.

54. K. Khazanov, *V. I. Lenin i Turkbiuro TsK RKP* (Tashkent, 1970); K. A. Gafurova, *Bor'ba za internatsional'noe splochenie trudiashchikhsia Srednei Azii i Kazakhstana v pervye gody Sovetskoi vlasti (1917–1924)* (Moscow, 1972); A. Shukman, "The Turkestan Commission, 1919–1920," in *Central Asian Review* 12, no. 1 (1964): 5–16.

55. F. Willfort, *Turkestanisches Tagebuch* (Vienna, 1930), pp. 274–75.

56. Zuev, *Ferganskoe basmachestvo*, pp. 45–48.

57. Skalov, *Sotsial'naia priroda*; Ginzburg, *Basmachestvo*, pp. 142–52.

58. Zuev, *Ferganskoe basmachestvo*, pp. 63–70; Ginzburg, *Basmachestvo*, pp. 142–52.

59. L. Vasil'ev, *Puti sovetskogo imperializma* (New York, 1954), pp. 55–66. Vasil'ev quotes a local farmer as having said, "Violence is not necessary; violence is bad; violence means that there will be Basmachis." See also J. Mikhal'skii, *Vragi chelovechestva* (Buenos Aires, 1951), pp. 105–06.

60. L. Soloveichik, *Basmachestvo v Bukhare* (Moscow, 1923); Di-Mur, "Grazhdanskaia voina v Tadzhikistane," in *Tadzhikistan* (Tashkent, 1925); S. Ayniy, *Materialy po istorii Bukharskoi revoliutsii* (Moscow, 1926); F. Khojaev, *K istorii revoliutsii v Bukhare* (Tashkent, 1926).

61. M. N., "Pod znakom Islama," *Novyi Vostok* 4 (1923): 92–97; N. E. Kakurin, "Boevye operatsii v Bukhare (1922 g.), in *Grazhdanskaia voina*, pp. 93–94; Hélène Carrière d'Encausse, "Civil War and New Governments," in *Central Asia: A Century of Russian Rule*, ed. Edward Allworth (New York, 1967), pp. 250–52.

62. G. Skalov, "Khivinskaia revoliutsiia 1920 goda," *Novyi Vostok* 3 (1923); A. Vinograda, "Khorezmskaia Narodnaia Sovetskaia Respublika," *Zhizn natsional'nostei* 1 (1923); G. Gumeniuk, *Bor'ba za Petro-Aleksandrovsk. Piataia godovshchina Krasnoi Armii* (Tashkent, 1923); I. Kutiakov, *Krasnaia konnitsa i Vozdushnyi flot v pustyne v 1924 godu* (Moscow and Leningrad, 1930); A. Sheehy, "The End of the Khanate of Khiva," *Central Asian Review* 1, no. 15 (1967).

13. Political Trends in Soviet Islam after the Afghanistan War

Marie Broxup

This study will first try to describe some of the recent trends in Soviet Islam generally, among the official Muslim establishment, among the native elites, and in "parallel Islam." The second part will attempt to determine the extent of the impact of the war in Afghanistan and of the Afghan resistance on these developments. In order to fully appreciate the present situation, it may be worth briefly recapitulating the official position of Islam in the USSR.

Marxism-Leninism and Islam

In the Soviet Union, religion is a private matter that, in principal, does not concern the state. However, Marxism is doctrinally committed to fighting all religions considered "superstructural phenomena of capitalist or precapitalist eras, deflecting the working masses from constructive tasks." It is the "moral duty" of all Soviet citizens, especially of the members of the *komsomol* (youth organization), of the trade unions, of the educational institutions from kindergarten to highest university level, in short, of the entire state apparatus, to conduct antireligious propaganda. Also, Soviet mass media, periodical and nonperiodical press, theatre, exhibitions, museums, television, radio, and, of course, thousands of private talks dwell extensively on atheism. It represents a massive effort employing an enormous and costly bureaucratic machine.

The basic themes of anti-Muslim propaganda have varied little since 1924. It includes Marxist arguments used against all religions: Islam is the "opiate of the toiling masses, distracting them from the social struggle against the exploiting parasites"; "it plays a reactionary role being an instrument for the spiritual oppression of the workers"; "it

inculcates in man a spirit of resignation distracting him from revolutionary activity"; "it is an antiscientific creed projecting the dream of
paradise into an imaginary other world" while Marxism is building paradise on this earth; and as a mere hangover from the presocialist past,
religion is a survival doomed to disappear. Added to these there are
specific objections to Islam: it is a "foreign" religion brought by alien
invaders, it has a strong anti-Russian character, it is the most conservative of religions and the least social, sanctifying the authority of the
elders, humiliating women, exalting fanaticism and intolerance. By setting "believers" against "infidels" it is an obstacle to friendship between
different people and to "internationalism" and Soviet patriotism. Islamic
rites such as circumcision and fasting during Ramadan are criticized as
primitive, barbarian, and unhealthy. Marxism-Leninism and religious
ideology are, therefore, incompatible and the Communist Party cannot
remain neutral toward religion.

In 1968, the Soviet Union reappeared on the political scene of the
Middle East with a new "Muslim face." The Kremlin began, at first cau-
tiously, to use its muftis as roving ambassadors and spokesmen to the
Muslim world at large. The objective was to testify to the freedom, welfare, and general prosperity of Islam in the Soviet Union, and, thus, to
demonstrate that the Soviet Union is the best friend and partner of the
Islamic world.

Official Muslim Establishment

Despite this dramatic change in its foreign Muslim policy, the official
attitude of the Soviet Union toward Islam and the Muslims at home
did not change, save for some minor concessions to the Muslim religious boards and changes of emphasis in the domestic anti-Islamic propaganda. The best opportunity to correctly appreciate the present prosperity of Islam in the USSR is to consider its legal status and the number
of "working" mosques in the country.

In 1942 Abdurahman Rasulaev, Mufti of Ufa, approached Stalin in
order to normalize relations between the Soviet government and Islam. A
concordat was signed, granting Islam a legal status and an official administration, modeled on the Central Spiritual Muslim Directorate, created
in Orenburg by Catherine II in 1783. This administration, which has no
equivalent in any other Muslim country, is divided into four spiritual
boards, in Tashkent, Ufa, Baku, and Makhach-Qala (Makhachkala). The
religious boards have a staff of approximately 2,000 people, two *madras-
sahs* (Mir-i Arab in Bukhara and Imam Ismail Al-Bukhari in Tashkent),

and one periodical publication, *Muslims of the Soviet East*, aimed exclusively at a foreign Muslim audience.[1] They also control the official, "working" mosques. No official data have been published since the Second World War, and the fragmentary figures given by representatives of the Soviet government and leaders of Soviet Islam are contradictory.

Before the 1917 Revolution there were about 25,000 mosques in Russia, and another several thousand in the Amirate of Bukhara and the Khanate of Khiva. By 1942, this number had declined to about 1,200, and declined even further under CPSU First Secretary Nikita S. Khrushchev and his antireligious campaign. According to the official *Spravochnik Propagandista i Agitatora*,[2] there were 400 working mosques in the Soviet Union in 1966. Ten years later, in May 1976, V. Furov, chairman of the Council for Religious Affairs of the USSR Council of Ministers, put the number at 300 "registered" and 700 "unregistered" mosques.[3] In the same year, an executive of the Spiritual Board of Tashkent, when speaking to a Western visitor, gave the number of 143 "working" mosques for the whole of Central Asia and Kazakhstan, which seems a reasonable figure.

What has happened over the last 20 years? Soviet sources are contradictory. Figures put forth by the leaders of Soviet Islam for the benefit of the Muslim world abroad are too optimistic. They claim that the number of mosques is slowly but steadily growing.[4] In 1979, an executive of the Council for Religious Affairs, Abdullah Nurulaev, gave the figure of "more than a thousand registered Muslim parishes, each with a mosque."[5] This optimistic image is contradicted by figures for domestic consumption which describe, on the contrary, a rapid decline of the number of "working" mosques. For example, *Komsomolets Uzbekistana*, analyzing the situation of Islam in the Khwarezm region of the Uzbek SSR, wrote, "Today, there are three working mosques in the Khwarezm region. This number is still too high, but it is incomparably lower than ten years ago."[6] In 1979 the total Muslim population of the Khwarezm region was 732,000. Today, it has probably reached 840,000. This means that there is one mosque for every 280,000 Muslims in the region. Khwarezm is one of the areas of Central Asia where Islam has especially deep roots. In other Muslim territories, there is a similar situation.

–In Turkmenistan, several recent sources mention the existence of only four small working mosques for a total Muslim population of 2,500,000 (1979 census), or one mosque for every 625,000 individuals.

–In Kirghizia, there remained only one working mosque in the entire valley of Talas (northern Kirghizia) in 1987.[7]
–In Daghestan, out of 2,100 mosques existing before the revolution, only 27 remain today.
–In Azerbaijan, there were 16 working mosques in 1980 for a Muslim population of over 5,000,000, or one mosque for every 320,000 people.
–In Tatarstan, only 13 mosques were working, according to figures published in 1978.
–In Tajikistan, 18 mosques were functioning for a total Muslim population of over 3,800,000 in 1979, and probably over 4,000,000 today.

Several mosques have been closed over the last seven years in Tajikistan (since the invasion of Afghanistan). The current proportion of working mosques to the total population must be about one mosque for every 400,000 individuals. In an issue of *Nauka i Religiia* a Tajik antireligious propagandist, M. Mirrakhimov, obviously disgusted by the destruction of his people's national patrimony, admitted that in the Leninabad region alone "there are 400 non-working mosques—the majority are historical monuments. Some are crumbling into dust, others have been transformed into warehouses. The regional authorities do not care."[8]

A prominent Soviet Islamologist, Igor Beliaev, in his article "Islam i politika," advances the figure of "365 open mosques full of believers."[9] For a total Muslim population of 50,000,000 (the dedicated atheists representing probably less than 15 percent), this is a ridiculously small number.

Considering the relentless anti-Islamic propaganda, the paucity of the religious administration and the fact that religious activity is totally outlawed outside the official establishment, how is it that Islam could not only survive but flourish in the USSR, as it undoubtedly does, judging by the increasing number of Soviet reports devoted to the Islamic problem?[10] There are several reasons for this, as will be set out below.

Islam and Nationalism

One of the most important admissions of Soviet specialists in recent years is that in Central Asia and the Caucasus the notions of Islam and nationalism are inextricably mixed. A leading Soviet specialist, T. S. Saidbaev, gives a remarkable insight into this situation: "A section of the population . . . still considers religion and nationalism as similar and looks at religion as being part of national life. It is judged compulsory to follow the prescriptions of Islam. To reject them is disapproved as showing a lack of respect to the memory of one's ancestors, to the nation, and national culture. This is why in the traditional areas of Islam, not only believers but a section of the nonbelievers as well, look favorably at religious rituals."[11]

More recently, at the Uzbek Communist Party Congress in January 1986, the former first secretary, Usmankhodjaev, attacked the low level of ideological work and the tolerance shown to Islam by party cadres, stressing that "it must be constantly remembered that religion clears the way for nationalism and chauvinism." He went on to specify that "popular traditions must be respected and a sense of love for the homeland history must be fostered in the rising generation, but the past of the Uzbek people . . . is not of course patriarchal traditions and the dogma of the Shariʿa."[12] Similar statements were echoed in all the last plenums of the communist parties of the other Central Asian republics.

Because of this confusion between national and religious loyalties, Soviet sources now make it eminently clear that the overwhelming majority of the population of the Muslim republics to this day performs certain religious rituals. The most commonly observed are the "family rites," such as circumcision, religious marriages, and, above all, religious funerals, but also the 'Id festivals and the fast during Ramadan. Saidbaev estimates that 40 percent of elderly believers fast during the whole month, the majority limiting themselves to three days at the beginning, middle, and end of the month. He adds that "the number of people performing religious rituals exceeds the number of believers and, unfortunately, among those who identify religious and national identities and pretend that Islam does not do any harm, one finds those people . . . who are supposed to implement atheistic propaganda."

He also emphasizes that "the bearers of the ideas of community between religions and nationalism are frequently people who do not participate in daily religious life, who are not believers."[13] This was also officially confirmed by Usmankhodjaev at the Uzbek plenum of January 1986. "One of the serious problems facing the republican party organization is that of antireligious propaganda and atheistic education. Some party organizations connive and sometimes openly flirt with religion and pander to backward traditions. Party committees do not notice, or else refuse to notice that goods bearing religious symbols and the sayings of theologians are produced in state enterprises. Religious rites, with their extravagance, have captivated many people. There are by no means isolated cases of communists, komsomol members and leading personnel taking part in the performance of religious rites."

On 4 March 1987 *Sovettik Kirgizstan* published a long article about Takht-e Suleyman, one of the most venerated holy places of Turkistan, in which it was stated that "members of the intelligentsia . . . are attempting to idealize harmful old customs and rites, including religious superstition. Under the influence of religious superstitions they go as far as convincing themselves that the nonobservance of Islamic religious festivals, customs, and rites is not less than a betrayal of national honor."[14]

Similar condemnation of "negative phenomena" and ideological failings among native cadres have been reported regularly in the republican press for the last year, but since the riots in Alma-Ata the reports have become more specific. Individual communist party members are now nominally singled out for attacks and accused not merely of participating in religious rituals but in several cases of organizing them.[15]

There are many historical reasons why, for a Turkistanian (or a North Caucasian), the notions of Islam and nation are intertwined. To expand on them would be outside the scope of this chapter.

For centuries, since the earliest years of Islam, Turkistan was the cradle of the greatest Muslim dynasties, brilliant theologians, philosophers, saints, poets, and Sufis. *Miras*—the rehabilitation of the national patrimony—which has been steadily growing since Stalin's death, and has allowed the Turkistanians to rediscover their past so deeply imbued with the glories and spirit of Islam, and has certainly helped to enhance the prestige of their ancestors' religion among the modern Soviet intelligentsia.

The Role of the Sufi Tariqa

The specific role of defender of Islam against infidel invaders played by the Sufi *tariqa* in Turkistan since the time of the Mongol invasions, and their fierce resistance to the Russian conquest in the nineteenth century gives to Islam in the USSR a strong mobilizing appeal for those who feel oppressed or who resent Russian domination.[16]

The fact that, unlike Communism, Islam, especially in its popular Sufi form, which is so perfectly adapted to local conditions, has not insisted on the total destruction of the social and cultural originality of the Central Asian societies, but instead has tried to accommodate them, accounts not only for its persistent vitality but for its continuous role of custodian of national values.[17]

In areas where official Islam is weak, the basic needs of the believers have been assumed by what some call "parallel Islam," represented in most cases by the Sufi *tariqa*. There are four main *tariqa*s in the USSR: the Naqshbandiya, the Qadiriya, the Yasawiya, and the Kubrawiya.[18]

North Caucasus

Sufi Islam (muridism) is better known in the North Caucasus where the *tariqas* are well structured and have completely taken over all aspects of the religious life, including the official religious establishment. "Over the last few years religious groups of murids have become more active and begun to meddle in public affairs which have nothing to do with the religious feelings of the believers" wrote I. Makatov, a specialist on Islam in the Caucasus in 1978.[19]

The Sufis are accused of a variety of activities—all totally illegal and likely to attract criminal prosecution under Soviet legislation. They allegedly spread anti-Russian propaganda and xenophobia. "The clergy represents Islam as the only repository of moral and national virtues and preaches the exclusiveness of Islam thereby trying to induce . . . a negative attitude toward the Soviet way of life and the friendship among nationalities of different creeds. At the same time, religious traditions are shown as being part of the eternal national patrimony."[20] Not only do the *tariqas* run Qur'ânic schools and distribute illegal religious literature, but some "fanatics" are also accused of forbidding their children to attend Soviet schools or go to the theater or cinema, and in some cases, they even refuse military service. They collect *zakat* (legal alms), have clandestine mosques, control local places of pilgrimage, and organize religious ceremonies—*zikr*—in public places, often in the presence of children and officials, during which "they brainwash the adepts with religious propaganda which sometimes acquires a purely nationalistic color."[21] They are accused of various economic crimes such as parasitism, nonlabor illicit profits and vagrancy, but also more specifically of encouraging believers to plunder socialist state property, of banditism and killings.[22] According to an article by Kh. Bokov, the chairman of the Presidium of the Supreme Soviet of the Chechen-Ingush ASSR, published in *Nauka i Religiia* in 1987, religious tribunals formed by Sufi sheikhs and clan elders still operate in the North Caucasus. Their authority often overrules that of the Soviet tribunals and their decisions are abided by punctiliously. Bokov also revealed that 60,000 people of working age in the republic completely escape all social production: "These people belong to the murid groups who provide them work and moral satisfaction."[23] This number is exactly the same as the number of murids in 1917 in the whole of North Caucasus.

Finally, the Sufis reject the Soviet system, do not take part in public life, and do not join the party or komsomol. They are said to advocate the private use of land and free enterprise, and to redistribute land according to precollectivization ownership.

Central Asia

The same crimes of antisocial behavior, fanaticism, xenophobia, are alleged against parallel Islam in Turkistan, although until the early 1980s it appeared, for lack of information, more diffuse than in the North Caucasus. Observers now have a better picture, although of course only partial. However, the glimpses allowed from the official Soviet media are enough to draw an amazing scene—amazing because of its wide-scale implications and the speed with which events seem to be unfolding and positions hardening.

First, quotes from Din-Muhammad Kunaev's reports to the last two congresses of the Communist Party of Kazakhstan: "The incidence of religious sentiments among the population remains relatively high and is even tending to increase in southern regions";[24] "in a series of districts of the southern region, wandering mullahs feel free to practice their religion."[25] The southern districts of Kazakhstan are those populated mostly by Kazakhs—former nomads whose attachment to Islam had always been lower than that of other Muslims of Russia. Some weeks after Kunaev's political demise, *Kazakhstanskaia Pravda* confirmed that "the effectiveness of many ideological measures is low. The religious situation remains disturbing and the harmfulness of Islam is often underestimated. Backward customs and habits, incompatible with the socialist way of life, are being revived in some places."[26]

Makhkamov, First Secretary of the Communist Party of Tajikistan, at a meeting of the ideological *aktiv* of the Tajik SSR, held in Dushanbe on 30 August 1986,[27] said that due to the poor motivation of atheist *agitpropchiks*, "a part of the population, especially in rural areas, unquestioningly follows the prescriptions of Shariʿa. . . . As a consequence, the leaders of various sectarian trends have become more active. . . . The level of religiosity of the population of our republic has noticeably increased. Numerous facts show that the antisocial activity of Muslim clerics is growing and that the education of children in Islamic dogma is increasing. Production and distribution of ideologically dangerous literature is growing. Also, more religious video films which are brought from abroad are being shown. The most reactionary members of the clergy are trying to revitalize nationalistic survivals and give new life to nefarious rites and customs."[27]

Numerous *mazars* and historical monuments with a religious significance, such as the mausoleum of Sultan Sanjar who died fighting the infidels, are being restored by Sufi groups with illicitly acquired state funds and building materials, houses of prayer for pilgrims disguised as "guest houses" are being built near ancestral holy places on similarly ill-gained money, while atheist clubs and government "houses of culture" face years of delay before construction. For every official mullah in the Navai district of Uzbekistan there are 15 "self-appointed" ones,[28] and thousands of "pseudo-mullahs" altogether operating in the republic.[29]

Of all the Muslim republics, Uzbekistan has the highest concentration of official clergy. Therefore, it could logically be assumed that there would be less need for parallel Islam than elsewhere. Even the *chaykhana*s have become illegal mosques. In several *raion*s of Gharm (Tajikistan) mullahs gathered the copies of the republican newspaper *Tojikistoni Soveti* which had published antireligious articles and burned them in spectacular autos-da-fe.[30]

Islam as a Political Weapon

Not only have the attacks on Islam increased in numbers, but they reveal a new militant, almost political trend among the Muslims of Turkistan and the Caucasus. The following are four new themes in the Soviet press which support this statement:

1. Soviet authors now talk of Sufism as a potential political opposition. This is a totally new phenomenon (previously Sufis were only branded as antisocial "fanatics" and "obscurantists"). Makatov states that "murid groups [in the North Caucasus] are influenced by foreign propaganda. . . . We must not forget that foreign religious propaganda centers and foreign intelligence centers are expecting murid and other extremist organizations to create a political opposition in our country."[31] According to Churlanova, Secretary of the Daghestan *obkom,* the weakness of atheistic propaganda has led to the reactivization in certain cities of "reactionary religious elements and the direct intrusion of Muslim clerics in the socio-political life of our country." These "nonregistered clerics" she adds, "escape all control."[32]

In what would appear a case of paranoiac overreaction, some innocuous Muslim rituals, such as *nikah* (religious marriage) which are adhered to by the great majority of people in Central Asia and the Caucasus, including members of the komsomol and Communist Party, are described as subversive plots by ideological enemies to destroy the Soviet Union. According to L. Berdyeva and Dzh. Khommatdurdyev, writing in *Sovet Turkmenistany:*

Muslim clerics and especially pseudo-mullahs have begun to concentrate on traditions of *nikah* actively. . . . Unfortunately, young
people do not pause to think that the givers of blessing to their
marriage also have zealous prompters, moreover not from their
neighbors' yard, but from much further—from beyond the border.
They are those people who work out radio broadcasts of a reactionary religious and instigatory nature, for example at Gorgan and
Bandar Turkmen radio stations. This 'spiritual' food in many places
is aimed at the population of the Central Asian republics. . . . Foreign
radio stations, strengthened with ill intentions, have perfected their
Islamic propaganda and rely on immature listeners. The main aim of
the ideological subversives, to put it plainly, is to achieve the social
and economic disintegration of the multinational Central Asian republics and consequently to eradicate their socialist structure. The
antiSoviets regard the practice of religion which develops cultural
narrow-mindedness and nationalist tendencies as something which
will initiate the collapse of the USSR. . . . In other words, in the
present ideological and political struggle against communism. . . .
Islam has turned into a live weapon in the hands of our enemies."
Thus, the authors conclude that "in our time a simple village wedding party held according to old customs might seem far from these
thoughts, but this is the picture which emerges from behind the
scene." That is to say, a wedding feast turns out to be seasoned with
poison.[33]

2. A high level of religiosity and adherence to Sufi *tariqa* is not predominant anymore in the backward rural areas. Many authors report the
appearance of radical religious groups in the cities, in urban and indus-
trialized areas, and significantly in places where Muslims are living in
close contact with Russians.

3. Religious extremists and Sufi brotherhoods are said to be interested
mainly in recruiting adherents among the young and the intellectuals. A
recent survey (1985–86) on the level of religiosity of students of the pedagogical schools in Kurgan-Tube (Tajikistan) gave the following results:
16.8 percent of the students claimed to be believers, 39.5 percent hesitant, 28.6 percent nonbelievers, 6.9 percent atheists, and 8.2 percent refused to answer. Supposedly, the 8.2 percent who refused to answer were
believers. The "hesitating," according to the survey, "may well ask for the
help of religion if placed in exceptional situations." These are very high
figures, especially when compared to a similar study conducted in 1973
in Nukus (Karakalpakistan) when the answer given by the 18–30 age
group were: believers 0 percent, hesitant 1.4 percent, nonbelievers 50.8

percent, and atheist 47.8 percent.[34] The striking discrepancy between the two surveys is due not to territorial differences—Karakalpakistan has always been a highly religious area of USSR where Sufi orders were active, certainly as religious as Tajikistan—but to chronological differences. It means that since the war in Afghanistan there has been a real, extraordinary, powerful religious revival.

In order to increase their influence on the young, clerics are said to pay particular attention to the religious education of women. The appearance of women shaykhs and preachers has been noted in the North Caucasus and Turkistan: "If until recent times the role of religious mentor was played by women believers in the circle of their families, today in a number of places one may see them speaking publicly, openly intruding into the spiritual life of other families. Their attempts at interference in the process of the moral development of members of labor collectives has been observed."[35] The fact that Islam is gaining ground among young well-educated people, and in the cities, will automatically lead to its greater politicization, a phenomenon seen in other parts of the Muslim world.

4. Finally, Igor Beliaev admitted, five months after the events, that Sufis were involved in the riots of Alma-Ata: "The young people in Alma-Ata who took part in the well-known December [1986] events were also manipulated by Muslim fanatics—Sufis—who infiltrated the student milieu. I mean students in the senior grades and even the teaching staff. What is most disturbing is that many young people who did not even know anything about the plenum of the Communist Party of Kazakhstan Central Committee of 16 December submitted so readily to certain forces who could not risk speaking out openly, but who appeared on the scene carrying sticks."[36]

Influence of the Afghan Resistance

In Tajikistan a new trend has developed where elements of "fanaticism," puritanism, and a political commitment to Islam are blended. The Soviets call it wrongly Wahhabism and describe it as a "religious political movement, extremely reactionary and nationalistic." Some of the leaders of this movement were tried and sentenced in 1986. They were said to find much of their inspiration and arguments in radio broadcasts from Iran, and were accused among other things of demanding the establishment of an Islamic republic based on the Shari'a, of opposing Soviet intervention in Afghanistan and of claiming that Soviet troops are trying "to turn the Afghans into infidels." Whether this movement has been directly sponsored by the Afghan Resistance, or whether it is a spontaneous development in response to events in Afghanistan, the similarities between these Tajiks (as described by the Soviet press) and their Afghan cousins are striking: in the social background and age of the "activists"—the Tajik preachers are particularly popular among young people with higher education, especially teachers, while cadres of parties like Jamiat-e Islami and Hizb-e Islami are also provided by school teachers and engineers; in the fact that in Tajikistan Islam is being politicized with demands for an Islamic state; in the Tajik preachers' desire to revive the original purity of Islam; and in their rejection of Soviet education. The arrest of one of the leaders, Mullah Abdullah Saidov, in Kurgan-Tube in August 1986 provoked street demonstrations and assaults on the police station and court rooms by the local population. Such developments would have appeared unbelievable some ten years ago.[37]

On 30 December 1987, *Kommunist Tadzhikistana* published the report of the chairman of the Tajikistan SSR KGB, V. V. Petkel, to the eighth plenum of the Communist Party of the Tajikistan Central Committee. His speech, which is reproduced in part below, officially confirms, at long last, reports from the Afghan Resistance which, up till now, have only been hinted at in Soviet sources:

Tajikistan's Chekists are resolving tasks of safeguarding state security in a complex situation. The situation is explained by the fact that there is a complex tangle of contradictions in the regions bordering on the republic—Afghanistan, Pakistan, Iran, and other countries. The situation in the republic of Afghanistan has become more complex in connection with the implementation by that country's government of the policy of national reconciliation. Counterrevolutionary gangs continue to be sent into that country from Pakistan. . . .

Imperialist circles, their special services and the bandit formations associated with them, are doing their utmost to try to exploit this tangle of contradictions to expand their subversive activity against Afghanistan and the Soviet Union. To this end the *Dushman* gangs are stepping up their activity in provinces bordering on the USSR. The enemy is trying to transfer armed forms of struggle to Soviet territory. That is why, in March and April of this year, on the special services' direct instructions, the *Dushman*s carried out armed actions on the border and on the territory of Kurgan-Tube and Kulab *oblast'*.

In connection with these provocations, Comrade V. M. Chebrikov, member of the Politburo of the CPSU Central Committee and Chairman of the USSR State Security Committee, visited the scene of the events. He set state security organs and border guards the task of preventing armed actions and other hostile manifestations on the border.

How is this task being carried out? The republic's Chekists are carrying out a great volume of work under the leadership of the CP of Tajikistan's Central Committee. A number of intelligence officers, agents of enemy special services and emissaries of enemy ideological centers among foreign citizens have been exposed with the help of the working people. . . . Dozens of attempts to violate the state border by criminal elements trying to go abroad have been stopped.

Open and organized hostile manifestations by religious extremists have been prevented in the republic.

However, there are also certain shortcomings in our work. We do not always succeed in fully controlling the existing situation and detecting certain emergent undesirable processes in time.

In conditions of restructuring and broadening democracy and *glasnost'* in Soviet society, preemptive, preventive work assumes especially great significance for KGB organs. Our actions must be understandable to working people and supported by them. The existence of crimes like cross-border smuggling illustrates the need to improve preventive work further with the border troops and law enforcement organs.

It must be admitted that, in view of the serious shortcomings and omissions in the organization of patriotic, internationalist, and atheistic education in the republic, hostile foreign ideological centers and organizations are able to find fertile ground. This is illustrated by the dozens of trials held in 1986–87 of ringleaders, unofficial [*zashtatnyi*] Muslim clerics who not only fanned religious sentiments but also called for a "jihad" against the existing system. They are setting the goal of infiltrating party, Soviet, and law enforcement organs in order to facilitate the implementation of hostile designs.

I want to take one important sector from the broad range of issues regarding the military-patriotic education of the republic's population, where there are very many shortcomings and unsolved problems. The flaws in patriotic, internationalist, and atheistic education are mirrored in the process of conscripting young men for service in the armed forces. In particular, there is no reduction in the number of people evading conscription. We must all be alerted by the very existence of cases where 18-year old citizens evade the performance of their sacred constitutional obligation and patriotic duty—service in the army and the defense of their fatherland. The reasons for these criminal actions cannot leave us indifferent.

Some young people think it is better to get a two-year suspended sentence, get married, and have a couple of children in that time than do military service right away. Some people take this step for fear of going to the Republic of Afghanistan. Others do not want to leave the republic for religious and regionalist motives or under the negative influence of relatives.

Unfortunately, there is no reduction in the number of young men susceptible to religious prejudices. Material at *raion* military commissariats shows that there are many such people each year among the draft-dodgers in Kurgan-Tube and Kulab *oblasts* and Ordzhonikidzeabad, Gharm and other *raions* under republican jurisdiction.

For instance, some conscripts from Kommunisticheskiy, Vakhsh, Dzhilikul, and Kabodien *raions*, without taking themselves off the register at local military commissariats, went to other *raions* in the oblast and republic where they began to study the dogmas of Islam, and thus evaded military service. . . .

There has been no fall in the number of draft-dodgers in Kurgan-Tube Oblast. . . .

The main cause of these shortcomings is that the CP of Tajikistan Central Committee's good comprehensive program on education matters has not been followed up with effective organizational measures to ensure its implementation by all responsible organs from top to bottom. It is time to move from talk to action and boost exactingness. . . .

Cross-border smuggling refers in particular to publications, printed in Peshawar by the Afghan Resistance specifically for Soviet Muslims, which often include highly politicized works such as those of Mawdudi and Said Qotb.[38] Other political and religious leaflets are produced directly by various resistance fronts in the north of Afghanistan. In June 1987, the cultural committee of Jamiat-e Islami Afghanistan, in close cooperation with Commander Ahmed Shah Massud's Alliance of the North, began publishing a remarkable newspaper, *Golos Islama* (entirely in Russian). The quality and interest of the news and analysis in this paper outweigh by far that of many similar Pashto and Dari papers from Peshawar. It is highly political and has only passing references to religious matters.

The "dozens of attempts to violate the State border by criminal elements trying to go abroad," mentioned by Petkel, refer to demonstrations which took place in 1984 in the Soviet Central Asian republics bordering Afghanistan (which were not reported by the Soviet press). Observers have been fortunate to receive an interview by a young Uzbek teacher from Termez who took part in the demonstrations and later joined the Afghan Resistance. Better than any analysis, his testimony explains the feelings of Soviet Muslims:

> As everybody knows, a movement of discontent spread over the Soviet Union after the invasion of Afghanistan. . . . Popular dissatisfaction grew and became a generalized movement. At the end of April 1984, mass demonstrations took place in the *oblast'* of Termez. Entire crowds came out to demonstrate. They were attacked by Soviet combat helicopters. There were many deaths and many arrests. Some people were certainly executed in prison. Having taken part in the demonstrations, I could not stay in the Soviet Union. I went underground. During several days, I stayed in the border area, then with the help of people who were in contact with the Afghan Mujahidin, I tried to escape to Afghanistan. Thanks to the help of the Afghan Mujahidin, who often cross the border for military raids on Soviet territory in Uzbekistan, Tajikistan, and Turkmenistan, I managed my escape. Once in Afghanistan I joined the resistance. . . .

> Muslims living in the USSR have not forgotten their past and their lost freedom. They also remember the lives sacrificed to defend their lost liberty. The Russian occupants have grabbed our countries, have exploited them ruthlessly, and, after the October Revolution, have forced them to be part of the land of the Soviets. But the Muslim people all aspire to freedom and want to liberate themselves from the yoke of the Communists and of the Russian tyrants. Because of this, Soviet Muslims consider the war in Afghanistan as a continuation of the war which brought the subjugation of Central Asia. The Afghan nation is fighting for her freedom, and we, the Muslims of the Soviet Union, we know that the Afghan people will win, and their victory will bring the liberation of Central Asia. . . .

Conclusion

Turkistan has played a leading role in the history of the Muslim world since the early days of Islam. For centuries, Muslims in Turkistan, in the Caucasus and Tatarstan have belonged to the ʿUmma, the community of believers. It is naive to expect that mere decades of forcibly imposed foreign rule and alien ideology would wipe out memories of a glorious past and create a new Soviet man. Those Muslims still belong to the ʿUmma, Islam remains a common denomination among the Turko-Iranian peoples of Central Asia and the Caucasus. As such, they feel attuned to movements and aspirations existing elsewhere in the Muslim world, and it is inconceivable that they could remain unaffected by the turmoil just across the borders. On the other hand, it would be a mistake to believe that events in Afghanistan and Iran contributed to something that was not already there in substance. This is indicated by the fact that the greatest Islamic militancy is to be found not only in Tajikistan, where observers undoubtedly see a direct influence of the Afghan mujahiddin, but also in the North Caucasus, with its rich, long jihad tradition; likewise, around all the old traditional religious centers such as Osh in the Farghana Valley, where demands for an Islamic state have also been heard recently.

Simply put, the Afghan war acted as a catalyst by proving that Russians were not invincible and that resistance could be worthwhile. In this context it is significant that the unrest, regularly described as "negative phenomena" by Soviet officials, increased in the Muslim republics of that country after 1986. It was a turning point in the Afghan war, when Stinger missles began to appear in Afghanistan, and the resistance became confident in their ultimate military victory.

Notes

1. The four religious boards are: Muslim Religious Board for Central Asia and Kazakhstan in Tashkent (Sunni, Hanafi school), Muslim Religious Board for European Russia and Siberia in Ufa (Sunni, Hanafi school), Muslim Religious Board of the North Caucasus and Daghestan in Makhach Qala (Sunni, Shafei school), and Muslim Religious Board of Transcaucasia in Baku (mixed Shia of Jafari rite and Sunni of Hanafi school). *Muslims of the Soviet East* is published by the Muslim Religious Board for Central Asia and Kazakhstan in English, French, Arabic, Uzbek (in Arabic script), Persian, Dari (Afghan Persian, since 1984), and Urdu (since 1987).

2. (Moscow, 1966), p. 149.

3. A secret report presented to the editorial board of the *Bol'shaia Sovetskaia En-*

tsiklopediia, reported by the samizdat publication *Khronika Tekushchikh Sobytii*, no. 41 (1976): 7.

4. *Muslims of the Soviet East*, April 1978, p. 16.

5. *Frankfurter Allgemeine Zeitung*, 4 May 1979.

6. *Komsomolets Uzbekistana*, Tashkent, 10 October 1966.

7. *Sovetskaia Kirgiziia*, 11 March 1987.

8. *Nauka i Religiia*, no. 5 (1987), p. 23.

9. *Literaturnaia Gazeta*, 13 and 20 May 1987.

10. See, in this context, Alexandre Bennigsen, "Mullahs, Mujahidin and Soviet Muslims," *Problems of Communism*, November/December 1984, pp. 28–44.

11. T. S. Saidbaev, *Islam: istoriia i sovremennost'* (Moscow: Znanie, 1985).

12. *Pravda Vostoka*, 31 January 1986.

13. Saidbaev, *Islam*, p. 41.

14. The same article appeared in *Sovetskaia Kirgiziia*, in Russian, 16 March 1987 (L. Kriuchkova and A. Sadykov, "Sheikhi na Suleiman-gore").

15. See, for instance, *Sovet Uzbekistoni*, 15 January 1987.

16. For example, the North Caucasian wars from Sheikh Mansur to Shamil (from 1783 to 1859), and later in 1920 the great uprising of Daghestan and Chechnia, also led by the Naqshbandi *tariqa*; the resistance of the Tekke tribes at Geok Tepe in 1881, led by Kurban Said—a Naqshbandi; the Andizhan uprising led by Ishan Madali in 1898.

17. On the question of national identity and the role of Islam, see Nazif Shahrani and Chantal Lemercier-Quelquejay's articles "From Tribe to 'Umma," *Central Asian Survey* 3, no. 3 (1985).

18. For a detailed study of Sufism in the USSR, see A. Bennigsen and S. E. Wimbush, *Mystics and Commissars, Sufism in the Soviet Union* (London: C. Hurst, 1985).

19. I. Makatov, "V ushcherb interesam obshchestva i lichnosti," *Sovetskii Dagestan*, no. 6 (1987): 37.

20. Sh. Ismailov, "Vyshe uroven' ateisticheskoi raboty," in *Sovetskii Dagestan*, no. 1 (1982): 1–2.

21. S. Murtazalieva, "Bor'ba idei i sovesti," in *Sovetskii Dagestan*, no. 2 (1981): 53.

22. Ibid. See also by the same author: "Uchityvaia mestnye osobennosti," *Sovetskii Dagestan*, no. 5 (1982): 46–50.

23. Kh. Bokov, "Uroki istorii," *Nauka i Religiia*, no. 5 (1987): 3–6.

24. D.-M. Kunaev, Report to the Fifteenth Congress of the Communist Party of Kazakhstan.

25. D.-M. Kunaev, Report to the Sixteenth Congress of the Communist Party of Kazakhstan.

26. *Kazakhstanskaia Pravda*, 8 February 1987.

27. Reported in *Agitator Tadzhikistana*, no. 20, October 1986.

28. *Pravda Vostoka*, 26 October 1986.

29. *Sovet Uzbekistoni*, 7 January 1987.

30. Mentioned in the Tajik, but not the Russian report of the 6th plenum of the Central Committee of the Communist Party of Tajikistan, *Tojikistoni Soveti*, 9 April 1987.

31. I. Makatov, "V ushcherb," p. 42.

32. P. Churlanova, "Perestroivaia ideologicheskuiu rabotu," in *Sovetskii Dagestan*, no. 4 (1986): 1–4.

33. *Sovet Turkmenistany,* 23 November 1986.

34. T. Vasneva, "Vospityvat' ubezhdennykh ateistov," in *Agitator Tadzhikistana,* no. 13 (1986): 24–26; and J. Bazarbaev, *Sekuliarizatsiia naseleniia sotsialisticheskoi Karakalpakii* (Nukus, 1973), p. 50.

35. S. Murtazalieva, "Uchityvaia mestnye osobennosti," p. 48. See also *Kommunist Tadzhikistana,* 23 November 1986.

36. Igor Beliaev, "Islam i politika," *Literaturnaia Gazeta,* 13 and 20 May 1987.

37. See on this subject *Kommunist Tadzhikistana,* 31 January 1987 and 12 February 1987, and *Tojikistoni Soveti,* 14 February 1987.

38. For further information on these publications, see A. Bennigsen, "Mullah, Mujahidin, and Soviet Muslims."

14. Islamic Movements in Yugoslavia

Alexandre Popović

An analysis of Yugoslavia's Islamic movements must first set out to define what is meant by *Yugoslav Muslims.* In a short space, however, it is difficult to describe the situation of that group of citizens designated by the term *Yugoslav Muslims* to readers who may not be familiar with the complexities of that country. This difficulty stems from the fact that this is a term devoid of meaning, as will become clear. Moreover, a good grasp of Balkan history is necessary for an understanding of the situation of these remarkably diverse groups in terms of their relationships with one another, with other population groups in the country and with the authorities.

Finally, a correct analysis of the concept of Yugoslav Muslims must delve beyond the misinformation given by the official Yugoslav media: by certain journalists, pseudohistorians, and the like. For several decades these presentations have been marred by taboos and intentional "forgetting," in fact, by a systematic deformation of the truth, if not by outright falsification.

These statements bear some explanation. The term *Yugoslav Muslims* actually applies to a great variety of groups of people, differing in ethnicity, language, social stratification, and, finally, degree of religiousness (as denoted, for example, in the secular term *Muslimani*, as opposed to Muslims—adherents of the Islamic faith). This vagueness allows for a certain number of manipulations. Strictly from the point of view of "nationality" and "ethnicity," according to current Yugoslav terminology, the following groups must be considered, all of them differing significantly in some aspects: Muslim Serbs, Muslim Croats, Muslim Macedonians, Muslim Montenegrins, Muslim Albanians, Muslim Turks, Muslim Gypsies (currently called "Romis"), and, finally, Muslim Muslimani.[1]

Those in the latter category consist of Muslim citizens of Herzegovina who, some time ago, opted not to choose either Serbian or Croatian nationality, which categories were considered to have too much to do with the Orthodox and Catholic churches, and declared themselves to be "undefined" (*neopredeleny*). In 1969, the Yugoslav government finally recognized a Muslim nation, partly in an attempt to remedy this situation, but more important, in fact, in order to use this devious means to weaken once more the position of the Serbs, who at that time comprised the nation with the largest population—not only in Yugoslavia but within the boundaries of Bosnia-Herzegovina. This Muslim nation, however, only included the Muslims of Bosnia-Herzegovina: the others remained Muslim Serbs, Croats, Macedonians, Montenegrins, and the like.[2]

The necessary criticism of the representation of facts by local Yugoslav media, as well as by numerous local bureaucrats, relates to the available documentation. Two sets of problems must be born in mind: the first, those originating in the centers of political power; the second, problems originating among the diverse groups of Muslims themselves. The first set of problems has to do with attitudes, actions, and official declarations by the authorities—and of their political writers—reflecting the official version of the facts. There is, of course, a political discourse that is dictated by the immediate situation and is susceptible to frequent shifts of orientation. A participant in this type of discourse can assert and support in like manner, and in suitable language, both truths and half-truths, lies and half-lies.

The second set of problems involves the documentation issuing from these diverse groups. Three major difficulties arise in this regard: (1) the absence of documents, where the group has no access to a periodical, whether official or not, in order to express itself; (2) censure and self-censure, where facts and situations may be distorted, diluted, or omitted in order to avoid displeasing authorities; (3) monolithic images that take no account of existing tensions, clashes, and factions. Such images may be created when one group of individuals gains so much influence that it controls the media and thus can willfully distort, dilute, or omit facts and events.[3]

Historical Problems

Historical problems can be linked to one major factor: Ottoman domination, which varied in duration from four to five centuries in different regions. It was a powerful shaping force in the country, creating deep divisions between people on the basis of religious faith. Deriving from the first, another factor that had profound consequences was the germination and, subsequently, the proliferation of local nationalisms that were inextricably linked to local churches, whether Serbian Orthodox or Catholic. The conflicts between the two Christian confessions became marked as early as the end of the seventeenth and the beginning of the eighteenth centuries, in part because of the Habsburg attempt to "reconquer" the region, described below.

The national ideologies of all the non-Muslim populations of Yugoslavia developed outside the realm of Islam (synonymous among these populations with the Ottoman Empire), if not wholly against it. For the purposes of this discussion, it will be useful to examine these influences on the country in two distinct regions: that of western and central Yugoslavia and that of eastern Yugoslavia.

Western and Central Yugoslavia

The western and northern part of the country, including some territories of Dalmatia and Croatia, as well as Slavonia and Voivodine, was occupied by the Ottoman Empire for some time. At the end of the seventeenth and beginning of the eighteenth centuries, following the Habsburgs' defeat of the Ottomans at Vienna in 1683, the Habsburgs sought to gain power in this region by supporting the Serbian population. In the process of this so-called "reconquest," much of the Muslim population was wiped out, through forced migration and conversions as well as massacres.

The situation was completely different, however, in the central regions of Bosnia-Herzegovina, which has remained the main bastion of Slavic Muslims in the Balkans. Toward the end of Ottoman rule the population of this region was 43 percent Orthodox, 39 percent Muslim and 18 percent Catholic.

In 1878, in accordance with the Congress of Berlin, Austria-Hungary occupied Bosnia-Herzegovina militarily, and annexed it in 1908. For forty years, therefore, the region's Muslim population was at the mercy of Austrian Balkan policy or, more accurately, of its anti-Serbian policy. Earlier, this population had had to endure not only the dislocation of the Ottoman Empire, but that of Ottoman society, undermined as it was by countless internal woes, one of which was the matter of local nationalisms that were just beginning to spring up.

There was another problem, much more delicate, that had held these people back for a long time. The members of both the Orthodox and the Catholic churches effectively regarded the Muslims of Bosnia-Herzegovina as "Turks," assimilated to that ethnic group. Consequently, these Muslims, although knowing full well that this conception was incorrect, had no means of self-determination, in view of the triumphant nationalisms around them. The total disarray that becomes apparent in nineteenth-century texts, and which has been depicted so well in several subsequent literary works, such as *The Dervish and Death*, by Mesa Selimovic (1910–82), created a particularly complex atmosphere. This atmosphere provided the context for the Austrian political ideology of "Bosnianism," or of "Bosnian particularism," which later caused so much damage.

The situation changed considerably after the demise of the Habsburg Empire, with the creation of the "Kingdom of Serbs, Croats and Slovenians" on 1 December 1918. As the name of the new state suggests, however, the only possibilities for identification it provided the Muslims of Bosnia-Herzegovina rested on a forced choice between Serbian and Croatian nationality. Under these new conditions, the Muslim community of these regions, and especially the local intelligentsia, were courted with bids by Pan-Serbian and Pan-Croatian movements, and works appeared with titles such as "Famous Serbian Muslims" and "Famous Croatian Muslims," presumably containing biographies of such individuals.

Most significantly, all of Yugoslavian Islam during these decades (1918–41) contributed to the complex dynamic between Serbian and Croatian nationalism: a dynamic in which the "Muslim problem" was one component. The scope of this chapter does not permit the extensive and thoughtful treatment that this fascinating subject deserves, because of the multiplicity of political views involved. These views were the outcome of very diverse interests and were expressed by innumerable short-lived and vague coalitions, which their partisans tried to shape together under circumstances that were often precarious and sometimes even completely absurd. The Yugoslavian government, for example, in its attempt to forge national unity, had tried in vain to promote the well-known slogan "Brat je mio koje vere bio," which translates roughly, "We are all brothers, regardless of our creed." This slogan, apparently generous and "democratic," came into conflict from the start with everyday situations that local Muslims found absolutely unacceptable.

Although a great number of the Muslims of Bosnia-Herzegovina declared themselves Serbians of Muslim faith, Serbian ideology was unacceptable for many others, because it cast these Muslims in the unenviable role of "renegades," by glorifying Saint Sava, the "Myth of the Nemanids" and the "Myth of Kosovo." In this role the Muslims bore the burden of the "treason" of their ancestors *ad vitam aeternam* and were thus forever excluded from participation in national glory.

During the subsequent period of 1941–44, atrocious events further embittered the situation, when an important party of Muslims (several of whom resigned publicly from October 1941 onward) participated actively in the Croat Ustasha State and in the terrible massacres ending in the deaths of several hundreds of thousands of the Orthodox Serbian population of the region. Some of the Četniki, monarchist and anti-Communist Serbian resistance fighters, retaliated by destroying Muslim cities and towns. Adequate and objective documentation is lacking for this sad and difficult period.

Numerous publications since 1945 have discussed the role of Muslims in the resistance, as well as the actions of the Četniki, who have been invariably depicted as disgraceful traitors. But until recently there has been no analysis of the role of an important group of Muslims in Bosnia-Herzegovina who collaborated very closely with the occupying German forces in the fascist Croatian state. To this author's knowledge, the first to speak about this situation was Meša Selimović in his memoirs, "Sjećanja";[4] the first text to venture into this taboo subject to be published in Yugoslavia was "Parergon,"[5] by Derviš Sušić, which will be discussed below.

Eastern Yugoslavia

Among the diverse groups of Muslims of eastern Yugoslavia—those of Sanjak, Kosovo, Montenegro, southern Serbia, and Macedonia—circumstances were different, and were often much worse than that of their coreligionists in Bosnia-Herzegovina. One source of difference is the fact that these Muslims endured—for the most part as helpless onlookers—the long agony and ultimate disintegration of "The Sick Man of Europe" (the Ottoman Empire). For this same reason Western and Central European progress in such areas as technology, science, culture, and hygiene only reached them much later, which explains why these "eastern" Muslims trail behind those of the west in all respects, even today. For it is an undeniable fact that Austrian occupation, seeking its own ends, of course, rather than any humanitarian aims, did much more to raise the cultural level of Bosnia-Herzegovina than did the lethargic, backward, and moribund Ottoman Empire of that time.

Another factor that served to worsen the situation in the east derived from the liberation of these eastern regions from the Turks by the Serbian army in the course of the Russo-Turkish War of 1877–78 and the Balkan Wars of 1912 and 1913. "Southern Serbia," the heart of the medieval Serbian state, was where the most important sanctuaries of medieval Serbian history were located, and its liberation prolonged for several decades the explosion of Pan-Serbian nationalism. In the exhilaration of recovering "ancestral lands" from over five centuries of Ottoman control, the proponents of this type of nationalism treated the Muslims of these regions—particularly those of Turkic and Albanian origin—as second-rate citizens, much inferior to the Slavic Muslims of Bosnia-Herzegovina.

A third reason, long ignored in scholarship, for the unfortunate state of affairs in the east was the ancient and fierce animosity of part of the Serbian population, generally Orthodox, toward the Albanian Muslims, whom they had always considered a Balkan police force in the service of the Ottomans. This animosity has been reciprocated by the Albanians, for whom, quite logically, Serbian nationalism was, and still is, a primary enemy.

Current Problems

At the close of the Second World War, the policies of the Yugoslavian government were marked by extreme antireligious sentiment, as was the case in the other people's republics. In Yugoslavia's case, this sentiment, however, took on slightly different tones with regard to the various religions of the country. In this campaign, led by the Yugoslav Communist Party under the famous slogan "Religion is the Opiate of the People," a tripartite concern became apparent.

The first consideration—that of avoiding direct conflict with the Muslim populations—had already become apparent among the Yugoslav Communist Party at the time of the resistance, as is clear in the great number of brochures written to placate the country's Muslims. The second consideration was the need to tread lightly on the toes of the Catholic high clergy, keeping in mind, presumably, the power of the Vatican, which the affair of Cardinal Stepinac demonstrated. The third objective was the dismantling of the Orthodox Church, which would not provoke any significant foreign reaction at all.

Beginning in 1948, the date of the rupture between Belgrade and Moscow, however, this situation began to change in an unexpected and dramatic fashion. Until 1979 there was a steady evolution toward religious liberalism, deriving its impetus from local nationalisms, in conjunction with economic problems and the bourgeoisie gained increasing political power. This religious liberalism, in turn, gave rise to a formidable religious revival, in which religion served, above all, as the sole "legal" means of affirming the power and the aspirations of local nationalisms.

What motivated this revival of religion among the Muslims of Yugo-slavia, which could not have been foreseen in 1945? A number of factors were involved, but their relative importance is difficult to assess, par-ticularly since they were ambiguous and ill-defined—a fact that allowed Muslims in different areas to apply them according to the circumstances and political situation of the moment.

The most significant of these factors was the deep religiousness of a great majority of the Muslims, combined with the need for religion that may be found at the popular level, both in towns and in rural areas. This sentiment may be pleasing or displeasing, according to the observer's convictions, but what must be emphasized here is the fact that the press vacillated in its treatment, sometimes seeking to minimize the role of religious spirit; at other times speaking about it quite openly in order to prove the liberalism of the system.

The second factor, no less important, was rooted in the necessity of affirming a local nationalism which, for the inhabitants of Bosnia-Herzegovina who were of Muslim background, could only refer to Islam. The concept of Islam, however, tended to vary in emphasis on secular socialism or spiritual faith according to the moment.

These two factors came to light because of a complex constellation of internal circumstances, created by the long-standing existence of mul-tiple problems transcending both nation and religious belief, further aggravated by a precarious economic situation. Most prominent among these difficulties, however, were a number of political decisions that the government had believed sound, but whose consequences later brought about suffering.

These problems will be outlined briefly: after Marshal Tito (Josip Broz) had decided to play a leading role in the bloc of "Non-Engaged" —later, "Non-Aligned"—nations, which were predominantly Muslim states, Yugoslavia was compelled to reinforce its position through the support of its own Muslim community. The Yugoslav Muslims were thus granted freedoms and material advantages, with the evident goal of eventually exploiting this situation in foreign policy, in relations with Arabic and other Muslim countries.

The leaders of the Supreme Islamic Authority of Yugoslavia regularly applied this "normalization of relations" (the euphemism frequently used by the Muslim press) between the government and the Muslim community to their own advantage. These leaders succeeded in securing their position and in gaining a solid structure for their entire organiza-tion: in effect, they achieved a more stable situation than they had ever had before. They were successful because they proceeded with utmost caution, and they were careful to represent each new initiative as the normal offshoot of the needs of the Muslim community and as wholly in accord with the constitutional rights of that community. Finally, by putting themselves under the protection of the state and its laws from the very beginning, they also took measures against any eventual attacks.

This action, in other words, was so effectively utilized by the Muslim authorities that it greatly surpassed the primitive schemes of the government, which found itself completely outmaneuvered. The reactions of the press conveyed the awkwardness of the state of affairs in the Yugoslav Communist Party (which had in the meantime become the League of Yugoslav Communists). The party was obliged to devise new plans, publishing texts that seemed convincing, but its intentions had no practical effect whatsoever. In the main Yugoslavian journals, for example, a reader might find a statement to the effect that: "because certain indices point to a remarkable revival of religion," a certain central committee of the party, or some directors of the Socialist Union, had met to discuss what measures to take. A glance through the Muslim periodicals, however, would reveal the extent to which daily events surpassed the information furnished by these indices.

The euphoric period of the Yugoslav Muslim community lasted twenty-five years, and it was well publicized by the press in the international community. The Yugoslav authorities seemed to be taken by surprise, and the question arose as to whether they would ever be able to take control of the situation again. The leaders of the Muslim community, now stronger than ever, portrayed socialism not only as a sort of outgrowth of Islamic ideology, but as a flawed by-product, lacking any spiritual component.

When the government finally reached a decision, the matter was conducted with great fanfare and was under control within a short time. Beginning in August 1979, the journal *Oslobodjenje* published a series of articles entitled "Parergon," extracted from the work of a Muslim communist, Dervis Sušić. One of the targets of the author's attacks was a part of the Yugoslav Muslim "clergy," on account of the role it had played between the two World Wars and during the German occupation. The presentation of these events by current Muslim authorities was treated with particular scorn.

Those toward whom the criticism was directed responded immediately, but feebly. Several responses were published, accompanied by a photograph showing Marshal Tito receiving important Muslim religious figures, a gesture that no longer had any importance. Some time afterward, Marshal Tito made a speech that set the tone for the new situation. On 23 September 1979, the dedication of a new mosque, in a village in Bosnia near Bugoino, served as a pretext for speeches that were actually part of a campaign to denigrate two of the principal leaders of the Yugoslav Muslim community. One of the leaders was reproached, among other things, for his conduct during the Second World War. Need it be repeated that these same leaders must have made dozens of speeches of this type and that, in any case, they had occupied their respective positions for twenty or even thirty years? (Subsequently, one of the two, shortly before his death, regained a high-ranking official position, while the other ultimately kept his post.)

No great fuss was made about this affair. Several people were forced into early retirement; there were changes in the staffs of the main Muslim religious publications, and constraints were placed on official Muslim delegations to other countries, as well as on the reception of such delegations. After a brief period of uncertainty, however, a new cadre took charge. It is very difficult at this time to form a clear idea of these men's inclinations, opportunities and aspirations, both for the middle and long range. What is certain is that there are a number of factions (as is attested by the relatively recent stepping-down of one prominent leader, as well as of the community spokesman), and that each faction has its own following.

It is difficult to predict what the situation will be in the future. It is true that the government was able to take control when required. After the death of Marshal Tito in 1980, however, the government has had to face other critical problems in the economic, social, and political spheres. Like all governments, it must play its cards on several tables at once, taking account of the value of oil in considering its relations with Arab and other Muslim countries.

The task of the leaders of the Muslim religious community appears to be much simpler. There is only one thing they need to do, regardless of who is in power in the state government: they must organize themselves, consolidating their position and trying to win back their 'lost advantages bit by bit. This purpose is best served, on the one hand, by playing the card of "Islamic socialism" and, on the other, by drawing maximum benefit from the Yugoslav government's need to make a good impression on the Arab and Muslim world.

Islamic Movements

Yugoslavia comprises five groups of Muslims: three small (Macedonian Muslims, those of Montenegro, and the Turkish minority) and two large (the Albanian Muslims of Kosovo and the Muslims, or Muslimani, of Bosnia-Herzegovina). No radicalism, whether religious or national, is to be expected among the first three groups, which are numerically small and relatively unorganized. Rather, as might well be expected, it is in the two larger groups that radical movements have arisen.

It is impossible to know exactly how many Muslims there are in Yugoslavia, for the most recent censuses give no data on religious belief. Their number must surpass—perhaps widely—the figure of 2.67 million given by the 1981 census. The three principal groups of Muslims are in Bosnia-Herzegovina, Serbia, and Macedonia. Those in Bosnia-Herzegovina include people of Muslim nationality (Muslimani), but not necessarily of the Muslim faith, as well as Serbian and Croatian Muslims, numbering all together about two million. In Serbia, and particularly in the autonomous region of Kosovo, Albanian Muslims predominate, numbering over a million, but there are also some tens of thousands of Turkish Muslims. In Macedonia, the number of Macedonian Muslims is probably about one hundred thousand, with the addition of some hundreds of thousands of Albanian Muslims and over one hundred thousand Turkish Muslims. One other group needs to be added to these three: there are perhaps some tens of thousands of Muslims in Montenegro, both of Montenegrin and Albanian origin. Finally, scattered throughout the country, there are some tens of thousands of Muslim Gypsies, as well as approximately the same number of other Muslims of the nationalities cited above.

Montenegro

The Muslim community of Montenegro is of little concern here, because its members have an insignificant role in the leadership of the "Supreme Islamic authority of Yugoslavia," and they play an insignificant role in politics generally.

Macedonia

From 1945 onward, the Muslim community of Macedonia (comprising Macedonians,[6] Albanians, and Turks) has been little discussed: its situation, both now and in the recent past, has been a taboo subject. The riots in Kosovo in April 1981, as well as the Macedonian authorities' fear of the heavy infiltration of Albanians, lasting several decades, from Kosovo, touched off a series of activities that had a strong effect on this community. In September 1981, in the small town of Gostivar, an academic conference was hastily convened to study the Muslims of Macedonia; recently, a madrasah opened in Skopje; a Macedonian Muslim periodical has been issued. It is also rumored that a formerly taboo theme has been revived: that of the troubled circumstances under which part of the local Turkish population left so suddenly for Turkey, around the year 1950.[7]

Serbia

The Muslim community of Serbia is composed of Albanians, and is centered around Prishtina, the capital of the autonomous region of Kosovo. There has been a great surge of interest in this religious community, following the pro-Albanian riots in Kosovo in April 1981. The leaders of the local Muslim community appear to have played no role in these disturbances, which is easily explained by the fact that radical nationalist sentiments, without any religious component, were the motivating factor.

These events allowed the lifting of two other taboos of the Yugoslavian post-World War II period. The first taboo concerned the recognition of the awakening, and subsequent explosion, of pro-Albanian nationalism among part of the Albanian population of Kosovo. The second taboo was brought to light by a delayed, but official, statement by current Yugoslav leaders. It concerned the existence—for several decades—of the strong pressures on the region's Serbian and Montenegrin population, which have been exerted with the complicity of the authorities by some of the Albanian population of Kosovo. These pressures have forced the Serbs and Montenegrins in the region to emigrate, selling at very low prices— or simply abandoning—all their property: lands, houses, and livestock. Whether the local Albanian Muslim community played any role in these events is still not known.[8]

The case of Dobrica Ćosić, the well-known Serbian novelist and, at that time, politician, gives evidence of the strength of the second taboo. Ćosić broke this taboo, speaking about the situation among the Serbian and Montenegrin population in Kosovo, at the Fourteenth Congress of the Central Communist Party, on 29 May 1968; he was subsequently compelled to step down from his position. The text of what he said on 29 May 1968, was published in 1982, in an edition of several of his essays, which sold out in record time.[9] The authorities responded vigorously against the publishing house that had dared to issue this text.

Bosnia-Herzegovina

The Muslim community of Bosnia-Herzegovina comprises the most numerous and important Muslim population in Yugoslavia. Mention has been made above of the political courses of action taken since the Conference of Bandung of 1955 by the Yugoslavian government vis-à-vis Arab countries and those countries of the Third World with a Muslim majority.

These measures have allowed the Muslim community of Yugoslavia—and particularly that of Bosnia-Herzegovina, the home of all the high-level leaders—to benefit from a situation that was more stable than ever before, as was said above. It involved several types of freedom of action, as well as material advantages, but this privileged status was considerably reduced in 1979. There was subsequently a significant amelioration of that community's status and then, shortly thereafter, there were two consecutive internal crises, involving new factors that might be termed as follows: first, "the affair of secular Islamic radicalism" and, second, "the affair of religious Islamic radicalism." How can these two factors be evaluated?

Secular Islamic radicalism. This issue of secular Islamic radicalism is wrapped up in an escalation of Muslim nationalism, officially secular, "progressive," and "revolutionary," but in fact inextricably linked, in one way or another, to religious factors. This escalation, which has been taking place over the past few decades, has been especially apparent among one sector of the local Muslim intelligentsia. On the political and cultural plane, this escalation of nationalism is manifest in the perceived need to revise completely the history of the locality. Nationalism also shows itself in a need to reassess its cultural history, under the assumption that non-Muslims have underestimated—and perhaps even voluntarily deformed—that past. Because of the political climate, this reaction, which would otherwise be quite legitimate, soon came to involve excess and even aberrations.[10]

In effect, this movement had begun as a quest for increased recognition for the culture of the Muslimani of Bosnia-Herzegovina within the larger framework of Yugoslavian culture. The movement then shifted quickly toward a view privileging this particular culture. Among a certain number of its proponents (who received strong support from local Muslimani politicians), the movement culminated in the obscuring and, finally, the falsification of both the literary and the general cultural history of the locality.[11] The movement also sought to use any means available to discredit those who did not go along with these adulterations of history.

Discussion of this subject was completely taboo until a set of publications first brought it to light in the fall of 1981. These publications, consisting of articles in journals and magazines, literary reviews and even in several books, appeared in Belgrade and in Zagreb, were issued by well-known intellectuals and academicians, some—and perhaps all—of whom were members of the Communist Party.[12]

Using irrefutable and overwhelming evidence, these publications denounced the continual falsification of the local history, and literary history, of the nineteenth and twentieth centuries, by certain Muslimani intellectuals—that is to say, "laymen" and, in this particular case, party members—of Bosnia-Herzegovina. These intellectuals were said to be in collusion with the high-ranking Muslimani leaders of that Federal Republic, who supported and sanctioned their activities.

The other target of these articles' criticism was the surge of Islamic radicalism, not only among actual religious circles, but also among certain high-ranking Muslimani (again, "laymen" and members of the party) of Bosnia-Herzegovina. That radicalism was said to reveal a reprehensible sympathy toward the "eternal values" of Islam while offering no such sentiments toward the Catholic or Orthodox churches, and to be far too obliging in the search for "rapprochement" between Marxism and Islam.[13]

Defense of these Muslimani intellectuals was immediately assured by the highest political leaders of Bosnia-Herzegovina, at which point an extremely virulent polemic ensued, centering more and more around the "nationalist and religious political climate" that was said to prevail in Sarajevo.[14] The character of this polemic enabled these authors to bring out a number of facts that were well known, but which had not been previously discussed, such as the departure from Sarajevo of the famous Muslim of Serbian nationality (according to his own terms), Meša Selimović, and his installation at Belgrade.[15]

Above all else, however, this polemic opened the way for official recognition of another phenomenon: that of Muslim religious radicalism. Previously, this subject had only been treated in the most guarded terms, and it was now presented without precise information regarding either its features or its scope.

Religious Islamic radicalism. The history of contemporary Islamic religious radicalism in Bosnia-Herzegovina is extremely simple to describe. It follows three quite distinct phases: the phase of negation, the phase of threats and accusations, and, finally, the phase of trials and condemnations.

In the course of the first phase, lasting until the summer of 1982, the existence of Islamic radicalism was more or less categorically denied.[16] Prior to that date, of course, some published articles denounced certain individuals as "black sheep," but these articles typically called for vigilance against "interior and exterior enemies." They also followed faithfully the "three mandatory parts" principle: that of never attacking an imam or other Muslim religious official without also attacking—in the same article and in precisely analogous fashion—a member of the Catholic clergy and an Orthodox priest.[17]

The second phase began between summer and autumn of 1982. Examination of the situation at that time gives the distinct impression that political leaders, citing the "damage" caused by those who had denounced secular Islamic radicalism, determined to fight back. Their strategy involved showing the public that they could clean up their own yards and that they were able to protect the secular Muslimani intellectuals from the ceaseless attacks of their critics. A great deal of political posturing ensued, in which the most visible politicians of Bosnia-Herzegovina assailed in ever stronger attacks the individuals and groups who had fallen to the demon of Islamic radicalism (or, rather, of Pan-Islamism, according to the misguided terminology of the Yugoslav media), an insidious and partially imported disease, whose existence they had previously denied.[18]

The third phase began in April 1983, with the incarceration of eleven people at Sarajevo who had been convicted of "counterrevolutionary activities inspired by Muslim nationalism." They were accused of "conducting their activities on the basis of Muslim nationalist positions, with the goal of overthrowing the social order and establishing an Islamic power. . . . United around a platform [entitled] the Islamic Declaration. The group sought to transform Bosnia-Herzegovina into an ethnically pure Islamic state. It also attempted to gain the support of several foreign states by manipulating some of their institutions."[19] This phase came to an end on 20 August 1983, and after the lengthy trial, extracts of which the Yugoslavian press published daily, concluded in very heavy sentences ranging from five to fifteen years' imprisonment.[20] According to the press, the defense lawyers spoke in favor of the release of the defendants, on the basis of their belief that the trial had not provided unequivocal evidence of their guilt.[21]

At the time, everything seemed to be in order. The case of Islamic radicalism, both secular and religious, seemed to be closed. The problems broke out once again, however, with the publication of the new edition of the most important Yugoslav encyclopedia, *Enciklopedija Jugoslavija.* Soon after the second volume of this encyclopedia came out, it appeared that some of the articles about Bosnia-Herzegovina had been compiled and edited by adherents of secular Islamic radicalism, during the period of their invulnerability. Once again voices arose in protest against the mystification and falsification concerning the collusion of "Militant Islam" and "Militant Christianity," but this time the voices were those of Sarajevo intellectuals.[22] Then, as before, the principal political leaders of the region covered up the matter, attempting to defuse the situation, as well as issuing scarcely veiled threats against those who continued to raise an outcry.[23]

Final Remarks

The events in Yugoslavia call to mind a phrase from *La forêt en feu*, by Simon Leys, on the subject of China: "a totalitarian society, served by a greedy and corrupt bureaucracy that paralyzes all initiative."

This brief overview of events has not sought to draw conclusions, much less to make predictions concerning an unforeseeable future. The objective here has been merely to present one complex aspect of the Yugoslav puzzle that is generally little known, and about which much misinformation is published daily by both the Yugoslav media and the Arab and foreign Muslim press. The only thing that can be stated with certainty about Islamic radicalism in Yugoslavia is that it exists, to varying degrees, in the two forms that have been discussed. At the present time, however, no one can say precisely what its dimensions are today, much less what they will be tomorrow.

Notes

1. For information on all of these groups, see the excellent article by Marie-Paule Canapa, "L'islam et la question des nationalités en Yougoslavie," in *Radicalismes islamiques* 2, ed. Oliver Carré and Paul Dumont (Paris: L'Harmattan, 1986), pp. 100–50.

The term *Muslimani*, from the Serbo-Croatian, is used in this essay to designate those of Muslim nationality, independent of religious affiliation.

2. At this writing, it remains impossible to determine the origins of the idea of the "Muslim Nation." Apparently, this designation was supposed to apply only to the residents of Bosnia-Herzegovina, but there seems to have been no official act to that effect. The fact that the term was thus poorly defined has led to a whole series of problems, as in the case of the Macedonian Muslims.

Evidently, neither academic expertise nor local opinion was taken into consideration in determining who should belong to the "Muslim Nation," except to give the gloss of legitimacy to the decision once it was made. See, for example, "Um die Schaffung einer 'Mohammedanischen' Nation in Jugoslawien," *Osteuropa* 1 (1971): A43–A50; "Streit um die Anerkennung der bosnisch-herzegowinischen Mohammedaner als Nation," *Osteuropa* 4 (1975): A236–A241.

3. According to a frequently cited passage by P. Bourdieu, "L'histoire de la transfor-

mation du mythe en religion (idéologie) n'est pas séparable de l'histoire de la constitution d'un corps de producteurs de discours et de rites religieux, qui est luimême une
dimension du progrès de la division du travail social, que conduit entre autres consé-
quences à déposséder des laïcs des instruments de production symboliques." "Sur le
pouvoir symbolique," *Annales* (May–June 1977): 409.

4. It appeared in *Kritičari o Meši Selimoviću* (Sarajevo: Svjetlost, 1973), pp. 340–41.

5. In *Oslobodjenje* (Sarajevo, August 1970).

6. Cf. D. Hr. Konstantinov, "Makedonci muslimani," *Prilozi. Društvo za nauka i umetnost* (Bitola, 1970), pp. 139–146. This essay is among the very few works on the Macedonian community written prior to 1981.

7. Two observations should be added with regard to the Turkish community in Yugoslavia. The first is the existence of a local urban "intelligentsia," who are lay-persons, and often ostensibly nonreligious. This group, like other small ethnic minorities in Yugoslavia, has gained substantial benefits, particularly on the socio-cultural level.

Secondly, there has been slow but constant emigration of ethnic Turks—adherents of "traditional" Islam—from the villages of Yugoslavia to Turkey. This emigration has been especially heavy from Kosovo since 1981. Yugoslav authorities have tried to obscure the reasons for this trend by attributing it to unemployment. See, for example, Enver Nobırda, "Göç nedenleri çok fakat başlıcası issizlik," *Tan* 897 (Priština, 6 December 1986), p. 2; "Mamusa'dan göç olayını tam yansıtmayan bir yayın," *Tan* 898 (Priština, 13 December 1986), p. 15.

8. The summaries of the Kosovo trial published by the Belgrade press give only indirect evidence for a single case of possible participation by religious Albanian Muslims in the insurrections of April 1981 (see *Politika*, 8 August 1981, p. 8, concerning a trial in Peć). It is unclear, however, whether Albanian Muslims were actually not involved in these events, or whether the press conformed to official demands for silence on this subject.

9. D. Ćosić, *Stvarno i moguće, Članci i ogledi* (Rijeka: Otokar Kersovani, 1982), particularly the chapter "Kritika vladajuće ideološke koncepcije u nacionalnoj politici," pp. 54–70. On the Ćosić incident, see, for example, H. Flottau, "Neuer Bannstrahl gegen die Propheten," *Süddeutsche Zeitung*, 15 February 1983, p. 3. Innumerable publications have treated the "Kosovo Affair," three of which are worth mentioning here: Stevan K. Pavlovitch and Elez Beberaj, "The Albanian Problem in Yugoslavia: Two Views," in *Conflict Studies* 137/138 (London: Institute for the Study of Conflict, 1982); Dimitrije Bogdanović, "Kosovo u svetlu istorije albansko-južnoslovenskih odnosa," in *Savremenik* 56/12 (Belgrade, December 1982), pp. 523–37 (an extract of this essay can be found in *Knjiga o Kosovu* [Belgrade: Srpska Akademija Nauka i Umetnosti, 1985]); Batrić Jovanović, "Prisilno iseljavanje Srba i Crnogoraca sa Kosova je izuzetno tamna mrlja u istoriji SFRJ," *Intervju* 65 (Belgrade, 25 November 1983), pp. 8–11.

10. A number of political scientists specializing in Eastern Europe have described this dynamic as "the promotion of nationalism among minorities in order to create or strengthen a totalitarian regime."

11. The author of this chapter has discussed this phenomenon from the perspective of local Ottoman literature in a number of publications. For example, see A. Popović, "La littérature ottomane des musulmans yougoslaves," *Journal Asiatique* 259/3–4

(1971): 309–76; and "Le poète Servi Bosnavi a-t-il existé?" *Turcica* 9/2-X (1978): 30–38.

12. See especially two articles by P. Šimunović: "Stare zablude i novi zanosi," *Književnost* (Belgrade, 1982/9), pp. 1395–1413; and "Da li su u pitanju samo zanosi ili kako se postaje slučaj," *Književnost* (Belgrade, 1983/3–4), pp. 699–721. See also the following articles by V. Šešelj: "Univerzalne teorije i njihovi sledbenici," *Književna Reč* 175 (Belgrade, 25 October 1981), p. 5; "Ostvetnički pohod sljedbenika 'Univerzalne teorije," *Književna Reč*, 25 November 1981, p. 3; "O sarajevskoj kulturnoj razglednici," *Duga* 221 (Belgrade, 14 August 1982), p. 7; "U cara Trojana kozje uši," *Danas* I/26 (Zagreb, 17 August 1982), pp. 45–46. Other articles on the subject include M. Kalezić, "Jančićeva 'izdaja'," *Duga* 218 (Belgrade, 3–19 July 1982), pp. 54–55; I. Dacić, "Izazov za polemiku," *Danas* I/26 (Zagreb, 17 August 1982), p. 43; Z. Sekulić, "Lažov Bili," *Duga* 224 (Belgrade, 25 September 1982), pp. 20–22; Idem, "Istina jedini kriterijum," *Duga* 227 (Belgrade, 6–20 November 1982).

13. The most typical example of this type of literature is Atif Purivatra's "Libijska 'Zelena Knjiga'," *Odjek* 1 (1981): 17: a well-intended analysis of Mu'ammar Qaddafi's "Green Book." Atif Purivatra is a Marxist theoretician from Bosnia-Herzegovina. Before writing this essay, he had participated in an international symposium organized by Libya in Madrid.

14. See, especially, the immediate reaction by Fuad Muhić, "Zašto je 'Književna reč' podzemlje," *Politika* (6 January 1982), as well as his later articles, "Osumnjičeni za ajatoaštvo," *Danas* I/24 (3 August 1982), pp. 11–13; "Žal za unitarizmom," ibid. (31 August 1982), pp. 9–10. See also Branko Mikulić, "Neprincipijelna čeprkanja po prošlosti," *Oslobodjenje* (Sarajevo, 16 October 1982), as well as the discussions by Hamija Pozderac, Branko Mikulić, Hasan Grabčanovic, et al., concerning various TsK sessions of the Communist League of Bosnia-Herzegovina (see, for example, "Neuralgične tačke ili nacionalizam," *NIN* 1672 [Belgrade, 16 January 1983], pp. 26–27; "Ne postoji 'naš' i 'vaš' nacionalizam," *Politika* 26 [February 1983], p. 6). Finally, see several similar texts by "second-rate" authors; for example, M. Mujkić, "Bez zanastvene ocene," *Danas* I/28 (31 August 1982), pp. 43–44; Dr. V. D., "Opasna podjela etiketa," ibid., p. 44; M. H. Grabčanović, "Nisam ratni zločinac," ibid., pp. 44–45; M. Filipović, "Šešelj me nije iznenadio," *Danas* I/29 (7 September 1982), p. 42; M. Kovačević, "Šta nije sporno?" *Oslobodjenje* (Sarajevo, 15 October 1982); M. Imamovic, "Panislamizam i 'panislamizam'," *Odjek*, no. 20 (Sarajevo, 1982), pp. 3, 5.

15. Since that time, other intellectuals, such as V. Lubarda, have had to leave Sarajevo, apparently for similar reasons. On this subject, see the vehement reaction of Fuad Muhić, "Glavni junak tužne priče," *Svijet* 1252 (Sarajevo, 31 May 1982), pp. 24–26, as well as those of G. Jakšić, R. Petrov Nogo, and E. Ćimić. E. Ćimić's *Politika kao sudbina* (Belgrade: Velika edicija "Ideja," 1982) is a typical example of a "confession." It gave rise to several commentaries, some of the most interesting of which are: Kasim Prohić, "Istina kao fikcija," *NIN* 1675 (6 February 1983), pp. 4, 6, 15; Nikola Milošević, "Carstvo nebesko i carstvo zemaljsko," *NIN* 1675 (6 February 1983), pp. 4, 6, 20; Gojko Marinković, "Plač nad vlastitom sudbinom," *Danas* II/53 (22 February 1983), pp. 14–16; Fuad Muhić, "Igre s politikom," ibid., pp. 16–18.

16. One of the most recent articles of this type is by A. Smajlović, "U svijetu smo najsamostalniji," *Danas* 32 (Zagreb, 28 September 1982), pp. 11–13.

17. Among the numerous publications written on this subject, see, for example, D. Marić, "Daleko od molitve," *Politika* (9 September 1981), p. 11.

18. The first people to discuss this matter appear to have been F. Muhić, "Osumnjičeni za ajatolaštvo," *Danas* (3 August 1982), pp. 11–13, and H. Pozderac, as described by M. Durić in "Pusti snovi nacionalista," *Politika* (17 September 1982), p. 4. See also D. Lazarević, "Ponekad se crkva bavi i politikom," *Politika* (22 December 1982); the interview by H. Ištuk in *Intervju* 44, no. 176 (Belgrade, 4 February 1983), pp. 15–18; excerpts of a speech by B. Mikulić in *Politika* (24 March 1983), p. 6; M. Durić, "Referisanje 'borbenog islama'," *Politika* (6 April 1983); Durić, "Preko nacionalizma se dolazi u fašizam," and "O varijantama 'panislamizma,'" *Politika* (17 April 1983), p. 6; F. Muhić, "Paranoične ideje o 'muslimanskoj republici,'" *Nedeljna Borba* (30 April/3 May 1983), p. 13; Muhić, "Scila prošlosti-Haribda budućnosti," *Svijet* 1300 (Sarajevo, 2 May 1983), pp. 11, 14; H. Pozderac, "Recidivi panislamizma," *Borba* (18 May 1983), p. 2; Pozderac, "Zaverenički protiv sopstvene zemlje," *Politika* (19 May 1983), p. 6; Pozderac, "Rasprava o političkoj ulozi islama," *Politika* (19 May 1983), p. 4; Pozderac, "Manipuliše se verskim osećanjima," *Politika* (23 June 1983), p. 4; the interview by H. Pozderac, *Oslobodjenje* (Sarajevo, 11 June 1983), p. 2. Also of note are two important articles: S. Grozdanić, "O islamskom fundamentalizmu," *Odjek* 36/11 (Sarajevo, 1–15 June 1983), pp. 6–7, on Islamic radicalism in general; N. Duraković, "Otkud panislamizam na kraju 20. veka, pa još kod nas," *Intervju* 25, no. 8 (July 1983), pp. 44–45, on Islamic radicalism in Yugoslavia.

19. *Le Monde* (23 August 1983), p. 24. See the English translation of the Islamic Declaration: Alija A. Izetbegović, *Islam between East and West* (Indianapolis: American Trust Publications, 1984), and the Turkish translation: Ali Izzetbegović, *Doğu ve Batı arasında İslâm* (Istanbul: Nehir Yayınları, 1987) (400 pages, translated from the Serbo-Croatian text "Islam izedju Istoka i Zapada treća alternativa"). For a summary of the English translation, see Stevan K. Pavlović, "Muslimanska 'neprijateljska propaganda,'" *Naša reč*, no. 384 (Harrow/Middlesex, April 1987), p. 14.

20. It would be unhelpful and tedious to cite all of the numerous articles that appeared between 9 April and 11 November 1983. Since it is not the purpose of the present essay to put forth any judgment regarding those who were indicted, nor, certainly, to analyze the systems of Yugoslav jurisprudence, the reader is referred to the numerous documents on the subject that are available, particularly the observations of the Yugoslav press between July and August 1983. The author's careful study of these publications would seem to suggest that this trial conforms to the pattern of hundreds—perhaps even thousands—that have taken place in Yugoslavia in recent decades. In addition, it appears that some Yugoslav journalists are quite capable of traducing, in a base and sycophantic manner, the completely defenseless (current) enemies of the regime.

21. On the question of "Muslim radicalism" in Yugoslavia, see Jens Reuter, "Islam in Jugoslawien in der Offensive?" *Südosteuropa* 9 (1984): 482–90.

22. See, for example, M. Durić, "Osporeni autori i merila," *Politika* (1 October 1983), p. 13; Durić, "Odgovori autora kritikovanih tekstova," ibid. (18 October 1983), p. 10; Durić, "Istina o 'El Hidaji,'" *Politika* (19 October 1983), p. 12; "Spor iz Enciklopeije," *Večernje Novosti* (20 October 1983); "Književnost NOB u dvadeset redi,"

Politika Ekspres (29 October 1983). See also the much older, but very informative, article by M. Mišović, "Razmedjavanje prošlosti," *NIN* 1644 (4 July 1982), pp. 29–31.

23. See M. Durić, "Za dijalog bez zle namere," *Politika* (21 October 1983), p. 12; Durić, "Potrebne dalje rasprave," *Politika* (25 October 1983), p. 12; Durić, "I dalje različita mišljenja," *Politika* (28 October 1983), p. 10.

Appendix *Statistical Tables and Figures*

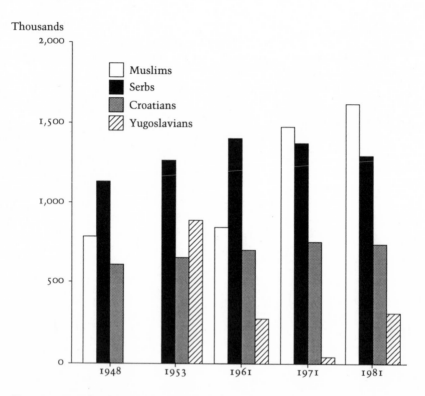

Figure 1   People of Bosnia-Herzegovina

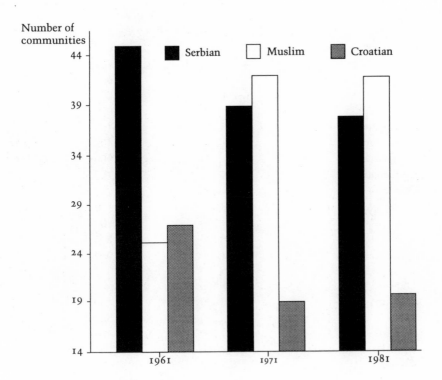

Figure 2   Communities of Bosnia-Herzegovina
According to Majority Groups

Table 1   Population of Ethnic Groups in the USSR
(existing boundaries)

	Total		
	1926	1939	1959
Total Population	147,027,900	170,557,100	208,826,700
Russians	77,791,100	99,591,500	114,113,600
Ukrainians	31,195,000	28,111,000	37,252,900
Belorussians	4,738,900	5,275,400	7,913,500
Lithuanians	41,500	32,600	2,326,100
Latvians	141,600	128,000	1,399,500
Estonians	154,700	143,000	988,600
Moldavians	278,900	260,400	2,214,100
Georgians	1,821,200	2,249,600	2,692,000
Armenians	1,567,600	2,152,900	2,786,900
Azerbaijanians	1,706,600	2,275,700	2,939,700
Uzbeks	3,904,600	4,845,100	6,015,400
Kazakhs	3,968,300	3,100,900	3,621,600
Turkmens	763,900	812,400	1,001,600
Tajiks	978,700	1,229,200	1,396,900
Kirghiz	762,700	884,600	968,700
Tatars	2,916,300	4,313,500	4,967,700
Chuvash	1,117,400	1,369,600	1,469,800
Mordvins	1,340,400	1,456,300	1,285,100
Maris	428,200	481,600	504,200
Udmurts	504,200	606,300	624,800
Komi/Komi Permyaks	375,900	422,300	430,900
Karelians	248,100	252,700	167,300
Kalmyks	132,000	134,400	106,100
Chechens	318,500	408,000	418,800
Bashkirs	713,700	843,600	989,000
Kabardins	139,900	164,200	203,600
Balkars	33,300	42,700	42,400
Ossetins	272,200	354,800	412,600
Ingush	74,100	92,100	106,000
Karachays	55,100	75,800	81,400
Cherkess	65,300	—	30,500
Avars	158,800	252,800	270,400
Lezgins	134,500	221,000	223,100
Dargins	109,000	153,800	158,100
Kumyks	94,600	112,600	135,000
Laks	40,400	56,100	63,500
Nogays	36,300	36,600	38,600
Tabasarans	32,000	33,600	34,700

		Percent Increase			
1970	1979	1926–39	1939–59	1959–70	1970–79
241,720,100	262,084,700	15.7	9.5[a]	15.8	8.4
129,015,100	137,397,100	28.0	13.7[a]	13.0	6.5
40,753,200	42,347,400	−9.9	4.6[a]	9.4	3.9
9,051,800	9,462,700	11.3	−4.4[a]	14.4	4.5
2,664,900	2,850,900	−21.4	14.4[a]	14.6	7.0
1,429,800	1,439,000	−9.6	−14.1[a]	2.2	0.6
1,007,400	1,019,900	−7.2	−13.6[a]	1.9	1.2
2,698,000	2,968,200	−6.6	7.5[a]	21.8	10.0
3,245,300	3,570,500	23.5	19.7	20.5	10.0
3,559,200	4,151,200	37.3	29.4	27.7	16.6
4,379,900	5,477,300	33.3	29.2	49.0	25.1
9,195,100	12,456,000	24.1	24.2	52.8	35.5
5,298,800	6,556,400	−21.9	16.8	46.3	23.7
1,525,300	2,027,900	6.3	23.3	52.2	33.0
2,135,900	2,897,700	25.6	13.6	52.9	35.7
1,452,200	1,906,300	16.0	9.5	49.9	31.3
5,930,700	6,317,500	47.9	15.2	19.4	6.5
1,694,400	1,751,400	22.6	7.3	15.2	3.4
1,262,700	1,191,800	8.4	−11.8	−1.7	−5.6
598,600	622,000	12.5	4.7	18.8	3.9
704,300	713,700	20.2	3.1	12.7	1.3
475,300	477,500	12.0	2.0	10.2	0.5
146,100	138,400	1.8	−33.8	−12.7	−5.3
137,200	146,600	1.8	−21.1	29.1	6.9
612,700	755,800	28.1	2.6	46.3	23.4
1,239,700	1,371,500	18.2	17.2	25.4	10.6
279,900	321,700	17.4	24.0	37.3	15.0
59,500	66,300	28.2	−0.7	40.3	11.4
488,000	541,900	30.3	16.3	18.3	11.0
157,600	186,200	24.3	15.1	48.7	18.1
112,700	131,100	37.6	7.4	38.4	16.3
39,800	46,500	—	—	30.5	16.8
396,300	482,900	59.2	7.0	46.6	21.9
323,800	382,600	64.3	1.0	45.1	18.2
230,900	287,300	41.1	2.8	46.1	24.4
188,800	228,400	19.0	19.9	39.8	20.8
85,800	100,100	38.9	13.2	35.1	16.7
51,800	59,500	0.8	5.5	34.2	14.9
55,100	75,200	5.0	3.3	58.8	36.5

Table 1 (continued)

	Total		
	1926	1939	1959
Tats	28,700	—	11,500
Adygeis	65,300	88,100	79,600
Abazins	13,800	15,300	19,600
Abkhaz	57,000	59,000	65,400
Karakalpaks	146,300	185,800	172,600
Buryats	237,500	224,700	253,000
Yakuts	240,700	242,100	236,700
Tuvins	—	800	100,100
Altays	37,600	47,900	45,300
Khakass	45,600	52,800	56,800
Shors	12,600	16,300	15,300
Evenks	32,800	29,700	24,700
Nenets	18,800	24,800	23,000
Khantys	19,700	18,500	19,400
Chukchis	13,100	13,900	11,700
Evens	—	9,700	9,100
Jews	2,600,900	3,028,500	2,267,800
Germans	1,238,500	1,427,200	1,619,700
Poles	782,300	630,100	1,380,300
Bulgarians	111,200	113,500	324,200
Greeks	213,800	286,400	309,300
Hungarians	5,500	—	154,700
Roumanians	4,600	—	106,400
Gypsies	61,200	88,200	132,000
Uyghurs	42,600	—	95,200
Gagauz	800	—	123,800
Koreans	87,000	182,300	313,700
Kurds	54,600	45,900	58,800
Finns	134,700	143,100	92,700
Turks	8,600	—	35,300
Dungans	14,600	—	22,000

a. Based on census data gathered after the occupation of the western territories. Figures for the population (in thousands) of ethnic groups in the western part of the USSR at the end of 1940 are as follows: Russians: 100,392; Ukrainians: 35,611; Belorussians: 8,275; Lithuanians: 2,033; Latvians: 1,628; Estonians: 1,144; Moldavians: 2,060. Taken from *Narodny SSSR: Kratkii Spravochnik* (Moscow, 1958).

Sources: *Itogi Vsesoyuznoi perepisi naseleniia 1959 goda*, 16 vols. (Moscow, 1962–63); *Itogi Vsesoyuznoi perepisi naseleniia 1970 goda*, vol. 4 (Moscow, 1973); *Naselenie SSSR. Po dannym*

1970	1979	Percent Increase			
		1926–39	1939–59	1959–70	1970–79
17,100	22,400	—	—	48.7	31.0
99,900	108,700	39.8	−9.6	25.5	8.8
25,400	29,500	10.9	28.1	29.6	16.1
83,200	90,900	3.5	10.8	27.2	9.3
236,000	303,300	27.0	−7.1	36.8	28.5
314,700	352,600	−5.4	12.6	24.4	12.0
296,200	328,000	0.6	−2.2	25.1	10.74
139,400	166,100	—	—	39.3	19.2
55,800	60,000	27.4	−5.4	23.2	7.5
66,700	70,800	15.8	7.6	17.4	6.1
16,500	16,000	29.4	−6.1	7.8	−3.0
25,100	27,500	−9.5	−16.8	1.6	9.6
28,700	29,900	31.9	−7.3	24.5	4.2
21,100	20,900	4.3	4.9	8.8	−0.9
13,600	14,000	6.1	−15.8	16.2	2.9
12,000	12,300	—	−16.2	31.9	2.5
2,150,700	1,810,900	16.4	−25.1	−5.2	−15.8
1,846,300	1,936,200	15.2	13.5	14.0	4.9
1,167,500	1,151,000	−19.5	119.1	−15.5	−1.4
351,200	361,100	2.1	185.6	8.3	2.8
336,900	343,800	34.0	8.0	9.0	2.0
166,500	170,600	—	—	7.6	2.5
119,300	128,800	—	—	12.2	8.0
175,300	209,200	44.1	49.6	32.8	19.3
173,300	210,600	—	—	82.0	21.5
156,600	173,200	—	—	26.5	10.6
357,500	388,900	109.5	72.1	14.0	8.8
88,900	115,900	−15.9	28.1	51.4	30.4
84,800	77,100	6.2	−35.2	−8.5	−9.1
79,000	92,700	—	—	123.8	17.3
38,600	51,700	—	—	75.5	33.9

Vsesoyuznoi perepisi naseleniia 1979 goda (Moscow, 1980); *Chislenost' i sostav naseleniia SSSR. Po dannym Vsesoyuznoi perepisi naseleniia 1979 goda* (Moscow, 1984); V. I. Kozlov, *Natsional'nosti SSSR* (Moscow, 1975), pp. 249–50. Taken from Gerhard Simon, *Nationalismus und Nationalitätenpolitik in der Sowjetunion: Von der totalitären Diktatur zur nachstalinischen Gesellschaft*, ed. Bundesinstitut für ostwissenschaftliche und internationale Studien, Köln (Baden-Baden, 1986).

Table 2   Population of Ethnic Groups in the Muslim
Republics of the USSR (1979)

	Population		Muslims (estimated)	
	Total	Percent	Total	Percent
1. Union Republics				
Uzbek SSR	15,389,000		13,081,000	85.0
Uzbeks	10,569,000	68.7		
Tatars	649,000	4.2		
Kazakhs	620,000	4.0		
Tajiks	595,000	3.9		
Karakalpaks	298,000	1.9		
Kirghiz	142,000	0.9		
Turkmens	92,000	0.6		
Azerbaijanians	60,000	0.4		
Uyghurs	25,000	0.2		
Persians	20,000	0.1		
Russians	1,666,000	10.8		
Kazakh SSR	14,684,000		6,314,000	43.0
Kazakhs	5,289,000	36.0		
Tatars	313,000	2.1		
Uzbeks	263,000	1.8		
Uyghurs	148,000	1.0		
Azerbaijanians	73,000	0.5		
Dungans	22,000	0.2		
Russians	5,991,000	40.8		
Germans	900,000	6.1		
Azerbaijan SSR	6,027,000		5,002,000	83.0
Azerbaijanians	4,709,000	78.1		
Dagestanians	205,000	3.4		
Tatars	31,000	0.5		
Kurds	30,000	0.5		
Turks	28,000	0.5		
Tats	9,000	0.1		
Armenians	475,000	7.9		
Russians	475,000	7.9		
Tajik SSR	3,806,000		3,273,000	86.0
Tajiks	2,237,000	58.8		
Uzbeks	873,000	22.9		
Tatars	80,000	2.1		
Kirghiz	48,000	1.3		

Table 2 (continued)

	Population		Muslims (estimated)	
	Total	Percent	Total	Percent
Turkmens	14,000	0.4		
Russians	395,000	10.4		
Kirghiz SSR	3,523,000		2,325,000	66.0
Kirghiz	1,687,000	47.9		
Uzbeks	426,000	12.1		
Tatars	72,000	2.0		
Uyghurs	30,000	0.8		
Kazakhs	27,000	0.8		
Dungans	27,000	0.8		
Tajiks	23,000	0.7		
Russians	912,000	25.9		
Turkmen SSR	2,765,000		2,323,000	84.0
Turkmens	1,892,000	68.4		
Uzbeks	234,000	8.5		
Kazakhs	80,000	2.9		
Tatars	40,000	1.5		
Azerbaijanians	24,000	0.9		
Baluches	19,000	0.7		
Dagestanians	12,000	0.4		
Russians	349,000	12.6		

2. Autonomous Republics

a. *RSFSR*

	Population		Muslims (estimated)	
Bashkir ASSR	3,849,000		1,886,000	49.0
Bashkirs	936,000	24.3		
Tatars	940,000	24.4		
Russians	1,547,000	40.2		
Tatar ASSR	3,436,000		1,649,000	48.0
Tatars	1,636,000	47.6		
Russians	1,510,000	43.9		
Dagestan ASSR	1,628,000		1,388,000	85.0
Dagestanians	1,266,000	77.8		
Azerbaijanians	65,000	4.0		
Chechen	49,000	3.0		
Tats	7,000	0.5		
Russians	189,000	11.6		

Table 2 (continued)

	Population		Muslims (estimated)	
	Total	Percent	Total	Percent
Chechen-Ingush ASSR	1,154,000		773,000	67.0
Chechens	611,000	52.9		
Ingush	135,000	11.7		
Dagestanians	22,000	1.9		
Russians	336,000	29.1		
Kabardin-Balkar ASSR	674,000		373,000	55.0
Kabardins	304,000	45.1		
Balkars	60,000	8.9		
Russians	234,000	34.7		
Severo-Ossetin ASSR	597,000		179,000	30.0
Ossetins				
(up to 50% Muslims)	301,000	50.5		
Ingush	24,000	4.0		
Russians	201,000	33.7		
b. *Uzbek SSR*				
Karakalpak ASSR	904,000		868,000	96.0
Karakalpaks	281,000	31.1		
Uzbeks	285,000	31.5		
Kazakhs	243,000	26.9		
Turkmens	49,000	5.4		
c. *Georgian SSR*				
Ajar ASSR	354,000		156,000	44.0
Georgians (up to 55%				
Muslims = Ajars)	284,000	80.1		
Russians	35,000	9.9		
Abkhaz ASSR	505,000		45,000	9.0
Abkhazians				
(up to 50% Muslims)	85,000	16.8		
Georgians	215,000	42.6		
Russians	82,000	16.2		
Armenians	75,000	14.9		
Azerbaijan SSR				
Nakhichevan ASSR	239,000		229,000	96.0
Azerbaijanians	229,000	95.6		
a. *RSFSR*				
Karachay-Cherkess				
Autonomous Oblast	368,000		180,000	49.0

Table 2 (continued)

	Population		Muslims (estimated)	
	Total	Percent	Total	Percent
Karachays	109,000	29.6		
Cherkess	33,000	9.0		
Abaz	24,000	6.5		
Nogavs	12,000	3.2		
Russians	165,000	44.8		
Adygei Autonomous Oblast	405,000		89,000	22.0
Adygeis	86,000	21.2		
Russians	285,000	70.4		
b. *Tajik SSR*				
Gorno-Badakhshan				
Autonomous Oblast	127,000		123,000	97.0
Tajiks	115,000	90.5		
Kirghiz	8,000	6.3		

Source: Contemporary Statistical Yearbooks.

Table 3 Population of Ethnic Groups of
Bosnia-Herzegovina and Kosovo (1981)

	Population		Muslims (estimated)	
	Total	Percent	Total	Percent
Republic of Bosnia-Herzegovina	4,124,000		1,650,000	40.0
Muslims (ethnic)	1,630,000	39.5		
Albanians	4,000	0.1		
Serbs	1,321,000	32.0		
Croatians	758,000	18.4		
"Yugoslavians"	326,000	7.9		
Autonomous Province of Kosovo	1,584,000		1,300,000	82.0
Albanians	1,227,000	77.5		
Muslims (ethnic)	59,000	3.7		
Turks	13,000	0.8		
Serbs	209,000	13.2		

Source: Contemporary Statistical Yearbooks.

Table 4   Regional Distribution of Muslims, 1971–1981
(percent in parentheses)

	1971	1981
Total number of Muslims	1,729,932	1,998,890
Bosnia-Herzegovina	1,482,430 (85.7)	1,629,924 (81.5)
Serbia	124,482 (7.2)	151,674 (7.6)
Montenegro	70,236 (4.1)	78,080 (3.9)
Macedonia	1,248 (0.07)	39,555 (2.0)
Kosovo	26,357 (1.4)	58,948 (2.9)
Slovenia	3,231 (0.19)	13,425 (0.7)
Croatia	18,457 (1.1)	23,740 (1.2)

Source: Statistički godišnjak SFRJ, 1972 and 1984.

Table 5   Communist Party Members in Bosnia-Herzegovina (percent)

	1965	1968	1976	1981
Total Members	132,696	158,110	221,621	391,244
Muslims	26.0	26.2	33.1	35.5
Serbs	57.1	55.0	48.2	44.0
Croatians	12.0	11.3	11.5	12.3
"Yugoslavians"	—	4.5	4.8	6.3

Sources: SKJ u uslovima samoupravljanja (Belgrade, 1967), p. 789; Klasno-socijalna struktura SKJ (Belgrade, 1984), pp. 528–29.

Table 6   People of Bosnia-Herzegovina, 1965–1978 (percent)

	1965	1967	1969	1974	1978
Muslims	0.5	1.0	15.8	33.4	35.3
Serbs	54.4	43.4	49.4	35.0	34.4
Croatians	21.8	17.3	18.8	20.9	20.0
"Yugoslavians"	14.2	11.2	—	3.1	7.8
No response	—	25.6	—	—	—

Sources: Statistički bilten br. 372, pp. 15–16; Stat. bilten br. 590, pp. 15–16; Stat. bilten br. 888, p. 49; Stat. bilten br. 1140, p. 65.

Notes on the Contributors
and Editors

Edward A. Allworth, Professor of Turko-Soviet Studies, Special Lecturer, and Head of the Executive Committee, Central Asia Center, Columbia University. General Editor, Central Asia Book Series. Recent publications: *Tatars of the Crimea: Their Struggle for Survival*, editor (Durham, N.C., 1988): *Central Asia: 120 Years of Russian Rule*, editor (Durham, N.C., 1989); *The Modern Uzbeks from the Fourteenth Century to the Present: A Cultural History* (Stanford, 1990); "A Theory of Soviet Nationality Policies," in *Soviet Nationality Policies: Ruling Ethnic Groups in the USSR*, ed. Henry R. Huttenbach (London 1990); "Abdalrauf Fitrat's Argument," *Central and Inner Asian Studies*, no. 1 (1991).

Hans Bräker, Emeritus Head Research Director, Bundesinstitut für ostwissenschaftliche und internationale Studien, Cologne; Honorary Professor, University of Trier. Major publications: *Kommunismus und Weltreligion Asiens*, 2 vols. (Tübingen, 1969–71); *Südostasien: Kulturführer* (1974); *Der Weg nach Asien* (Freiburg, 1978); "Moskaus orientalische Frage," *Osteuropa* (1988–89); "India's Relationship with Its Communist Neighbors," *Indoasia* (1989–90).

Marie Broxup, Director, Society for Central Asian Studies; Editor-in-Chief, *Central Asian Survey*, Oxford, England. Major publications: *The Islamic Threat to the Soviet State* (with Alexandre Bennigsen) (London, 1983); "The Basmachis," *Central Asian Survey* 2 (1983).

George Brunner, Professor of Administration Law, Government and Eastern Affairs, University of Cologne. Major publications: *Kontrolle in Deutschland* (Cologne, 1972); *Politische Soziologie der UdSSR*, 2 vols. (Wiesbaden, 1977); *Vergleichende Regierungslehre*, vol. 1 (Paderborn, 1979); *Before Reforms: Human Rights in the Warsaw Pact States, 1971–1988* (London, 1990).

Bert G. Fragner, Professor of Iranian and Central Asian Studies, University of Bamberg, Germany. Major publications: *Persische Memoirenliteratur als Quelle zur neueren Geschichte Irans* (Wiesbaden, 1979); "Sowjetmacht und Islam: Die Revolution von Buchara," *Festschrift Hans Robert Roemer* (Beirut, 1979); "Zur Erforschung der kulinarischen Kultur Irans," *Die Welt des Islams* 23–24 (1984); "Die 'Wiederentdeckung' des

Persischen in Mittelasien: Sprachpolitik und Sprachentwicklung in Tadschikistan," in *Festschrift A. Falaturi* (Cologne-Vienna, 1991).

Ewe Halbach, Fellow, Bundesinstitut für ostwissenschaftliche und internationale Studien, Cologne. Major publications: *Die altrussische Fürstenhof vor dem 16. Jahrhundert* (Stuttgart, 1985); "Sowjetische Nationalitätenproblematik: Zu ihrer Rezeption in der sowjetischen Öffentlichkeit," *Osteuropa* 4 (1988); "Die Bergvölker als Gegner und Opfer: Der Kaukasus in Der Wahrnehmung Russlands," in *Kleine Völker in der Geschichte Osteuropas: Festschrift fur G. Stökl* (Stuttgart, 1991).

Wolfgang Höpken, Fellow and Deputy Director, Georg Eckert Institut für Internationale Schulbuchforschung, Braunschweig. Major publications: *Sozialismus und Pluralismus Tito*, coeditor, 2 vols. (Munich 1984–86); "Modernisierung und Nationalismus: Sozialgeschichtliche Aspekte der bulgarischen Minderheitenpolitik gegenüber den Türken," *Sudosteuropa* 35 (1986); *Die ungeliebte Minderheit—Bulgariens Türken, 1978–1990* (Munich, 1992).

Andreas Kappeler, Professor of East European History, University of Cologne. Major publications: *Russlands erste Nationalitäten: Das Zarenreich und die Völker der Mittleren Wolga vom 16. bis 19. Jahrhundert* (Cologne, 1982); *Die Russen: Ihr Nationalbewusstsein in Geschichte und Gegenwart*, editor (Cologne, 1990); *Russland als Vielvölkerreich—Entstehung, Geschichte, Zerfall* (Munich, 1992).

Edward J. Lazzerini, Professor of Russian and Asian History, University of New Orleans. Research specialties in the cultural and intellectual history of European Russia's major Turkic peoples (Azerbaijanis, Crimean Tatars, Volga Tatars) since the eighteenth century. Recent publications: "From Bakhchisarai to Bukhara in 1893: Ismail Bey Gasprinskii's Journey to Central Asia," *Central Asian Survey* 3 (1984); "Beyond Renewal: The *Jadid* Response to Pressure for Change in the Modern Age," in *Muslims in Central Asia: Expressions of Identity and Change*, ed. Jo-Ann Gross (Durham, N.C., 1992). In preparation: a study of Ismail Bey Gasprinskii, nineteenth-century Crimean Tatar reformer.

Richard Lorenz, Professor of Modern East European History, University of Kassel. Major publications *Anfänge der bolschewistischen Industriepolitik* (Cologne, 1965); *Sozialgeschichte der Sowjetunion 1: 1917–1945* (Frankfurt am Main, 1976); *Die russische Revolution 1917. Der Aufstand der Arbeiter, Bauern und Soldaten: Eine Dokumentation*, editor (Munich, 1981).

Alexandre Popović, Director of Research, Centre National de la Recherche Scientifique, Paris. Major publications: *L'Islam balkanique* (Berlin, 1986); "'Le radicalisme islamique' en Yougoslavie," in *Radicalismes Islamiques*, vol. 2 (Paris, 1986); "Les turcs en Bulgarie (1878–1985)," *Cahiers du monde russe et soviètique* 27 (1986); "Les derviches balkaniques: La zifa'iyya," *Zeitschrift für Balkanologie* 25–26 (1989–90); *Les musulmans yougoslaves, 1945–1989 (médiateurs et métaphores)* (Lausanne, 1990).

Sabrina Petra Ramet, Associate Professor of International Studies, University of Washington, Seattle. Recent publications: *Social Currents in Eastern Europe: The Sources and Meaning of the Great Transformation* (Durham, N.C., 1991); *Balkan Babel: Politics, Culture, and Religion in Yugoslavia* (Boulder, Colo., 1992); *Nationalism and*

Federalism in Yugoslavia, 1962–1991, 2d ed. (Bloomington, 1992). Also, two other books individually, eight volumes as editor, and numerous articles.

Azade-Ayşe Rorlich, Associate Professor of Russian History, University of Southern California. Major publications: *The Volga Tatars: A Profile in National Resilience* (Stanford, 1986); "Islam and Atheism: Dynamic Tension in Central Asia," in *Soviet Central Asia: The Failed Transformation*, ed. William Fierman (Boulder, Colo., 1991).

Gerhard Simon, Research Director, Bundesinstitut für ostwissenschaftliche und internationale Studien; Professor, University of Cologne. Major publications: *Die Kirchen in Russland* (Munich, 1970); *Neue Wege der Sowjetunion-Forschung* (with Astrid von Borcke) (Baden-Baden, 1980); *Nationalism and Policy Toward the Nationalities in the Soviet Union* (Boulder, Colo., 1991).

Tadeusz Swietochowski, Professor of History, Monmouth College. Major publications: "The Himmat Party. Socialism and the National Question in Russian Azerbaijan, 1904–1920," *Cahiers du monde russ et soviètique*, nos. 1–2 (1978); *Russian Azerbaijan 1905–1920: The Shaping of National Identity in a Muslim Community* (Cambridge, 1985); "Azerbaijan: Between Ethnic Conflict and Irredentism," *Armenian Review*, nos. 2–3 (1990); "Islam and Nationality in Tsarist Russia and Soviet Union," in *Soviet Nationality Policies: Ruling Ethnic Groups in the USSR*, ed. Henry R. Huttenbach (London, 1990).

Index

Library of Congress Cataloging-in-Publication Data
Die Muslime in der Sowjetunion und in Jugoslawien. English
Muslim communities reemerge : historical perspectives on
nationality, politics, and opposition in the former Soviet
Union and Yugoslavia / Andreas Kappeler, Gerhard Simon, Georg
Brunner, editors of the German edition ; Edward Allworth,
editor of the English edition ; translations from the German
by Caroline Sawyer.—English supplemented and translated ed.
p. cm.—(Central Asia book series)
Includes index.
ISBN 0-8223-1447-9 (cloth : alk. paper).—
ISBN 0-8223-1490-8 (pbk. : alk. paper)
1. Muslims—Soviet Union. 2. Muslims—Yugoslavia.
3. Islam—Europe, Eastern.   I. Allworth, Edward.
II. Title.   III. Series.
DK34.M8M8713   1994
947'.008'82971—dc20   93-43021 CIP